THE *CRISIS* READER

THE *CRISIS* READER

STORIES, POETRY, AND ESSAYS FROM THE N.A.A.C.P.'S *CRISIS* MAGAZINE

Sondra Kathryn Wilson

THE MODERN LIBRARY

NEW YORK

LIBRARY OF CONGRESS CATALOGING-IN-PUBLICATION DATA
The Crisis Reader : stories, poetry, and essays from the N.A.A.C.P.'s
Crisis magazine/Sondra Kathryn Wilson.
p. cm.
Excerpts from the period 1918–1930.
Includes bibliographical references.
ISBN 0-375-75231-5 (acid-free paper)
1. American literature—Afro-American authors.   2. Afro-Americans—
Literary collections.   3. American literature—20th century.
I. Wilson, Sondra K.   II. Crisis (New York, N.Y.)   III. National
Association for the Advancement of Colored People.
PS508.N3C69   1999
810.8'0896073—dc21   98-31436

Printed in the United States of America
Modern Library website address: www.modernlibrary.com

2 4 6 8 9 7 5 3

First Edition

For

Mildred Bond Roxborough,

valiant keeper of the N.A.A.C.P. tradition

I dare to say that it is now more or less generally acknowledged that the only things artistic that have sprung from American soil and out of American life, and been universally recognized as distinctively American products, are the folk creations of the Negro.

JAMES WELDON JOHNSON, 1928

ACKNOWLEDGMENTS

I wish to thank Manie Barron of Random House for conceiving the idea of this work and for his invaluable advice and support.

I wish to thank the Crisis Publishing Company, the publisher of the magazine of the National Association for the Advancement of Colored People, for authorizing the use of these works.

The poems "Helene," "The River," "Moods," and "A Passing Melody" by James Weldon Johnson are published here by permission of Sondra Kathryn Wilson.

Contents

Part Two: Fiction

LITERARY AND CULTURAL ESSAYS

SOCIAL ESSAYS

INTRODUCTION

O Black and unknown bards of long ago,
How came your lips to touch the sacred fire?
How, in your darkness, did you come to know
The power and beauty of the minstrel's lyre?
Who first from midst his bonds lifted his eyes?
Who first from out the still watch, lone and long?
Feeling the ancient faith of prophets rise
Within his dark-kept soul, burst into song?

Heart of what slave poured out such melody
As "Steal away to Jesus"? On its strains
His spirit must have nightly floated free,
Though still about his hands he felt his chains,
Who heard great "Jordan Roll"?[1]

In his poem "O Black and Unknown Bards," James Weldon Johnson reveals African Americans as creators of the Negro spirituals who lived and died captives of a system of slave labor. Johnson wrote pointedly, "But from whom did these songs spring—these songs unsurpassed among the folk songs of the world and, in the poignancy of their beauty, unequalled?"[2] The composers and lyricists of the Negro spirituals were the faceless, nameless slaves—the "black and unknown bards."

Notwithstanding their enslavement, America's unlettered African Americans had contributed worlds of music, art, and poetry to this nation centuries before the Harlem Renaissance of the 1920s. In acknowledging the "black and unknown bards," perhaps an African proverb serves as the best epitaph: "If you know well the beginning, the end will not trouble you much."

I want in this introduction to explain the roles of the N.A.A.C.P. and its official organ, *The Crisis* magazine, in the birth and early development of the black literary movement of the 1920s known as the Harlem Renaissance. The selection of *Crisis* poems, short stories, plays, and essays in this volume illustrates the magazine's role as a literary and intellectual outlet for black writers. The brilliance and effectiveness of the writings presented here illuminate a principal objective of the N.A.A.C.P.: to break the stubborn stereotype that had misrepresented and malformed implicitly every external view of African-American life.

In 1910, the N.A.A.C.P., founded one year before, established *The Crisis* magazine as its official organ and named Atlanta University professor William Edward Burghardt Du Bois the editor. He reported for work in the organization's New York City headquarters in August of 1910, and the first issue of the magazine appeared that November. Articulating a general purpose of his work, the editor said, "with *The Crisis,* I essayed a new role of interpreting to the world the hindrances and aspirations of American Negroes."[3] He soon made *The Crisis* one of the most influential journals on social and political thought ever seen in America. Under his editorship, *The Crisis* became widely read even beyond N.A.A.C.P. membership.

It is apparent that the N.A.A.C.P., for most of this century, can certainly claim almost monopolistic credit for civil-rights achievements. The organization's role in the birth of the Harlem Renaissance, however, proved uniquely significant in that it provoked both the production of a body of black literature and the improvement of race relations. As scholar David Levering Lewis has noted, "The Harlem Renaissance was a somewhat forced phenomenon, a cultural nationalism of the parlor, institutionally encouraged and directed by leaders of the national civil rights establishment for the paramount purpose of improving race relations."[4]

By 1920, the N.A.A.C.P. had accumulated a myriad of court victories, making the civil-rights organization a powerful advocate for the disenfranchised. Du Bois wrote that "the N.A.A.C.P. proved between 1910 and the first world war to be one of the most effective organizations of the liberal spirit and the fight for social progress which America has known."[5] Due in large measure to the work of the N.A.A.C.P., certain blacks experienced a new self-confidence, which spawned a greater degree of intellectual freedom. Notwithstanding this optimism, there was still some disillusionment. But a new hope was abounding, and this hope gave birth to the Harlem Renaissance.

Writer Arna Bontemps divided the literary movement into two phases. Phase one (1921–1924) represents the period of primary black propaganda. Bontemps cites *The Crisis* and the Urban League's official organ, *Opportunity: A Journal of Negro Life*, as the most important supporters of phase two (1924–1931).[6] These two influential journals devoted space to literature and social and political writings. Their efforts must be credited for generating interest in the artistic and intellectual side of Harlem. Phase two eventually connected Harlem writers to the white intelligentsia who had access to establishment publishing entities. This connection between black writers and white publishers proved essential in promulgating the Harlem Renaissance. (*The* Crisis *Reader* will be followed by *The* Opportunity *Reader,* which will examine *Opportunity's* role in the birth and development of the Harlem Renaissance.)

Notwithstanding the talent and contributions of black artists, barriers based on race prejudice had long made black writers pariahs in the white publishing world. They had often been reduced to publishing either with obscure or dubious publishing outfits or out of their own pockets because most establishment white publishers believed black writings were substandard. This opinion, according to David Levering Lewis, was evidenced by the fact that no more than five African Americans had published significant literary writings between 1908 and 1923: Sutton Grigg's *Pointing the Way* (1908), W. E. B. Du Bois's *The Quest of the Silver Fleece* (1911); James Weldon Johnson's critically acclaimed *The Autobiography of an Ex-Colored Man* (1912); Du Bois's *Darkwater* (1920); Claude McKay's *Harlem Shadows* (1922); and Jean Toomer's *Cane* (1923).[7]

Following the end of World War I, gifted black writers such as Arna Bontemps, Claude McKay, Wallace Thurman, Zora Neale Hurston, Nella Larson, and Langston Hughes arrived in Harlem. By this time, there were more African-American journalists, intellectuals, poets, composers, dramatists, and actors of note and distinction in Harlem than in all American cities (other than New York City) combined.[8] In spite of this unprecedented and spirited collection of black talent, white America, for the most part, remained unconvinced that writings by blacks were worthy of being published. "What was necessary was a revolution and a revelation sufficient to disturb the age-old customary cynicisms."[9] It became critically vital to convince an incredulous world of a race's mental and intellectual parity.

As long as blacks had been in America, the questions surrounding race had run the gamut from whether or not black people were even human beings to whether full citizenship was a right that they should enjoy. What is it, then, that can change the heart and attitude of white America? asked black leadership of the day. W. E. B. Du Bois addressed this question in the early 1920s by noting that "until the art of black folk compels recognition they will not be regarded as human." James Weldon Johnson proclaimed that there had to be another means to conquer American injustices, after several approaches had been tried through the work of the N.A.A.C.P. He regarded the artistic approach as a significant means to advance the cultural dignity of African Americans in national and international life.

Even after World War I, such distinguished white writers as Octavus Roy Cohen, Irvin Cobb, and Julia Peterkin continued to portray African-American characters as buffoons who could not pronounce even the simplest words. Johnson argued that just as these stereotypes had been shaped, propagated, and bolstered by a white literary system, they could be smashed as well by similar means. "Each book, play, poem, or canvas by an Afro-American would become a weapon against old racial stereotypes."[10] This challenge, Johnson believed, would have to be accomplished by a group of writers reared by the race. Johnson's forecast of what a black literary movement could do for the status of African-American life was insightful. He wrote:

> The final measure of the greatness of all peoples is the amount and standard of the literature and art they have produced. The world does not know that a people is great until that people produces great literature and art. No people that has produced great literature and art has ever been looked upon by the world as distinctly inferior. . . . And nothing will do more to change the mental attitude and raise his status than a demonstration of intellectual parity by the Negro through the production of literature and art.[11]

Johnson understood the power of the Negro spirituals in changing the attitude of white America. When white Americans first heard the spirituals, they felt sympathy for the "pitiful Negroes." However, by the

1920s, white Americans felt not pity but deference for the creative genius of the race.

The intellectual and literary prosperity of blacks in the 1920s can be seen as the result of the efforts of four brilliant black writers on the N.A.A.C.P.'s staff who shared a strong conviction that the power of literature and art could diminish racial prejudice: James Weldon Johnson, W. E. B. Du Bois, Jessie Redmon Fauset, and Walter White.

James Weldon Johnson, poet, novelist, essayist, lyricist, and leader of the N.A.A.C.P., was unique as a black man because even prior to the advent of the Harlem Renaissance he was lauded in sophisticated white literary circles. Johnson's role as a leader of the black literary movement of the 1920s while simultaneously running the N.A.A.C.P. is legend. As poet and essayist Sterling Brown put it, "By his interpretations of Negro poetry and music, by occasional essays on the problems of Negro writers, and by his own creative work, James Weldon Johnson succeeded more than any predecessor in furthering the cause of Negro artists."[12] N.A.A.C.P. Assistant Secretary Walter White pointed out that "there is hardly a Negro artist who is not indebted to . . . [Johnson] for spiritual and material assistance."[13]

In their fifties during the height of the Harlem Renaissance, Johnson and Du Bois were among the older and more experienced writers. Years before this period, Du Bois, like Johnson, was widely acclaimed as an author, a noted scholar, and an intellectual of international status. Du Bois was deeply committed to addressing the political and social questions of the day, and the bulk of his writings in *The Crisis* centered on those issues.

Realizing that *The Crisis* needed a strong literary voice, Du Bois found in Jessie Redmon Fauset the qualities required for the job of literary editor. Considered a midwife of the Harlem Renaissance, Fauset not only encouraged and nurtured new writers but wrote the majority of her own vast literary works during the 1920s. Shortly after she assumed her duties as literary editor in 1919, Fauset began to attract and publish such great writers as Langston Hughes, Georgia Douglas Johnson, Jean Toomer, Claude McKay, Fenton Johnson, Countee Cullen, and Gwendolyn Bennett.

As N.A.A.C.P. assistant secretary during the 1920s, Walter White rose to great heights as a leader and artist of the Harlem Renaissance because of his own published works and his superb public-relations skills. He was adept at making friends in high places, and his Harlem apartment, used for social gatherings, became known as the place "where interracial contracts and contacts were sealed over bootleg spirits."[14]

The N.A.A.C.P. and *The Crisis* had most certainly accepted the challenge to reclaim through art and literature the status of black Americans. The civil-rights organization understood that what black writers needed was an organized forum with specific guidelines and a system of rewards. Therefore, in 1924, *The Crisis* instituted the Amy Einstein Spingarn Prizes in Literature and Art to attract and promote black writers. Amy Spingarn, wife of N.A.A.C.P. board member and philanthropist Joel Elias Spingarn, served as program funder and literary judge. Other judges included such popular writers as Sinclair Lewis, Witter Bynner, Edward Bok, Charles Waddell Chesnutt, and Robert Morss Lovett.

James Weldon Johnson and Walter White not only mentored many new writers and encouraged them to publish in *The Crisis* but also used their broad contacts in the white world to secure publishing contracts for some of them. Therefore, by the mid-1920s, influential white Americans were patronizing black artists and writers. After a long history of struggling, of being rejected, of being despised or pitied, black creative artists were finally being courted by white patrons and white publishers.[15]

Many of the brilliant and beautiful writings presented here were anomalous in that they sprung out of the repulsive and perilous conditions that served as the backdrop of black life. Handed down from slavery, this African-American literary tradition was dependent on its ability to relate to the situations of oppressed people in general and African Americans in particular. To the extent that these black writers conveyed this empathy is the extent to which they were really successful.

In 1928, at the meridian of the Harlem Renaissance, James Weldon Johnson, citing such music as spirituals, ragtime, the blues, and other black art forms, contended that "it is now more or less generally acknowledged that the only things artistic that have sprung from American soil and out of American life, and been universally recognized as distinctively American products, are the folk creations of the Negro."[16] Today, acclaimed black art in such fields as jazz, gospel, and rap music substantiate Johnson's pronouncement. Certainly, no one can deny that black American art and literature have been amalgamated into world culture.

In this volume, I have included some writings that predate the advent of the Harlem Renaissance. Writers like Charles W. Chesnutt, Fenton

Johnson, Jessie Redmon Fauset, Benjamin Brawley, and James Weldon Johnson were publishing poems and literary and social essays in *The Crisis* from shortly after its 1910 inception. These writings are the seeds of the Harlem Renaissance.

When one thinks of the Harlem Renaissance, names like Langston Hughes, Countee Cullen, James Weldon Johnson, and Alain Locke come quickly to mind. However, writings by lesser known but equally talented authors such as Marita O. Bonner, Allison Davis, Charles Bertram Johnson, Anita Scott Coleman, and others are also included here. And, as a special treat, I have included four unpublished poems by James Weldon Johnson.

For some, this volume will be a reintroduction to well-known persons and their writings; for others, it will be an introduction to unfamiliar figures and their works. But for all, this rich collection of *Crisis* writings, written during some of the most egregiously racist times in American history, will be an affirmation that black American literature has long been among the most sophisticated in the world.

NOTES

1. James Weldon Johnson, ed., *The Books of American Negro Spirituals* (New York: Viking Press, 1964), p. 11.
2. Ibid., p. 12.
3. W. E. B. Du Bois, *The Autobiography of W. E. B. Du Bois* (New York: International Publishers, 1968), p. 256.
4. David Levering Lewis, *The Portable Harlem Renaissance* (New York: Viking, 1994), p. xv.
5. Du Bois, *Autobiography of W. E. B. Du Bois*, p. 256.
6. Arna Bontemps, ed., *The Harlem Renaissance Remembered* (New York: Dodd, Meade, 1972), pp. 272–73.
7. David Levering Lewis, *When Harlem Was in Vogue* (New York: Oxford University Press, 1989), p. 86.
8. James Weldon Johnson, *Black Manhattan* (New York: DaCapo Press, 1991 [1930]), p. 5.
9. Bontemps, *Harlem Renaissance Remembered*, p. 222.
10. Lewis, *When Harlem Was in Vogue*, p. 86.
11. James Weldon Johnson, ed., *The Book of American Negro Poetry* (New York: Harcourt Brace Jovanovich, 1969 [1922]), p. 9.
12. Sterling Brown, Arthur P. Davis, and Ulysees Lee, *The Negro Caravan* (New York: Dryden Press, 1941), p. 834.
13. Walter White, "James Weldon Johnson," N.A.A.C.P. pamphlet, 1938.

14. Lewis, *When Harlem Was in Vogue,* p. 136.
15. Nathan Irvin Huggins, *Harlem Renaissance* (New York: Oxford University Press, 1971), p. 118.
16. James Weldon Johnson, "Race Prejudice and the Negro Artist," *Harper's* 157 (1928): 769–76.

EDITING *THE CRISIS*

W. E. B. Du Bois was editor of *The Crisis* from its inception in 1910 to 1934. He returned in 1944 and remained until 1948. In the following, Du Bois offers some historical insights and discusses the objectives and outcomes of the N.A.A.C.P.'s official organ during his tenure as editor. Du Bois published this essay in March 1951.

From the time I entered High School at Great Barrington, Massachusetts, in 1880, I have had the itch to edit something. The first fruition was a school paper, in manuscript, called the "High School Howler," edited by me and illustrated by Art Benham, who could draw caricatures. It had as I remember but one issue.

My next effort was while I was a student as Fisk University and I became, first, exchange editor and then editor of the *Fisk Herald,* during my junior and senior years, 1887–1888.

The next adventure was the monthly called *The Moon,* which was published by Harry Pace and Edward Simon in Memphis and edited by me in Atlanta in 1906. From 1907 to 1910, I was joint editor of a miniature magazine, published monthly in Washington, D.C. My colaborers were H. M. Hershaw and F. H. M. Murray.

In 1910, I came to New York as Director of Publications and Research in the NAACP. The idea was that I should continue the kind of research into the Negro problem that I had been carrying on in Atlanta and that eventually I should become Secretary of the NAACP. But I did not want to raise money, and there were no funds for research; so that from the first, I urged that we have a monthly organ.

This seemed necessary because the chief Negro weekly *The New York Age* was then owned by friends of Mr. Washington, and the Tuskegee organization had tight hold of most of the rest of the Negro press. The result was that the NAACP got a pretty raw deal from the colored press and none at all from the white papers.

In addition to that the Negro press was at the time mainly organs of opinion and not gatherers of news.

I had the idea that a small publication would be read which stressed the facts and minimized editorial opinion, but made it clear and strong; and also published the opinion of others.

There were many on the board of directors who did not agree with me. I remember Albert Pillsbury, former Attorney General of Massachusetts, wrote to me and said: If you have not already determined to publish a magazine, for heavens' sake drop the idea. The number of publications now is as many as the "plagues of Egypt!" But I was firm, and back of me stood William English Walling, Paul Kennedy, Charles Edward Russell and John E. Milholland and other members of the board.

But there again the matter of money was difficult. It was hard enough to raise the salaries of our two executive officers, and certainly we had no capital for investment in a periodical. I was persistent and two persons helped me: Mary Maclean, an English woman who was a writer on the *New York Times* and a loyal and efficient friend; and Robert N. Wood, a printer who was head of the Negro Tammany organization at that time.

Wood knew about printing and I knew nothing. He advised me, helped me to plan the magazine, and took the risk of getting me credit for paper and printing. The Board agreed that it would be responsible for debts up to but not exceeding $50.00 a month. It has always been a matter of pride to me that I never asked for that $50.00.

Finally after what seemed to me interminable delays on various accounts, the first number of the CRISIS appeared in November, 1910. It had sixteen 5x8 pages, with a cover which carried one little woodcut of a Negro child; as one of my critics facetiously said: "It is a shame to take the ten cents which this issue costs."

First because of the news which it contained, in 4 pages of "Along the Color Line"; then because of some blazing editorials which continually got us into hot water with friends and foes; and because of the pictures of Negroes which we carried in increasing number and often in color, the CRISIS succeeded.

We condensed more news about Negroes and their problems in a month than most colored papers before this had published in a year. Then we had four pages of editorials, which talked turkey. The articles were at first short and negligible but gradually increased in number, length, and importance; but we were never able to pay contributors. Pictures of colored people were an innovation; and at that time it was the rule of most white papers never to publish a picture of a colored person except as a criminal and the colored papers published mostly pictures of celebrities who sometimes paid for the honor. In general the Negro race was just a little afraid to see itself in plain ink.

The circulation growth of the CRISIS was extraordinary, even to us who believed in it. From a monthly net paid circulation of 9,000 copies in 1911, it jumped to 75,000 copies in 1918, and from an income of $6,500 to an income of $57,000. In January, 1916, the CRISIS became entirely self-supporting, paying all items of its cost including publicity, light, heat, rent, etc., and the salaries of an editor and business manager and nine clerks. It circulated in every state in the Union, in all the insular possessions, and in most foreign countries including Africa.

We doubled the size of the tiny first issue in December, 1910. We increased the number of pictures, trying two-color jobs on the cover in 1911 and three colors in 1912, 1917–1918. Our special education and children's numbers began in 1914. From time to time we issued special numbers on localities like Chicago and New Orleans; on "Votes for Women" and the pageant "Star of Ethiopia."

During this period two persons were indispensable in the conduct of the CRISIS: Mary Maclean, editorial assistant, who died in harness and worked without pay; and Augustus Dill, business manager, who organized a model office. In November, 1919, Jessie Fauset became literary editor and gave us inestimable help for seven years. Mattie Allison and Lotte Jarvis as secretaries, and Hazel Branch as head of the clerical staff, helped make an ideal family. Frank Turner was our bookkeeper from 1910 until the NAACP took him over in 1922.

We reached a circulation of 100,000 in 1919, following my revelation of the attitude of American army officers toward the Negroes in France. I shall never forget the circumstances of that scoop. I was in the office of Blaise Diagne in the spring of 1919. Diagne was a tall, thin, black Senegalese, French Under-Secretary of State of Colonies, and during the war, French Commissioner in West Africa, out-ranking the Colonial Governor. Diagne saved France by the black shock troops which he brought from Africa and threw against German artillery. They held the Germans until the Allies could get ready for them.

Diagne was consequently a great man and it was his word which induced Prime Minister Clemenceau to let the First Pan-African Congress meet in Paris against the advice of the Americans. Diagne did not like white Americans.

"Did you see," he stormed, "what the American Mission told the French about the way Negroes should be treated?" Then he showed me the official document. I read it and sat very still. Then I said, as carelessly as possible, "Would it be possible to obtain a copy of this?" "Take that," said Diagne.

Having the precious document, the problem was what to do with it. I dare not carry it nor trust it to the mails. But a white friend who was sailing home offered to take anything I wished to send. I handed him the document sealed, neglecting to say what dynamite was in it. The CRISIS office and NAACP officials read it and dropped it until I returned. I published it in May, 1919. The Post Office promptly held the CRISIS up in the mails. But it proved too hot for them; if the Government held it that would be acknowledging its authorship. They let it go. We sold 100,000 copies!

Our income in 1920, was $77,000, that was our high-water mark. Then began a slump which brought the circulation down to 35,000 copies in 1924 and a cash income of $46,000.

The causes of this were clear and strike every modern periodical: the reading public is not used to paying for the cost of the periodicals which they read; often they do not pay even for the cost of the paper used in the edition. Advertisers pay for most of the costs and advertisers buy space in periodicals which circulate widely among well-to-do persons able to buy the wares offered. The CRISIS was known to circulate among Negro workers of low income. Moreover it antagonized many white powerful interests; it had been denounced in Congress and many respectable Negroes were afraid to be seen reading it. Mississippi passed laws against it and some of our agents were driven from home.

We got some advertising, especially from Negro businesses; some advertisers we refused because we did not like the wares they offered or suspected fraud. The "Big" advertisers remained aloof; some looked us over, but nearly all fell back on the rule not to patronize "propaganda" periodicals. Besides they did not believe the Negro market worth entering.

Our only recourse was to raise our price of subscription. In December, 1919, we raised our price to a dollar and a half for a year and fifteen cents a copy; also we increased our size to 64 pages and cover. This might have extricated us if the prices of everything else had not gone up, while wages went down. The Depression which burst on the nation in 1929, started among Negro workers as early as 1926. It struck the workers of the Negro race long before the country in general dreamed of it. I remember bringing the matter to the attention of the president of the board of directors, but he said "the country is unusually prosperous!" Nevertheless, I retorted, the Negro worker is losing old jobs and not getting new ones.

There was a wider underlying cause: How far was the CRISIS an organ of opinion and propaganda; and of whose opinion and just what propaganda? Or how far was it an organ of an association catering to its immediate plans and needs? The two objects and methods were not incompatible with each other in the earlier days of beginnings. Indeed from 1910 to 1925 or later the CRISIS was the predominant partner, with income and circulation larger than the NAACP. For just this reason the NAACP became known outside its membership, and with the energetic work of Shillady, Johnson, and White, the membership and income increased and the question of the future relation of the CRISIS and the NAACP had to be settled. Their complete separation was proposed; or if the income of the CRISIS continued to fall, the subsidy of the CRISIS by the NAACP; or further attempt to prolong the present relations and increase CRISIS income and circulation.

From 1925 to 1934, the latter method was tried. Various efforts were made to increase CRISIS circulation, by change of form and content. Considerable success ensued, but the Depression which now fell heavier on the nation convinced me that the CRISIS could not be made to pay again for a long period and that meantime the only way to keep it alive was by subsidy from the NAACP. For this reason in 1934, I gave up my position as editor and publisher of the CRISIS and went back to teaching and writing at Atlanta University.

In the nature of the case, there is a clear distinction between an organ of an organization and a literary magazine. They have different objects and functions. The one is mainly a series of reports and record of organizational technicalities and news notes of methods and routine notices. All large organizations need such a publication. But it is never self-supporting nor widely read. So far as it tries to be literary and artistic, it misses its main function and is too narrow to achieve any other.

On the other hand, a literary and news journal must be free and uncontrolled; in no other way can it be virile, creative, and individual. While it must follow an ideal, and one of which one or more organizations approve, yet its right to deviate in particulars must be granted, else it misses its function of provoking thought, stimulating argument, and attracting readers. For many years the NAACP gave me such freedom and the public repaid them and me by wide support. But when public support lagged and the NAACP must furnish a large part of the supporting funds, it would have called for more faith than any organization was likely to have in one man, to leave me still in untrammeled control. And as for me, I had no interest in a conventional organ; I must be Free Lance or nothing.

Against, therefore, the strong pleas of close friends like Joel Spingarn; and against the openly expressed wish of the whole Board, which did not wholly agree with me, but were willing to yield much to retain me, I resigned. And I resigned completely and not in part. I was not only editor and head of a department which was separate from that of the Executive Secretary, with my own office and staff and separate bank account; I was also one of the incorporators of the NAACP and member of the Board of Directors since its beginning. Its officials from the first had come to consideration and election on my recommendation. I was a member of the Spingarn Medal Committee, and chief speaker at every annual conference. It was fair to say that the policy of the NAACP from 1910 to 1934 was largely of my making.

I would not have been honest therefore with my successors to have resigned in part and hung on to remnants of my former power. I went out completely. I think some sighed in relief. But many were genuinely sorry. Among the latter was myself. For I was leaving my dream and brainchild; my garden of hope and highway to high emprise. But I was 65; my life work was practically done. I looked forward to a few final years of thought, advice and remembrance, beneath the trees and on the hills beside the graves and with the friends where first my real life-work had begun in 1897.

—*March, 1951*

PART ONE

POETRY

GWENDOLYN BENNETT

To Usward

Let us be still
As ginger jars are still
Upon a Chinese shelf.
And let us be contained
By entities of Self....
Not still with lethargy and sloth,
But quiet with the pushing of our growth.
Not self-contained with smug identity
But conscious of the strength in entity.
If any have a song to sing
That's different from the rest,
Oh let them sing
Before the urgency of Youth's behest!
For some of us have songs to sing
Of jungle heat and fires,
And some of us are solemn grown
With pitiful desires,
And there are those who feel the pull
Of seas beneath the skies,
And some there be who want to croon
Of Negro lullabies.
We claim no part with racial dearth;
We want to sing the songs of birth!
And so we stand like ginger jars
Like ginger jars bound round
With dust and age;
Like jars of ginger we are sealed
By nature's heritage.
But let us break the seal of years
With pungent thrusts of song,
For there is joy in long-dried tears
For whetted passions of a throng!

"TO USWARD" WAS PUBLISHED IN MAY 1924.

ARNA BONTEMPS

Hope

Lone and dismal; hushed and dark,
Upon the waves floats an empty bark.

The stars go out; the raindrops fall,
And through the night comes a ghostly call—

My lone and dismal life's a-float
Upon the seas like an empty boat.

Above the heights where the sea-gulls soar,
The thunder lifts its resonant roar.

Like a jagged arrow a flash is sent,
That splits the clouds with a double rent.

And just beyond my bark that drifts,
Moonbeams steal through the kindly rifts.

Dirge

Oh bury my bones in the dark of the moon,
In a place where the soil is bare,
And none will say that I mar the clay
Or the vine buds there too soon.
But the worm will think me sweet somehow.
As he gnaws away I'll hear him say,
"I scorn the taste of white flesh now".

"HOPE" AND "DIRGE" WERE PUBLISHED
IN AUGUST 1924 AND MAY 1926, RESPECTIVELY.

WILLIAM STANLEY BRAITHWAITE

Scintilla

I kissed a kiss in youth
    Upon a dead man's brow;
And that was long ago,—
    And I'm a grown man now.

It's lain there in the dust,
    Thirty years and more;—
My lips that set a light
At a dead man's door.

"SCINTILLA" WAS PUBLISHED IN APRIL 1915.

BENJAMIN GRIFFITH BRAWLEY

The Freedom of the Free

When the people of Jehovah to the promised land would go,
They were shown a valiant leader for the conflict with the foe;
But they wandered many weary years and faced the raging sea,
Ere their children won the harvest of the Freedom of the Free.

When the black men of the wilderness were wanted of the Lord,
From America to Europe flashed the word with one accord;
And the Christian nations hankered for the glitter of the gain,
While the screaming of the eagle dulled the clanking of the chain.

But the captive on the slaver's deck beneath the lightning's flash—
Unto him were only scourging and the stinging of the lash;
But such things as these must be, they say, and such the pruning be,
Ere our children win the harvest of the Freedom of the Free.

Far across the deep Atlantic speeds the vessel on its way,
And the nights are wild with weeping, and the days with tempests gray,
Till at length within the glory of the dawn the shore appears,
And the slave takes up the burden and the battle of the years.

In the fury of the auction runs the clamor on and on:
"Going! Going! Who bids higher? Going! Going! Going! Gone!"
And the mocking bird is singing, and the lilies dance in glee,
And the slave alone is sighing for the Freedom of the Free.

Now the wide plantation shimmers in the freshness of the morn,
And the dusky workers scatter through the cotton and the corn,
With the problems of the ages in the yearning of their eyes,
While the slave whip sings forever underneath the azure skies.

In the silence of the night and from the weird assembled throng
Comes the beauty and the wailing of the dirge and Sorrow Song:
"I've been listenin' all the night long for to hear some sinner pray;
I've been waitin' all the night long for the breakin' of the day."

Till at length from Maine to Mexico peals forth the trumpet blast,
And a wild expectant nation at the fury stands aghast;
While the young men in their glory feel the fever of the fight,
And the blood drops of the firstborn stain the doorposts in the night.

In the crimson of the carnage, in the deluge of the flame,
Come the black men to the trenches for the honor and the fame;
And they sell their hearts' blood dearly for humanity's decree,
That their sons should have the promise of the Freedom of the Free.

"THE FREEDOM OF THE FREE," SUBTITLED "EMANCIPATION EXPOSITION
POEM," WAS PUBLISHED IN NOVEMBER 1913.

STERLING BROWN

After the Storm

There is pathetic beauty in it all;
    O'erhead the murky, sullen rain clouds pass,
    The sun's first darting rays have pierced the mass,
Just now so grim, so gray. Again the call
Is heard of storm hushed robins. Maples tall,
    To show the regal silver of their class,
    Rustle their thirst-slaked leaves and on the grass,
Drenched into higher color, some last drops fall.

'Tis like that heart, whose happiness excelled
    All others, which, with its gay threshold crossed
        At last by sorrow's gloom, has fitly learned
To stifle throes of pain, has ne'er rebelled
        In angry bitterness, has merely turned
    Gayness to pathos, with no beauty lost.

"AFTER THE STORM" WAS PUBLISHED IN APRIL 1927.

JAMES D. CORROTHERS

The Road to the Bow

Ever and ever and anon,
　　After the black storm, the eternal, beauteous bow!
Brother, to rosy-painted mists that arch beyond,
　　Blithely I go.

My brows men laureled and my lyre
　　Twined with immortal ivy for one little rippling song;
My "House of Golden Leaves" they praised and "passionate fire"—
　　But, Friend, the way is long!

Onward and onward, up! away!
　　Though Fear flaunt all his banners in my face,
And my feet stumble, lo! the Orphean Day!
　　Forward by God's grace!

These signs are still before me: "Fear,"
　　"Danger," "Unprecedented," and I hear black "No".
Still thundering, and "Churl." Good Friend, I rest me here—
　　Then to the glittering bow!

Loometh and cometh Hate in wrath,
　　Mailed Wrong, swart Servitude and Shame, with bitter rue,
Nathless a Negro poet's feet must tread the path
　　The winged god knew.

Thus, my true Brother, dream-led, I
　　Forefend the anathema, following the span.
I hold my head as proudly high
　　As any man.

"THE ROAD TO THE BOW" WAS PUBLISHED IN APRIL 1915.

JOSEPH S. COTTER, SR.

Shakespeare's Sonnet

I read a sonnet from the magic pen,
And in that sonnet was a lilting line,
And from that line I culled a haunting word,
And through that word I saw a crystal mountain,
And from that mountain rose a million voices—
I heard them singly and I heard them jointly—
And some were whispering and some were shouting,
And some were squeaking like a trothsome fieldmouse,
And some were fluting like the Hamelin piper,
And some were singing like a thrush at evening.
And some were wroth or sad and some were merry,
And some lipped notes that rose and splintered sky-ward,
And some tongued tunes that fell and fused the world-heart,
And all the insects halted, strained and listened,
And all the bird-folk trilled a wonder chorus,
And Spring, in sandals, sidled up to Summer,
And Summer, laughing, gripped the hand of Autumn,
And Autumn filled her lap with grief and greetings,
And, when I saw "mailed Winter doff his doublet,"
I hurried back, O Shakespeare to thy sonnet.

"SHAKESPEARE'S SONNET" WAS PUBLISHED IN SEPTEMBER 1923.

COUNTEE CULLEN

Dad

His ways are circumspect and bound
With trite simplicities;
His is the grace of comforts found
In homely hearthside ease.
His words are sage and fall with care,
Because he loves me so;
And being his, he knows, I fear,
The dizzy path I go.
For he was once as young as I,
As prone to take the trail,
To find delight in the sea's low cry,
And a lone wind's lonely wail.
It is his eyes that tell me most
How full his life has been;
There lingers there the faintest ghost
Of some still sacred sin.
So I must quaff Life's crazy wine,
And taste the gall and dregs;
And I must spend this wealth of mine,
Of vagrant wistful legs;
And I must follow, follow, follow
The lure of a silver horn,
That echoes from a leafy hollow,
Where the dreams of youth are born.
Then when the star has shed its gleam,
The rose its crimson coat;
When Beauty flees the hidden dream,
And Pan's pipes blow no note;
When both my shoes are worn too thin,
My weight of fire to bear,
I'll turn like dad, and like him win
The peace of a snug arm-chair.

Bread and Wine

From death of star to new star's birth
This ache of limb, this throb of head,
This sweaty shop, this smell of earth;
For this we pray, "Give daily bread".

Then tremulous with dreams the night,
The feel of soft, brown hands in mine,
Strength from your lips for one more fight:
Bread's not so dry when dipped in wine.

Sonnet to Her

How have I found this favor in her sight,
And will the flame burn steady to the end,
Until we round that dark and dangerous bend
Where there is such a crying need for light;
Or will it flare up now so clear and bright,
Sunlike its wealth so far and wide distend
That nothing will remain for us to spend
When toll is taken by the dismal night?
Why should I harrow up my mind like this,
To tarnish with a doubt each golden kiss?
This is the Day most certainly! This bars
Us now from any hidden darkness spun;
Sufficient to the day let be the sun,
And to the night the spear-points of the stars.

"DAD," "BREAD AND WINE," AND "SONNET TO HER" WERE PUBLISHED IN
NOVEMBER 1922, JUNE 1923, AND MARCH 1927, RESPECTIVELY.

ALLISON DAVIS

Gospel for Those Who Must

One lone bird,
Small and brown,
Singing in the morning
One clear note,

Singing to the high church-steeple
With its needle spire
Pointing to the infinite heaven,
Merging with the far blue sky,

In the fresh vigor of the morning
His one clear call,
Harsh, unvarying, but
Beautiful.

Oh, all sweeter, fuller singers,
All loud and busy noises of the mid-day
Drown his voice;

But in the quiet cool of dusk,
By the spire pointing to the far blue
    vault,
I hear him singing still,

Lonely
With his one unfaltering call,
Beautiful
With his one clear note
Following the spire.

"GOSPEL FOR THOSE WHO MUST" WAS PUBLISHED IN JULY 1928.

JESSIE FAUSET

Again It Is September

Again it is September!
It seems so strange that I who made no vows
Should sit here desolate this golden weather
    And wistfully remember—

A sigh of deepest yearning,
A glowing look and words that knew no bounds,
A swift response, an instant glad surrender
    To kisses wild and burning!

Ay me!
Again it is September!
It seems so strange that I who kept those vows
Should sit here lone, and spent, and mutely praying
    That I may not remember!

Rencontre

My heart, which beat so passionless,
    Leaped high last night when I saw you.
Within me surged the grief of years
    And whelmed me with its endless rue.
My heart which slept so still, so spent,
    Awoke last night—to break anew.

"Courage!" He Said

Ulysses, debarking in the Lotus Land,
Struck the one note that the hapless Ithacans
Travel-sick, mazed, bemused, could understand,
And understanding, follow.

"Courage," he said, "remember, is not Hope!"
He left the worn, safe ship, spumestained and hollow.
"To be courageous is to face despair."
And through the groves and 'thwart the ambient air
Resounded reedy echoes:
"Face despair!"

But this they understood.
And plunging on prepared for best, and most prepared
For worst, found only in their stride
A deep umbrageous wood,
And grassy plains where they disported; eased
And bathed lame feet within a purling stream
And murmured: "Here, Odysseus, would we fain abide!"

But neither the stream's sweet ease
Nor the shade of the vast beech-trees,
Nor the blessed sense
Of the sweet, sweet soil
Beneath feet salt-cracked and worn
Brought to them even then,
(Still fainting and frayed and forlorn),
Such complete recompense
As the knowledge that once again
Facing the new and untried,
They had kept the courage of men!

For he who is courageous
Seeks no meed. Naught flashing nor white
Blazons the fortitude
With which he bears his burden,
Signalling him to the world
For all men's seeing.
His heart is calmly conscious of its might.
The fact of courage,—a sufficient guerdon,—
Like beauty, is its own excuse for being.

"AGAIN IT IS SEPTEMBER," "RENCONTRE," AND " 'COURAGE!' HE SAID"
WERE PUBLISHED IN SEPTEMBER 1917, JANUARY 1924, AND
NOVEMBER 1929, RESPECTIVELY.

LESLIE PINCKNEY HILL

The Teacher

Lord, who am I to teach the way
To little children day by day,
So prone myself to go astray?

I teach them *Knowledge,* but I know
How faint they flicker, and how low
The candles of my knowledge glow.

I teach them *Power* to will and do,
But only now to learn anew
My own great weakness through and through.

I teach them *Love* for all mankind
And all God's creatures; but I find
My love comes lagging still behind.

Lord, if their guide I still must be,
O let the little children see
The teacher leaning hard on thee!

Vision of a Lyncher

Once looked I into hell—'twas in a trance
Throughout a horrid night of soul-wrought pain;
Down through the pit I saw the burning plain,
Where writhed the tortured swarm, without one glance
Upward to earth or God. There in advance
Of all the rest was one with lips profane
And murderous, bloody hands, marked to be slain
By peers that would not bear him countenance:
"God," cried I in my dream, "what soul is he
Doomed thus to drain the utmost cup of fate,
That even the cursed of Tartarus expel?"
And the great Voice replied: "The chastity
Of dear, confiding Law he raped; now Hate,
His own begotten, drives him forth from hell."

"THE TEACHER" AND "VISION OF A LYNCHER" WERE PUBLISHED IN
JANUARY 1911 AND JANUARY 1912, RESPECTIVELY.

FRANK HORNE

Letters Found Near a Suicide

To All of You

My little stone
Sinks quickly
Into the bosom of this deep, dark pool
Of oblivion...
I have troubled its breast but little.
Yet those far shores
That knew me not
Will feel the fleeting, furtive kiss
Of my tiny concentric ripples.....

To Lewellyn

You have borne full well
The burden of my friendship—
I have drunk deep
At your crystal pool,
And in return
I have polluted its waters
With the bile of my hatred,
I have flooded your soul
With tortuous thoughts,
I have played Iscariot
To your Pythias.....

To Mother

I came
In the blinding sweep
Of ecstatic pain,
I go
In the throbbing pulse
Of Aching Space,
In the eons between
I piled upon you
Pain on pain
Ache on ache
And yet as I go
I shall know

That you will grieve
And want me back . . . . .

To Bennetti
You have freed me—
In opening wide the doors
Of flesh—
You have freed me
Of the binding leash.
I have climbed the heights
Of white disaster.
My body screaming
In the silver crash of passion . . . . .
Before you gave yourself
To him
I had chained myself
For you.
But when at last
You lowered your proud flag
In surrender complete
You gave me too, as hostage—
And I have swept my joy
At the dawn-tipped shrine
Of many breasts.

To Jean
When you poured your love
Like molten flame
Into the throbbing mold
Of her pulsing veins
Leaving her blood a river of fire
And her arteries channels of light,
I hated you . . .
Hated with that primal hate
That has its wells
In the flesh of me
And the flesh of you
And the flesh of her

I hated you—
Hated with envy
Your mastery of her being . . .
With one fleshy gesture
You pricked the irridescent bubble
Of my dreams
And so to make
Your conquest more sweet
I tell you now
That I hated you.

To Catalina
Love thy piano, Oh girl,
It will give you back
Note for Note
The harmonies of your soul.
It will sing back to you
The high songs of your heart.
It will give
As well as take . . . . .

To Mariette
I sought consolation
In the sorrow of your eyes.
You sought reguerdon
In the crying of my heart . . .
We found that shattered dreamers
Can be bitter hosts . . . . .

To ———
You call it
Death of the Spirit
And I call it Life . . .
The vigor of vibration,
The muffled knocks,
The silver sheen of passion's flood,
The ecstacy of pain . . .
You call it

Death of the Spirit
And I call it Life.

To Telie
You have made my voice
A rippling laugh
   But my heart
   A crying thing . . .
   'Tis better thus,
   A fleeting kiss
   And then,
   The dark . . .

To "Chick"
Oh Achilles of the moleskins
And the gridiron
Do not wonder
Nor doubt that this is I
That lie so calmly here—
This is the same exultant beast
That so joyously
Ran the ball with you
In those far flung days of abandon.
You remember how recklessly
We revelled in the heat and the dust
And the swirl of conflict?
You remember they called us
The Terrible Two?
And you remember
After we had battered our heads
And our bodies
Against the stonewall of their defense,—
You remember the signal I would call
And how you would look at me
In faith and admiration
And say "Let's go", . . .
How the lines would clash
And strain,

And how I would find an opening,
A wee small space,
Amidst tangling arms and torsos,
And how I would slip through
Fighting and squirming
Over the line
To victory.
You remember, Chick? . . .
When you gaze at me here
Let that same light
Of faith and admiration
Shine in your eyes
For I have battered the stark stonewall
Before me. . . .
I have kept faith with you
And now
I have called my signal,
Found my opening
And slipped through
Fighting and squirming
Over the line
To victory. . . .

To Wanda
To you, so far away
So cold and aloof,
To you, who knew me so well,
This is my last Grand Gesture
This is my last Great Effect
And as I go winging
Through the black doors of eternity
Is that thin sound I hear
Your applause? . . . . .

Harlem

The Black Minstrel Sings:—
You ain't been there, brother?
Don't tell me so!
"... Tell 'im 'bout it ... tell 'im 'bout it ..."
Han' me ma sax
An lemme go
Taint nothin' to 'im
Lemme tell 'im so—
Han' me ma sax
An' lemme go ...
Harlem ... Harlem
Black, black Harlem
Boody ... see hootchiepep
Hootchiepep ... See boody—
... I'll sing 'im 'bout it—

Harlem ... Harlem
Black, black Harlem
Niggers, Jigs an' shiney spades
Highbrowns, yallers, fagingy-fagades
"... Oh say it, brother
Say it ..."
Pullman porters, shipping clerks an' monkey chasers
Actors, lawyers, Black Jews an' fairies
Ofays, pimps, low-downs an' dicties
Cabarets, gin an' number tickets
All mixed in
With gangs o'churches—
Sugar-foot misters an' sun-dodgin' sisters
Don't get up
Till other folks long in bed ...
... Hey! ... Hey!
"Say it, brother
Say it ..."

"LETTERS FOUND NEAR A SUICIDE" AND "HARLEM" WERE PUBLISHED IN
NOVEMBER 1925 AND JUNE 1928, RESPECTIVELY.

LANGSTON HUGHES

The Negro Speaks of Rivers

I've known rivers:
I've known rivers ancient as the world and older than the flow of human
    blood in human veins.

My soul has grown deep like the rivers.

I bathed in the Euphrates when dawns were young.
I built my hut near the Congo and it lulled me to sleep.

I looked upon the Nile and raised the pyramids above it.
I heard the singing of the Mississippi when Abe Lincoln went down to
    New Orleans, and I've seen its muddy bosom turn all golden in the
    sunset.

I've known rivers;
Ancient, dusky rivers.

My soul has grown deep like the rivers.

The South

The lazy, laughing South
With blood on its mouth;
The sunny-faced South,
    Beast-strong,
    Idiot-brained;
The child-minded South
Scratching in the dead fire's ashes
For a Negro's bones.
    Cotton and the moon,
    Warmth, earth, warmth,
    The sky, the sun, the stars,
    The magnolia-scented South;
Beautiful, like a woman,
Seductive as a dark-eyed whore,
    Passionate, cruel,
    Honey-lipped, syphilitic—
    That is the South.
And I, who am black, would love her

But she spits in my face;
And I, who am black,
Would give her many rare gifts
But she turns her back upon me;
 So now I seek the North—
 The cold-faced North,
 For she, they say,
 Is a kinder mistress,
And in her house my children
May escape the spell of the South.

Being Old

It's because you are so young,—
You do not understand.
 But we are old
 As the jungle trees
 That bloomed forever,
 Old as the forgotten rivers
 That flowed into the earth.
Surely we know what you do not know:
 Joy of living,
 Uselessness of things.
You are too young to understand yet.
Build another skyscraper
Touching the stars.
We sit with our backs against a tree
And watch skyscrapers tumble
And stars forget.
 Solomon built a temple
 And it must have fallen down.
 It isn't here now.
We know some things, being old,
You do not understand.

"THE NEGRO SPEAKS OF RIVERS," "THE SOUTH," AND
"BEING OLD" WERE PUBLISHED IN JUNE 1921, JUNE 1922,
AND OCTOBER 1927, RESPECTIVELY.

ROSCOE C. JAMISON

Negro Soldiers

These truly are the Brave,
These men who cast aside
Old memories, to walk the blood-stained pave
Of Sacrifice, joining the solemn tide
That moves away, to suffer and to die
For Freedom—when their own is yet denied!
O Pride! O Prejudice! When they pass by,
Hail them, the Brave, for you now crucified!

These truly are the Free,
These souls that grandly rise
Above base dreams of vengeance for their wrongs,
Who march to war with visions in their eyes
Of Peace through Brotherhood, lifting glad songs
Aforetime, while they front the firing-line.
Stand and behold! They take the field today,
Shedding their blood like Him now held divine,
That those who mock might find a better way!

"NEGRO SOLDIERS" WAS PUBLISHED IN SEPTEMBER 1917.

CHARLES BERTRAM JOHNSON

Old Things

I love old faces mellow wise,
    That smile; their young-old laughing eyes
Undimmed, still view, in sheer pretense
    Of youth, their own sweet innocence.

I love old hands that trembling bless
    Youth's wild impetuous duress;
That find in childhood's tangled cares,
    Life's answers to unuttered prayers.

Old things to me are dear and best:
    Old faith—that after life is rest;
That somehow, from above our will,
    God works His gracious marvels still.

True Wealth

What though no castles grand
In somber grandeur stand
Entitled in my name;
What though uncrowned by fame
I sing in humble state;
I don't bemoan my fate:
The April-haunted lea
Is wealth enough for me.

"OLD THINGS" AND "TRUE WEALTH" WERE PUBLISHED IN
MARCH 1923 AND APRIL 1924, RESPECTIVELY.

FENTON JOHNSON

My Love

Young gallant from the fairer race of men,
　　Have you a love as comely as the maid
To whom I chant my lyre-strung passion songs?
　　Has she large eyes that gleam from out the shade,
And voice as low as when Ohio's stream
Glides silently along a summer dream?

Her face is golden like the setting sun,
　　Her teeth as white as January's snow,
Her smile is like a gleam from Paradise,
　　Her laugh the sweetest music that I know,
And all the wide, wide world is but a mite
When she, my darling elf, is in my sight.

Let Sorrow wring the blood from out my heart,
　　Let Melancholy be my daily book,
Let all the earth be like a sinner's grave,
　　And let my wand'ring spirit never look
Upon the Kingdom if my damozel
From out my soul the charm of love dispel.

"MY LOVE" WAS PUBLISHED IN MARCH 1913.

GEORGIA DOUGLAS JOHNSON

Prejudice

These fell miasmic rings of mist, with ghoulish menace bound,
Their noose-horizons tightening my little world around,
They still the throbbing will to sing, to dance, to speed away,
And fling the soul insurgent back into its shell of clay:
Beneath these crusted silences a seething Etna lies,
The fire of whose furnaces may sleep—but never dies!

Motherhood

Don't knock on my door, little child,
I cannot let you in;
You know not what a world this is,
Of cruelty and sin.
Wait in the still eternity
Until I come to you.
The world is cruel, cruel, child,
I cannot let you through.

Don't knock at my heart, little one,
I cannot bear the pain
Of turning deaf ears to your call,
Time and time again.
You do not know the monster men
Inhabiting the earth.
Be still, be still, my precious child,
I cannot give you birth.

Decay

Swift-footed Time, how eagerly you go
Across the swaying summer grasses bed
As on in breathless haste you hurry me
To Winter with its chilling winds and snow.

The noontide hour is fading—in my hair
The furtive shadows caper and recline.
I tell my beads of amethyst and gold
So near at end, so passing dear and fair.

Courier

Where are the brave men?
Where are the strong men?
Pygmies rise and spawn the earth,
Weak-kneed, weak-hearted and afraid!
Afraid to face the counsel of their timid hearts.
Afraid to look men squarely—
Down they gaze
With fatal fascination—
Down,
Down
Into the whirling maggot-sands
Of prejudice!

"PREJUDICE" AND "MOTHERHOOD" WERE PUBLISHED IN
SEPTEMBER AND OCTOBER 1922, RESPECTIVELY.
"DECAY" AND "COURIER" WERE PUBLISHED IN NOVEMBER 1926.

JAMES WELDON JOHNSON

Father, Father Abraham

Father, Father Abraham,
    To-day look on us from above;
On us, the offspring of thy faith,
    The children of thy Christlike love.

For that which we have humbly wrought,
    Give us to-day thy kindly smile;
Wherein we've failed or fallen short,
    Bear with us, Father, yet a while.

Father, Father Abraham,
    To-day we lift our hearts to thee,
Filled with the thought of what great price
    Was paid, that we might ransomed be.

To-day we consecrate ourselves
    Anew in hand and heart and brain,
To send this judgment down the years:
    The ransom was not paid in vain.

Father, Father Abraham,
    To-day send on us from above
A blessing of thy gentle strength,
    Of thy large faith, of thy deep love.

Brothers

See! There he stands; not brave, with an air
Of sullen stupor. Mark him well! Is he
Not more like brute than man? Look in his eye!
No light is there, none, save the light that shines
In the now glaring, and now shifting orbs
Of some wild animal in the hunter's trap.

    How came this beast in human shape and form?

Speak man!—We call you man because you wear
His shape—How are you thus? Are you not from
That docile, child-like, tender-hearted race
Which we have known three centuries? Not from

That more than faithful race which through three wars
Fed our dear wives and nursed our helpless babes
Without a single breach of trust? Speak out?

    I am, and am not.
        Then who, why are you?
    I am a thing not new, I am as old
As human nature. I am that which lurks,
Ready to spring whenever a bar is loosed;
The ancient trait which fights incessantly
Against restraint, balks at the upward climb;
The weight forever seeking to obey
The law of downward pull,—and I am more:
The bitter fruit am I of planted seed,
The resultant, the inevitable end
Of evil forces and the powers of wrong.

    Lessons in degradation taught and learned,
The memories of cruel sights and deeds,
The pent up bitterness, the unspent hate
Filtered through fifteen generations have
Sprung up and found in me sporadic life.
In me the muttered curse of dying men,
On me the stain of conquered women, and
Consuming me the fearful fires of lust,
Lit long ago by other hands than mine.
In me the down-crushed spirit, the hurled-back prayers
Of wretches now long dead,—their dire bequests,—
In me the echo of the stifled cry
Of children for their bartered mothers' breasts.

    I claim no race, no race claims me; I am
No more than human dregs; degenerate;
The monstrous offspring of the monster, Sin;
I am—just what I am—The race that fed
Your wives and nursed your babes would do the same

To-day, but I—
    Enough, the brute must die!
Quick! Chain him to that oak! It will resist
The fire much longer than this slender pine.
Now bring the fuel! Pile it 'round him! Wait!
Pile not so fast or high! or we shall lose
The agony and terror in his face.

And now the torch! Good fuel that! the flames
Already leap head-high. Ha! hear that shriek!
And there's another wilder than the first.
Fetch water! Water! Pour a little on
The fire, lest it should burn too fast. Hold so!
Now let it slowly blaze again. See there!
He squirms, he groans, his eyes bulge wildly out,

Searching around in vain appeal for help.
Another shriek, the last! Watch how the flesh
Grows crisp and hangs till, turned to ash, it sifts
Down through the coils of chain that hold erect
The ghastly frame against the bark-scorched tree.

    Stop! to each man no more than one man's share
You take that bone, and you this tooth; the chain
Let us divide its links; this skull, of course,
In fair division, to the leader comes.

    And now his fiendish crime has been avenged;
Let us back to our wives and children.—Say,
What did he mean by those last muttered words,
"Brothers in spirit, brothers in deed are we"?

Helene

I walk by day, I wake by night,
Thirsting, panting for your beauty—
And ever, ever at my side
There stalks a spectre men call Duty.

I turn aside, I turn about,
And still love beckons, burning bright—
And ever, ever facing me
There hands a sword that men call Right.

I fight the battle in my heart,
And wavering is the victory;
And then I pray to God for strength,
In this, my own Gethsemane.

Oft in my agony of soul
I wonder if God hears my prayers,
And—may He now forgive the thought—
I sometimes wonder if God cares.

The River

When the earth was young this river
Was a thing of unsoiled beauty.
It gurgled down from the hill,
And hymned its way through the valley.
A pageant in the sunlight,
A mystery under the moon,
And a symbol of all eternity
Where it lost itself in the ocean.

I crossed the river the other day
On a hideous ferryboat,
I leaned on the rail and watched the wheel
Savagely churn up the water.
It churned up time and boxes,
Jute bags and rotten cabbages,
A cat some seven days drowned
And a stench that went to the stomach.

The river hissed and frothed
In piteous indignation.
I thought: Why this hissing and frothing,
Do you not know
That the ultimate end of all beautiful rivers
Is to carry sewage to the sea?

Moods

I love the sea when it is windswept
The ships ploughing up the foam,
The sailor man loudly swearing
From sheer excess of joy,
The shrill cry of a solitary sea bird,
And the smell of the sharp, salt spray.

I love the melancholy beach
Under the shimmering magic of the moon.
When just above the ocean's rim
One lone star marks a path for me;
And the waves are moaning to the shore
Their monotoned love melody.

A Passing Melody

A chord was touched on the harp of my heart,
On the delicate strings at the core;
A tender, hesitating part
I had never heard before.

It quivered there one moment brief,
Awakening hopes and fears,
Imparting joy, suggesting grief,
Then melted into tears.

Oh! was it a long lost love that cleaven
To the dead, forgotten past?
Or but the rustling of the leaves,
Stirred by the winter's blast?

"FATHER, FATHER ABRAHAM" AND "BROTHERS" WERE PUBLISHED IN
FEBRUARY 1913 AND FEBRUARY 1916, RESPECTIVELY.
"HELENE," "THE RIVER," "MOODS," AND "A PASSING MELODY" ARE
UNPUBLISHED POEMS, WRITTEN CIRCA 1920S.

CLAUDE MCKAY

The International Spirit

As flower dust is driven down the wind
To touch and quicken the green life of earth,
As birds spread wings and leave cold lands behind,
For regions of sweet warmth and singing mirth:
So shall thy thought be carried surely forth
To the remotest dwellings of mankind,
Reaching its inmost self to give new birth,
New strength, new purpose to man's boundless mind.

The birds of time shall wing thee down the ways
Of man's abode. The progress will be keen
Against the heavy mist of stormy days,
As ever progress through the years has been.
Even as strong-winged messengers are seen,
In these amazing times with fine amaze,
Threading the tides of space that roll between
The earth and heavens that ever hold man's gaze.

The nations will be stricken at thy word,
And grand old prejudices crumble down,
That ancient pride in warring breasts has stirred.
The noblest men shall work for any renown.
Thy truest heralds do not fear the frown
Of legioned bigots leagued by fear and spurred
To crush thy truth, but more the shouting clown,
The standard-flocking of the sheeplike herd.

"THE INTERNATIONAL SPIRIT" WAS PUBLISHED IN JUNE 1928.

ALICE DUNBAR NELSON

Sonnet

I had not thought of violets of late,
The wild, shy kind that spring beneath your feet
In wistful April days, when lovers mate
And wander through the fields in raptures sweet.
The thought of violets meant florists' shops,
And cabarets and soaps, and deadening wines.
So far from sweet real things my thoughts had strayed,
I had forgot wide fields; and clear brown streams;
The perfect loveliness that God has made,—
Wild violets shy and Heaven-mounting dreams.
And now—unwittingly, you've made me dream
Of violets, and my soul's forgotten gleam.

The Proletariat Speaks

I love beautiful things:
Great trees, bending green winged branches to a velvet lawn,
Fountains sparkling in white marble basins,
Cool fragrance of lilacs and roses and honeysuckle
Or exotic blooms, filling the air with heart-contracting odors;
Spacious rooms, cool and gracious with statues and books,
Carven seats and tapestries, and old masters.
Whose patina shows the wealth of centuries.

And so I work
In a dusty office, whose grimed windows
Look out in an alley of unbelievable squalor.
Where mangy cats, in their degradation, spurn
Swarming bits of meat and bread;
Where odors, vile and breath taking, rise in fetid waves
Filling my nostrils, scorching my humid, bitter cheeks.

I love beautiful things:
Carven tables laid with lily-hued linen
And fragile china and sparkling irridescent glass;
Pale silver, etched with heraldies,
Where tender bits of regal dainties tempt,
And soft-stepped service anticipates the unspoken wish.

And so I eat
In the food-laden air of a greasy kitchen,
At an oil-clothed table:
Plate piled high with food that turns my head away,
Lest a squeamish stomach reject too soon
The lumpy gobs it never needed.
Or in a smoky cafeteria, balancing a slippery tray
To a table crowded with elbows
Which lately the bus boy wiped with a grimy rag.

I love beautiful things:
Soft linen sheets and silken coverlet,
Sweet coolth of chamber opened wide to fragrant breeze;
Rose shaded lamps and golden atomizers,
Spraying Parisian fragrance over my relaxed limbs,
Fresh from a white marble bath, and sweet cool spray.

And so I sleep
In a hot hall-room whose half opened window,
Unscreened, refuses to budge another inch;
Admits no air, only insects, and hot choking gasps,
That make me writhe, nun-like, in sackcloth sheets and lumps of straw.
And then I rise
To fight my way to a dubious tub
Whose tiny, tepid stream threatens to make me late;
And hurrying out, dab my unrefreshed face
With bits of toiletry from the ten cent store.

"SONNET" AND "THE PROLETARIAT SPEAKS" WERE PUBLISHED IN
AUGUST 1919 AND NOVEMBER 1929, RESPECTIVELY.

EFFIE LEE NEWSOME

Exodus

Rank fennel and broom
Grow wanly beside
The cottage and room
We once occupied,
But sold for the snows!
The dahoon berry weeps in blood,
I know,
Watched by the crow—
I've seen both grow
In those weird wastes of Dixie!

Bluebird

I just heard your soft smothered voice today!
I'm sure you'll flit on in your light-winged way,
Unmindful, undreaming of me,
Who have not yet seen you in blue and brown,
But just heard your lush notes drip down, drip down
As showers from the black ash tree.

The Little Page

And then some others ring the bell
Who seem to like us very well.
They like our dogs and like our cats,
And give them little friendly pats,
And ask their names and all,
Right down there in the hall.
We watch them from upstairs,
Then slip down easily,
When they are friends of ours
That we are glad to see,
Especially when they know our names
And have a lot to talk about,
Our running and our different games—
Some others just leave children out—
And all about your birthdays,
And who's the oldest now.
They're not real favorites with the rest.
But they suit us somehow.

"EXODUS," "BLUEBIRD," AND "THE LITTLE PAGE" WERE PUBLISHED IN
JANUARY 1925, APRIL 1927, AND JUNE 1928, RESPECTIVELY.

ANNE SPENCER

Dunbar

Ah, how poets sing and die!
Make one song and Heaven takes it:
Have one heart and Beauty breaks it:
Chatterton, Shelley, Keats, and I—
Ah, how poets sing and die!

White Things

Most things are colorful things—the sky, earth, and sea.
Black men are most men; but the white are free!
White things are rare things; so rare, so rare
They stole from out a silvered world—somewhere.
Finding earth-plains fair plains, save greenly grassed,
They strewed white feathers of cowardice, as they passed;
    The golden stars with lances fine,
    The hills all red and darkened pine,
They blanched with their wand of power;
And turned the blood in a ruby rose
To a poor white poppy-flower.

They pyred a race of black, black men,
And burned them to ashes white; then,
Laughing, a young one claimed a skull,
For the skull of a black is white, not dull,
    But a glistening awful thing;
    Made it seems, for this ghoul to swing
In the face of God with all his might,
And swear by the hell that sired him:
    "Man-maker, make white!"

"DUNBAR" AND "WHITE THINGS" WERE PUBLISHED IN NOVEMBER 1920 AND
MARCH 1923, RESPECTIVELY.

JEAN TOOMER

Song of the Son

Pour, O pour, that parting soul in song,
O pour it in the saw-dust glow of night,
Into the velvet pine-smoke air tonight,
And let the valley carry it along,
And let the valley carry it along.

O land and soil, red soil and sweet-gum tree
So scant of grass, so profligate of pines,
Now just before an epoch's sun declines
Thy son, in time, I have returned to thee,
Thy son, I have in time returned to thee.

In time, for though the sun is setting on
A song-lit race of slaves, it has not set;
Though late, O soil it is not too late yet
To catch thy plaintive soul, leaving, soon gone,
Leaving, to catch thy plaintive soul soon gone.

O Negro slaves, dark-purple ripened plums,
Squeezed, and bursting in the pine-wood air,
Passing, before they stripped the old tree bare
One plum was saved for me, one seed becomes

An everlasting song, a singing tree,
Carrolling softly souls of slavery,
All that they were, and that they are to me,—
Carrolling softly souls of slavery.

Banking Coal

Whoever it was who brought the first wood and coal
To start the fire, did his part well;
Not all wood takes to fire from a match,
Nor coal from wood before it's burned to charcoal.
The wood and coal in question caught a flame
And flared up beautifully, touching the air
That takes a flame from anything.

Somehow the fire was furnaced,
And then the time was ripe for some to say,
"Right banking of the furnace saves the coal."
I've seen them set to work, each in his way,
Though all with shovels and with ashes,
Never resting till the fire seemed most dead;
Whereupon they'd crawl in hooded night-caps
Contentedly to bed. Sometimes the fire left alone
Would die, but like as not spiced tongues
Remaining by the hardest on till day would flicker up,
Never strong, to anyone who cared to rake for them.
But roaring fires never have been made that way.
I'd like to tell those folks that one grand flare
Transferred to memory tissues of the air
Is worth a life, or, for dull minds that turn in gold,
All money ever saved by banking coal.

"SONG OF THE SON" AND "BANKING COAL" WERE PUBLISHED IN
APRIL 1922 AND JUNE 1922, RESPECTIVELY.

PART TWO

FICTION

THE SERVANT

In this short story, Fenton Johnson introduces the reader to Elizabeth (Eliza) Jan, an African-American servant. Liza, a Southerner, finds herself working for an "uppity" Chicago black family. Although the indignities of racism have always been part of her existence, she now experiences a feeling of separation based on social class within her own race. This short story was published in August 1912.

"Ah sho' ain't gwine tuh wohk foh dese hyar cullud folks no mo'. 'Deed ah isn't."

And in these words, spoken during great emotional stress, Eliza Jane, three weeks removed from the Southland, announced to herself her dissatisfaction with the Crawfords.

"It's nuffin' but wohk, wohk, wohk all de' time as if ah nevah gits tiahed. It's 'Liza dis and 'Liza dat an' nevah do dey say when de day am done: 'Won't you come wif us to de festival or de 'vival meetin'?' Ah's gwine tuh quit dese high-toned folks, an' git in some white fam'ly. Ah's too lonely heah."

The Crawfords were well-to-do Chicago Negroes. Mr. Crawford was a lawyer, who in recent years had acquired a fortune through real estate. His wife was the daughter of a Southern Congressman of reconstruction days, and was consequently proud of her money and family. They had two children, Wallace and Aline, who were students of the university, and very popular among the young people of their race. According to their point of view those who were inferior to them intellectually were not their equals socially and the servant's position was the lowest plane of society. Mrs. Crawford was a prominent clubwoman and intimate with the leading social workers of both races. Mr. Crawford belonged to the Elmore Club, an organization of colored professional and business men, who had purchased a neat little clubhouse where they could play billiards and entertain their wives and friends at dances and whist parties. He had received his education at Fisk University and a Chicago law school, and was looked upon with high respect by the black world.

Eliza came to them from the backwoods of Georgia with one gingham dress and a pair of squeaky new shoes. Mrs. Crawford engaged her partly on account of her pretty face and her seeming willingness to do as she was bidden; and for a day or two the little Georgian appeared satisfied, for she was in financial straits and the liberal wages were uppermost in her mind. But when Mrs. Crawford advanced her half of her wages the irresponsible creature had enough to satisfy her few wants and began to discover the faults in her situation. Mrs. Crawford was too haughty; Aline too proud and cold; Wallace never had a pleasant word for her or asked her to go out with him; and Mr. Crawford was splenetic and hard to please. The work was too confining; she longed for the open air and for the freedom of her own Georgia land. Every night the lights on State Street shone so brightly, emphasizing her loneliness in a city where she had neither friends nor acquaintances.

In Georgia she was not confronted with the social problem. There she worked for the whites and associated with the blacks; there the color line obliterated every other line society should wish to draw. No rich Negroes asserted their superiority over her; she was just plain Eliza and they were Moses or Mandy, as the case might be. And now that she was up North, where money was the basis of social stratum, inferiority within the race was sickening and disappointing.

That was the situation that confronted her that Friday evening as she sat before the little mirror in her room.

Softly to her ears came the low strains of a violin. Music! How it touched her soul! Could she resist the spell? Could she, who loved to hear the drowsy humming of the bees and the endless song of the brook back there in Georgia, refrain from listening to the melody of rosin and bow? With low, measured step she left her room and went upstairs to the library, where the Friday Evening Culture Club, a young people's organization, was being entertained by Wallace and Aline. With a slight tremor, for she feared that she was breaking some social rule, she knocked on the door, which was presently opened by Wallace himself, standing before her with bow and violin.

" 'Scuse me, please. Ah jes' wants tuh heah de music, dat's all. Ah laks music so," she said, her voice trembling with fear.

"Oh, it is you," was all that Wallace said, as he motioned her to a seat in the corner.

There were about twenty young people in the library and the music room. They were elegantly dressed, intelligent in countenance, and many of them handsome. At the time Eliza entered Aline was playing a selection from Chopin on the piano, and the members of the club were conversing in low tones. Eliza could not understand the drift of their conversation; such names as Ibsen, Galsworthy and Shaw were mentioned. The problem novel was discussed, and current politics was made the ground for friendly argument among the boys. All this was Greek to the little unlettered girl in the corner, and her large black eyes opened wide with astonishment and her breath heaved with wonder.

Presently a young octoroon girl, who had acquired some reputation among her people as a concert singer, was called upon by the presiding officer to render a contribution to the program. Aline accompanied her as in a voice both sweet and technically correct she rendered a love song from Schubert, and for an encore sang in a tone of passionate tenderness the "Swing Low, Sweet Chariot," of plantation days.

The singer was followed by Wallace, who said: "I might give you something from the masters, but as we have music of our own I think it is better that we should cultivate that."

And so the young musician tuned his instrument and started to play the sorrow songs that can never die, because they are the genuine expression of American life. As the wild passionate music came forth, trembling with its pathos, a tear glistened in Eliza's eye. She saw the little cabin that she called home, the burning sand where the Negro children played, the cotton field with its wealth of snowy blossoms, and the lane on a moonlight night when the dusky lovers plighted their troth, free from the problem of color. She saw the grave where her mother lay, gone to sleep too soon because poverty had preyed on her and won the battle. She saw the river winding its way through eternity, bringing as its tribute the body of her father, given to the water by a crowd of hilarious poor whites, drunk with cheap corn whiskey.

And he, who thus played the old plantation songs, was he not more than she? He could throw on the screen of her mind pictures of her home life by means of an instrument that she could not even wield. He and his sister were versed in the lore and the music of civilization. Within her bosom was nothing save the emotions that she could feel so vividly but could not express. To him culture had granted the gift to interpret the joys and sorrows of the human soul; and some mysterious power had denied her that sweet privilege.

As all this flashed across her mind, she realized her utter littleness.

Rising, her face wet with tears, she left the room so quietly that no one noticed her departure.

When she had reached her room she threw herself across the bed and sobbed as if her heart were bursting.

"Ah wants tuh luhn! Ah wants tuh luhn! Ah's so po' an' nuffin' lak. Ah wants tuh luhn."

EMMY

This story by Jessie Fauset was published in two parts for the December 1912 and January 1913 issues of *The Crisis*. Emmy, a beautiful golden-brown girl of central Pennsylvania, falls in love with Archie Ferrers, a young African American whose blackness isn't at all visible. Archie has a promising future as an engineer, but only because his boss, a white man, believes that Archie is of foreign extraction. Archie has to decide whether he will negate his blackness and pursue his career or hold on to the love of his life, Emmy.

I.

"There are five races," said Emmy confidently. "The white or Caucasian, the yellow or Mongolian, the red or Indian, the brown or Malay, and the black or Negro."

"Correct," nodded Miss Wenzel mechanically. "Now to which of the five do you belong?" And then immediately Miss Wenzel reddened.

Emmy hesitated. Not because hers was the only dark face in the crowded schoolroom, but because she was visualizing the pictures with which the geography had illustrated its information. She was not white, she knew that nor had she almond eyes like the Chinese, nor the feathers which the Indian wore in his hair and which, of course, were to Emmy a racial characteristic. She regarded the color of her slim brown hands with interest—she had never thought of it before. The Malay was a horrid, ugly-looking thing with a ring in his nose. But he was brown, so she was, she supposed, really a Malay.

And yet the Hottentot, chosen with careful nicety to represent the entire Negro race, had on the whole a better appearance.

"I belong," she began tentatively, "to the black or Negro race."

"Yes," said Miss Wenzel with a sigh of relief, for if Emmy had chosen to ally herself with any other race except, of course, the white, how could she, teacher though she was, set her straight without embarrassment? The recess bell rang and she dismissed them with a brief but thankful "You may pass."

Emmy uttered a sigh of relief, too, as she entered the schoolyard. She had been terribly near failing.

"I was so scared," she breathed to little towheaded Mary Holborn. "Did you see what a long time I was answering? Guess Eunice Leeks thought for sure I'd fail and she'd get my place."

"Yes, I guess she did," agreed Mary. "I'm so glad you didn't fail—but, oh, Emmy, didn't you mind?"

Emmy looked up in astonishment from the orange she was peeling.

"Mind what? Here, you can have the biggest half. I don't like oranges anyway—sort of remind me of niter. Mind what, Mary?"

"Why, saying you were black and"—she hesitated, her little freckled face getting pinker and pinker—"a negro, and all that before the class." And then mistaking the look on Emmy's face, she hastened on. "Everybody in Plainville says all the time that you're too nice and smart to be a—er—I mean, to be colored. And your dresses are so pretty, and your hair isn't all funny either." She seized one of Emmy's hands—an exquisite member, all bronze outside, and within a soft pinky white.

"Oh, Emmy, don't you think if you scrubbed real hard you could get some of the brown off?"

"But I don't want to," protested Emmy. "I guess my hands are as nice as yours, Mary Holborn. We're just the same, only you're white and I'm brown. But I don't see any difference. Eunice Leeks' eyes are green and yours are blue, but you can both see."

"Oh, well," said Mary Holborn, "if you don't mind——"

If she didn't mind—but why should she mind?

"Why should I mind, Archie," she asked that faithful squire as they walked home in the afternoon through the pleasant "main" street. Archie had brought her home from school ever since she could remember. He was two years older than she; tall, strong and beautiful, and her final arbiter.

Archie stopped to watch a spider.

"See how he does it, Emmy! See him bring that thread over! Gee, if I could swing a bridge across the pond as easy as that! What d'you say? Why should you mind? Oh, I don't guess there's anything for us to mind about. It's white people, they're always minding—I don't know why. If any of the boys in your class say anything to you, you let me know. I licked Bill Jennings the other day for calling me a 'guiney.'

Wish I were a good, sure-enough brown like you, and then everybody'd know just what I am."

Archie's clear olive skin and aquiline features made his Negro ancestry difficult of belief.

"But," persisted Emmy, "what difference does it make?"

"Oh, I'll tell you some other time," he returned vaguely. "Can't you ask questions though? Look, it's going to rain. That means uncle won't need me in the field this afternoon. See here, Emmy, bet I can let you run ahead while I count fifteen, and then beat you to your house. Want to try?"

They reached the house none too soon, for the soft spring drizzle soon turned into gusty torrents. Archie was happy—he loved Emmy's house with the long, high rooms and the books and the queer foreign pictures. And Emmy had so many sensible playthings. Of course, a great big fellow of 13 doesn't care for locomotives and blocks in the ordinary way, but when one is trying to work out how a bridge must be built over a lop-sided ravine, such things are by no means to be despised. When Mrs. Carrel, Emmy's mother, sent Céleste to tell the children to come to dinner, they raised such a protest that the kindly French woman finally set them a table in the sitting room, and left them to their own devices.

"Don't you love little fresh green peas?" said Emmy ecstatically. "Oh, Archie, won't you tell me now what difference it makes whether you are white or colored?" She peered into the vegetable dish. "Do you suppose Céleste would give us some more peas? There's only about a spoonful left."

"I don't believe she would," returned the boy, evading the important part of her question. "There were lots of them to start with, you know. Look, if you take up each pea separately on your fork—like that— they'll last longer. It's hard to do, too. Bet I can do it better than you."

And in the exciting contest that followed both children forgot all about the "problem."

II.

Miss Wenzel sent for Emmy the next day. Gently but insistently, and altogether from a mistaken sense of duty, she tried to make the child see wherein her lot differed from that of her white schoolmates. She felt herself that she hadn't succeeded very well. Emmy, immaculate in a white frock, her bronze elfin face framed in its thick curling black hair, alert with interest, had listened very attentively. She had made no comments till toward the end.

"Then because I'm brown," she had said, "I'm not as good as you." Emmy was at all times severely logical.

"Well, I wouldn't—quite say that," stammered Miss Wenzel miserably. "You're really very nice, you know, especially nice for a colored girl, but—well, you're different."

Emmy listened patiently. "I wish you'd tell me how, Miss Wenzel," she began. "Archie Ferrers is different, too, isn't he? And yet he's lots nicer than almost any of the boys in Plainville. And he's smart, you know. I guess he's pretty poor—I shouldn't like to be that—but my mother isn't poor, and she's handsome. I heard Céleste say so, and she has beautiful clothes. I think, Miss Wenzel, it must be rather nice to be different."

It was at this point that Miss Wenzel had desisted and, tucking a little tissue-wrapped oblong into Emmy's hands, had sent her home.

"I don't think I did any good," she told her sister wonderingly. "I couldn't make her see what being colored meant."

"I don't see why you didn't leave her alone," said Hannah Wenzel testily. "I don't guess she'll meet with much prejudice if she stays here in central Pennsylvania. And if she goes away she'll meet plenty of people who'll make it their business to see that she understands what being colored means. Those things adjust themselves."

"Not always," retorted Miss Wenzel, "and anyway, that child ought to know. She's got to have some of the wind taken out of her sails, some day, anyhow. Look how her mother dresses her. I suppose she does make pretty good money—I've heard that translating pays well. Seems so funny for a colored woman to be able to speak and write a foreign language." She returned to her former complaint.

"Of course it doesn't cost much to live here, but Emmy's clothes! White frocks all last winter, and a long red coat—broadcloth it was, Hannah. And big bows on her hair—she has got pretty hair, I must say."

"Oh, well," said Miss Hannah, "I suppose Céleste makes her clothes. I guess colored people want to look nice just as much as anybody else. I heard Mr. Holborn say Mrs. Carrel used to live in France; I suppose that's where she got all her stylish ways."

"Yes, just think of that," resumed Miss Wenzel vigorously, "a colored woman with a French maid. Though if it weren't for her skin you'd never tell by her actions what she was. It's the same way with that Archie Ferrers, too, looking for all the world like some foreigner. I must say I like colored people to look and act like what they are."

She spoke the more bitterly because of her keen sense of failure. What she had meant to do was to show Emmy kindly—oh, very kindly—her proper place, and then, using the object in the little tissue-wrapped parcel as a sort of text, to preach a sermon on humility without aspiration.

The tissue-wrapped oblong proved to Emmy's interested eyes to contain a motto of Robert Louis Stevenson, entitled: "A Task"—the phrases picked out in red and blue and gold, under glass and framed in passepartout. Everybody nowadays has one or more of such mottoes in his house, but the idea was new then to Plainville. The child read it through carefully as she passed by the lilac-scented "front yards." She read well for her age, albeit a trifle uncomprehendingly.

"To be honest, to be kind, to earn a little and to spend a little less;"—"there," thought Emmy, "is a semi-colon—let's see—the semi-colon shows that the thought"—and she went on through the definition Miss Wenzel had given her, and returned happily to her motto:

"To make upon the whole a family happier for his presence"—thus far the lettering was in blue. "To renounce when that shall be necessary and not be embittered"—this phrase was in gold. Then the rest went on in red: "To keep a few friends, but these without capitulation; above all, on the same given condition to keep friends with himself—here is a task for all that a man has of fortitude and delicacy."

"It's all about some man," she thought with a child's literalness. "Wonder why Miss Wenzel gave it to me? That big word, cap-it-u-la-tion"—she divided it off into syllables, doubtfully—"must mean to spell with capitals I guess. I'll say it to Archie some time."

But she thought it very kind of Miss Wenzel. And after she had shown it to her mother, she hung it up in the bay window of her little white room, where the sun struck it every morning.

III.

Afterward Emmy always connected the motto with the beginning of her own realization of what color might mean. It took her quite a while to find it out, but by the time she was ready to graduate from the high school she had come to recognize that the occasional impasse which she met now and then might generally be traced to color. This knowledge, however, far from embittering her, simply gave to her life keener zest. Of course she never met with any of the grosser forms of prejudice, and her personality was the kind to win her at least the respect and sometimes the wondering admiration of her schoolmates. For unconsciously she made them see that she was perfectly satisfied with being colored. She could never understand why anyone should think she would want to be white.

One day a girl—Elise Carter—asked her to let her copy her French verbs in the test they were to have later in the day. Emmy, who was both by nature and by necessity independent, refused bluntly.

"Oh, don't be so mean, Emmy," Elise had wailed. She hesitated. "If you'll let me copy them—I'll—I tell you what I'll do, I'll see that you get invited to our club spread Friday afternoon."

"Well, I guess you won't," Emmy had retorted. "I'll probably be asked anyway. 'Most everybody else has been invited already."

Elise jeered. "And did you think as a matter of course that we'd ask you? Well, you have got something to learn."

There was no mistaking the "you."

Emmy took the blow pretty calmly for all its unexpectedness. "You mean," she said slowly, the blood showing darkly under the thin brown of her skin, "because I'm colored?"

Elise hedged—she was a little frightened at such directness.

"Oh, well, Emmy, you know colored folks can't expect to have everything we have, or if they do they must pay extra for it."

"I—I see," said Emmy, stammering a little, as she always did when she was angry. "I begin to see for the first time why you think it's so awful to be colored. It's because you think we are willing to be mean and sneaky and"—with a sudden drop to schoolgirl vernacular—"soup-y. Why, Elise Carter, I wouldn't be in your old club with girls like you for worlds." There was no mistaking her sincerity.

"That was the day," she confided to Archie a long time afterward, "that I learned the meaning of making friends 'without capitulation.' Do you remember Miss Wenzel's motto, Archie?"

He assured her he did. "And of course you know, Emmy, you were an awful brick to answer that Carter girl like that. Didn't you really want to go to the spread?"

"Not one bit," she told him vigorously, "after I found out why I hadn't been asked. And look, Archie, isn't it funny, just as soon as she wanted something she didn't care whether I was colored or not."

Archie nodded. "They're all that way," he told her briefly.

"And if I'd gone she'd have believed that all colored people were sort of—well, you know, 'meachin'—just like me. It's so odd the ignorant way in which they draw their conclusions. Why, I remember reading the most interesting article in a magazine—the *Atlantic Monthly* I think it was. A woman had written it and at this point she was condemning universal suffrage. And all of a sudden, without any warning, she spoke of that 'fierce, silly, amiable creature, the uneducated Negro,' and—think of it, Archie—of 'his baser and sillier female.' It made me so angry. I've never forgotten it."

Archie whistled. "That was pretty tough," he acknowledged. "I suppose the truth is," he went on smiling at her earnestness, "she has a colored cook who drinks."

"That's just it," she returned emphatically. "She probably has. But, Archie, just think of all the colored people we've both seen here and over in Newtown, too; some of them just as poor and ignorant as they can be. But not one of them is fierce or base or silly enough for that to be considered his chief characteristic. I'll wager that woman never spoke to fifty colored people in her life. No, thank you, if that's what it means to belong to the 'superior race,' I'll come back, just as I am, to the fiftieth reincarnation."

Archie sighed. "Oh, well, life is very simple for you. You see, you've never been up against it like I've been. After all, you've had all you wanted practically—those girls even came around finally in the high school and asked you into their clubs and things. While I—" he colored sensitively.

"You see, this plagued—er—complexion of mine doesn't tell anybody what I am. At first—and all along, too, if I let them—fellows take me for a foreigner of some kind—Spanish or something, and they take me up hail-fellow-well-met. And then, if I let them know—I hate to feel I'm taking them in, you know, and besides that I can't help being curious to know what's going to happen—"

"What does happen?" interrupted Emmy, all interest.

"Well, all sorts of things. You take that first summer just before I entered preparatory school. You remember I was working at that camp in Cottage City. All the waiters were fellows just like me, working to go to some college or other. At first I was just one of them—swam with them, played cards—oh, you know, regularly chummed with them. Well, the cook was a colored man—sure enough, colored you know—and one day one of the boys called him a—of course I couldn't tell you, Emmy, but he swore at him and called him a Nigger. And when I took up for him the fellow said—he was angry, Emmy, and he said it as the worst insult he could think of—'Anybody would think you had black blood in your veins, too.'

"Anybody would think right," I told him.

"Well?" asked Emmy.

He shrugged his shoulders. "That was all there was to it. The fellows dropped me completely—left me to the company of the cook, who was all right enough as cooks go, I suppose, but he didn't want me any more than I wanted him. And finally the manager came and told me he was sorry, but he guessed I'd have to go." He smiled grimly as at some unpleasant reminiscence.

"What's the joke?" his listener wondered.

"He also told me that I was the blankest kind of a blank fool—oh, you couldn't dream how he swore, Emmy. He said why didn't I leave well enough alone.

"And don't you know that's the thought I've had ever since—why not leave well enough alone?—and not tell people what I am. I guess you're different from me," he broke off wistfully, noting her look of disapproval; "you're so complete and satisfied in yourself. Just being Emilie Carrel seems to be enough for you. But you just wait until color keeps you from the thing you want the most, and you'll see."

"You needn't be so tragic," she commented succinctly. "Outside of that one time at Cottage City, it doesn't seem to have kept you back."

For Archie's progress had been miraculous. In the seven years in which he had been from home, one marvel after another had come his way. He had found lucrative work each summer, he had got through his preparatory school in three years, he had been graduated number six from one of the best technical schools in the country—and now he had a position. He was to work for one of the biggest engineering concerns in Philadelphia.

This last bit of good fortune had dropped out of a clear sky. A guest at one of the hotels one summer had taken an interest in the handsome, willing bellboy and inquired into his history. Archie had hesitated at first, but finally, his eye alert for the first sign of dislike or superiority, he told the man of his Negro blood.

"If he turns me down," he said to himself boyishly, "I'll never risk it again."

But Mr. Robert Fallon—young, wealthy and quixotic—had become more interested than ever.

"So it's all a gamble with you, isn't it? By George! How exciting your life must be—now white and now black—standing between ambition and honor, what? Not that I don't think you're doing the right thing—it's nobody's confounded business anyway. Look here, when you get through look me up. I may be able to put you wise to something. Here's my card. And say, mum's the word, and when you've made your pile you can wake some fine morning and find yourself famous simply by telling what you are. All rot, this beastly prejudice, I say."

And when Archie had graduated, his new friend, true to his word, had gotten for him from his father a letter of introduction to Mr. Nicholas Fields in Philadelphia, and Archie was placed. Young Robert Fallon had gone laughing on his aimless, merry way.

"Be sure you keep your mouth shut, Ferrers," was his only enjoinment.

Archie, who at first had experienced some qualms, had finally completely acquiesced. For the few moments' talk with Mr. Fields had intoxicated him. The vision of work, plenty of it, his own chosen kind—and the opportunity to do it as a man—not an exception, but as a plain ordinary man among other men—was too much for him.

"It was my big chance, Emmy," he told her one day. He was spending his brief vacation in Plainville, and the two, having talked themselves out on other things, had returned to their old absorbing topic. He went on a little pleadingly, for she had protested. "I couldn't resist it. You don't know what it means to me. I don't care about being white in itself any more than you do—but I do care about a white man's chances. Don't let's talk about it any more though; here it's the first week in September and I have to go the 15th. I may not be back till Christmas. I should hate to think that you—you were changed toward me, Emmy."

"I'm not changed, Archie," she assured him gravely, "only somehow it makes me feel that you're different. I can't quite look up to you as I used. I don't like the idea of considering the end justified by the means."

She was silent, watching the falling leaves flutter like golden butterflies against her white dress. As she stood there in the old-fashioned garden, she seemed to the boy's adoring eyes like some beautiful but inflexible bronze goddess.

"I couldn't expect you to look up to me, Emmy, as though I were on a pedestal," he began miserably, "but I do want you to respect me, because—oh, Emmy, don't you see? I love you very much and I hope you will—I want you to—oh, Emmy, couldn't you like me a little? I—I've never thought ever of anyone but you. I didn't mean to tell you all about this now—I meant to wait until I really was successful, and then come and lay it all at your beautiful feet. You're so lovely, Emmy. But if you despise me—" he was very humble.

For once in her calm young life Emmy was completely surprised. But she had to get to the root of things. "You mean," she faltered, "you mean you want"—she couldn't say it.

"I mean I want you to marry me," he said, gaining courage from her confusion. "Oh, have I frightened you, Emmy, dearest—of course you couldn't like me well enough for that all in a heap—it's different with me. I've always loved you, Emmy. But if you'd only think about it."

"Oh," she breathed, "there's Céleste. Oh, Archie, I don't know, it's all so funny. And we're so young. I couldn't really tell anything about my feelings anyway—you know, I've never seen anybody but you." Then as his face clouded—"Oh, well, I guess even if I had I wouldn't like him any better. Yes, Céleste, we're coming in. Archie, mother says you're to have dinner with us every night you're here, if you can."

There was no more said about the secret that Archie was keeping from Mr. Fields. There were too many other things to talk about—reasons why he had always loved Emmy; reasons why she couldn't be sure just yet; reasons why, if she were sure, she couldn't say yes.

Archie hung between high hope and despair, while Emmy, it must be confessed, enjoyed herself, albeit innocently enough, and grew distractingly pretty. On the last day as they sat in the sitting room, gaily recounting childish episodes, Archie suddenly asked her again. He was so grave and serious that she really became frightened.

"Oh, Archie, I couldn't—I don't really want to. It's so lovely just being a girl. I think I do like you—of course I like you lots. But couldn't we just be friends and keep going on—so?"

"No," he told her harshly, his face set and miserable; "no, we can't. And, Emmy—I'm not coming back any more—I couldn't stand it." His voice broke, he was fighting to keep back the hot boyish tears. After all he was only 21. "I'm sorry I troubled you," he said proudly.

She looked at him pitifully. "I don't want you to go away forever, Archie," she said tremulously. She made no effort to keep back the tears. "I've been so lonely this last year since I've been out of school—you can't think."

He was down on his knees, his arms around her. "Emmy, Emmy, look up—are you crying for me, dear? Do you want me to come back—you do—you mean it? Emmy, you must love me, you do—a little." He kissed her slim fingers.

"Are you going to marry me? Look at me, Emmy—you are! Oh, Emmy, do you know I'm—I'm going to kiss you."

The stage came lumbering up not long afterward, and bore him away to the train—triumphant and absolutely happy.

"My heart," sang Emmy rapturously as she ran up the broad, old-fashioned stairs to her room—"my heart is like a singing bird."

IV.

The year that followed seemed to her perfection. Archie's letters alone would have made it that. Emmy was quite sure that there had never been any other letters like them. She used to read them aloud to her mother.

Not all of them, though, for some were too precious for any eye but her own. She used to pore over them alone in her room at night, planning to answer them with an abandon equal to his own, but always finally evolving the same shy, almost timid epistle, which never failed to awaken in her lover's breast a sense equally of amusement and reverence. Her shyness seemed to him the most exquisite thing in the world—so exquisite, indeed, that he almost wished it would never vanish, were it not that its very disappearance would be the measure of her trust in him. His own letters showed plainly his adoration.

Only once had a letter of his caused a fleeting pang of misapprehension. He had been speaking of the persistent good fortune which had been his in Philadelphia.

"You can't think how lucky I am anyway," the letter ran on. "The other day I was standing on the corner of Fourth and Chestnut Streets at noon—you ought to see Chestnut Street at 12 o'clock, Emmy—and someone came up, looked at me and said: 'Well, if it isn't Archie Ferrers!' And guess who it was, Emmy? Do you remember the Higginses who used to live over in Newtown? I don't suppose you ever knew them, only they were so queer looking that you must recall them. They were all sorts of colors from black with 'good' hair to yellow with the red, kinky kind. And then there was Maude, clearly a Higgins, and yet not looking like any of them, you know; perfectly white, with blue eyes and fair hair. Well, this was Maude, and, say, maybe she didn't look good. I couldn't tell you what she had on, but it was all right, and I was glad to take her over to the Reading Terminal and put her on a train to New York.

"I guess you're wondering where my luck is in all this tale, but you wait. Just as we started up the stairs of the depot, whom should we run into but young Peter Fields; my boss's son and heir, you know. Really, I thought I'd faint, and then I remembered that Maude was whiter than he in looks, and that there was nothing to give me away. He wanted to talk to us, but I hurried her off to her train. You know, it's a queer thing, Emmy; some girls are just naturally born stylish. Now there are both you and Maude Higgins, brought up from little things in a tiny inland town, and both of you able to give any of these city girls all sorts of odds in the matter of dressing."

Emmy put the letter down, wondering what had made her grow so cold.

"I wonder," she mused. She turned and looked in the glass to be confronted by a charming vision, slender—and dusky.

"I am black," she thought, "but comely." She laughed to herself happily. "Archie loves you, girl," she said to the face in the glass, and put the little fear behind her. It met her insistently now and then, however, until the next week brought a letter begging her to get her mother to bring her to Philadelphia for a week or so.

"I can't get off till Thanksgiving, dearest, and I'm so lonely and disappointed. You know, I had looked forward so to spending the 15th of September with you—do you remember that date, sweetheart? I wouldn't have you come now in all this heat—you can't imagine how hot Philadelphia is, Emmy—but it's beautiful here in October. You'll love it, Emmy. It's such a big city—miles and miles of long, narrow streets, rather ugly, too, but all so interesting. You'll like Chestnut and Market Streets, where the big shops are, and South Street, teeming with Jews and colored people, though there are more of these last on Lombard Street. You never dreamed of so many colored people, Emmy Carrel—or such kinds.

"And then there are the parks and the theatres, and music and restaurants. And Broad Street late at night, all silent with gold, electric lights beckoning you on for miles and miles. Do you think your mother will let me take you out by yourself, Emmy? You'd be willing, wouldn't you?"

If Emmy needed more reassurance than that she received it when Archie, a month later, met her and her mother at Broad Street station in Philadelphia. The boy was radiant. Mrs. Carrel, too, put aside her usual reticence, and the three were in fine spirits by the time they reached the rooms which Archie had procured for them on Christian Street. Once ensconced, the older woman announced her intention of taking advantage of the stores.

"I shall be shopping practically all day," she informed them. "I'll be so tired in the afternoons and evenings, Archie, that I'll have to get you to take my daughter off my hands."

Her daughter was delighted, but not more transparently so than her appointed cavalier. He was overjoyed at the thought of playing host and of showing Emmy the delights of city life.

"By the time I've finished showing you one-fifth of what I've planned you'll give up the idea of waiting 'way till next October and marry me Christmas. Say, do it anyway, Emmy, won't you?" He waited tensely, but she only shook her head.

"Oh, I couldn't, Archie, and anyway you must show me first your wonderful city."

They did manage to cover a great deal of ground, though their mutual absorption made its impression on them very doubtful. Some things though Emmy never forgot. There was a drive one wonderful, golden October afternoon along the Wissahickon. Emmy, in her perfectly correct gray suit and smart little gray hat, held the reins—in itself a sort of measure of Archie's devotion to her, for he was wild about horses. He sat beside her ecstatic, ringing all the changes from a boy's nonsense to the most mature kind of seriousness. And always he looked at her with his passionate though reverent eyes. They were very happy.

There was some wonderful music, too, at the Academy. That was by accident though. For they had started for the theatre—had reached there in fact. The usher was taking the tickets.

"This way, Emmy," said Archie. The usher looked up aimlessly, then, as his eyes traveled from the seeming young foreigner to the colored girl beside him, he flushed a little.

"Is the young lady with you?" he whispered politely enough. But Emmy, engrossed in a dazzling vision in a pink décolleté gown, would not in any event have heard him.

"She is," responded Archie alertly. "What's the trouble, isn't to-night the 17th?"

The usher passed over this question with another—who had bought the tickets? Archie of course had, and told him so, frankly puzzled.

"I see. Well, I'm sorry," the man said evenly, "but these seats are already occupied, and the rest of the floor is sold out besides. There's a mistake somewhere. Now if you'll take these tickets back to the office I can promise you they'll give you the best seats left in the balcony."

"What's the matter?" asked Emmy, tearing her glance from the pink vision at last. "Oh, Archie, you're hurting my arm; don't hold it that tight. Why—why are we going away from the theatre? Oh, Archie, are you sick? You're just as white!"

"There was some mistake about the tickets," he got out, trying to keep his voice steady. "And a fellow in the crowd gave me an awful dig just then; guess that's why I'm pale. I'm so sorry, Emmy—I was so stupid, it's all my fault."

"What's the matter with the tickets?" she asked, incuriously. "That's the Bellevue-Stratford over there, isn't it? Then the Academy of

Music must be near here. See how fast I'm learning? Let's go there; I've never heard a symphony concert. And, Archie, I've always heard that the best way to hear big music like that is at a distance, so get gallery tickets."

He obeyed her, fearful that if there were any trouble this time she might hear it. Emmy enjoyed it all thoroughly, wondering a little, however, at his silence. "I guess he's tired," she thought. She would have been amazed to know his thoughts as he sat there staring moodily at the orchestra. "This damnation color business," he kept saying over and over.

That night as they stood in the vestibule of the Christian Street house Emmy, for the first time, volunteered him a kiss. "Such a nice, tired boy," she said gently. Afterward he stood for a long time bareheaded on the steps looking at the closed door. Nothing he felt could crush him as much as that kiss had lifted him up.

V.

Not even for lovers can a week last forever. Archie had kept till the last day what he considered his choicest bit of exploring. This was to take Emmy down into old Philadelphia and show her how the city had grown up from the waterfront—and by means of what tortuous self-governing streets. It was a sight at once dear and yet painful to his methodical, mathematical mind. They had explored Dock and Beach Streets, and had got over into Shackamaxon, where he showed her Penn Treaty Park, and they had sat in the little pavilion overlooking the Delaware.

Not many colored people came through this vicinity, and the striking pair caught many a wondering, as well as admiring, glance. They caught, too, the aimless, wandering eye of Mr. Nicholas Fields as he lounged, comfortably smoking, on the rear of a "Gunner's Run" car, on his way to Shackamaxon Ferry. Something in the young fellow's walk seemed vaguely familiar to him, and he leaned way out toward the sidewalk to see who that he knew could be over in this cheerless, forsaken locality.

"Gad!" he said to himself in surprise, "if it isn't young Ferrers, with a lady, too! Hello, why it's a colored woman! Ain't he a rip? Always thought he seemed too proper. Got her dressed to death, too; so that's how his money goes!" He dismissed the matter with a smile and a shrug of his shoulders.

Perhaps he would never have thought of it again had not Archie, rushing into the office a trifle late the next morning, caromed directly into him.

"Oh, it's you," he said, receiving his clerk's smiling apology. "What d'you mean by knocking into anybody like that?" Mr. Fields was facetious with his favorite employees. "Evidently your Shackamaxon trip upset you a little. Where'd you get your black Venus, my boy? I'll bet you don't have one cent to rub against another at the end of a month. Oh, you needn't get red; boys will be boys, and everyone to his taste. Clarkson," he broke off, crossing to his secretary, "if Mr. Hunter calls me up, hold the 'phone and send over to the bank for me."

He had gone, and Archie, white now and shaken, entered his own little room. He sat down at the desk and sank his head in his hands. It had taken a moment for the insult to Emmy to sink in, but even when it did the thought of his own false position had held him back. The shame of it bit into him.

"I'm a coward," he said to himself, staring miserably at the familiar wall. "I'm a wretched cad to let him think that of Emmy—Emmy! and she the whitest angel that ever lived, purity incarnate." His cowardice made him sick. "I'll go and tell him," he said, and started for the door.

"If you do," whispered common sense, "you'll lose your job and then what would become of you? After all Emmy need never know."

"But I'll always know I didn't defend her," he answered back silently.

"He's gone out to the bank anyhow," went on the inward opposition. "What's the use of rushing in there and telling him before the whole board of directors?"

"Well, then, when he comes back," he capitulated, but he felt himself weaken.

But Mr. Fields didn't come back. When Mr. Hunter called him up, Clarkson connected him with the bank, with the result that Mr. Fields left for Reading in the course of an hour. He didn't come back for a week.

Meanwhile Archie tasted the depths of self-abasement. "But what am I to do?" he groaned to himself at nights. "If I tell him I'm colored he'll kick me out, and if I go anywhere else I'd run the same risk. If I'd only knocked him down! After all she'll never know and I'll make it up to her. I'll be so good to her—dear little Emmy! But how could I know that he would take that view of it—beastly low mind he must have!" He colored up like a girl at the thought of it.

He passed the week thus, alternately reviling and defending himself. He knew now though that he would never have the courage to tell. The economy of the thing he decided was at least as important as the principle. And always he wrote to Emmy letters of such passionate adoration that the girl for all her natural steadiness was carried off her feet.

"How he loves me," she thought happily. "If mother is willing I believe—yes, I will—I'll marry him Christmas. But I won't tell him till he comes Thanksgiving."

When Mr. Fields came back he sent immediately for his son Peter. The two held some rather stormy consultations, which were renewed for several days. Peter roomed in town, while his father lived out at Chestnut Hill. Eventually Archie was sent for.

"You're not looking very fit, my boy." Mr. Fields greeted him kindly; "working too hard I suppose over those specifications. Well, here's a tonic for you. This last week has shown me that I need someone younger than myself to take a hand in the business. I'm getting too old or too tired or something. Anyhow I'm played out.

"I've tried to make this young man here"—with an angry glance at his son—"see that the mantle ought to fall on him, but he won't hear of it. Says the business can stop for all he cares; he's got enough money anyway. Gad, in my day young men liked to work, instead of dabbling around in this filthy social settlement business—with a lot of old maids."

Peter smiled contentedly. "Sally in our alley, what?" he put in diabolically. The older man glared at him, exasperated.

"Now look here, Ferrers," he went on abruptly. "I've had my eye on you ever since you first came. I don't know a thing about you outside of Mr. Fallon's recommendation, but I can see you've got good stuff in you—and what's more, you're a born engineer. If you had some money, I'd take you into partnership at once, but I believe you told me that all you had was your salary." Archie nodded.

"Well, now, I tell you what I'm going to do. I'm going to take you in as a sort of silent partner, teach you the business end of the concern, and in the course of a few years, place the greater part of the management in your hands. You can see you won't lose by it. Of course I'll still be head, and after I step out Peter will take my place, though only nominally I suppose."

He sighed; his son's business defection was a bitter point with him. But that imperturbable young man only nodded.

"The boss guessed right the very first time," he paraphrased cheerfully. "You bet I'll be head in name only. Young Ferrers, there's just the man for the job. What d'you say, Archie?"

The latter tried to collect himself. "Of course I accept it, Mr. Fields, and I—I don't think you'll ever regret it." He actually stammered. Was there ever such wonderful luck?

"Oh, that's all right," Mr. Fields went on, "you wouldn't be getting this chance if you didn't deserve it. See here, what about your boarding out at Chestnut Hill for a year or two? Then I can lay my hands on you any time, and you can get hold of things that much sooner. You live on Green Street, don't you? Well, give your landlady a month's notice and quit the 1st of December. A young man coming on like you ought to be thinking of a home anyway. Can't find some nice girl to marry you, what?"

Archie, flushing a little, acknowledged his engagement.

"Good, that's fine!" Then with sudden recollection—"Oh, so you're reformed. Well, I thought you'd get over that. Can't settle down too soon. A lot of nice little cottages out there at Chestnut Hill. Peter, your mother says she wishes you'd come out to dinner to-night. The youngest Wilton girl is to be there, I believe. Guess that's all for this afternoon, Ferrers."

VI.

Archie walked up Chestnut Street on air. "It's better to be born lucky than rich," he reflected. "But I'll be rich, too—and what a lot I can do for Emmy. Glad I didn't tell Mr. Fields now. Wonder what those 'little cottages' out to Chestnut Hill sell for. Emmy—" He stopped short, struck by a sudden realization.

"Why, I must be stark, staring crazy," he said to himself, standing still right in the middle of Chestnut Street. A stout gentleman whom his sudden stopping had seriously incommoded gave him, as he passed by, a vicious prod with his elbow. It started him on again.

"If I hadn't clean forgotten all about it. Oh, Lord, what am I to do? Of course Emmy can't go out to Chestnut Hill to live—well, that would be a give-away. And he advised me to live out there for a year or two—and he knows I'm engaged, and—now—making more than enough to marry on."

He turned aimlessly down 19th Street, and spying Rittenhouse Square sat down in it. The cutting November wind swirled brown, crackling leaves right into his face, but he never saw one of them.

When he arose again, long after his dinner hour, he had made his decision. After all Emmy was a sensible girl; she knew he had only his salary to depend on. And, of course, he wouldn't have to stay out in Chestnut Hill forever. They could buy, or perhaps—he smiled proudly—even build now, far out in West Philadelphia, as far as possible away from Mr. Fields. He'd just ask her to postpone their marriage—perhaps for two years. He sighed a little, for he was very much in love.

"It seems funny that prosperity should make a fellow put off his happiness," he thought ruefully, swinging himself aboard a North 19th Street car.

He decided to go to Plainville and tell her about it—he could go up Saturday afternoon. "Let's see, I can get an express to Harrisburg, and a sleeper to Plainville, and come back Sunday afternoon. Emmy'll like a surprise like that." He thought of their improvised trip to the Academy and how she had made him buy gallery seats. "Lucky she has that little saving streak in her. She'll see through the whole thing like a brick." His simile made him smile. As soon as he reached home he scribbled her a note:

"I'm coming Sunday," he said briefly, "and I have something awfully important to ask you. I'll be there only from 3 to 7. When Time lets slip one little perfect hour,' that's that Omar thing you're always quoting, isn't it? Well, there'll be four perfect hours this trip."

All the way on the slow poky local from Harrisburg he pictured her surprise. "I guess she won't mind the postponement one bit," he thought with a brief pang. "She never was keen on marrying. Girls certainly are funny. Here she admits she's in love and willing to marry, and yet she's always hung fire about the date." He dozed fitfully.

As a matter of fact Emmy had fixed the date. "Of course," she said to herself happily, "the 'something important' is that he wants me to marry him right away. Well, I'll tell him that I will, Christmas. Dear old Archie coming all this distance to ask me that. I'll let him beg me two or three times first, and then I'll tell him. Won't he be pleased? I shouldn't be a bit surprised if he went down on his knees again." She flushed a little, thinking of that first wonderful time.

"Being in love is just—dandy," she decided. "I guess I'll wear my red dress."

Afterward the sight of that red dress always caused Emmy a pang of actual physical anguish. She never saw it without seeing, too, every detail of that disastrous Sunday afternoon. Archie had come—she had gone to the door to meet him—they had lingered happily in the hall a few moments, and then she had brought him in to her mother and Céleste.

The old French woman had kissed him on both cheeks. "See, then it's thou, my cherished one!" she cried ecstatically. "How long a time it is since thou art here."

Mrs. Carrel's greeting, though not so demonstrative, was no less sincere, and when the two were left to themselves "the cherished one" was radiant.

"My, but your mother can make a fellow feel welcome, Emmy. She doesn't say much but what she does, goes."

Emmy smiled a little absently. The gray mist outside in the sombre garden, the fire crackling on the hearth and casting ruddy shadows on Archie's hair, the very red of her dress, Archie himself—all this was making for her a picture, which she saw repeated on endless future Sunday afternoons in Philadelphia. She sighed contentedly.

"I've got something to tell you, sweetheart," said Archie.

"It's coming," she thought. "Oh, isn't it lovely! Of all the people in the world—he loves me, loves me!" She almost missed the beginning of his story. For he was telling her of Mr. Fields and his wonderful offer.

When she finally caught the drift of what he was saying she was vaguely disappointed. He was talking business, in which she was really very little interested. The "saving streak" which Archie had attributed to her was merely sporadic, and was due to a nice girl's delicacy at having money spent on her by a man. But, of course, she listened.

"So you see the future is practically settled—there's only one immediate drawback," he said earnestly. She shut her eyes—it was coming after all.

He went on a little puzzled by her silence; "only one drawback, and that is that, of course, we can't be married for at least two years yet."

Her eyes flew open. "Not marry for two years! Why—why ever not?"

Even then he might have saved the situation by telling her first of his own cruel disappointment, for her loveliness, as she sat there, all glowing red and bronze in the fire-lit dusk, smote him very strongly.

But he only floundered on.

"Why, Emmy, of course, you can see—you're so much darker than I—anybody can tell at a glance what you—er—are." He was crude, he knew it, but he couldn't see how to help himself. "And we'd have to live at Chestnut Hill, at first, right there near the Fields', and there'd be no way with you there to keep people from knowing that I—that—oh, confound it all—Emmy, you must understand! You don't mind, do you? You know you never were keen on marrying anyway. If we were both the same color—why, Emmy, what is it?"

For she had risen and was looking at him as though he were some-one entirely strange. Then she turned and gazed unseeingly out the window. So that was it—the "something important"—he was ashamed of her, of her color; he was always talking about a white man's chances. Why, of course, how foolish she'd been all along—how could he be white with her at his side? And she had thought he had come to urge her to marry him at once—the sting of it sent her head up higher. She turned and faced him, her beautiful silhouette distinctly outlined against the gray blur of the window. She wanted to hurt him—she was quite cool now.

"I have something to tell you, too, Archie," she said evenly. "I've been meaning to tell you for some time. It seems I've been making a mistake all along. I don't really love you"—she was surprised dully that the words didn't choke her—"so, of course, I can't marry you. I was wondering how I could get out of it—you can't think how tiresome it's all been." She had to stop.

He was standing, frozen, motionless like something carved.

"This seems as good an opportunity as any—oh, here's your ring," she finished, holding it out to him coldly. It was a beautiful diamond, small but flawless—the only thing he'd ever gone into debt for.

The statue came to life. "Emmy, you're crazy," he cried passionately, seizing her by the wrist. "You've got the wrong idea. You think I don't want you to marry me. What a cad you must take me for. I only asked you to postpone it a little while, so we'd be happier afterward. I'm doing it all for you, girl. I never dreamed—it's preposterous, Emmy! And you can't say you don't love me—that's all nonsense!"

But she clung to her lie, desperately.

"No, really, Archie, I don't love you one bit; of course I like you aw-fully—let go my wrist, you can think how strong you are. I should have told you long ago, but I hadn't the heart—and it really was interesting." No grand lady on the stage could have been more detached. He should know, too, how it felt not to be wanted.

He was at her feet now, clutching desperately, as she retreated, at her dress—the red dress she had donned so bravely. He couldn't be-lieve in her heartlessness. "You must love me, Emmy, and even if you don't you must marry me anyway. Why, you promised—you don't know what it means to me, Emmy—it's my very life—I've never even dreamed of another woman but you! Take it back, Emmy, you can't mean it."

But she convinced him that she could. "I wish you'd stop, Archie," she said wearily; "this is awfully tiresome. And, anyway, I think you'd better go now if you want to catch your train."

He stumbled to his feet, the life all out of him. In the hall he turned around: "You'll say good-by to your mother for me," he said mechanically. She nodded. He opened the front door. It seemed to close of its own accord behind him.

She came back into the sitting room, wondering why the place had suddenly grown so intolerably hot. She opened a window. From somewhere out of the gray mists came the strains of "Alice, Where Art Thou?" executed with exceeding mournfulness on an organ. The girl listened with a curious detached intentness.

"That must be Willie Holborn," she thought; "no one else could play as wretchedly as that." She crossed heavily to the armchair and flung herself in it. Her mind seemed to go on acting as though it were clockwork and she were watching it.

Once she said: "Now this, I suppose, is what they call a tragedy." And again: "He did get down on his knees."

VII.

There was nothing detached or impersonal in Archie's consideration of his plight. All through the trip home, through the long days that followed and the still longer nights, he was in torment. Again and again he went over the scene.

"She was making a plaything out of me," he chafed bitterly. "All these months she's been only fooling. And yet I wonder if she really meant it, if she didn't just do it to make it easier for me to be white. If that's the case what an insufferable cad she must take me for. No, she couldn't have cared for me, because if she had she'd have seen through it all right away."

By the end of ten days he had worked himself almost into a fever. His burning face and shaking hands made him resolve, as he dressed that morning, to 'phone the office that he was too ill to come to work.

"And I'll stay home and write her a letter that she'll have to answer." For although he had sent her one and sometimes two letters every day ever since his return, there had been no reply.

"She must answer that," he said to himself at length, when the late afternoon shadows were creeping in. He had torn up letter after letter—he had been proud and beseeching by turns. But in this last he had laid his very heart bare.

"And if she doesn't answer it"—it seemed to him he couldn't face the possibility. He was at the writing desk where her picture stood in its little silver frame. It had been there all that day. As a rule he kept it locked up, afraid of what it might reveal to his landlady's vigilant eye. He sat there, his head bowed over the picture, wondering dully how he should endure his misery.

Someone touched him on the shoulder.

"Gad, boy," said Mr. Nicholas Fields, "here I thought you were sick in bed, and come here to find you mooning over a picture. What's the matter? Won't the lady have you? Let's see who it is that's been breaking you up so." Archie watched him in fascinated horror, while he picked up the photograph and walked over to the window. As he scanned it his expression changed.

"Oh," he said, with a little puzzled frown and yet laughing, too, "it's your colored lady friend again. Won't she let you go? That's the way with these black women, once they get hold of a white man—bleed 'em to death. I don't see how you can stand them anyway; it's the Spanish in you, I suppose. Better get rid of her before you get married. Hello—" he broke off.

For Archie was standing menacingly over him. "If you say another word about that girl I'll break every rotten bone in your body."

"Oh, come," said Mr. Fields, still pleasant, "isn't that going it a little too strong? Why, what can a woman like that mean to you?"

"She can mean," said the other slowly, "everything that the woman who has promised to be my wife ought to mean." The broken engagement meant nothing in a time like this.

Mr. Fields forgot his composure. "To be your wife! Why, you idiot, you—you'd ruin yourself—marry a Negro—have you lost your senses? Oh, I suppose it's some of your crazy foreign notions. In this country white gentlemen don't marry colored women."

Archie had not expected this loophole. He hesitated, then with a shrug he burnt all his bridges behind him. One by one he saw his ambitions flare up and vanish.

"No, you're right," he rejoined. "White gentlemen don't, but colored men do." Then he waited calmly for the avalanche.

It came. "You mean," said Mr. Nicholas Fields, at first with only wonder and then with growing suspicion in his voice, "you mean that you're colored?" Archie nodded and watched him turn into a maniac.

"Why, you low-lived young blackguard, you———" he swore horribly. "And you've let me think all this time—" He broke off again, hunting for something insulting enough to say. "You Nigger!" he hurled at him. He really felt there was nothing worse, so he repeated it again and again with fresh imprecations.

"I think," said Archie, "that will do. I shouldn't like to forget myself, and I'm in a pretty reckless mood to-day. You must remember, Mr. Fields, you didn't ask me who I was, and I had no occasion to tell you. Of course I won't come back to the office."

"If you do," said Mr. Fields, white to the lips, "I'll have you locked up if I have to perjure my soul to find a charge against you. I'll show you what a white man can do—you——"

But Archie had taken him by the shoulder and pushed him outside the door.

"And that's all right," he said to himself with a sudden heady sense of liberty. He surveyed himself curiously in the mirror. "Wouldn't anybody think I had changed into some horrible ravening beast. Lord, how that one little word changed him." He ruminated over the injustice—the petty, foolish injustice of the whole thing.

"I don't believe," he said slowly, "it's worth while having a white man's chances if one has to be like that. I see what Emmy used to be driving at now." The thought of her sobered him.

"If it should be on account of my chances that you're letting me go," he assured the picture gravely, "it's all quite unnecessary, for I'll never have another opportunity like that."

In which he was quite right. It even looked as though he couldn't get any work at all along his own line. There was no demand for colored engineers.

"If you keep your mouth shut," one man said, "and not let the other clerks know what you are I might try you for a while." There was nothing for him to do but accept. At the end of two weeks—the day before Thanksgiving—he found out that the men beside him, doing exactly the same kind of work as his own, were receiving for it five dollars more a week. The old injustice based on color had begun to hedge him in. It seemed to him that his unhappiness and humiliation were more than he could stand.

VIII.

But at least his life was occupied. Emmy, on the other hand, saw her own life stretching out through endless vistas of empty, useless days. She grew thin and listless, all the brightness and vividness of living toned down for her into one gray, flat monotony. By Thanksgiving Day the strain showed its effects on her very plainly.

Her mother, who had listened in her usual silence when her daughter told her the cause of the broken engagement, tried to help her.

"Emmy," she said, "you're probably doing Archie an injustice. I don't believe he ever dreamed of being ashamed of you. I think it is your own wilful pride that is at fault. You'd better consider carefully—if you are making a mistake you'll regret it to the day of your death. The sorrow of it will never leave you."

Emmy was petulant. "Oh, mother, what can you know about it? Céleste says you married when you were young, even younger than I—married to the man you loved, and you were with him, I suppose, till he died. You couldn't know how I feel." She fell to staring absently out the window. It was a long time before her mother spoke again.

"No, Emmy," she finally began again very gravely, "I wasn't with your father till he died. That is why I'm speaking to you as I am. I had sent him away—we had quarrelled—oh, I was passionate enough when I was your age, Emmy. He was jealous—he was a West Indian—I suppose Céleste has told you—and one day he came past the sitting room—it was just like this one, overlooking the garden. Well, as he glanced in the window he saw a man, a white man, put his arms around me and kiss me. When he came in through the side door the man had gone. I was just about to explain—no, tell him—for I didn't know he had seen me when he began." She paused a little, but presently went on in her even, dispassionate voice:

"He was furious, Emmy; oh, he was so angry, and he accused me—oh, my dear! He was almost insane. But it was really because he loved me. And then I became angry and I wouldn't tell him anything. And finally, Emmy, he struck me—you mustn't blame him, child; remember, it was the same spirit showing in both of us, in different ways. I was doing all I could to provoke him by keeping silence and he merely retaliated in his way. The blow wouldn't have harmed a little bird. But—well, Emmy, I think I must have gone crazy. I ordered him from the house—it had been my mother's—and I told him never, never to let me see him again." She smiled drearily.

"I never did see him again. After he left Céleste and I packed up our things and came here to America. You were the littlest thing, Emmy. You can't remember living in France at all, can you? Well, when your father found out where I was he wrote and asked me to forgive him and to let him come back. 'I am on my knees,' the letter said. I wrote and told him yes—I loved him, Emmy; oh, child, you with your talk of color; you don't know what love is. If you really loved Archie you'd let him marry you and lock you off, away from all the world, just so long as you were with him.

"I was so happy," she resumed. "I hadn't seen him for two years. Well, he started—he was in Hayti then; he got to New York safely and started here. There was a wreck—just a little one—only five people killed, but he was one of them. He was so badly mangled, they wouldn't even let me see him."

"Oh!" breathed Emmy. "Oh, mother!" After a long time she ventured a question. "Who was the other man, mother?"

"The other man? Oh! that was my father; my mother's guardian, protector, everything, but not her husband. She was a slave, you know, in New Orleans, and he helped her to get away. He took her to Hayti first, and then, afterward, sent her over to France, where I was born. He never ceased in his kindness. After my mother's death I didn't see him for ten years, not till after I was married. That was the time Emile— you were named for your father, you know—saw him kiss me. Mr. Pechegru, my father, was genuinely attached to my mother, I think, and had come after all these years to make some reparation. It was through him I first began translating for the publishers. You know yourself how my work has grown."

She was quite ordinary and matter of fact again. Suddenly her manner changed.

"I lost him when I was 22. Emmy—think of it—and my life has been nothing ever since. That's why I want you to think—to consider—" She was weeping passionately now.

Her mother in tears! To Emmy it was as though the world lay in ruins about her feet.

IX.

As it happened Mrs. Carrel's story only plunged her daughter into deeper gloom.

"It couldn't have happened at all if we hadn't been colored," she told herself moodily. "If grandmother hadn't been colored she wouldn't have been a slave, and if she hadn't been a slave— That's what it is, color—color—it's wrecked mother's life and now it's wrecking mine."

She couldn't get away from the thought of it. Archie's words, said so long ago, came back to her: "Just wait till color keeps you from the thing you want the most," he had told her.

"It must be wonderful to be white," she said to herself, staring absently at the Stevenson motto on the wall of her little room. She went up close and surveyed it unseeingly. "If only I weren't colored," she thought. She checked herself angrily, enveloped by a sudden sense of shame. "It doesn't seem as though I could be the same girl."

A thin ray of cold December sunlight picked out from the motto a little gilded phrase: "To renounce when that shall be necessary and not be embittered." She read it over and over and smiled whimsically.

"I've renounced—there's no question about that," she thought, "but no one could expect me not to be bitter."

If she could just get up strength enough, she reflected, as the days passed by, she would try to be cheerful in her mother's presence. But it was so easy to be melancholy.

About a week before Christmas her mother went to New York. She would see her publishers and do some shopping and would be back Christmas Eve. Emmy was really glad to see her go.

"I'll spend that time in getting myself together," she told herself, "and when mother comes back I'll be all right." Nevertheless, for the first few days she was, if anything, more listless than ever. But Christmas Eve and the prospect of her mother's return gave her a sudden brace.

"Without bitterness," she kept saying to herself, "to renounce without bitterness." Well, she would—she would. When her mother came back she should be astonished. She would even wear the red dress. But the sight of it made her weak; she couldn't put it on. But she did dress herself very carefully in white, remembering how gay she had been last Christmas Eve. She had put mistletoe in her hair and Archie had taken it out.

"I don't have to have mistletoe," he had whispered to her proudly.

In the late afternoon she ran out to Holborn's. As she came back 'round the corner she saw the stage drive away. Her mother, of course, had come. She ran into the sitting room wondering why the door was closed.

"I will be all right," she said to herself, her hand on the knob, and stepped into the room—to walk straight into Archie's arms.

She clung to him as though she could never let him go.

"Oh, Archie, you've come back, you really wanted me."

He strained her closer. "I've never stopped wanting you," he told her, his lips on her hair.

Presently, when they were sitting by the fire, she in the armchair and he at her feet, he began to explain. She would not listen at first, it was all her fault, she said.

"No, indeed," he protested generously, "it was mine. I was so crude; it's a wonder you can care at all about anyone as stupid as I am. And I think I was too ambitious—though in a way it was all for you, Emmy; you must always believe that. But I'm at the bottom rung now, sweetheart; you see, I told Mr. Fields everything and—he put me out."

"Oh, Archie," she praised him, "that was really noble, since you weren't obliged to tell him."

"Well, but in one sense I was obliged to—to keep my self-respect, you know. So there wasn't anything very noble about it after all." He couldn't tell her what had really happened. "I'm genuinely poor now, dearest, but your mother sent for me to come over to New York. She knows some pretty all-right people there—she's a wonderful woman, Emmy—and I'm to go out to the Philippines. Could you—do you think you could come out there, Emmy?"

She could, she assured him, go anywhere. "Only don't let it be too long, Archie—I—"

He was ecstatic. "Emmy—you—you don't mean you would be willing to start out there with me, do you? Why, that's only three months off. When—" He stopped, peering out the window. "Who is that coming up the path?"

"It's Willie Holborn," said Emmy. "I suppose Mary sent him around with my present. Wait, I'll let him in."

But it wasn't Willie Holborn, unless he had been suddenly converted into a small and very grubby special-delivery boy.

"Mr. A. Ferrers," he said laconically, thrusting a book out at her. "Sign here."

She took the letter back into the pleasant room, and A. Ferrers, scanning the postmark, tore it open. "It's from my landlady; she's the only person in Philadelphia who knows where I am. Wonder what's up?" he said incuriously. "I know I didn't forget to pay her my bill. Hello, what's this?" For within was a yellow envelope—a telegram.

Together they tore it open.

"Don't be a blooming idiot," it read; "the governor says come back and receive apologies and accept job. Merry Christmas.

"PETER FIELDS."

"Oh," said Emmy, "isn't it lovely? Why does he say 'receive apologies,' Archie?"

"Oh, I don't know," he quibbled, reflecting that if Peter hadn't said just that his return would have been as impossible as ever. "It's just his queer way of talking. He's the funniest chap! Looks as though I wouldn't have to go to the Philippines after all. But that doesn't alter the main question. How soon do you think you can marry me, Emmy?"

His voice was light, but his eyes—

"Well," said Emmy bravely, "what do you think of Christmas?"

THE END.

A MAN THEY DIDN'T KNOW

Published in December 1913, James D. Corrothers's
story tells of U.S. President Nefferman, who is suddenly confronted by a civil war in Mexico, revolt in
Hawaii, unrest among black Americans, and imminent
war with Japan. President Nefferman enlists the support of African-American leaders. He is persuaded to
secure the help and cooperation of Jed Blackburn, a
discredited black pugilist.

The opposition was right.

President Nefferman had blundered. In fact, he had not understood
the situation at all. *Now* the people realized this. A crisis was at hand.
War seemed inevitable. An appalled and anxious nation looked for a
way out—with *honor.*

Yet, at the beginning of all this, President Nefferman had laughed,
flouting all thought of serious possibilities. The chief mouthpiece of
the opposition, stung to hysteria by the president's bungling, merci-
lessly assailed him, urging his immediate impeachment, and stood not
upon the order of its flaming and virulent denunciation. Bristling in-
vective, scathing rebuke, scourgings and knoutings, it volleyed and
showered upon him in the fury of its wrath. Perhaps this great paper, a
veritable "thunderer" among its kind, was most dangerous to the interests of the president and his friends when it condescended to ridicule,
and malignantly played the fierce light of its derision upon the pitiful
man. Again and again it shouted:

"Nefferman laughed!"

"Laughed in the face of this black and ominous storm, thick-
belching from the noxious shores of hell! Laughed and could not be
made to understand the oncoming, dreadful thing. He laughed, actually *laughed!* And all the mountebanks, mimes, grafters and money bags
of his senile administration laughed with him, in unison. *They* had

made 'theirs' and were content. So doubtless, too, was poor, fat-witted Nefferman. He laughed until his own private money bags rumbled and burst and laughed. This was caught up and echoed by the money bags of the protected 'interests.' It became the laugh of millions, as if every bag had a golden mouth, and all the bags had burst. But from the tormented, seething populace it evoked no merriment; awoke no answer; provoked no response but malediction. To the anxious, fearing people the fearful levity of Nefferman and his friends was as mocking and hateful as the bacchanalia of devils who lead the doomed to hell, among echoing rocks, and beside murmurous rivers of pitch.

"But it was all very funny to Nefferman. His lazy brain reported: All is well. He *laughed*—amid these flashings from Sheol! He actually threw back his beefy, Midaseared head; wrinkled his butcher-hued face in complacent, Neffermanian smiles; opened his big mouth wide, and—*laughed*! Had it not been for a little isthmus at the back of his neck the whole top of his head would have been an island.

"Dolt!

"Already the Orientals, through their secret treaties with Mexico, were at the beginning of things. The American consulate in Mexico City had been damaged; several Americans in Mexico had been imprisoned, tortured and killed; shots, always 'random shots,' had been fired across the border into the United States, wounding our citizens and destroying property; American soldiers had been hit, and skirmishes were frequent until forbidden by the American government. Then began the desertions of our Negro soldiers to Mexican ranks. There these trained men, of a race never before disloyal to their land or flag, manned the machine guns for the 'Mexicans,' and sent vindictive volleys crashing back into American homes and towns.

" 'Mere straws!' observed Nefferman, not realizing that 'straws' tell which way the *winds* blow.

"Next came the California 'land law' movement, against which Japan formally protested to this government—*her only open move.*

"Then came the remarkable *'votes for Negroes; justice NOW!'* movement of the blacks throughout the country. Great mass meetings and restless bands of men and women, with black, agonized faces, marching through our cities and from town to town.

"Again Nefferman laughed!

" 'Mere imitation!' he reassured us. 'Sambo and Topsy,' he explained, 'trying to mimic the English suffragettes. That is—all but the "hunger strike." Ha! ha! Sambo loves his po'k chops too well for that!'

"Still Nefferman laughed!

"But now 'a change came o'er the spirit of his dream.' Ten American soldiers and three citizens were shot on American soil during a raid by Mexican rebels. Six of those wounded died. The American government demanded from Mexico proper reparation and apology. This the Mexican government seemed reluctant to grant, disclaiming federal responsibility, and claiming also that the rebels were assisted by American adventurers and mercenaries. Upon this some American State troops and a few regulars surreptitiously plunged over the Mexican border by night and captured the entire rebel band, of necessity shooting a few in the drastic transaction. All Mexico is flaming white hot over the 'outrage.' War may be declared upon us at any moment, and united Mexico, backed by her cunning and powerful ally, will bristle to the assault.

"Now Nefferman's levity subsided, and a look of determination clouded his Napoleonic brow. His pride was aroused. He would end this thing at once, and decisively.

"But now came the second greater shock: The 'peaceful' revolution of Hawaii, voted in by 20,000 Hawaiian-born Japanese youths, real 'American citizens,' who had a right to vote, and who, together with certain renegade whites and a wholesale importation of Negroes, formed a new political balance of power in the islands, thus assuring the success of their audacious plot. It is anticipated that the next move will be an annexation to Japan. A Hawaiian republic can hardly stand alone. Americans are leaving the islands.

"The government at Washington, beyond furnishing transports for the departing Americans, has done little other than to demand that the authority of the United States be recognized, as heretofore. It is asserted that the Atlantic fleet may be ordered to the scene to enforce our demands. Meanwhile, it is rumored that a dozen Japanese cruisers are already secreted in secluded Hawaiian waters awaiting the attack of the American squadron. There is, however, no confirmation of this report.

"Nefferman is not laughing *now*!

"*Later:* A most disquieting report reaches us to the effect that Charles H. Bowden, the American aviator, soaring over the supposedly unfrequented waters of the lower California gulf, on Friday, made the startling discovery of a secret Japanese coaling station situated on a quiet bay. Some cruisers of lighter draft were hiding nearby. There appeared to be great activity on board.

"*Ft. Bayard, N. M.,* April 18.—Nearly half a company of United States colored troops stationed here deserted to the enemy when ordered to prepare for action against the Mexicans. Disloyalty is spreading among the Negro troops. Further desertions seem imminent. The yellow peril is upon us. Behind all that has happened may *now* be discerned the hand of the plotting East.

"*Chicago,* April 19.—At a mass meeting held here last night more than 2,000 Negroes, among whom were some of the leading colored people of this city, passed resolutions demanding *'votes for Negroes,'* and *'the immediate cessation of lynching in the United States.'* The Negroes declared they would not bear arms in the impending conflict unless the national government took steps for their relief. Similar meetings were held in Detroit, Cincinnati and St. Louis. The Negroes asserted that meetings of like nature will take place soon in other leading cities, especially in the East and Northwest. The leaders of last night's meeting were arrested, but the disaffection continues to spread. It is a grave and alarming state of affairs. Severe punishment of the leaders will only inflame the blacks. Something must be done to win the Negroes over."

—

A tall, athletic, sun-browned man, emerging from a field of rustling corn, received a letter from the rural postman. It was noon. The dinner bell at the farmhouse had rung, and thither, letter in hand, the man started with swinging strides. The letter had originally been sent to X——, Mass. After repeated forwarding, it had finally reached him in Eastern Pennsylvania. It was from the President of the United States, and was as follows:

The Rev. Grant Noble,
Pastor Baptist Church,
X——, Mass.

Rev. Sir:

In the present crisis, which threatens to become a national calamity, it is deemed advisable for the President to call together some of the representative men of your race with whom he may take counsel concerning the unprecedented attitude which colored citizens are assuming toward the national government. Your name was suggested by a gentleman from Massachusetts as that of a sagacious and resourceful man of unusual attainments and character. It is to such men as yourself that the President turns in this our country's hour of need. No other President of the United States has had such a problem on his hands. Will you not meet with the President in Washington on the evening of April 21, at 8 o'clock? The expense of the trip will be met. No publication of this matter should be made at present. Sincerely yours,

Rodney Morris.
Secretary to President Martin Carlos Nefferman.

Grant Noble decided to go, though it might involve for him no small sacrifice. In a few words he set forth the matter before the good German folk for whom he worked, and with whom he and his little son enjoyed one of the pleasantest homes in which they had found shelter, on their gradual journey westward, since his unfortunate losses in Massachusetts.

"Chess," assented the good farmer, a staunch Nefferman man, "dot vill pe alright. Go unt dalk mit him all vat he vants. Unt der chob, unt der liddle, mudderless poy vill pe here alright, ven pack you come."

That night Grant Noble was in Washington, and, a few minutes after 8, was shown into the President's office. Three other colored men, all strangers to him, were already waiting. At nearly 9 o'clock another colored man, a bishop of pompous mien, was ushered in. Out of fifty who were asked to come but five were present.

The President, burdened and worn, though not precisely upon the minute, came promptly, without the slightest hint of ceremony, and, arrogating to himself no air of Saxon superiority, got immediately to business.

"Gentlemen," he said, "I want your help, and your sympathy. I *know* your race has been abused; I know we have lost its confidence. *Can it be restored?*"

The prelate, to whom all deferred, spoke first—a set speech, and an *old* one—grandiloquent; vain, he threw no light upon the subject. Plainly, his sole desire was to "show off"—to get advertised. He had not the intelligence nor sense to know that he had failed. And upon the impenetrable face of Nefferman there was no sign.

One after one, three other Negroes spoke, and in their talk that long telegraph pole of a capital letter "I" was indubitably apparent. Evidently each thought that *he* could lead his race back to loyalty—and whithersoever he chose.

"Do you not think, gentlemen, that Dr. Packer T. Jefferson would be the proper leader to carry through any plans upon which we might decide?" asked the President.

It was Grant Noble who answered.

"There is just one man," he declared, "who can prevail with my people *now.* That man is not Dr. Jefferson. They would follow Dr. Jefferson through *life,* to progress and success, but I doubt if Mr. Jefferson himself would presume that he could lead them into *death. That* requires a warrior soul! There is one mighty black man whom my people would follow into death. *That* man is Jed Blackburn, the discredited Negro boxer. I am aware of his mistakes and of his limitations. I know he is in great disfavor. But, if you would win back the American Negro, get *this* man into action. He is lion hearted and patriotic."

"Do you know this man personally?"

"Yes, slightly."

"If this plan is decided upon," asked the President, "would you be willing to undertake its negotiation?"

"I think so, sir."

"And what boon would you offer him—what reward?"

"*Redemption,* through the battlefield; a patriot's bright glory, perhaps a patriot's death, but—*REDEMPTION.*"

"The plan will be considered," announced the President. "I shall need your help, gentlemen, for whatever line of action we decide upon; and I thank you sincerely for coming. My secretary will see each one of you. You will not object, I trust, if we secure the co-operation of Dr. Jefferson."

In the envelope containing his expense allowance Grant Noble found a request to call upon the President the following morning.

In the interim of a night Grant Noble had made a hurried trip into Pennsylvania. When he arrived at the White House in the morning he led by the hand a wondering little boy whom he left in the outer room, when finally he was admitted to see the President.

"Ah! *so!*" exclaimed President Nefferman, glancing up. "Answer two questions: Your plans? And the *reason* for this state of affairs?"

"The reason, Mr. President," Grant Noble replied, "is the failure of white Americans to keep the golden rule in their dealings with colored people; the inability to believe that we are no less human than they. Three hundred years ago Shakespeare made Shylock ask: 'If you prick us, do we not bleed? If you poison us, do we not die? If you wrong us, shall we not revenge?' But these memorable heart cries of another race merely *amuse* your own. *They should make you shiver!* 'Vengeance is mine, saith the Lord, and I *will* repay!' You have been buying, buying, buying, with bullet and rope and roaring, red flame! These, and every agonized victim's cry, are *legal tender* with *God!* Strangely, the despised black man has at last turned from, or upon, his tormentors, resolved to die."

"But they must be won back!" interrupted the President. "What is your remedy?"

"Simply *inspiring JUSTICE.*"

"Is this disaffection really as general among your people, Mr. Noble, as it would appear?"

"I presume you want the *truth?* I have myself been approached by—. Well, secret agents of another government. I was offered tempting things—a professorship in their great university and a *man's* chance among them. I was at the point of wavering. Your letter, and that alone, caused me to reflect that *yet hope* might dawn for my race—in *America,*" he said with emotion. "It is my duty to tell you, Mr. President," he added, "that this entire country has been mapped by pretended 'students.' Every important road, stream, forest and hill is known, and the location of the remotest hamlet. The subjugation of the whole country is planned. The yellow race has shaken hands upon the prospect. Only God's providence can save us, with all we may do."

"What would your plan require?"

"A colonelship for Jed Blackburn."

"And for yourself, what?"

"A common soldier's fare."

President Nefferman was strangely moved. "Permit me to shake your hand!" he exclaimed. "I did not know there were such men in your race. I and my people have sinned!"

The glaring sign on a Chicago street announced the name *"Jed Blackburn."* But the place was closed, and the ebon giant, standing before the door, had a downcast look. He extended his hand to Grant Noble with a "Glad to meet you, parson." Noble explained his mission.

"What!" roared the scowling giant. "Fight fer *this* country? Well, I'm d—d if I do! Excuse *me,* parson. But ain't there some more interestin' subject?—prayer meetin', missions, measles, cholera morbus, an' th' like. Anything *pleasant*'ll do. Fightin' fer white folks is whut ruined *me!* They say I'm a bad man. Well, I'm just whut white men *developed* me into. See? Did *I* want to be a prize-fighter? *No!* I wanted to be a wheelwright, like my father. I was a brawny lad. White men saw me. 'Be a fighter,' sez they. I fought. 'Now, be a sport,' they sez. I sported. 'Git tough,' sez they. 'Th' tougher you be th' better you'll fight; an' maybe you'll git to be champeen.' Say! I moved right over on to *Tough Street.* Th' further you went th' tougher it got. An' I lived in th' last *house!*

"Well, whut does my champeenship 'mount to? After I licked th' champeen, th' white folks got it in fer me. I'm disgraced to-day, an' almost broke. Wish I'd never *seen* a glove! I could have been useful an' happy down South in th' little ole shop. But I ain't got no trade, ner no fr'en's, parson. That's all!"

"My friend," agreed Grant Noble, "you've been a big fool. But there's a way of atonement for you. You are a brave man. Will you take it?"

Thereupon he narrated his plan.

"Parson," declared the pugilist with emotion, "I'll *go* you! The' ain't no yaller in me! I never *saw* this thing before. If I've hurt my race I'll atone. An' thank God fer th' chance!" And his eyes filled with tears.

"All my life I've tried, in my way, to be somebody," he continued. "I meant to win glory fer my race. I starved, stalled, fought under wraps, played silly—till my chance come, when they sent me ag'inst the champeen. Before that fight I prayed to God. Between every round I prayed. The champeen wuz almost killin' me. My punishment wuz awful. His strength wuz as the strength of twenty men; his blows were murder. Ag'inst his ponderous bulk an' strength I pitted my skill an' *toughness,* and fought toe to toe. Three of my ribs were crushed, my teeth loosened an' my lips bleedin'; an' I bled inwardly, but I joked an' smiled an' fought on. I knew my good, ole mother wuz prayin'. I knew all my race wuz hopin', an' I went in to win or die. I'm a tough guy, parson, but I went to th' hospital after that fight. The champeen nearly finished me, 'stead o' me gittin' him. As I lay in that hospital, sufferin' th' tortures uv th' damned, I thanked my lucky stars, an' thanked th' dear, good God. It's tough, ain't it, parson, when a feller's disgraced his race? Well, Jeddie Blackburn in a colonel's uniform'll look *swell.* Aye?"

The country responded gallantly to the President's call for volunteers—Germans, Jews, Irish, Italians, Negroes, men of nearly every race, a million Americans sprang bravely to arms, proudly augmenting the regular troops. Gen. Frederick R. Gant, son of the illustrious "Hero of Athernox," was placed in supreme command.

As the ranking officer of his race, Jed Blackburn was allowed to attend the conference of officers, and to listen while plans were discussed for "the defeat of the enemy on his own grounds." Little attention was paid to Blackburn. In fact, he was merely tolerated. Someone, in pure consideration, however, suggested that he be allowed a word.

Blackburn spoke briefly, but as decisively as a veteran.

"Always let your man come *to* you," he declared, in heavy bass; "let 'im come on, an' nail 'im without a return. How you goin' to fight anybody you can't find? Let th' geesers come over here. They're comin' fast enough! Save your energy, an' cut loose when you're sure. An', depend upon it, they'll feint, an' try to smash you where you don't expect it. Jes' like boxin'!"

Strange to tell, this was the very plan the enemy pursued. The Philippines had yielded; Hawaii was gone. Suddenly a small Japanese squadron, appearing off San Francisco, began a heavy bombardment. Repelled, they sullenly drew off, in apparent discomfiture, steaming swiftly westward, out of sight. Almost immediately a withering bombardment was begun at San Diego, crumpling the town. The invaders landed, pushed rapidly north, and formed a juncture with their land forces, marching north from lower California. Within three days the vanishing fleet which had withdrawn from the Golden Gate was hurled back, like a thunderbolt, upon Santa Monica, the port of Los Angeles, wreaking untold vengeance there.

"Do you go, gen'al, an' say 'howdy' to 'em down there!" exclaimed Blackburn, joyfully. "Me an' my men 'll troll these others off to a nice little place I know—a deep valley in th' Santa Rosa Mountains. I found it when I used to be trainin'. It's a reg'lar death trap. When we fellers git 'em there we'll settle with *some* of 'em; an' you'se come back an' do th' rest."

Then he stepped out before *his* "army"—200,000 blacks. "Who's goin' along with *me*?" he asked quietly. "It may mean death, men. Will you go? Will *you* go, McVey? Will *you*, Langford? You, Jeannette?" To which they assented—"Yes."

"An' who else?" Jed Blackburn cried.

With a tremendous roar, 200,000 Negro throats gave back a thunderous "I—I—I!"

"Good boys!" avowed Blackburn, "but you've too many. I'll take every twentieth man."

Thus, of those named, were counted out all but McVey. Grant Noble was counted out, and bidden to "come on with th' reinforcements."

"Men," announced Jed Blackburn to the 10,000 who should go, "we shell move at once ag'inst th' enemy. There's not much hope uv us comin' back. But, if we die in this fight, we'll be dyin' fer our race. Maybe we'll make it better fer them that's lef' to tell."

Then, like desperate wasps, they stung the hurrying yellow flank, harassing, retreating, harrying; interfering with their march; luring them always toward the "death trap"—on and on. At last the great moment was near. "Colonel" Blackburn sent this message to General Gant:

"Send reinforcements now. We'll end the war here."

Northeast in the Santa Rosa range is a narrow defile, flanked and overbrowed with beetling cliffs. It is like a rocky throat. Straight north it leads into a valley, a precipitous, dreary enclosure, several miles in circumference. This is the stomach. Thither Jed Blackburn retreated, close pressed by the invaders, and made his only stand. This was "the death trap." From this valley there was no retreat, save by the pass by which they came.

Now came the victorious whites, like the swift eagles of Rome, swooping to the prey. The black reinforcement came with them, straining upon the leash, madly eager for the fray. Grant Noble, among them, wore the uniform of a common soldier. Eyes ablaze, breath quick, he stood waiting for the command. Over in the "death trap" the sound of grim slaughter was heard. The loyal blacks were dying now. Under that lurid sky the fierce arm of Nippon was bared; the sword of Nippon drank blood, and leaden missiles sang of death. The smoking valley reeled beneath the awful cannonade. It was horrible for the black men within!—400,000 yellow men against 10,000 blacks.

Now! now, the command was given! In an impetuous charge 10,000 black, battle-glaring demons dashed through the blazing pass and rushed upon the foe. A hundred thousand Germans followed, like the resistless legions of Barbarossa; 90,000 more Negro troops followed these, and then still other and other American soldiers came—Jews, Frenchmen, English-Americans, Italians, Irish, Swedes; and from the heights American cannon boomed, while American aviators, hovering aloft, skilfully dropped explosives upon the army of Nippon. The effect was horrible. Brave devils! whole Japanese regiments crumpled and curled up in the withering fire. Raked every way with belching cannon and rattling musketry, bayonetted and slashed by the ever-charging black troops, no human power could long endure the fearful plight of the yellow warriors. The fight was soon over. A dash by the Irish troopers gained the day. The war was ended.

The correspondents who accompanied the troops heralded the magnificent victory, and agreed that Gen. Frederick R. Gant vied with President Nefferman as the "man of the hour." But General Gant himself stated that he must agree with President Nefferman who had generously avowed that much credit was due to a colored man of the name of Grant Noble. But Noble, when sought out upon the battlefield, pointed to a gigantic black man lying among the slain.

"There, gentlemen," he declared, "is a man they didn't know."

THE DOLL

Written by Charles W. Chesnutt in April 1912, this short story relates a dilemma that a successful African-American entrepreneur faces: whether to avenge the death of a loved one at the hands of a racist or to protect the lives and future of his family and members of his race.

When Tom Taylor, proprietor of the Wyandot Hotel barber shop, was leaving home, after his noonday luncheon, to return to his work, his daughter, a sprightly, diminutive brown maid, with very bright black eyes and very curly, black hair, thrust into his coat pocket a little jointed doll somewhat the worse for wear.

"Now, don't forget, papa," she said, in her shrill childish treble, "what's to be done to her. Her arms won't work, and her legs won't work, and she can't hold her head up. Be sure and have her mended this afternoon, and bring her home when you come to supper; for she's afraid of the dark, and always sleeps with me. I'll meet you at the corner at half-past six—and don't forget, whatever you do."

"No, Daisy, I'll not forget," he replied, as he lifted her to the level of his lips and kissed her.

Upon reaching the shop he removed the doll from his pocket and hung it on one of the gilded spikes projecting above the wire netting surrounding the cashier's desk, where it would catch his eye. Some time during the afternoon he would send it to a toy shop around the corner for repairs. But the day was a busy one, and when the afternoon was well advanced he had not yet attended to it.

———

Colonel Forsyth had come up from the South to attend a conference of Democratic leaders to consider presidential candidates and platforms. He had put up at the Wyandot Hotel, but had been mainly in the hands of Judge Beeman, chairman of the local Jackson club, who was charged with the duty of seeing that the colonel was made comfortable and given the freedom of the city. It was after a committee meeting, and about 4 in the afternoon, that the two together entered the lobby of the Wyandot. They were discussing the platforms to be put forward by the two great parties in the approaching campaign.

"I reckon, judge," the colonel was saying, "that the Republican party will make a mistake if it injects the Negro question into its platform. The question is primarily a local one, and if the North will only be considerate about the matter, and let us alone, we can settle it to our entire satisfaction. The Negro's place is defined by nature, and in the South he knows it and gives us no trouble."

"The Northern Negroes are different," returned the judge.

"They are just the same," rejoined the colonel. "It is you who are different. You pamper them and they take liberties with you. But they are all from the South, and when they meet a Southerner they act accordingly. They are born to serve and to submit. If they had been worthy of equality they would never have endured slavery. They have no proper self-respect; they will neither resent an insult, nor defend a right, nor avenge a wrong."

"Well, now, colonel, aren't you rather hard on them? Consider their past."

"Hard? Why, no, bless your heart! I've got nothing against the nigger. I like him—in his place. But what I say is the truth. Are you in a hurry?"

"Not at all."

"Then come downstairs to the barber shop and I'll prove what I say."

———

The shop was the handsomest barber shop in the city. It was in the basement, and the paneled ceiling glowed with electric lights. The floor was of white tile, the walls lined with large mirrors. Behind ten chairs, of the latest and most comfortable design, stood as many colored barbers, in immaculate white jackets, each at work upon a white patron. An air of discipline and good order pervaded the establishment. There was no loud talking by patrons, no unseemly garrulity on the part of the barbers. It was very obviously a well-conducted barber shop, frequented by gentlemen who could afford to pay liberally for superior service. As the judge and the colonel entered a customer vacated the chair served by the proprietor.

"Next gentleman," said the barber.

The colonel removed his collar and took his seat in the vacant chair, remarking, as he ran his hand over his neck, "I want a close shave, barber."

"Yes, sir; a close shave."

The barber was apparently about forty, with a brown complexion, clean-cut features and curly hair. Committed by circumstances to a career of personal service, he had lifted it by intelligence, tact and industry to the dignity of a successful business. The judge, a regular patron of the shop, knew him well and had often, while in his chair, conversed with him concerning his race—a fruitful theme, much on the public tongue.

"As I was saying," said the colonel, while the barber adjusted a towel about his neck, "the Negro question is a perfectly simple one."

The judge thought it hardly good taste in the colonel to continue in his former strain. Northern men might speak slightingly of the Negro, but seldom in his presence. He tried a little diversion.

"The tariff," he observed, "is a difficult problem."

"Much more complicated, suh, than the Negro problem, which is perfectly simple. Let the white man once impress the Negro with his superiority; let the Negro see that there is no escape from the inevitable, and that ends it. The best thing about the Negro is that, with all his limitations, he can recognize a finality. It is the secret of his persistence among us. He has acquired the faculty of evolution, suh— by the law of the survival of the fittest. Long ago, when a young man, I killed a nigger to teach him his place. One who learns a lesson of that sort certainly never offends again, nor fathers any others of his breed."

The barber, having lathered the colonel's face, was stropping his razor with long, steady strokes. Every word uttered by the colonel was perfectly audible to him, but his impassive countenance betrayed no interest. The colonel seemed as unconscious of the barber's presence as the barber of the colonel's utterance. Surely, thought the judge, if such freedom of speech were the rule in the South the colonel's contention must be correct, and the Negroes thoroughly cowed. To a Northern man the situation was hardly comfortable.

"The iron and sugar interests of the South," persisted the judge, "will resist any reduction of the tariff."

The colonel was not to be swerved from the subject, nor from his purpose, whatever it might be.

"Quite likely they will; and we must argue with them, for they are white men and amenable to reason. The nigger, on the other hand, is the creature of instinct; you cannot argue with him; you must order him, and if he resists shoot him, as I did.

"Don't forget, barber," said the colonel, "that I want a close shave."

"No, sir," responded the barber, who, having sharpened his razor, now began to pass it, with firm and even hand, over the colonel's cheek.

"It must have been," said the judge, "an aggravated case, to justify so extreme a step."

"Extreme, suh? I beg yo' pardon, suh, but I can't say I had regarded my conduct in that light. But it was an extreme case so far as the nigger was concerned. I am not boasting about my course; it was simply a disagreeable necessity. I am naturally a kind-hearted man, and don't like to kill even a fly. It was after the war, suh, and just as the reconstruction period was drawing to a close. My mother employed a Negro girl, the child of a former servant of hers, to wait upon her."

The barber was studying the colonel's face as the razor passed over his cheek. The colonel's eyes were closed, or he might have observed the sudden gleam of interest that broke through the barber's mask of self-effacement, like a flash of lightning from a clouded sky. Involuntarily the razor remained poised in midair, but, in less time than it takes to say it, was moving again, swiftly and smoothly, over the colonel's face. To shave a talking man required a high degree of skill, but they were both adepts, each in his own trade—the barber at shaving, the colonel at talking.

"The girl was guilty of some misconduct, and my mother reprimanded her and sent her home. She complained to her father, and he came to see my mother about it. He was insolent, offensive and threatening. I came into the room and ordered him to leave it. Instead of obeying, he turned on me in a rage, suh, and threatened me. I drew my revolver and shot him. The result was unfortunate; but he and his people learned a lesson. We had no further trouble with bumptious niggers in our town."

"And did you have no trouble in the matter?" asked the judge.

"None, suh, to speak of. There were proceedings, but they were the merest formality. Upon my statement, confirmed by that of my mother, I was discharged by the examining magistrate, and the case was never even reported to the grand jury. It was a clear case of self-defense."

———

The barber had heard the same story, with some details ignored or forgotten by the colonel. It was the barber's father who had died at the colonel's hand, and for many long years the son had dreamed of this meeting.

He remembered the story in this wise: His father had been a slave. Freed by the Civil War, he had entered upon the new life with the zeal and enthusiasm of his people at the dawn of liberty, which seem, in the light of later discouragements, so pathetic in the retrospect. The chattel aspired to own property; the slave, forbidden learning, to educate his children. He had worked early and late, had saved his money with a thrift equal to that of a German immigrant, and had sent his children regularly to school.

The girl—the barber remembered her very well—had been fair of feature, soft of speech and gentle of manner, a pearl among pebbles. One day her father's old mistress had met him on the street and, after a kindly inquiry about his family, had asked if she might hire his daughter during the summer, when there was no school. Her own married daughter would be visiting her, with a young child, and they wanted some neat and careful girl to nurse the infant.

"Why, yas ma'am," the barber's father had replied. "I reckon it might be a good thing fer Alice. I wants her ter be a teacher; but she kin l'arn things from you, ma'am, that no teacher kin teach her. She kin l'arn manners, ma'am, an' white folks' ways, and nowhere better than in yo' house."

So Alice had gone to the home of her father's former mistress to learn white folks' ways. The lady had been kind and gracious. But there are ways and ways among all people.

When she had been three weeks in her new employment her mistress's son—a younger brother of the colonel—came home from college. Some weeks later Alice went home to her father. Who was most at fault the barber never knew. A few hours afterward the father called upon the lady. There was a stormy interview. Things were said to which the ears of white ladies were unaccustomed from the lips of black men. The elder son had entered the room and interfered. The barber's father had turned to him and exclaimed angrily:

"Go 'way from here, boy, and don't talk ter me, or I'm liable ter harm you."

The young man stood his ground. The Negro advanced menacingly toward him. The young man drew his ready weapon and fatally wounded the Negro—he lived only long enough, after being taken home, to gasp out the facts to his wife and children.

The rest of the story had been much as the colonel had related it.

As the barber recalled it, however, the lady had not been called to testify, but was ill at the time of the hearing, presumably from the nervous shock.

That she had secretly offered to help the family the barber knew, and that her help had been rejected with cold hostility. He knew that the murderer went unpunished, and that in later years he had gone into politics, and became the leader and mouthpiece of his party. All the world knew that he had ridden into power on his hostility to Negro rights.

The barber had been a mere boy at the time of his father's death, but not too young to appreciate the calamity that had befallen the household. The family was broken up. The sordid details of its misfortunes would not be interesting. Poverty, disease and death had followed them, until he alone was left. Many years had passed. The brown boy who had wept beside his father's bier, and who had never forgotten nor forgiven, was now the grave-faced, keen-eyed, deft-handed barber, who held a deadly weapon at the throat of his father's slayer.

How often he had longed for this hour! In his dreams he had killed this man a hundred times, in a dozen ways. Once, when a young man, he had gone to meet him, with the definite purpose of taking his life, but chance had kept them apart. He had imagined situations where they might come face to face; he would see the white man struggling in the water; he would have only to stretch forth his hand to save him; but he would tell him of his hatred and let him drown. He would see him in a burning house, from which he might rescue him; and he would call him murderer and let him burn! He would see him in the dock for murder of a white man, and only his testimony could save him, and he would let him suffer the fate that he doubly deserved! He saw a vision of his father's form, only an hour before thrilling with hope and energy, now stiff and cold in death; while under his keen razor lay the neck of his enemy, the enemy, too, of his race, sworn to degrade them, to teach them, if need be, with the torch and with the gun, that their place was at the white man's feet, his heel upon their neck; who held them in such contempt that he could speak as he had spoken in the presence of one of them. One stroke of the keen blade, a deflection of half an inch in its course, and a murder would be avenged, an enemy destroyed!

For the next sixty seconds the barber heard every beat of his own pulse, and the colonel, in serene unconsciousness, was nearer death than he had ever been in the course of a long and eventful life. He was only a militia colonel, and had never been under fire, but his turbulent political career had been passed in a community where life was lightly valued, where hot words were often followed by rash deeds, and murder was tolerated as a means of private vengeance and political advancement. He went on talking, but neither the judge nor the barber listened, each being absorbed in his own thoughts.

To the judge, who lived in a community where Negroes voted, the colonel's frankness was a curious revelation. His language was choice, though delivered with the Southern intonation, his tone easy and conversational, and, in addressing the barber directly, his manner had been courteous enough. The judge was interested, too, in watching the barber, who, it was evident, was repressing some powerful emotion. It seemed very probable to the judge that the barber might resent this cool recital of murder and outrage. He did not know what might be true of the Negroes in the South, but he had been judge of a police court in one period of his upward career, and he had found colored people prone to sudden rages, when under the influence of strong emotion, handy with edged tools, and apt to cut thick and deep, nor always careful about the color of the cuticle. The barber's feelings were plainly stirred, and the judge, a student of human nature, was curious to see if he would be moved to utterance. It would have been no novelty—patrons of the shop often discussed race questions with the barber. It was evident that the colonel was trying an experiment to demonstrate his contention in the lobby above. But the judge could not know the barber's intimate relation to the story, nor did it occur to him that the barber might conceive any deadly purpose because of a purely impersonal grievance. The barber's hand did not even tremble.

In the barber's mind, however, the whirlwind of emotions had passed lightly over the general and settled upon the particular injury. So strong, for the moment, was the homicidal impulse that it would have prevailed already had not the noisy opening of the door to admit a patron diverted the barber's attention and set in motion a current of ideas which fought for the colonel's life. The barber's glance toward the door, from force of habit, took in the whole shop. It was a handsome shop, and had been to the barber a matter of more than merely personal pride. Prominent among a struggling people, as yet scarcely beyond the threshold of citizenship, he had long been looked upon, and had become accustomed to regard himself, as a representative man, by whose failure or success his race would be tested. Should he slay this man now beneath his hand, this beautiful shop would be lost to his people. Years before the whole trade had been theirs. One by one the colored master barbers, trained in the slovenly old ways, had been forced to the wall by white competition, until his shop was one of the few good ones remaining in the hands of men of his race. Many an envious eye had been cast upon it. The lease had only a year to run. Strong pressure, he knew, had been exerted by a white rival to secure the reversion. The barber had the hotel proprietor's promise of a renewal; but he knew full well that should he lose the shop no colored man would succeed him; a center of industry, a medium of friendly contact with white men, would be lost to his people—many a good turn had the barber been able to do for them while he had the ear—literally had the ear—of some influential citizen, or held some aspirant for public office by the throat. Of the ten barbers in the shop all but one were married, with families dependent upon them for support. One was sending a son to college; another was buying a home. The unmarried one was in his spare hours studying a profession, with the hope of returning to practice it among his people in a Southern State. Their fates were all, in a measure, dependent upon the proprietor of the shop. Should he yield to the impulse which was swaying him their livelihood would be placed in jeopardy. For what white man, while the memory of this tragic event should last, would trust his throat again beneath a Negro's razor?

Such, however, was the strength of the impulse against which the barber was struggling that these considerations seemed likely not to prevail. Indeed, they had presented themselves to the barber's mind in a vague, remote, detached manner, while the dominant idea was present and compelling, clutching at his heart, drawing his arm, guiding his fingers. It was by their mass rather than by their clearness that these restraining forces held the barber's arm so long in check—it was society against self, civilization against the primitive instinct, typifying, more fully than the barber could realize, the great social problem involved in the future of his race.

He had now gone once over the colonel's face, subjecting that gentleman to less discomfort than he had for a long time endured while undergoing a similar operation. Already he had retouched one cheek and had turned the colonel's head to finish the other. A few strokes more and the colonel could be released with a close shave—how close he would never know!—or, one stroke, properly directed, and he would never stand erect again! Only the day before the barber had read, in the newspapers, the account of a ghastly lynching in a Southern State, where, to avenge a single provoked murder, eight Negroes had bit the dust and a woman had been burned at the stake for no other crime than that she was her husband's wife. One stroke and there would be one less of those who thus wantonly played with human life!

The uplifted hand had begun the deadly downward movement—when one of the barbers dropped a shaving cup, which was smashed to pieces on the marble floor. Fate surely fought for the colonel—or was it for the barber? Involuntarily the latter stayed his hand—instinctively his glance went toward the scene of the accident. It was returning to the upraised steel, and its uncompleted task, when it was arrested by Daisy's doll, hanging upon the gilded spike where he had left it.

If the razor went to its goal he would not be able to fulfil his promise to Daisy! She would wait for him at the corner, and wait in vain! If he killed the colonel he himself could hardly escape, for he was black and not white, and this was North and not South, and personal vengeance was not accepted by the courts as a justification for murder. Whether he died or not, he would be lost to Daisy. His wife was dead, and there would be no one to take care of Daisy. His own father had died in defense of his daughter; he must live to protect his own. If there was a righteous God, who divided the evil from the good, the colonel would some time get his just deserts. Vengeance was God's; it must be left to Him to repay!

The jointed doll had saved the colonel's life. Whether society had conquered self or not may be an open question; but it had stayed the barber's hand until love could triumph over hate!

The barber laid aside the razor, sponged off the colonel's face, brought him, with a movement of the chair, to a sitting posture, brushed his hair, pulled away the cloths from around his neck, handed him a pasteboard check for the amount of his bill, and stood rigidly by his chair. The colonel adjusted his collar, threw down a coin equal to double the amount of his bill and, without waiting for the change, turned with the judge to leave the shop. They had scarcely reached the door leading into the hotel lobby when the barber, over-wrought by the long strain, collapsed heavily into the nearest chair.

"Well, judge," said the colonel, as they entered the lobby, "that was a good shave. What a sin it would be to spoil such a barber by making him a postmaster! I didn't say anything to him, for it don't do to praise a nigger much—it's likely to give him the big head—but I never had," he went on, running his hand appreciatively over his cheek. "I never had a better shave in my life. And I proved my theory. The barber is the son of the nigger I shot."

The judge was not sure that the colonel had proved his theory, and was less so after he had talked, a week later, with the barber. And, although the colonel remained at the Wyandot for several days, he did not get shaved again in the hotel barber shop.

MR. TAYLOR'S FUNERAL

In this short story, published by Charles W. Chesnutt in 1915, David Taylor, who is from a small town near the Great Lakes, was not on board when his ship arrived home. The drowning of a man who bears a striking resemblance to Taylor leads to a series of complications and confusion.

Mr. David Taylor had been for many years chief steward, during the season of navigation, upon a steamboat running between Groveland and Buffalo, on one of the Great Lakes. The salary and perquisites made the place a remunerative one, and Mr. Taylor had saved considerable money. During the wintertime he ran a coal yard, where he supplied poor people with coal in small quantities at a large profit. He invested his savings in real estate, and in the course of time became the owner of a row of small houses on a side street in Groveland, as well as of a larger house on the corner of the adjacent main street.

Mr. Taylor was a stout mulatto, with curly hair and a short grey mustache. He had been a little wild in his youth, but had settled down into a steady old bachelor, in which state he remained until he was past forty-five, when he surprised his friends by marrying a young wife and taking her to live with him in the corner house.

Miss Lula Sampson was a very personable young woman, of not more than twenty-two or twenty-three. She had not been without other admirers; but Mr. Taylor's solid attractions had more than counterbalanced the advantages of these others in the way of youth and sprightliness. For Miss Sampson, while not without her sentimental side, had a practical vein as well, and concluded that on the whole it would be better to be a rich old man's darling than a poor young man's slave.

They lived together very comfortably in the corner house, and Mrs. Taylor enjoyed to the full such advantages as regular rents and savings bank dividends carried in their train. Mr. Taylor had been for many years a leading member of the Jerusalem Methodist Church, in which he had at various times acted as class-leader, trustee and deacon, and of which he had been at all times the financial backer and manager. Mrs. Taylor had been brought up, so to speak, in the Mt. Horeb Baptist Church, and had at one time sung in the choir; but after her marriage, she very dutifully attended service with her husband, only visiting the Baptist Church on special occasions, such as weddings or funerals, or other events of general public interest.

One day in May, 1900, a month or more after the opening of navigation in the spring, Mr. Taylor left Groveland on the steamer *Mather* for Buffalo, on one of her regular semiweekly trips to that port. When the steamer returned several days later without him, his wife and friends felt some concern at his nonappearance, as no message had been received from him in the meantime. Inquiry on the steamer merely brought out the fact that Taylor had not been on hand when the boat was ready to leave port, and that she had sailed without him; in fact, he had not been missed until the *Mather* was some miles out.

When several days more elapsed without news from the absent man, his wife's uneasiness became a well-defined alarm. She could account for his absence on no hypothesis except that some harm had befallen him. And, upon reading an item in a newspaper, about a week after Mr. Taylor's disappearance, to the effect that the body of a middle-aged mulatto had been found floating in Buffalo harbor, she divined at once that her husband had been the victim of accident, or foul play, and that it was his body that had been recovered. With a promptitude born of sincere regret and wifely sorrow, she requested the company of Deacon Larkins, the intimate personal friend and class-leader of her husband, and with him took the train for Buffalo. Arriving there, they found the body at an undertaking establishment. It had evidently been in the water several days, and the features were somewhat disfigured, but nevertheless, Mrs. Taylor had no difficulty in identifying the body as that of her late husband. She had the remains prepared for shipment, and the day after her arrival at Buffalo, accompanied them back to Groveland. She had telegraphed for a hearse to be at the depot, and when she saw the coffin placed in it, she took a carriage with Deacon Larkins and drove to her home.

"Brother Larkins," she said, in griefstricken accents, as she thought of her good friend and husband and of the narrow cell in which he must soon be laid, "I wish you would t-t-take charge of the arrangements for the f-f-funeral. I know my dear dead David loved you, and would have wished you to attend to it."

"I shall be glad to, Sister Taylor. It is the last service I can perform for my dear friend and brother. His loss will be a sad blow to the church, and to us all."

In pursuance of his instructions Deacon Larkins engaged an undertaker, inserted in the newspapers a notice announcing the date of the funeral, requested six of the intimate friends of the deceased to act as pallbearers, and telegraphed the pastor of the Methodist Church, who was out of town, to be on hand on Wednesday at 2 o'clock in the afternoon to conduct the services and preach the funeral sermon.

Several friends of the family called on Mrs. Taylor during the day preceding the funeral, among them the Reverend Alonzo Brown, pastor of the Mt. Horeb Baptist Church. Mr. Brown was a youngish man, apparently not more than thirty, and had himself suffered a bereavement several years before, in the loss of a wife to whom he had made a model husband, so excellent a husband indeed that more than one lady had envied his wife when living—and when she died, had thought that her successor would be indeed a fortunate woman. In addition to possessing these admirable domestic qualities, the Reverend Alonzo was a very handsome man, of light brown complexion, and with large and expressive black eyes and very glossy curly hair. Indeed, Mrs. Taylor herself had several times thought that if an over-ruling Providence in its inscrutable wisdom should see fit to remove her dear David from his earthly career while she was yet a young woman—which was not at all unlikely, since he was twenty-five years her senior—there was no man of her acquaintance with whom she could more willingly spend the remainder of her days and the money her good David would leave her, than the Reverend Alonzo Brown. Of course, this had been only one of the vague daydreams of a lively imagination; but it is not surprising, when the central figure in this vision called on her upon the heels of the very event upon which the daydreams had been predicated, that the idea should penetrate even the veil of grief that surrounded her, and assume something of the nature of a definite probability.

Mr. Brown was a man of tact, and consoled the widow very beautifully in her bereavement.

"Yes, Sister Taylor," he said, pressing her hand with soothing friendliness, "your loss is indeed great, for your husband was a man of whom any woman might have been proud. You displayed excellent taste and judgment, too, Sister Taylor, in selecting as your companion a man of steady habits and settled character, who could leave you suitably provided for during the rest of your life."

The widow sobbed at the magnitude of her loss, but was not unmindful of the compliment to her own taste and judgment.

"But the saddest feature about our dear brother's taking off is not *your* loss"; he said, again pressing her hand consolingly, "it is what he, himself, has lost—the companionship of one who made his household a model for his friends to imitate, and the despair of those who could not hope to be so fortunate. It is true," he added, with proper professional consistency, "that he has gone to his reward; but I am sure he would willingly have waited for it a few years longer in this terrestrial paradise."

The minister, as he said this, looked around appreciatively at the very comfortable room in which they sat. There was handsome paper on the walls, a bright red carpet on the floor, lace curtains at the windows, a piano, a well-filled bookcase,—and in fact, all the evidences of solid prosperity, based on landed proprietorship. And by his side, too, sat the weeping young widow, to whom tears and weeds were by no means unbecoming.

While he had been speaking, an idea had occurred to Mrs. Taylor. She was before her marriage a member of his church. The pastor of the Methodist Church, she had learned since her return from Buffalo, was out of town, in attendance on the general conference of his denomination in session at New York. It would be a very nice thing indeed to have Mr. Brown preach the funeral sermon.

"Brother Brown," she said, on the impulse of the moment, "I want you to do me a favor. Will you preach my dear David's funeral sermon?"

He reflected a moment. It was an opportunity to secure that influence which would enable him to lead back into his fold this very desirable sheep.

"If you don't think it will be taken amiss by his own church," he answered, "it would give me great pleasure to perform the last sad rites over our departed friend."

"There will be no trouble about that," she replied. "Elder Johnson has gone to general conference, and there is no one else whom I would prefer to yourself. I ask it as a personal favor."

"It shall be done at any cost," he said determinedly, again pressing her hand in farewell.

"And if you will ask the choir to sing, I shall be under still greater obligations," she said. "They are all my friends, and I have often joined with them on similar occasions, before I was married, and I'm sure you would prefer them."

About an hour after Mr. Brown went away, Deacon Larkins called to make a final report of the arrangements he had made.

"I've requested several of the brethren to act as pallbearers," he said, naming them, "and have asked the choir to furnish the music. Elder Johnson telegraphed this afternoon that he would be here in time to preach the sermon. He has already started, and will get here by half-past one, and come right up from the depot."

Mrs. Taylor scented trouble. "But I thought he couldn't come, and I've invited Elder Brown to preach the sermon," she said.

Deacon Larkins looked annoyed. "There'll be trouble," he said. "You asked me to make arrangements and I acted accordingly."

"What can we do about it?" she asked, anxiously.

"Don't ask me," he said. "I'm not responsible for the difficulty."

"But you can help me," she said. "I see no way out of it but to explain the situation to Elder Brown and ask him to retire. Please do that for me."

Deacon Larkins grumbled a little and went away, intending to do as requested. But the more he thought about the matter, the more displeased he felt at the widow's action. She had not only been guilty of disrespect to him, in asking a minister to conduct the services without consulting the man in whose charge she had placed the arrangements, but she had committed the far more serious offense of slighting the Methodist church. He could hardly think of a graver breach of propriety than to ask the minister of a rival denomination to officiate at this funeral. If it had been some obscure member of the congregation the matter would have been of less consequence; but to request the Baptist minister to preach Brother David's funeral sermon was something like asking Martin Luther to assist at the Pope's interment. The more Deacon Larkins thought of it the less he liked it; and finally he concluded that he would simply wash his hand of the entire business—if the widow wanted to call off Elder Brown, she would have to do it herself.

He wrote a note to this effect and sent it by his younger son, a lad of ten, with instructions to deliver it to Mrs. Taylor. The boy met a companion and went off to play, and lost the note. His father was away when he got back home. In the meantime, the boy had forgotten about the note, and left his father to infer that it had been delivered.

About a quarter of two on the day of the funeral the friends began to arrive. The undertaker in charge seated them. When the Baptist choir came it was shown to the place provided beforehand for the singers. When a few minutes later the Methodist choir arrived and stated what their part in the service was to be, the undertaker, supposing they were an addition to the number already on hand, gave them the seats nearest those occupied by the Baptist choir. There was some surprise apparent, but for a while nothing was said, the members of the two bodies confining themselves to looks not altogether friendly. Some of them thought it peculiar that, if the two choirs had been asked to cooperate, there had been no notice given and no opportunity to practice together; but all waited for the coming of the officiating minister to solve the difficulty. Meantime the friends of the family continued to arrive, until the room where the remains were placed was filled to overflowing, and there were people standing in the hall and seated in other rooms from which they would be able to see or hear very little of the exercises.

At just five minutes to two a livery carriage drove up to the gate, and deposited on the pavement a tall dark man, wearing a silk hat, a high vest, and a coat of clerical cut—it was Elder Johnson, of the Jerusalem Methodist Church. The elder paid the driver his fee, and went in at the front gate. At the same moment the pastor of the Baptist Church came in at the side gate and drew near the front door. The two preachers met on the porch, and bowed to one another stiffly. The undertaker's assistant came forward and took their hats.

"Which of you gentlemen is to conduct the service?" asked the undertaker, with a professionally modulated voice.

"I shall conduct the service," answered Elder Johnson in a matter-of-fact tone.

"I am to conduct the service," said Mr. Brown firmly, in the same breath.

Elder Johnson looked surprised, Mr. Brown looked determined, and they glared at each other belligerently.

"May I ask what you mean, sir?" said Elder Johnson, recovering somewhat from his surprise.

"I mean, sir, that I'm going to conduct the funeral exercises," replied the other.

The undertaker began to feel uneasy. It was his first funeral in that neighborhood, and he had expected to make a reputation by his success in directing it.

"There's evidently some misunderstanding here," he said, in a propitiatory tone.

"There's no misunderstanding on my part, said Elder Johnson. "I was telegraphed to by Deacon Larkins, at the widow's request, and have left important business and come five hundred miles at considerable expense to preach this funeral, and I intend to preach it, or know the reason why."

"There can be no possible misunderstanding on my part," replied Mr. Brown. "People may send telegrams without authority, or under a mistaken impression; but I was asked by the widow, personally, to conduct the funeral services, and I propose to do so."

"The deceased was a member of my church before the widow was born," retorted Elder Johnson, making in his warmth a mistake of several years. "I was requested by the widow's agent to conduct this service, and have come here prepared to do it. Every consideration of duty and decency requires me to insist. Even the wishes of the widow should hardly be permitted to stand in the way of what, in this case, is the most obvious propriety."

"The widow," said Mr. Brown, "is the principal one concerned. Her wishes should be sacred on such an occasion, to say nothing of her rights. I'll not retire until I am personally requested by her to do so. I received my commission from her, and I'll resign it to her only."

"Wait a moment, gentlemen," said the undertaker, hopefully, "until I go and speak to the widow."

The colloquy on the porch had not gone unnoticed. Through the half-closed Venetian blinds a number of the guests had seen the group apparently engaged in animated discussion, though their voices had been pitched in low tones; and there was considerable curiosity as to what was going on.

In a few moments the undertaker returned. "Gentlemen," he said in desperation, "something must be done. I can't get anything out of the widow. She is almost hysterical with grief, and utterly unfit to decide on anything. You must come to some agreement. Why can't you divide the services between you?"

The rival clergymen set their faces even more rigidly.

"I can submit to no division," said Elder Johnson, "that does not permit me to preach the sermon. No man could know Brother Taylor as well as I did, and no man could possibly be so well prepared to pronounce a fitting eulogy on his life. It would be an insult to my church for any one but Brother Taylor's pastor to preach his funeral; in fact, it seems to me not only in bad taste, but bordering on indecency for the pastor of another church, of another denomination, to take advantage of a widow's grief and irresponsibility, and try to force himself where the most elementary principles of professional courtesy would require him to stay away. However, I'm willing to overlook that, under the circumstances, if Brother Brown will be content to read the Scriptures and lead in one of the prayers."

"I repel Brother Johnson's insinuations with scorn; their animus is very plain," said the Baptist minister, with some heat. "I will accept of no compromise that does not allow me to deliver the discourse. I was personally requested to do so; I have prepared a sermon with special reference to the needs of this particular case. If I don't use it my labor is wasted. My brother seems to think there's nobody to be considered in this matter but the deceased, whereas I am of quite the contrary opinion."

It was very apparent that no such compromise as the one proposed was possible. Meanwhile the curiosity on the inside was rising to fever heat; a number of eyes were glancing through the blinds, and several late comers had collected about the steps leading up to the porch and were listening intently.

Pending this last statement by the reverend gentlemen of their respective positions, the undertaker had had time to think. He was a man of resources, and the emergency brought out his latent powers. A flash of professional inspiration came to his aid.

"Gentlemen," he said soothingly, "I think I can see a way out of this difficulty, which will give each of you an opportunity to officiate, and prevent the funeral from being spoiled. Here are two large rooms, opening by wide doors from opposite sides of a central hall. There are people enough to fill the two rooms easily. The remains can be placed in the hall between the two rooms, where they can be seen from both. Each of you conduct a service in a separate room, and all the guests can be comfortably seated, in a position to hear or participate in one service or the other."

The proposition was a novel one, but it possessed the merit of practicability, and after some brief demure, both ministers reluctantly consented to the arrangement. The body was quickly removed to the hall, and disposed in a position where it would be visible from both rooms. The undertaker made a brief statement of the situation, and announced that two services would be held. The company divided according to their individual preferences, some taking seats in the other room, others remaining where they were. The Baptist choir of course went with their own minister, the Methodist choir remained with theirs. When the widow came out, clad in deepest weeds and sobbing softly, she took her seat, whether by inadvertence or choice did not appear, in the room where Mr. Brown had elected to conduct his part of the ceremony.

Each service opened with singing. The Methodist choir sang "Rock of Ages." The Baptist choir softly chanted "Asleep in Jesus," until they were compelled to sing louder in order to be heard at all. Each of the ministers then read a passage of Scripture; there was no conflict in this, as they were far enough apart to avoid confusion.

Each then offered prayer. The Methodist minister rendered thanks for the blessing of a beautiful life that had been spared so long among them as an example of right living. Mr. Brown, on the other side of the hall, with equal fervor asked for comfort to the sorrowing widow in her bereavement. And each in his own words prayed that the event they had come together to mourn over might be a warning to those present of the transitoriness of all earthly good, and that by calling attention to the common mortality it might humble their souls and drive out jealousy and envy and malice and all uncharitableness.

At the close of the prayers there was another musical number—or rather two of them. The Baptist choir rendered an anthem breathing resignation and comfort. The Methodist choir sang a hymn of triumph over death and the grave. Some one discreetly closed one of the doors during the singing, so that no discord marred the harmony of this part of the service.

When the two addresses were well under way, a man came up the street and entered the premises by the front gate. There had been several late arrivals, but until this one appeared they had all found seats in the house. As the newcomer approached he saw the crepe upon the door, noted the half-drawn blinds, and glanced across the lot at the row of carriages drawn up on the side street. With an expression of mingled wonder and alarm, he drew nearer the door and heard the sound of preaching. He stepped softly upon the porch but paused before he reached the door, and, after hesitating a moment, came down again, and going around to the side of the house stood on tiptoe and peered curiously through the half-closed blinds at the scene within. First he noticed the coffin, piled high with flowers. Then the sermon fixed his attention, and clutching the window-sill with his elbows he stood listening for several minutes.

"Indeed, my dear brethren and sisters," Elder Johnson was saying, "we may well mourn the death of our dear brother, and look upon it as an irreparable loss. Where will we find a man who was so generous in his contributions to the church, so devoted to his family, or who set a better example of the Christian life? In him we have lost a leader in every good work, a faithful friend, a dear brother, a strong pillar in the church, a champion of his race, a man whom we all loved and admired. Cut off in the prime of life, in the full tide of his usefulness, we mourn his departure, and we rejoice that he has lived—we celebrate his virtues and we revere his memory."

The man outside dropped from his somewhat constrained position, and the puzzled expression on his face became even more pronounced. But he had heard the voice, though indistinctly, of the minister across the hall, and he went softly around the rear of the house and picking up a small box which lay in the yard, placed it under a window of the other room. Looking through the slats, he saw a woman dressed in deepest mourning. Her face was concealed by the heavy crepe veil that fell before it, but her form was shaken by convulsive sobs. Grouped around the room was an audience equally as large as the one across the hall, and the young Baptist minister was saying, with great unction:

"There are no words, my hearers, by which we can adequately express the sympathy we feel for this bereaved widow in this, her hour of deepest earthly sorrow. Our hearts go out to this beloved sister, whose mainstay has been cut off, and who has been left to tread the thorny path of life in loneliness and desolation. I know that if the departed can look down from that upper sphere which he now adorns, upon this scene of his late earthly career, no more painful thought could mar the celestial serenity of his happiness than the reflection that he had left behind him in inconsolable grief the companion of his earthly joys and sorrows. We feel for our sister; we commend her to the source of all comfort; we assure her of such friendly offices as are within our weak power. And we hope that in time the edge of her grief will lose its sharpness, and that she may feel resigned to the decree of Heaven, and find such consolation as a life of usefulness may yet have to offer her."

The two sermons came to an end almost simultaneously, and again the two audiences were led in prayer. While the eyes of the two ministers were raised on high in supplication, and those of their hearers were piously turned to earth, the man on the outside, unable to restrain his curiosity longer, stepped down from his box, came around to the front door, opened it, walked softly forward, and stopped by the casket, where he stood looking down at the face it contained.

At that moment the two prayers came to an end, the eyes of the ministers sought a lower level, while those of the guests were raised, and they saw the stranger standing by the coffin.

Some nervous women screamed, several strong men turned pale, and there was a general movement that would probably have resulted in flight if there had been any way out except by passing through the hall.

The man by the casket looked up with even greater wonderment than he had before displayed.

"Whose funeral is this, anyhow?" he asked, addressing himself to nobody in particular.

"Why," responded several voices in chorus, "it's your funeral!"

A light dawned on the newcomer, and he looked much relieved.

"There's some mistake here," he said, "or else if I'm dead I don't know it. I was certainly alive when I came in on the train from Buffalo about thirty minutes ago."

The drowning in Buffalo harbor of a man resembling Taylor had been, of course, a mere coincidence. It might be said, in passing, that Mr. Taylor never explained his prolonged absence very satisfactorily. He did tell a story, or rather a vague outline of a story, lacking in many of the corroborative details which establish truthfulness, about an accident and a hospital. As he is still a pillar in the Jerusalem Methodist Church, and trying hard to live up to the standard set by his funeral sermons, it would be unbecoming to do more than suggest, in the same indefinite way, that when elderly men, who have been a little wild in their youth, are led by sudden temptation, when away from the restraining influences of home, to relapse for a time into the convivial habits of earlier days, there are, in all well-governed cities, institutions provided at the public expense, where they may go into retreat for a fixed period of time, of such length—say five or ten or twenty or thirty days—as the circumstances of each particular case may seem to require.

THE MARKED TREE

Published by Charles W. Chesnutt in the December 1924 and January 1925 issues of *The Crisis*, this story centers on the so-called marked tree on the Spencer plantation. The tree is seemingly tied to the fate of the entire Spencer family.

I had been requested by my cousin, whose home was in Ohio, to find for him, somewhere in my own neighborhood in the pine belt of North Carolina, a suitable place for a winter residence. His wife was none too strong; his father, who lived with him, was in failing health; and he wished to save them from the raw lake winds which during the winter season take toll of those least fitted to resist their rigor. My relative belonged to the fortunate class of those who need take no thought today for tomorrow's needs. The dignity of labor is a beautiful modern theory, in which no doubt many of the sterner virtues find their root, but the dignity of ease was celebrated at least as long ago as the days of Horace, a gentleman and philosopher, with some reputation as a poet.

Since my cousin was no lover of towns, and the term neighborhood is very elastic when applied to rural life, I immediately thought of an old, uncultivated—I was about to say plantation, but its boundaries had long since shrunk from those which in antebellum times would have justified so pretentious a designation. It still embraced, however, some fifteen or twenty acres of diversified surface—part sand-hill, part meadow; part overgrown with scrubby shortleaf pines and part with a scraggy underbrush. Though the soil had been more or less exhausted by the wasteful methods of slavery, neglected grapevines here and there, and gnarled and knotted fruit-trees, smothered by ruder growths about them, proved it to have been at one time in a high state of cultivation.

I had often driven by the old Spencer place, as it was called, from the name of the family whose seat it had been. It lay about five miles from my vineyard and was reached by a drive down the Wilmington Road and across the Mineral Spring swamp. Having brought with me to North Carolina a certain quickness of decision and promptness of action which the climate and *laissez faire* customs of my adopted state had not yet overcome, upon receipt of my cousin's letter I ordered old Julius to get out the gray mare and the rockaway and drive me over to the old Spencer place.

When we reached it, Julius left his seat long enough to take down the bars which guarded the entrance and we then drove up a short lane to the cleared space, surrounded by ragged oaks and elms, where the old plantation house had once stood. It had been destroyed by fire many years before and there were few traces of it remaining—a crumbling brick pillar here and there, on which the sills of the house had rested, and the dilapidated, ivy-draped lower half of a chimney, of which the yawning, blackened fireplace bore mute witness of the vanished generations which had lived and loved—and perchance suffered and died—within the radius of its genial glow.

Not far from where the house had stood, there was a broad oak stump, in a good state of preservation, except for a hole in the center, due, doubtless, to a rotten heart, in what had been in other respects a sound and perfect tree. I had seated myself upon the top of the stump—the cut had been made with the axe, almost as smoothly as though with a saw—when old Julius, who was standing near me, exclaimed, with some signs of concern.

"Excuse me, suh, I know you come from de No'th, but did any of yo' folks, way back yonder, come from 'roun' hyuh?"

"No," I returned, "they were New England Yankees, with no Southern strain whatever. But why do you ask?" I added, observing that he had something on his mind, and having often found his fancies quaint and amusing, from the viewpoint of one not Southern born.

"Oh, nothin', suh, leas' ways nothin' much—only I seed you settin' on dat ol' stump, an' I wuz kind er scared fer a minute."

"I don't see anything dangerous about the stump," I replied. "It seems to be a very well preserved oak stump."

"Oh, no, suh," said Julius, "dat ain' no oak stump."

It bore every appearance of an oak stump. The grain of the wood was that of oak. The bark was oak bark, and the spreading base held the earth in the noble grip of the king of trees.

"It is an oak, Julius—it is the stump of what was once a fine oak tree."

"Yas, suh, I know it 'pears like oak wood, and it 'pears like oak bahk, an' it looked like a oak tree w'en it wuz standin' dere, fifty feet high, fohty years ago. But it wa'n't—no, suh, it wa'n't."

"What kind of a tree was it, if not an oak?"

"It was a U-pass tree, suh; yes, sah, dat wuz de name of it—a U-pass tree."

"I have never heard of that variety," I replied.

"No, suh, it wuz a new kind er tree roun' hyuh. I nevah heard er any but dat one."

"Where did you get the name?" I asked.

"I got it from ol' Marse Aleck Spencer hisse'f, fohty years ago—fohty years ago, suh. I was lookin' at dat tree one day, aftuh I'd heared folks talkin' 'bout it, an' befo' it wuz cut down, an' ole Marse Aleck come erlong, an' sez I, 'Marse Aleck, dat is a monst'us fine oak tree.' An' ole Marse Aleck up an sez, sezee, 'No, Julius, dat ain' no oak-tree—dat is a U-pass tree.' An' I've 'membered the name evuh since, suh—de U-pass tree. Folks useter call it a' oak tree, but Marse Aleck oughter a knowd;—it 'us his tree, an' he had libbed close to it all his life."

It was evident that the gentleman referred to had used in a figurative sense the name which Julius had remembered so literally—the Upas tree, the fabled tree of death. I was curious to know to what it owed this sinister appellation. It would be easy, I knew, as it afterwards proved, to start the old man on a train of reminiscence concerning the family and the tree. How much of it was true I cannot say; I suspected Julius at times of a large degree of poetic license—he took the crude legends and vague superstitions of the neighborhood and embodied them in stories as complete, in their way, as the Sagas of Iceland or the primitive tales of ancient Greece. I have saved a few of them. Had Julius lived in a happier age for men of his complexion, the world might have had a black Aesop or Grimm or Hoffman—as it still may have, for who knows whether our civilization has yet more than cut its milk teeth, or humanity has even really begun to walk erect?

Later in the day, in the cool of the evening, on the front piazza, left dark because of the mosquitoes, except for the light of the stars, which shone with a clear, soft radiance, Julius told my wife and me his story of the old Spencer oak. His low, mellow voice rambled on, to an accompaniment of night-time sounds—the deep diapason from a distant frog-pond, the shrill chirp of the cicada, the occasional bark of a dog or cry of an owl, all softened by distance and merging into a melancholy minor which suited perfectly the teller and the tale.

Marse Aleck Spencer uster be de riches' man in all dis neighborhood. He own' two thousan' acres er lan'—de ole place ovuh yonduh is all dat is lef'. Dere wus ovuh a hund'ed an' fifty slaves on de plantation. Marse Aleck was a magist'ate an a politician, an' eve'ybody liked him. He kep' open house all de time, an' had company eve'y day in de yeah. His hosses wuz de fastes' an' his fox-hounds de swiftes', his gamecocks de fierces', an' his servants de impidentes' in de county. His wife wuz de pretties' an' de proudes' lady, an' wo' de bes' clo's an' de mos' finguh-rings, an' rid in de fines' carriage. Fac', day alluz had de best er eve'ything, an' nobody did n' 'spute it wid 'em.

Marse Aleck's child'en wuz de apples er his eye—dere wuz a big fambly—Miss Alice an' Miss Flora, an' young Marse Johnny, an' den some yeahs latuh, little Marse Henry an' little Marse Tom, an' den dere wuz ol' Mis' Kathu'n, Marse Aleck's wife, an' de chilen's mammy.

When young Marse Johnny was bawn, and Aunt Dasdy, who had nussed all de child'en, put de little young marster in his pappy's arms, Marse Aleck wuz de happies' man in de worl'; for it wuz his fus' boy, an' he had alluz wanted a boy to keep up de fambly name an' de fambly rep'tation. An' eve'ybody on de plantation sheered his joy, fer when de marster smile, it's sunshine, an' when de marster frown, it's cloudy weather.

When de missis was well enough, an' de baby was ol' enough, de christenin' come off; an' nothing would do fer Marse Aleck but to have it under de fambly tree—dat wuz de stump of it ovuh yonduh, suh, dat you was setting on dis mawnin'.

"Dat tree," said Marse Aleck, "wuz planted when my great-gran'daddy wuz bawn. Under dat tree eve'y fus'-bawn son er dis fambly since den has be'n christen'. Dis fambly has growed an' flourish' wid dat tree, an' now dat my son is bawn, I wants ter hab him christen' under it, so dat he kin grow an' flourish 'long wid it. An' dis ole oak"—Marse Aleck useter 'low it wuz a oak, befo' he give it de new name—"dis ole oak is tall an' stout an' strong. It has weathe'd many a sto'm. De win' cant blow it down, an' de lightnin' ain't nevuh struck it, an' nothin' but a prunin' saw has ever teched it, ner ever shill, so long as dere is a Spencer lef' ter pertec' it.

"An' so my son John, my fus'-bawn, is gwineter grow up tall an' strong, an' be a big man' an' a good man' an' his child'en and his child'en's child'en an' dem dat follers shall be as many as de leaves er dis tree, an' dey shill keep de name er Spencer at de head er de roll as long as time shall las'."

De same day Marse Johnny wuz bawn, which wuz de fu'st er May—anudder little boy, a little black boy, wuz bawn down in de quahtahs. De mammy had worked 'roun' de big house de yeah befo', but she had give er mist'iss some impidence one day, an' er mist'iss had made Marse Aleck sen' her back ter de cotton-fiel'. An' when little Marse Johnny wuz christen', Phillis, dis yuther baby's mammy, wuz standin' out on de edge, 'long wid de yuther fiel'-hands, fuh dey wuz all 'vited up ter take part, an' ter eat some er de christenin' feas'. Whils' de white folks wuz eatin' in de house, de cullud folks all had plenty er good things pass 'roun' out in de yahd—all dey could eat an' all they could drink, fuh dem wuz de fat yeahs er de Spencers—an' all famblies, like all folks, has deir fat yeahs an' deir lean yeahs. De lean yeahs er de Spencers wuz boun' ter come sooner er later.

Little Marse Johnny growed an' flourish' just like the fambly tree had done, an' in due time growed up to be a tall an' straight an' smart young man. But as you sca'cely evuh sees a tree widout a knot, so you nevuh sees a man widout his faults. Marse Johnny wuz so pop'lar and went aroun' so much wid his frien's that he tuck ter drinkin' mo' dan wuz good for him. Southe'n gent'emen all drunk them days, suh—nobody had never dremp' er dis yer foolishness 'bout pro'bition dat be'n gwine roun' er late yeahs. But as a gin'ral rule, dey drunk like gent'emen—er else dey could stan mo' liquor dan folks kin dese days. An' young Marse Johnny had a mighty quick temper, which mo'd'n once got 'im inter quarrels which it give 'im mo' or less trouble to make up.

Marse Johnny wuz mighty fond er de ladies, too, an' wuz de pet of 'em all. But he wuz jus' passin' de time wid 'em, 'tel he met Miss Mamie Imboden—de daughter er de Widder Imboden, what own' a plantation down on Rockfish. Ole Mis' Imboden did n' spen' much time on huh place, but left it tuh a overseah, whils' she an' Miss Mamie wuz livin' in de big towns, er de wat'rin-places, er way up yonduh in de No'th, whar you an' yo' lady come fum.

When de Widder Imboden come home one winter wid huh daughter, Marse Johnny fell dead in lub wid Miss Mamie. He could n' ha'dly eat ner sleep fuh a week or so, an' he jus' natch'ly could n' keep way fum Rockfish, an' jus' wo' out Marse Aleck's ridin' hosses comin' an' going', day, night an' Sunday. An' wharevuh she wuz visitin' he'd go visitin'; an' when she went tuh town he'd go tuh town. An' Marse Johnny got mo' religious dan he had evuh be'n befo' an' went tuh de Prisbyte'ian

Chu'ch down tuh Rockfish reg'lar. His own chu'ch wuz 'Piscopal, but Miss Iboden wuz a Prisbyte'ian.

But Marse Johnny wa'n't de only one. Anudder young gentleman, Marse Ben Dudley, who come fum a fine ole fambly, but wuz monst'us wild an' reckless, was payin' co't tuh Miss Mamie at de same time, an' it was nip an' tuck who should win out. Some said she favored one, and some said de yuther, an' some 'lowed she did n' knowed w'ich tuh choose.

Young Marse Johnny kinder feared fuh a while dat she like de yuther young gentleman bes'. But one day Marse Ben's daddy, ole Marse Amos Dudley, went bankrup', an' his plantation and all his slaves wuz sol', an' he shot hisse'f in de head, and young Marse Ben wuz lef' po'. An' bein' too proud tuh work, an' havin' no relations ter live on, he tuck ter bettin' an' dicin' an' kyardplayin', an' went on jes' scan'lous. An' it wuz soon whispered 'roun' dat young Mistah Dudley wuz livin' on his winin's at kyards, an' dat he wa' n't partic'lar who he played wid, er whar er how he played. But I is ahead er my tale, fuh all dis hyuh 'bout Marse Ben happen' after Marse Johnny had cut Marse Ben out an' ma'ied Miss Mamie.

Ol' Marse Aleck wuz monst'us glad when he heared Marse Johnny wuz gwineter git ma'ied, for he wanted de fambly kep' up, an' he 'lowed Marse Johnny needed a wife fuh tuh he'p stiddy him. An' Miss Mamie wuz one of dese hyuh sweet-nachu'd, kin'-hearted ladies dat nobody could he'p lovin'. An, mo'over, Miss Mamie's Mammy wuz rich, an' would leave huh well off sume day.

Fuh de lean yeahs er de Spencers wuz comin', an' Marse Aleck 'spicioned it. De cotton crop had be'n po' de yeah befo', de cawn had ben wuss, glanders had got in the hosses an most of 'em had had ter be killed; an' old Marse Aleck wuz mo' sho't of money dan he'd be'n fur a long, long time. An' when he tried tuh make it up by spekilatin', he jus' kep' on losin' mo' an' mo' an' mo'.

But young Marse Johnny had ter hab money for his weddin', an' the house had to be fix' up fuh 'im an' his wife, an' dere had ter be a rich weddin' present an' a fine infair, an' all dem things cos' money. An' sence he did n' wanter borry de money, Marse Aleck 'lowed he s'posed he'd hafter sell one er his han's. An' ole Mis' Spencer say he should sell Phillis's Isham. Marse Aleck did n' wanter sell Isham, fur he 'membered Isham wuz de boy dat wuz bawn on de same day Marse Johnny wuz. But ole Mis' Spencer say she did n' like dat boy's looks nohow, an' dat his mammy had be'n impident tuh huh one time, an ef Marse Aleck gwine sell anybody he sh'd sell Isham.

Prob'bly ef ole Marse Aleck had knowed jus' what wuz gwineter happen he mought not 'a' sol' Isham—he'd 'a' ruther gone inter debt, er borried de money. But den nobody nevuh knows whats gwineter happen; an' what good would it do 'em ef dey did? It'd only make 'em mizzable befo' han', an' ef it wuz gwineter happen, how could dey stop it? So Marse Aleck wuz bettuh off dan ef he had knowed.

Now, dis hyuh Isham had fell in love, too, wid a nice gal on de plantation, an' wuz jus' 'bout making up his min' tuh ax Marse Aleck tuh let 'im marry her an' tuh give 'em a cabin tuh live in by deyse'ves, when one day Marse Aleck tuck Isham ter town, an' sol' 'im to another gent'eman, fuh tuh git de money fuh de expenses er his own son's weddin'.

Isham's mammy wuz workin' in de cottonfiel' way ovuh at de fah end er de plantation dat day, an' when she went home at night an' foun' dat Marse Aleck had sol' huh Isham, she run up to de big house an' wep' an' hollered an' went on terrible. But Marse Aleck tol huh it wuz all right, dat Isham had a good marster, an' wa'n't many miles erway, an' could come an' see his mammy whenevuh he wanter.

When de young ma'ied folks came back f'm dey weddin' tower, day had de infair, an' all de rich white folks wuz invited. An' dat same night, whils' de big house wuz all lit up, an' de fiddles wuz goin', an' dere wuz eatin' an' drinkin' an' dancin' an' sky-larkin' an' eve'body wuz jokin' de young couple an' wushin' 'em good luck, Phillis wuz settin' all alone in huh cabin, way at de fah end er de quarters, studyin' 'bout huh boy, who had be'n sol' to pay for it all. All de other cullud folks wuz up 'roun' de big house, some waitin' on de white folks, some he'pin in de kitchen, some takin' keer er de guest's hosses, an' de res' swa'min' 'roun' de yahd, gittin' in one anudder's way, an' waitin' 'tel de white folks got thoo, so dey could hab somethin' tuh eat too; fuh Marse Aleck had open' de big blade, an' wanted eve'body to have a good time.

'Bout time de fun wuz at de highes' in de big house, Phillis heared somebody knockin' at huh cabin do'. She did n' know who it could be, an' bein' as dere wa'nt' nobody e'se 'roun', she sot still an' did n' say nary word. Den she heared somebody groan, an' den dere wuz anudder knock, a feeble one dis time, an' den all wuz still.

Phillis wait' a minute, an' den crack' de do', so she could look out, an' dere wuz somebody layin' all crumple' up on de do'-step. An' den somethin' wahned huh what it wuz, an' she fetched a lighterd to'ch fum de ha'th. It wuz huh son Isham. He wuz wownded an' bleedin'; his feet wuz so' wid walkin'; he wuz weak from loss er blood.

Phillis pick' Isham up an' laid 'im on huh bed an' run an' got some whiskey an' give 'im a drap, an' den she helt camphire tuh his nost'ils, meanwhile callin' his name an' gwine on like a wild 'oman. An' bimeby he open' his eyes an' look' up an' says—"I'se come home, mammy,"— an' den died. Dem wuz de only words he spoke, an' he nevuh drawed anudder bref.

It come tuh light nex' day, when de slaveketchers come aftuh Isham wid deir dawgs an' deir guns, dat he had got in a 'spute wid his marster, an' had achully *hit his marster*! An' realizin' what he had done, he had run erway; natch'ly to'ds his mammy an' de ole plantation. Dey had wounded 'im an' had mos' ketched him, but he had 'scaped ag'in an' had reach' home just in time tuh die in his mammy's ahms.

Phillis laid Isham out wid her own han's—dere wa'n't nobody dere tuh he'p her, an' she did n' want no he'p nohow. An' when it wuz all done, an' she had straighten' his lim's an' fol' his han's an' close his eyes, an' spread a sheet ovuh him, she shut de do' sof'ly, and stahted up ter de big house.

When she drawed nigh, de visituhs wuz gittin' ready tuh go. De servants wuz bringin' de hosses an' buggies an' ca'iges roun', de white folks wuz laffin' an gwine on an' sayin' good-bye. An' whils' Phillis wuz standin' back behin' a bunch er rose-bushes in de yahd, listenin' an' waitin', ole Marse Aleck come out'n de house wid de young couple an' stood unduh de ole fambly tree. He had a glass er wine in his han', an' a lot er de yuthers follered:

"Frien's," says he, "drink a toas' wid me tuh my son an' his lady, hyuh under dis ole tree. May it last anudder hund'ed yeahs, an' den anudder, an' may it fetch good luck tuh my son an' his wife, an' tuh deir child'en an' deir child'en's child'en."

De toas' wuz drunk, de gues's depahted; de slaves went back tuh de quahtuhs, an' Phillis went home tuh huh dead boy.

But befo' she went, she *marked de Spencer tree*!

Young Marse Johnny an' his wife got 'long mighty well fuh de fust six mont's er so, an' den trouble commence' betwix' 'em. Dey wus at a pahty one night, an' young Marse Johnny seen young Marse Ben Dudley talking in a cawnuh wid Miss Mamie. Marse Johnny wuz mighty jealous-natu'ed, an did n' like dis at all. Endoyin' de same evenin' he overheard somebody say that Miss Mamie had th'owed Marse Ben ovuh beca'se he was po' an' married Marse Johnny beca'se he wuz rich. Marse Johnny did n' say nothin', but he kep' studyin' an studyin' 'bout dese things. An' it did n' do him no good to let his min' run on 'em.

Marse Ben Dudley kep' on gwine from bad ter wuss, an' one day Marse Johnny foun' a letter from Marse Ben in his wife's bureau drawer.

"You used ter love me" says Marse Ben in dis hyuh letter—"you know you did, and you love me yit—I know you does. I am in trouble. A few hun'ed dollahs'll he'p me out. Youer totin' mo' d'n dat 'roun' on yo' pretty little fingers. Git the money fuh me—it'll save my honor an' my life. I swear I'll pay it back right soon."

Den' all Marse Johnny's jealousy b'iled up at once, an' he seed eve'ything red. He went straight to Miss Mamie an' shuck de lettuh in her face an' 'cused her er gwine wid Marse Ben. Co'se she denied it. Den he ax' huh what had become er huh di'mon' 'gagement ring dat he had give huh befo' dey wuz ma'ied.

Miss Mamie look' at huh han' an' turn' white as chalk, fer de ring wa'n't dere.

"I tuck it off las' night, when I went tuh bed, an' lef' it on de bureau, an' I fuhgot tuh put it on dis mawnin".

But when she look' fer it on de bureau it wuz gone. Marse Johnny swo' she had give' it tuh Marse Ben, an' she denied it tuh de las'. He showed her de letter. She said she had n' answered it, an' had n't meant to answer it, but had meant to bu'n it up. One word led to another. Dere wuz a bitter quarrel, an' Marse Johnny swo' he'd never speak to his wife ag'in 'tel de di'mond ring wuz foun'. And he did n'.

Ole Marse Aleck wuz 'way from home dat winter, to congress or de legislator, or somewhar, an' Marse Johnny wuz de boss er de plantation whils' he wuz gone. He wuz busy all day, on de plantation, or in his of-fice, er in town. He tuck moster his meals by hisself, an' when he et wid Miss Mamie he manage' so as nevuh to say nothin'. Ef she spoke, he purten' not to hear her, an' so she did n't try mo' d'n once er twice. Oth-e'wise, he alluz treated her like a lady out a mile erway.

Miss Mamie tuck it mighty ha'd. Fuh she was tenduh as well as proud. She jus' moped an' pined erway. One day in de springtime, when Marse Johnny wuz in town all day, she wuz tuck ill sudden, an' her baby wuz bawn, long befo' its time. De same day one er de little black child'en clum up in de ole Spencer tree an' fetch' down a jaybird's nes', an' in de nes' dey foun' Miss Mamie's ring, whar de jaybird had stole it an' hid it. When Marse Johnny come home dat night he found his wife an' his chile bofe dead, an' de ring on Miss Mamie's finger.

Well, suh, you nevuh seed a man go on like Marse Johnny did; an' folks said dat ef he could 'a' foun' Marse Ben Dudley he sho' would a' shot 'im; but lucky fer Marse Ben he had gone away. Aftuh de fune'al, Marse Johnny shet hisse'f up in his room fer two er three days; an' as soon as Marse Aleck come home, Marse Johnny j'ind de ahmy an' went an' fit in de Mexican Wah an' wuz shot an' kill'.

Ole Marse Aleck wuz so' distress' by dese yer troubles, an' grieve' migh'ly over de loss er his fus' bawn son. But he got ovuh it after a while. Dere wuz still Marse Henry an Marse Tom, bofe un' 'em good big boys, ter keep up de name, an' Miss Alice an' Miss Flora who wuz bofe ma'ied an' had child'en, ter see dat de blood did n' die out. An' in spite er dis hyuh thievin' jaybird, nobody 'lowed dat de ole tree had anything ter do wid Marse Johnny's troubles, fer 'co'se nobody but Phillis knowed dat it had evuh been mark'.

But dis wuz only de beginnin'.

Next year, in the spring, Miss Alice, Marse Aleck's oldes' daughter, wuz visitin' the fambly wid her nuss an' chile—she had ma'ied sev'al yeahs befo' Marse Johnny—an' one day de nuss wuz settin' out in de yahd, wid de chile, under de ole tree, when a big pizen spider let hisse'f down from a lim' when de nuss wa'n't lookin', an' stung the chile. The chile swoll up, an' dey sent fer de doctuh, but de doctuh could n' do nothin', an' the baby died in spasms dat same night, an' de mammy went inter a decline fum grief an' died er consumption insid' er six mont's.

Of co'se de tree wuz watched close fer spiders aftah dis, but none er de white folks thought er blamin' de tree—a spider mought 'a' come from de ceilin' er from any other tree; it wuz jes' one er dem things dat could n' be he'ped. But de servants commence' ter whisper 'mongs' deyse'ves dat de tree wuz conju'ed an' dere'd be still mo' trouble from it.

It wa'n't long coming. One day young Marse Henry, de nex' boy ter Marse Johnny, went fishin' in de ribber, wid one er de naber boys, an' he clumb out too fah on a log, an' tip' de log up, an' fell in de ribber an' got drownded. Nobody could see how de ole tree wuz mix' up wid little Marse Henry's drownin', 'tel one er de house servants 'membered he had seed de boys diggin' bait in de shade er de ole tree. An' whils' they did n' say nothin' ter de white folks, leas'ways not jes' den, dey kep' it in min' an' waited tuh see what e'se would happen. Dey did n' know den dat Phillis had mark' de tree, but dey mo' den half s'picioned it.

Sho' 'nuff, one day de nex' fall, Miss Flora, Marse Aleck's secon' daughter, who wuz ma'ied an' had a husban', come home to visit her folks. An' one day whils' she wuz out walkin' wid her little boy, a sto'm come up, an' it stahted ter rain, an' dey did n' hab no umbreller, an' wuz runnin' ter de house, when jes' as dey got under de ole tree, de lightnin' struck it, broke a limb off'n de top, skun a little strip off'n de side all de way down, an' jump off an' hit Miss Flora an' de boy, an' killt 'em bofe on de spot—dey didn't have time ter draw anudder bref.

Still de white folks did n' see nuthin wrong wid de tree. But by dis time de cullud folks all knowed de tree had be'en conju'd. One un 'em said somethin' 'bout it one day ter old Marse Aleck, but he tol' 'em ter go 'long wid deir foolishness; dat it wuz de will er God; dat de lightnin' mought's well 'a' struck any yuther tree dey'd be'en under as dat one; an' dat dere would n' be no danger in de future, fer lightnin' nebber struck twice in de same place nohow.

It wus 'bout a yeah after dat befo' anything mo' happen', an' de cullud folks 'lowed dat mo' likely dey had be'n mistaken an' dat maybe de tree had n' be'n mark', er e'se de goopher wuz all wo' off, when one day little Marse Tom, de only boy dat wuz lef', wuz ridin' a new hoss Marse Aleck had give 'm, when a rabbit jump 'cross de road in front er him, an' skeered dis hyuh young hoss, an' de hoss run away an' thowed little Marse Tom up 'gins' de ole Spencer tree, an' bu'st his head in an' killt 'im.

Marse Aleck wuz 'mos' heartbroken, fer Marse Tom wuz de only son he had lef'; dere wa'n't none er his child'en lef' now but Miss Alice, whose husban' had died, an' who had come wid her little gal ter lib wid her daddy and mammy.

But dere wuz so much talk 'bout de ole tree 'tel it fin'lly got ter ole Miss Katherine's yeahs, an' she tol' Marse Aleck. He did n' pay no 'tention at fu'st, jes' 'lowed it 'uz all foolishness. But he kep' on hearin' so much of it, dat bimeby he wuz 'bleege' ter listen. An' he fin'lly 'lowed dat whether de tree was conju'd or not, it had never brought nuthin' but bad luck evuh sence Marse Johnny's weddin', an' he made up his min' ter git rid of it, in hopes er changin' de fambly luck.

So one day he ordered a couple er han's ter come up ter de house wid axes an' cut down de ole tree. He tol' 'em jes' how ter chop it, one on one side an' one on de yuther, so's ter make it fall a partic'lar way. He stood off ter one side, wid his head bowed down, 'tel de two cuts had 'mos' met, an' den he tu'ned his eyes away, fer he did n' wanter see de ole tree fall—it had meant so much ter him fer so long. He heared de tree commence crackin', an' he heared de axemen holler, but he did n' know dey wuz hollerin' at him, an' he did n' look roun'—he did n't wanter see de ole Spencer tree fall. But stidder fallin' as he had meant it ter, an' as by rights it could n' he'p fallin', it jes' twisted squar' roun' sideways to'ds ole Marse Aleck an' ketched 'im befo' he could look up, an' crushed 'im ter de groun'.

Well, dey buried Marse Aleck down in de fambly buryin'-groun'— you kin see it over at de ole place, not fur from de house; it's all growed up now wid weeds an' briars, an' most er de tombstones is fell down and covered wid green moul'. It wuz already pretty full, an' dere wa'n't much room lef'. After de fune'al, de ole tree wuz cut up inter firewood an' piled up out in de yard.

Ole Mis' Kathu'n an' her daughter, Mis' Alice, an' Mis' Alice's little gal, went inter mo'nin' an' stayed home all winter.

One col' night de house-boy toted in a big log fum de old Spencer tree, an' put it on de fire, an' when ole Mis' Kathu'n an' her daughter an' her gran' daughter went to bed, dey lef' de log smoulderin' on de ha'th. An' 'long 'bout midnight, when eve'ybody wuz soun' asleep, dis hyuh log fell out'n de fireplace an' rolled over on de flo' an' sot de house afire an' bu'nt it down ter de groun', wid eve'ybody in it.

Dat, suh, wuz de end er de Spencer fambly. De house wuz nebber rebuil'. De war come erlong soon after, an' nobody had no money no mo' ter buil' houses. De lan', or what little wuz lef' after de mogages an' de debts wuz paid off, went ter dis hyuh young gentleman, Mistuh Brownlow, down Lumberton, who wuz some kinder fo'ty-secon' cousin er nuther, an' I reckon he'd be only too glad ter sell it.

I wrote to young Mr. Brownlow, suggesting an appointment for an interview. He replied that he would call on me the following week, at an hour stated, if he did not hear from me beforehand that some other time would be more convenient.

I awaited him at the appointed house. He came in the morning and stayed to luncheon. He was willing to sell the old place and we agreed upon a price at which it was to be offered to my cousin.

He was a shallow, amiable young fellow, unmarried, and employed as a clerk in a general store. I told him the story of the Spencer oak, as related by old Julius. He laughed lightly.

"I believe the niggers did have some sort of yarn about the family and the old tree," he said, "but of course it was all their silly superstition. They always would believe any kind of foolishness their crazy imaginations could cook up. Well, sir, let me know when you hear from your friend. I reckon I'll drive past the old place on my way home, and take a last look at it, for the sake of the family, for it was a fine old family, and it was a pity the name died out."

An hour later there was an agitated knock at my library door. When I opened it old Julius was standing there in a state of great excitement.

"What is the matter, Julius?"

"It's done gone an' happen', suh, it's done gone an' happen'!"

"What has done gone and happened?"

"De tree, suh, de U-pass tree—de ole Spencer tree."

"Well, what about it?"

"Young Mistuh Brownlow lef' here an' went ovuh tuh de old place, an' sot down on de ole stump, an' a rattlesnake come out'n de holler an' stung 'im, an' killt 'im, suh. He's layin' ovuh dere now, all black in de face and swellin' up fas' ".

I closed my deal for the property through Mr. Brownlow's administrator. My cousin authorized me to have the land cleared off, preparatory to improving it later on. Among other things, I had the stump of the Spencer oak extracted. It was a difficult task even with the aid of explosives, but was finally accomplished without casualty, due perhaps to the care with which I inquired into the pedigree of the workmen, lest perchance among them there might be some stray offshoot of this illustrious but unfortunate family.

A Tale of the
North Carolina Woods

Arthur Huff Fauset published this short story in January 1922. He writes about a huge, oddly shaped tree in
the woods of North Carolina. The tree stretches across
a stream from one side to the other. The tree is a source
of wonderment for all who encounter it. Finally, one
day an old feebleminded woman who has lived in the
village for over sixty years tells the gruesome tale of the
tree.

North Carolina woods, where the tall, gaunt pines "mosey" upward
and stretch their towering tops to the blue skies, is a certain haven of
rest and comfort to the sojourner weary of the *pêle-mêle* and tedium of
American city life. Crickets and grasshoppers chirp and play at your
feet; toadstools of enormous size and wonderful colors arouse your curiosity and revive the drooping spirits which need so much a touch of
nature's tonic. Here and there, splashing the verdant earth with colors
as numerous as the rainbow are colonies of wild flowers—sometimes
a lonely daisy, or a gay, frisky cowbell looks up from its lowly station,
anxious, no doubt, for you to take notice of the part it plays in this
wonderful bit of nature's handiwork.

Any number of beautiful flowers surround one, large and small,
great and tiny, all of them tinted with the most delicate of nature's pig-
ments, some in a most complex manner with an almost inexplicable
medley of color; others, like the dew of the morning, simple, plain, refreshing to the eye, with a power that braces the heart and causes song,
even poetry, to burst forth from within—tiny creatures ofttimes, but
lovelier than the loveliest rose of the city's floral shop, and primmer
than the daintiest violet.

It is so cool and quiet in the North Carolina woods!

We used to enjoy the sparkling wafts of pine-laden breezes, seated
by (or over) a little muddy streamlet which coursed its way somewhere,

nowhere. Such a sluggish stream I have never seen in any other place. To take a casual look at it you would not know it was flowing water. Just when you had made up your mind that it was a stagnant pool, you perceived a dim, sluggish, almost imperceptible movement of the murky water. A tiny pine twig thrown on the crest of the stream would gradually move down, inch by inch, stopping on its tedious journey for half hours and even hours, and then slowly moving a few more inches.

The stream was only ten or twelve feet wide and scarcely six inches in depth. Occasionally you could see something dash through the muddy water, the distinctness of its outline dimmed by the sediment which saturated the water everywhere.

"It's a frog," I would cry.

"No, it's a water snake," would call another.

"You're seeing things," would be the taunt of Allan, who loved to talk but cared nothing about watching nature.

There was a huge tree stretched across the stream over which passersby could cross from one side to the other. This tree was a source of wonder to us because it had taken root on one side of the stream and then, as though prompted by Mother Nature herself, had grown straight across to the other side. There it lay, a living bridge, having for years served the people thereabouts.

We would often sit and puzzle about that bridge. We wondered whether the tree had just happened by chance, or whether some crafty woodsman, prompted by a deep civic spirit, had deliberately coerced nature into allowing the tree to assume such a course. Seated upon it, over the stream, we would speculate about it, until some person would come along and make it necessary for us to get off for a few moments while he crossed over. For a long time it did not occur to us that these people who lived in the woods might know something about the tree. A number of persons passed us regularly and we soon knew just who it was who was approaching.

One in particular became a special subject of interest. She would have interested anybody. She was an old colored woman, wild-eyed and fierce in the expression of her face, with the appearance of one who was half-witted. She always came by about the same time each day, near eventide. We could tell that she was coming by the songs she always sang as she passed through the woods. Such songs! And the voice of that poor creature! (She seemed happy enough, though.) They were old plantation songs, doubtless, though none of the more familiar ones, which have crept northward, seemed to appear among them.

Her whole appearance was odder than anything I have ever seen.

She always had something balanced on her head, whether it was a bundle of clothes or merely an old newspaper. Her face was dark brown in color, her eyes somewhat slanty, black and sparkling, with the fire of a maniac. Her clothing, if one may call it such, was a patchwork of rags as dirty as they were old; and her shoes barely acted as a covering for her feet—so ragged and worn were they.

Whenever she passed by us at the bridge she would stop her singing, eye us quickly and make a peculiar grimace or grain. Then as she gaily tripped across the natural passageway she would call out: "Good evenin' gen'mens." At which we would nod and perhaps tender a reply.

One hot August afternoon we had retreated to the cool of the stream and pines. We hardly knew what to do to pass the time away. While we were musing on the bridge we heard the familiar voice, loud and clear, echoing and re-echoing through the woods:

"Don' 'no wen I'se cum-in',
Don' 'no wen I'se cum-in',
Sun is still moughty high."

"Why not ask her about this tree?" suggested Chalfonte.

"Good," I replied, and we awaited her as she wended her way toward us.

"Good evenin' gen'mens," came the familiar greeting, together with a broad, expressive grin.

"Good evening," replied Chalfonte. "We heard you singing through the woods and we've been wondering what your name might be."

"Who, me? Don' yuh know me? I'se Queen of Sedalia," and then she went off into a loud laugh, half hysterical. "Yeh, Queen of Sedalia, bin livin' roun' dese parts mos' sixty yeahs."

"Well, well, perhaps you can tell us how this bridge came about. Can you?"

"Kin I? Well, I guess. I'se Queen of Sedalia, don' yuh know dat?"

Later we learned that the district about these woods was known locally as Sedalia.

"Queen, eh," Chalfonte answered. "How long have you been queen?"

The old woman eyed Chalfonte from shoe to cap, and then glanced at each one of us with suspicion. She must have thought we were quizzing her.

"Come," I said quickly, fearing we might lose her. "Could you tell us the story of this tree?"

Her eyes gleamed. Her whole body trembled with excitement. Then she gave one of those hideous hysterical laughs.

"Who, me? I'se Queen of Sedalia, don' yuh know dat? Sho I kin tell yuh! I knows all about ut. Does yuh reely want ter heah ut?"

"Do we?" we all cried. Chalfonte jingled some coins in his pocket. She never seemed to notice this, however.

"Set down, den, an' I'll tell yuh all."

We sat down on the grassy bank, lest some passerby disturb us as she recounted the story. She sat down with us.

This was the story. In the days when Grant was President, this stream was almost twice as wide as it now is, and considerably deeper. This was caused by the amount of rainfall in those days, which was greater by far than the amount of rainfall at the present time. All the land in this region was owned by one Squire Marks ("Ole Man Marks"), who allowed his neighbors to take the short cut through his land to the little village on the other side of the stream, but who steadfastly refused to build any sort of bridge across the stream.

It was necessary for persons who wished to cross, to wade over, either in bare feet or in rubber boots. Besides the inconvenience which this brought about, there was always the danger of snakes. The stream and its environs were known to be infested by moccasins. Still "Ole Man Marks" steadfastly refused to build a bridge.

Every now and then some child would come tearing through the woods yelling that a snake had bitten him. However it usually proved to be a hallucination on the child's part. Either it had pierced its foot with a thorn, or in some similar manner had done something which would give rise to the notion that a snake had bitten it.

One day however, the woods were rent with the terrific cries of some one in great terror or pain. Several villagers ran to the place from whence came the yells, and found on the shore of the stream the only son of "Ole Man Marks", prostrate, his limbs tense, his blue eyes glaring up to the burning sun. The "Queen of Sedalia" arrived just in time to see a friend make a deep incision, with some steel instrument, in the boy's leg.

"It was turrible. Blood black ez ink. . . . It flo'd all 'roun. 'Ole Man Marks' son, he kep' right still. Purty soon, along comes de Ole Man, pale ez a ghost en' shiverin' all over . . . No use ter weep—the boy wuz daid. . . .

"Ole Man Marks went crazy. . . . They did sumpin or other'n for him, killed him I guess, nebber see'd him no mo, po' ole fool. . . .

"Eb'rybody 'fraid ub de ribber from den on, 'cep me . . . I wuzn't 'fraid. Who, me? I'se Queen of Sedalia.

"Eb'ry day I comes to de same spot, jes' where dat boy's black blood done all flo'd about. I prays dere, ebery day, I does.... What yuh t'ink? Dis tree start sproutin' up. Up, up it shoots.... and den—when it grows so high (pointing about three inches) it starts shootin' dis-away. See!... Dat's all. De blood ub dat boy done made seed fo de good Lawd, and dis tree mus' be his body. Yes!"... and then she gave another of those laughs.

She wouldn't say another word about the tree. She wouldn't take any money. She looked at us and grinned.

"Good evenin' gen'mens," she said, and crossed the bridge singing hilariously:

"Bridge ub Heben—soul en body,
Pepul's gwine to leab yuh now!"

"High Yaller"

This prize-winning short story was published in two parts in the October and November 1925 issues of *The Crisis*. Author Rudolph Fisher discusses the social ramifications of skin color within the black community.

I

The timekeeper's venomous whistle killed the ball in its flight, halfway to the basket. There was a triumphant bedlam. From the walls of Manhattan Casino impatient multitudes swarmed on to the immense floor, congratulating, consoling, gibing; pouring endlessly from the surrounding terrace, like long restrained torrents at last transcending a dam; sweeping tumultuously in from all sides, till the dance floor sank beneath a sounding flood of dark-skinned people, submerged to its furthest corners save the distant platform that gave the orchestra refuge, like a raft. A sudden blare of music cut the uproar. The turbulence gradually ordered itself into dense, crawling currents, sluggish as jammed traffic, while the din of voices at length reluctantly surrendered to the rhythmic swish-swash of shuffling feet.

Looking down from a balcony on that dark mass of heads, close together as buckshot, Evelyn Brown wondered how they all managed to enjoy it. Why must they always follow a basket-ball game with a dance?—the one pleasurable enough, the other mob-torture, she knew.

"Game?" challenged MacLoed.

She couldn't refuse her escort, of course. "If you are."

They descended and struck out like swimmers in the sea. MacLoed surrounded her as closely as a lifesaver. She knew that he had to, but she hated it—this mere hugging to music, this acute consciousness of her partner's body. The air was vile—hot, full of breath and choking perfume. You were forever avoiding, colliding, marking time on the same spot. So insulating was the crush that you might sway for several minutes near a familiar couple, even recognize their voices, yet catch only the merest glimpse of their vanishing faces.

Something of the sort was happening now. Evelyn heard someone say her name, and the mordant intonation with the succeeding spiteful snatch-phrases made her forget the physical unpleasantness of the moment.

"Evelyn Brown?—Hmph!—got yellow fever—I know better—color struck, I tell you—girls she goes around with—all lily whites—even the fellows—Mac to-day—pass for white anywhere—Jeff, Rickmond, Stanley Hall, all of 'em—You? Shoot! You don't count—you're crazy 'bout high yallers anyhow."

The words were engulfed. Evelyn had not needed to look. Mayme Jackson's voice was unmistakable.

The dance number ended on an unresolved, interrogative chord that set off an explosion of applause. Jay Martin, who had just been defending Evelyn against Mayme's charge, spied the former's fluff of fair hair through several intervening thicknesses of straight and straightened black, and, dragging Mayme by the arm, he made for the other couple.

"Now say what you said about Evelyn!" he dared Mayme, mock-maliciously, quite unaware that Evelyn already knew.

"Sweetest old thing in the world," came Mayme's tranquil purr.

"Rake in the chips," gasped Jay. "Your pot." He addressed Evelyn. "How about the next wrestle?"

There was a ready exchange of partners. The orchestra struck up an air from a popular Negro comedy: "Yaller Gal's Gone Out o' Style". Soon the two couples were urged apart in increasingly divergent currents.

"Black sea," commented Jay.

But Evelyn was thoughtful. "Jay?"

"Nobody else."

"I heard what Mayme said."

"You did? Aw, heck—don't pay any attention to that kid. She's a nut."

"I'm not so sure she isn't right, Jay."

"Right? About what?"

"I've been thinking over my best friends. They're practically all 'passing' fair. Any one of them could pass—for a foreigner, anyway."

"Me, for instance," he grinned. "Prince Woogy-boogy of Abyssinia."

"I'm afraid you prove the rule."

He was serious. "Well, what of it?"

"Oh, I don't mean I've done it intentionally. I never realized it till just now. But, just as Mayme says, it looks bad."

"Hang what Mayme says. She's kind o' gone on yaller men, herself. See the way she melted into Mac's shirtfront? Hung round his neck like a chest-protector. Didn't drape herself over *me* that way."

"Jay! You're as bad as she is."

"That's what she said."

"What do you mean?"

"Claims I fall only for pinks."

"Oh. I didn't mean that."

"Neither did she. Point is, there aren't any more dark girls. Skin bleach and rouge have wiped out the strain. The blacks have turned sealskin, the sealskins are high-brown, the high-browns are all yaller, and the yallers are pink. How's a bird going to fall for what ain't?"

They jazzed on a while in noisy silence. Evelyn's tone was surprisingly bitter when at last she spoke again:

"I wish I looked like Mayme." Astonished, Jay stared at her as she went on: "A washerwoman can make half a million dollars turning dark skins light. Why doesn't someone learn how to turn light skins dark?"

And now, in addition to staring, he saw her: the averted blue eyes, the fine lips about to quiver, the delicate, high-bridged nose, the white cheeks, colorless save for the faintest touch, the incredible tawny, yellow-flecked, scintillant hair,—an almost crystalline creature, as odd in this dark company as a single sapphire in jet. He was quick to comprehend. "I know a corner—let's sit out the rest," he suggested.

When they achieved their place in a far end of the terrace, the orchestra was outdoing itself in the encore. One of its members sang through a megaphone in a smoky, half-talking voice:

"*Oh Miss Pink thought she knew her stuff,*
But Miss High Brown has called her bluff."

When the encore ended, the dancers demanded yet another. The rasp of syncopation and the ceaseless stridor of soles mingled, rose about the two refugees, seeming to wall them in, so that presently they felt alone together.

"Jay, can you imagine what it's like to be colored and look white?"

He tried to be trivial. "Very convenient at times, I should think."

"But oftener unbearable. That song—imagine—everyone looking at you—laughing at you. And Mayme Jackson—'yellow fever'! Can I help it?—Jeff—Rickmond—Stanley Hall—yes, they're light. But what can I do? I like the others. I'd be glad to go places with them. But they positively avoid me."

"I don't, Ev."

"No, you don't, Jay." But her bitterness recaptured her. "Oh, I've heard them talking: 'There goes Evelyn Brown—queen of the lily-whites—nothing brown about her but her name'!" A swiftly matured determination rendered her suddenly so grim that it seemed, fragile as she was, something about her must break. "Jay, no one's going to accuse me of jim-crowing again!"

"Shucks. What do you care as long as you don't mean to?"

"I'm not only not going to mean to. I'm not going to. I'm going to see to it that I don't."

"What the deuce—by cutting your gang?"

"No. By cultivating the others."

"Oh."

"Jay—will you help me?"

"Help you? Sure. How?"

"Come to see me oftener."

"Good night! Don't you see enough of me at the office every day?"

"Come oftener. Take me places when you're not too broke. Rush me!"

He grinned as he perceived her purpose. "Doggone good stunt!" he said slowly, with increasingly enthusiastic approval. "Blessed if I wouldn't like to see you put it over, Ev. It'll show Mayme something, anyhow."

"It'll show me something, too."

"You? What?"

She was about to answer when a sharp, indecent epithet rent the wall of noise that had until then isolated them. Looking involuntarily up, Jay saw two youngsters, quarreling vituperatively. They were too close to be ignored, and, since dancing was at its height, no one else was about.

"Excuse me a second," he said, rising before Evelyn could protest. The pair were but a few feet away. The evident aggressor was a hard-looking little black youth of indefinite age,—perhaps sixteen actual years, plus the accumulated bonus of worldly wisdom which New

York pays its children. He grew worse, word by word. Approaching, Jay spoke sharply, in a low voice so that Evelyn might not hear:

"Cut out that gutter-talk, boy!"

"Aw, go to hell!"

Jay stopped, less amazed than aggravated. He knew his Harlem adolescent, but he was not quite sure what to do with it. Meanwhile he was being advised: "This is a horse-race, big boy. No jackasses allowed!"

He seized the lad firmly by the shoulder and said, "Son, if you don't cover that garbage-trap of yours—" but the boy flung away and defied him in a phrase both loud and ugly. Thoroughly angered, Jay clapped one hand over the offending mouth and, catching the youngster around the waist with the other, forcibly propelled him through a tangle of empty, spindle-legged chairs to a place where two big policemen, one black and one red, were complacently watching the dancers. Here he released him with "Now—talk."

The boy scowled with wrath and impotence. So outraged in the street, he would have found a stone to throw. Now only a retaliative speech was left him, and the nearness of the law attenuated even that:

"Aw 'ight! Showin' off before 'at ole 'fay gal, huh? Aw 'ight, y' pink-chaser. Ah'm goan put y' both in." And he sidled darkly off, pulling at his disadjusted collar.

Evelyn, out of earshot, followed it all with her eyes. "Mac wouldn't have done that," she mused as she saw Jay turn from the boy and start back toward her. "Mac would have pretended he didn't hear." And before Jay reached her, she had decided something: "I certainly like Jay Martin. He's so—white."

II.

Over One Hundred and Thirty-fourth Street's sidewalks between Fifth and Lenox Avenues Jay Martin's roller-skates had rattled and whirred in the days when that was the northern boundary of Negro Harlem. He had grown as the colony grew, and now he could just recall the time when his father, a pioneer preacher, had been forever warning him never to cross Lenox Avenue and never to go beyond One Hundred and Thirty-fifth Street; a time when no Negroes lived on or near Seventh Avenue and when it would have been almost suicidal for one to appear unarmed on Irish Eighth.

School had been a succession of fist-fights with white boys who called him nigger, until, when he reached the upper grades, the colored boys began to outnumber the white; from that time until high school, pitched battles superseded individual contests, and he ran home bruised less often. His high school record had been good, and his father, anxious to make a physician of him, had sent him on to college. At the end of his third year, however, the looming draft menace, combined with the chance of a commission in the army, had urged him into a training camp at Des Moines.

He had gone to France as a lieutenant. When he returned, unharmed, he found his father fatally ill and his mother helpless. Further study out of the question, he had taken his opportunity with a Negro real estate firm, and for five years now he had been actively concerned in black Harlem's extension, the spread whose beginnings his earlier years had witnessed.

About Evelyn, of course, there had been hypothesis:

"Looks mighty funny to me when a woman Jennie Brown's color has a yaller-headed young one white as Evelyn."

"Daddy was white, so I understan'."

"Huh. An' her mammy, too, mos' likely. 'At's de way dese rich white folks do. Comes a wile oat dey doan want, dey ups an' gives it to one de servants—to adopt."

"Oh, I dunno. How come she couldn't been married to some white man 'nuther? Dey's plenty sich, right hyeh in Harlem."

"Plenty whut? Plenty common law, maybe. You know d' ain' no se'f-respectin' white man gonna—"

"Well, doan make no diff'nce. Cain' none of us go but so fur back in our fam'ly hist'ry 'fo we stops. An' doan nobody have t' ask us why we stops. We jes' stops. Evelyn's a good girl. Smart—works regular an' makes mo' out o' dem real estate niggers 'n she'd ever make in Miss Ann's kitchen. Bad 's her mother's asthma's gittin', no tellin' whut they'd do if 'twasn't f' Evelyn's job an' dem two women lodgers."

"Oh, I ain' sayin' nuthin' 'gins 'em. Only seem like to me—dey's a white man in de woodpile somewha'."

Her own singularity had become conscious early in Evelyn's life. There crept often into her mind of late an old, persistent recollection. She and Sookie Johnson, seven-year-old playmates, had been playing jacks on the front stoop. There arose a dispute as to whose turn it was. Sookie owned the ball and Evelyn the jacks; neither would surrender her possession to the other, and the game was deadlocked. Whereupon, the spiteful Sookie had resorted to abuse:

"Y' ole yaller thing, you! My mother say y' cain't 'speck nuthin' f'm yaller niggers nohow!"

Evelyn had thrown the jacks into Sookie's face and run heartbroken to her mother. Why didn't she have kinky hair and dark brown skin like Sookie's? "Why, honey, you're beautiful," her mother had comforted her. "Folks 'll call you names long as you live. They're just jealous, that's all."

Thus fortified, Evelyn had come to maturity, finding her mother's prophecy ever and again true. "They're just jealous" was but a fortification, however; within it Evelyn's spirit was still vulnerable, and she knew that under constant fire this stronghold could not stand forever. Mayme Jackson's thrust-in-the-back culminated what Sookie's sneer had begun. Evelyn felt her mother's defence crumbling rapidly and alarmingly, and her appeal to Jay Martin was a rather desperate effort to establish a defence of her own.

They sat now in the front room of her flat; a room too full of mock-mahogany furniture about to collapse; a room with gas light and a tacked-down carpet, with flower-figured wall-paper and a marble-topped walnut table in one corner, bearing a big brown morocco-bound Bible.

"Jay, will you?"

"Remember the time I pulled your hair in Sunday-School?"

"I'm going to pull your ears if you don't answer me!"

"Did you say something?"

"You make me tired."

"Aw, for Pete's sake, Ev, I can't take you to that dump."

"Have the last two weeks frozen your nerve?"

"No—but—"

"Well, this isn't like the others, you know. This is a colored place."

"But why go there? Let's go to Broadway's or Happy's."

"No. I want to see something new. Why isn't Hank's decent, anyway? It can't be any worse than the Hole in the Wall."

"Much worse. Regular rat-trap. No gentleman would take a lady—"

"You flatter us. Let's don't be a gentleman and lady tonight. I want to see the rat-trap."

"Why, Ev, the place was raided only last week!"

"You can't scare me that way. If it was it'll be all the safer this week."

"Lord! You girls know it all."

"I don't know anything about Hank's."

"But I'm trying to tell you—"

"Seeing is believing."

"There's nothing to see."

She introduced strategy. "All right. I guess Mac won't be so hard to persuade."

"Ev—please—for Pete's sake don't let anybody take you to that—"

"Jay, I'd really hate to have to go with anybody but you." He was growing helpless. "Just the tiniest peep into the place, Jay. We won't stay—cross my liver."

"Your mother wouldn't like it."

"Come here." She led him by the arm down the long hallway to the dining-room, where her mother was sewing.

"You may go any place you please, if you go with Jay," smiled Mrs. Brown.

———

Hank's, at first glance, presented nothing unique: a sedate old house in an elderly row of houses with high entrances, several steps above the sidewalk; houses that had once been private, but now, trapped in an extending matrix of business, stoically accepted their fates as real estate offices, printing shops and law rooms. Here and there a card peeped around the corner of a window and whispered, "Rooms"; but not the most suspicious eye would have associated those timid invitations with the bold vertical electric sign projecting over the doorway of the one lighted building in the row. Great letters, one above another, blazed the word "Café"; smaller horizontal ones across the top read "Hank's", and others across the bottom "Cabaret".

"This doesn't look so bad," commented Evelyn as they approached. "Police station right in the same block."

"Yes—convenient."

Several men stood about on the sidewalk, smoking and talking. One of these, a white man, looked sharply at Jay and Evelyn as they mounted the steps and entered.

"Why, this is like any restaurant," said Evelyn. "Just a lot of tables and folks eating."

"Only a blind," explained Jay. "The real thing is downstairs."

A dinner-coated attendant came toward them. "I'm sorry. Everything's gone in the cabaret. Would you care to wait a few minutes?"

Jay, eager for an excuse to flee, looked at Evelyn; but the blue eyes said, "Please," and he nodded. "Very well."

"This way, then."

They were led up a narrow flight of padded stairs, along a carpeted hallway with several mysterious closed doors on either side, and finally into a little room near the end. Against one wall of the room was a table with two chairs, and against the opposite a flat couch with two or three cushions. Curtains draped the one window, facing the door. The table was bare except for a small lamp with a parchment shade of orange and black, yielding a warm, dim light.

"M—m!" exclaimed Evelyn. "Cozy!"

"We can serve you here if you like," suggested the attendant.

"No, thanks," Jay answered quickly. "We'll wait."

The attendant seemed to hesitate a moment. Then, "All right," he said. "I'll let you know as soon as there's space in the cabaret." He went out and closed the door.

Evelyn was alive with interest. "Spiffy, isn't it?" She sat down on one of the chairs and looked about. "Couldn't get lost, could you?"

Jay thoughtfully took the other chair.

"You might," he said absently.

"What are you talking about? Goodness, what a lot of fun you're having!"

"I don't like this, that's a fact."

"What's wrong?"

Jay looked and noted that the door locked from within. He went over to the window, pulled the shade aside a crack, and made out the skeleton of a fire-escape in the darkness outside.

"Oh, nothing", he said, returning to his seat. "Not a thing."

"Heavens, you give me the shivers! What is it?"

He was not eager to answer. "I'm not sure but—I believe—that bird thinks you're ofay."

"White? What difference would that make?"

"Well, I'll tell you, Ev. This place, like some you already know about, has a mixed patronage, see? Part jigs, part ofays. That's perfectly all right as long as the jigs keep to their own parties and the ofays to theirs. But as soon as they begin to come mixed, trouble starts. The colored men don't like to see white men with colored women and the white men don't like to see colored men with white women. So the management avoids it. I don't believe that house-man was telling the truth when he said there was no room in the cabaret. It's too early in the evening and it's not a busy night. Fact is, the place is probably half full of ofays, and he figured that if we went down there together some drunk would get fly and I'd bounce him on the nose and right away there'd be a hullabaloo. So he took a chance that maybe we were more interested in each other than in the cabaret anyhow, and sidetracked us off up here."

"But he said he'd let us know—"

"Of course. He thought we'd be tickled silly to be in one of these rooms alone; but after I refused to be served up here, what else could he say? I don't think he has any more idea of coming back than Jack Johnson."

"Then what does he expect you to do?"

"Get tired waiting and beat it."

"Oh." A depressed silence. Then a tragic diminuendo: "Lord, what a misfit I am!"

He was contrite at once. "I'm a bum. I shouldn't have told you. I don't know—maybe I'm wrong. We're here, so let's wait awhile and see."

"Jay, if only I were one thing or the other! You can't imagine—"

He absolutely could not answer. From somewhere below a thin strain drifted to their ears, like a snicker: "Yaller Gal's Gone Out o' Style".

Jay rose. "Let's breeze. That shine isn't coming back."

"All right. I'm sorry to be such a nuisance."

"You're not the nuisance. It's—folks."

They went down the soft-carpeted hallway. Strange, low sounds behind the closed doors seemed to hush apprehensively as they approached and revive after they passed. Once a shrill laugh was abruptly cut off as if by a stifling hand. There was a thick atmosphere of suppression, a sense of unspoken fears and half-drawn breaths and whispers.

As they reached the head of the padded stairs they saw someone hurrying up and drew aside to let him pass. It was a youth in a white coat, bent on some errand. He looked at them as he went by. They resumed their course and proceeded down the stairs; but the boy halted in his, and turned to look again. Immediately, he left off his errand, and waiting until he heard the front door close behind them, retraversed the staircase. A minute later he was on the sidewalk talking in an undertone to the white man who had so sharply observed Evelyn and Jay when they entered, and who now stood smoking still, following their departure with his eyes.

"Ah know 'at sucker", scowled the little black youth. "Collects rents f' Hale an' Barker. See 'at 'fay wid 'im? Seen 'im pick 'uh up pre' near two weeks ago at Manhattan Casino."

The white man puffed a minute, while the boy looked up at him, side-long, expectant. "Hale and Barker, huh?—Hmph! All right, Shorty. I'll keep my eye on 'im. If you're on, I'll fix y' up as usual."

" 'At's the time papa." And the boy too stood eyeing the disappearing pair, an imp of malice and satisfaction.

III.

A young man leaned nonchalantly on the high foot of Jay's wooden bed, grinning goodnaturedly at him; a young man who looked exactly like Jay, feature for feature, with one important exception: his skin was white.

"Who in hell are you?" asked Jay.

"What you would be if you could," came the prompt, pleasant response.

"Liar."

"Straight stuff, brother. Think of the heights you might rise to if you were I."

"Hell!" grunted Jay.

"Eventually, of course. But I mean meanwhile. Why, now you'd be in a big firm downtown, on your way to wealth. Or you might be a practicing physician—your old man could have kept you out of the draft."

"Oh, well, I'm not doing so worse."

"No, nor so better. And then there's Evelyn."

"What about Evelyn? Why, I wouldn't even know her."

"You'd know somebody like her. Don't kid yourself, boy. You like 'em pink. Remember Paris?"

"You lie like a bookmaker. I like 'em intelligent. If they happen to be bright on the outside, too, why of course, I don't bar 'em."

"No—of course not." The sarcastic caller paused a thoughtful moment. "I've got a jawful of advice for you, old-timer."

"Swallow it and choke."

"Now listen. Don't you get to liking Evelyn, see. She's too damned white."

"What of it?"

"Be yourself, son. You ask me that, after these last two weeks?"

Jay reached up and wiped a mosquito from his forehead and smacked at another singing into his ear. They irritated him. "I'll like whoever I damn please!" he flared.

"Don't get high, now," soothed the other. "I'm only warning you. Pull up on the emergency before something hits you. That girl's too fair for comfort."

"But I like her."

The other disregarded this. "You're too dark, buddy. You're ultraviolet anyhow, alone. Beside her you become absolute black—invisible. The lady couldn't see you with an arc-lamp."

"Shucks! Evelyn doesn't care."

"You're wrong there. She does. She can't help it. But she doesn't want to, so she tries hard to make herself believe she doesn't. She takes up with you, tells herself how much she likes you, invites all sorts of embarrassments upon both of you. She might even marry you. It's like taking bad medicine she thinks she's got to take and telling herself it's sweet. She figures it's better to gulp it down than to sip it, and it's better to say it's sweet than to make faces."

"Well, maybe. But I'm just conceited enough to think she likes me."

"Of course she does. I'm not talking about you. I'm talking about your color. If you were I, now, she'd jump at you."

"Humph! I don't see her jumping at MacLoed."

"Mac isn't either of us, buddy. He hasn't got a thing but his looks, and Evelyn's too wise to fall for that alone."

"There are others."

"None who can make her forget what she's trying to do. She thinks it's a sort of duty to be colored, so she's going to make a thorough job of it—do it up brown, you might say. See? The only man that could unscramble her would be a real white man. She's not going to compromise."

"You're too deep for me. But I don't believe she cares about the color of a fellow's skin."

"You don't? Well, stay away from her anyhow."

"How come?"

"To save her feelings. Every time you two go out together you're in torture. Everybody stares at you—jigs and ofays both. You've tried it now for two weeks. What's happened? The first night you went to Coney Island and nearly got yourself mobbed. A couple of days later you went into an ice-cream parlor on One Hundred and Twenty-Fifth Street, a place where Evelyn goes anytime she likes, and the proprietor had the nerve to tell you *your* presence hurt his business. Then how about that crowd of jigs on the subway? And last night, when you wanted to get up and punch that shine waiter in the ear because he gave Evelyn the once over and then rolled his eyes at you behind her back, as much as to say, 'Oh, boy! How I envy you!'—and she looking at him all the time in the mirror! Tonight caps it all. You go out to enjoy yourself in a 'colored' place, and get jim-crowed by a man of your own color who's afraid to let the two of you be seen. Do you think Evelyn enjoys a string of things like that?"

"She enjoys 'em as much as I do."

"But it isn't the same. When people look at you, it's just with surprise. All their look says is, 'Wonder what that nigger is doing with a white woman?' But when they look at her, it's with contempt. They say, 'Humph! What a cheap drab she must be to tag around with a nigger!' No matter whether it's true or not. Do you suppose she enjoys being looked at like that?"

Jay was silent. Sounds came from the street below into his open window; an empty Coney Island bus, rumbling, clattering, shrieking, eager to get in before daybreak; gay singing of a joy-riding chorus, swelling, consummating, dying away; the night-clear whistle of a lone, late straggler—"Yaller Gal's Gone Out o' Style".

"What do you expect me to do about it?" he finally asked.

"Ease out. See less and less of her. When you breeze away for your vacation, forget to write."

"Simple, ain't it?"

"Quite." The devil straightened up. "And now that that's settled, suppose you go to sleep a while."

"Suppose you go to hell," suggested Jay glumly.

"With pleasure. See you again."

Jay closed his smarting eyes. His caller departed into the clothespress or the hall or up the airshaft, he wasn't sure where; he knew only that when again he looked about, he was alone.

Evelyn Brown, too, lay in bed, debating with a visitor—a sophisticated young woman who sat familiarly on the edge of the counterpane and hugged her knees as she talked, and who might have been Evelyn over again, save for a certain bearing of self-assurance which the latter entirely lacked.

"Well, you've tried it," said this visitor. "See what a mess you've made of it."

"I wish you'd let me alone."

"I think too much of you, dear. And you're thinking too much of Jay. Surely the last two weeks have shown you how impossible that is."

"Two weeks isn't a long enough test."

"Quite long enough. The only place you and Jay could be happy together would be on a desert island that nobody could find. You can't go to a single place together without sooner or later wishing the ground would swallow you."

"Oh, I'd get hardened to it."

"Would that be happiness? And even if you did, he wouldn't. You don't think he enjoys all this, do you?"

"No, I suppose not."

"No. And don't think he's dumb enough to put himself into it for life, either."

"He cares enough to, I think."

"Then you've got to care enough not to let him."

"How?"

"Drop him."

"I can't."

"You must. Don't you see now why you lily-whites seek each other? It's self-protection. Whether you do it consciously or not, you're really trying to prevent painful embarrassment."

"But I can't just shut myself away from everyone who happens to be a little darker than I am. If I did it before I didn't realize it, and I wasn't to blame. But if I do it now, intentionally, I'm just drawing the color-line, and that wouldn't be right. What can I do?"

Her visitor smiled. "Do? Get out. Pass. What else?"

"That's impossible. There's mother. Wherever I'd go I'd have to take her, and she couldn't pass for anything but American Negro—"

Her protest was drowned in her visitor's laughter. It was harsh, strident laughter, like the suddenly stifled outburst she'd heard at Hank's that night. It was long, loud laughter that left the visitor breathless, panting pitiably.

Of a sudden Evelyn sat upright, fearfully aware that the laughter of her dream had merged into something real and close. She listened a moment. It was her mother in the next room. Asthma again.

She met both the women lodgers in the hall, frightened, helpless.

"Did you hear her?"

Shortly Evelyn hurried from her mother's room, leaving the two women with her. She slipt on as little as she dared and sped out to get a physician.

A half hour passed before she returned with one. She noted a bright light in the front room and hastened to it, thinking the two women had taken her mother there for air; but she found only the two of them, huddled together on the sofa, shivering in their bathrobes, with something close to panic in their eyes.

IV

Jimmy MacLoed, red-eyed, stretchy, disconsolate, and broke, all the event of a prolonged and fatal night of stud-poker, got up at noontime, dressed, and strolled languidly into the street, wondering from whom he could bum four bits for breakfast. At the corner of One Hundred and Thirty-Fifth Street and the Avenue he encountered Jay Martin, hurrying to lunch. This was luck, for Jay always had bucks.

"See me go for breakfast?" he asked.

"No," grinned Jay, "but I'll add it to the five I'm by you already."

Dick's lunchroom seemed to have been designed so that the two waitresses could serve everybody without moving from where they stood. You could pass from the little front door to your stool before the counter without colliding with someone only when there was no one else there. Many a patron had unexpectedly thrust his knife further into his mouth than he intended because some damn fool, rushing out, squeezed between him and the wall. But one of the waitresses was pretty; and the ham with your eggs was cut thick, not shaved; and the French fried potatoes were really French fried, not boiled ones warmed over in grease. Jay and MacLoed considered themselves lucky to find two of the dozen stools still unoccupied.

They gave their orders and rested their elbows on the counter while the waitress that wasn't pretty threw down some pewter implements before them.

"Too bad about Evelyn's old lady, huh?" said MacLoed.

Jay became grave. "Too bad about Evelyn."

"Evelyn? Wha' d' y' mean?"

"Nobody's seen her since the funeral."

"No? Only three days. Maybe she's gone off for a rest."

"Didn't leave any notice at the office."

"Think she went dippy and jumped in the river or somethin'?"

"No. But I think she's jumped out of Harlem."

"You mean—passin'?"

"I don't know. The last time I saw her she was sick enough to do anything. Those two women roomers wouldn't stay in the house another night. None of her friends would either, even after her mother was safe in the undertaker's. She had three rotten days of it, except when my mother was there. Nobody much went to the funeral. I sent the only flowers. Next day, my mother went around to see how she was making out and found nobody home.—There hasn't been, since."

"Didn't leave word with nobody, huh?"

"Nope."

" 'S funny. 'D she have any relations?"

"Nope."

"Hm! Then that's what she's doin' all right."

"Passing?"

"Yea." Mac contemplated the ham and eggs that the homely waitress had just slid between his elbows. "Don't blame her. I'd do the same thing if I didn't have so damn much brownskin family."

"Why?"

"Why?—Why not? Wouldn't you?"

"Be white if I could?" Jay paid the waitress. "I don't know."

"The hell you don't. What would you be afraid of? Meetin' somebody? Hell! Don't see 'em. If they jump you, freeze 'em.—But you'd never meet anybody you knew. S'posin' you looked white and didn't have anything to stop you, what would be the hold-back?"

Jay chewed a minute thoughtfully. Then he looked at MacLoed as if wondering whether he was worth a reply. Finally he answered:

"Kids."

"Kids?" Mac ingested this with two pieces of the real French fried potatoes well swabbed in ham gravy. "You mean you might get married and have a little pickaninny to account for, huh? Well, you could get out o' that all right. Just tell her she'd been runnin' around with a nigger and quit."

Jay knew MacLoed too well to be shocked. "You might not want to quit," he said. "You might like her. Or you might have a conscience."

"Humph! Conscience and kids. Old stuff, buddy."

"And even if your scheme worked with a man who was passing, it wouldn't with a woman. She couldn't tell her white husband he'd been running around with a colored girl. That wouldn't explain the pickaninny."

"No.—The woman catches hell both ways, don't she?"

"It's a damned shame." Jay was speaking rather to himself than to MacLoed. "I know. I took her—places. That girl was white—as white as anybody could be. Lord only knows what she'll be now."

Three or four men had come in, standing in what little space they could find and reading the menu signs while they awaited seats. No one paid any particular attention to one of these who was "ofay". White patrons were not infrequent in Dick's. This one had moved close enough to Jay to hear his last statement. He touched him on the shoulder. As Jay turned the white man drew aside his coat, and Jay glimpsed a badge. When the officer motioned him to step outside, there was nothing else to do, and with an "Excuse me a minute, Mac—be right back," he preceded the other to the sidewalk.

Outside, Jay asked, "What's the idea?"

"Didn't want to start a row in that dump. Somebody might 'a had a gun."

"What's the idea?"

"Let's walk down this way." Jay knew better than to refuse, though "this way" led toward the police station. "So you think it's a damned shame, do you? Well, I think it's a damned shame, too."

"What the devil are you talking about?"

"Come down out o' that tree, son. I'm talking about you and the white girl you picked up at Manhattan Casino a while back. You y'self said just now she's white. That about settles it."

"White? Why, I only meant——"

"I heard you. You said 'white'. White's white, ain't it?"

Presently: "What's the charge?"

"Don't play dumb, bud. There's been too damn much of this thing goin' on here. We're goin' to stop it."

Suddenly Jay Martin laughed.

The two walked on in silence.

V.

From a point in the wide, deep balcony's dimness, Jay followed the quick-shifting scenes; not those on the screen at which he stared, but others, flashing out from his mind.

Coney Island. He and Evelyn arm in arm, inconsequent, hilarious, eating sticky popcorn out of the same bag, dipping in at the same time, gaily disputing the last piece. Their laughter suddenly chilled by an intentionally audible remark: "Look at that white girl with a nigger." A half-dozen lowering rowdies. Evelyn urging him away. People staring.

An ice-cream parlor. A rackety mechanical piano, tables with white tops and dappled wire legs; outside One Hundred and Twenty-fifth Street traffic shadowing past; Evelyn and he, wilted with the heat, waiting a couple of eternities for a waitress; he finally looking about impatiently, beckoning to one, who leers through him. The proprietor. "Of course we don't mind serving the lady, sir; but while we can't actually refuse, why—er—frankly your presence is unprofitable to us, sir." People staring.

The subway. He and Evelyn in a corner of the car. Above the rattle and bump of doors and clang of signal-gong, wild laughter, coarse, loud. Different. Negro laughter. Headlong into the car, stumbling over one another, a group of hilarious young colored people. Men contesting seats with women, and winning; women flouncing defiantly down on the men's knees. Conscious of the attention attracted by their loudness; pleased with it. Train starting, accelerating. Train-din rising. Negro-noise rising through and above it, like sharp pain through and above dull ache. "Oh, you high yaller!" Evelyn ashamed. People staring.

Finally a back room in the police station. Two or three red-faced ruffians in brass-buttoned uniforms, sneering, menacing, quite like those Coney Island rowdies. Himself, outraged, at bay, demanding to know on just what score he was there. Surly accusation, hot denial, scalding epithet—flame. A blow. Swift, violent struggle. "Now mebbe y'll leave white women alone!" Emptiness. After a time release; release raw with bodily anguish, raw with the recurrent sting of that cover-all charge of policemen, "resisting an officer".

What an enormity, blackness! From the demons and ogres and ravens of fairy tales on; storm-clouds, eclipses, night, the valley of the shadow, gloom, hell. White, the standard of goodness and perfection. Christ himself, white. All the angels. Imagine a black angel! A black angel with a flat nose and thick lips, laughing loudly. The devil! Standards, of course; but beneath the standards, what? An instinctive shrinking from the dark? He'd seen a little white child run in terror from his father once, the first black man the child had ever seen. Instinctive? He looked about. All this balcony full of fellow creatures instinctively shrinking from him. No help for it? Awful idea. Unbearable.

A general murmur of amusement refocussed his attention for a moment on the screen. Two chubby infants sat side by side on a doorstep; the one shiny black, with a head full of kinks and eyes of twinkling midnight; the other white, with eyes of gray and the noonday sun in its hair; both dimpled and grinning and happy. Kids. Old stuff, buddy. Evelyn—would she dare?

The thoughts that gathered and throbbed like an abscess were suddenly incised. Off to one side, a row or two ahead, he had caught sight of an oddly familiar face. The dimness seemed to lift mockingly, so that he should have no doubt. Evelyn, like an answer. Different, but— Evelyn. The attitude of the young man beside her was that of an escort, and something in his profile, in the fairness of his hair and skin, discernible even through the dusk, marked him to the staring Jay as unmistakably white. Watching with quickened pulse Jay saw the young man's hand move forward over Evelyn's arm, lying on the elbow-rest between them; move forward till it reached her own hand, which turned palm-upward to clasp it. Saw one white hand close firmly over the other.

He rose abruptly and made his way past stubborn knees to the aisle. The orchestra struck up a popular bit of Negro jazz. It fell on his ears like a guffaw: the familiar refrain of "Yaller Gal's Gone Out o' Style".

THE DEATH GAME

This short story received second prize in the *Crisis* contest of 1926. In "The Death Game," author Edwin Drummond Sheen relates the tragic life of "Home-breaking Nell" Bowen, a haggard white woman of the streets who is protected and supported by black, quick-tempered Joe Nixon. She cannot be true to one man; therefore, she enjoys flirting with Shug Lewis. This story was published in two parts in January and February 1927.

South Dearborn Street is not especially appealing to the esthetic eye. In the "Loop", of course, it boasts of thriving businesses and towering buildings, but below the railroad yards that lie behind the old Polk Street Station, it stretches untidily southward for miles and miles, an almost unrelieved expanse of cracked and dirty sidewalks, or none at all; badly paved streets, filled with gritty dust in dry weather and oozy slime in wet and sad looking old frame houses, their blackened boards unpainted for ages seemingly, their cracked windows stuffed with rags and paper and hung with dirty green blinds, sieve-like of appearance when the lamp light shines through at night, their doors wide open in warm weather, revealing a generous portion of cheerless interior, with bare, frequently crumbling walls, broken and home-made furniture, ragged carpets, general disorder and hopeless resignation. In the long summer evenings, after supper (for seven o'clock comes early in Chicago with its daylight saving time), there are little girls with their short hair in many dusty braids and little boys with hardly any hair at all; and there are loud-mouthed men who sit on the steps and pick guitars and dance and sing the blues; and there are bold women in loose-fitting, low-necked, sleeveless gingham house dresses, who chew tobacco and swear and allow the loud-mouthed men to handle them with shameless familiarity.

I

NELL BOWEN

Nell Bowen wasn't the girl she used to be. She admitted as much to herself almost every time she saw her likeness in the peeling mirror above her dresser, her hair thin and streaked with gray at twenty-eight, her eyes dull and sunken, with dark blue lids, bordered with ghastly pinkish half moons; her lips pale and twitching and her skin harsh and dry and covered with fine white hairs . . .

In the bright lights of Wilson Avenue and the Uptown district, where she once had known questionable notoriety as "Homebreaking Nell", high powered motor cars still purred with secretive mystery and slim white arms still twined about fat red necks and expensive furs and jewelry were still charged confidentially to prominent names and wives still sat alone at night; but Nell Bowen was buried—buried in the dirt and squalor of Dearborn Street, stripped of her glory, shorn of her power, forgotten by the world that once groveled at her feet.

It was only twelve years ago that she had run away from her quiet home in Indiana and come to the big city in quest of a thrill. She got it—in a cheap cabaret, where the admission was only a dime and the men came collarless and wore square toed shoes. She couldn't sing at all and her dancing was poor; but she wasn't afraid to undress and they told her she had personality; so her rise to fame was rapid. In less than two years she was entertaining at the rendezvous of the elite, where gunmen rubbed elbows with bankers' sons and saloon keepers hob-nobbed with the socially prominent.

She learned to be a "good pal". There were long rides in the country, piles of pretty clothes, numerous "little parties", now and then an "affair", ending in the divorce court, with her picture on the front pages of newspapers as co-respondent. She became the world's sweetheart. Lifelong friends fell out about her; wives sought their mothers; husbands hardened their hearts and looked out the window; one man hanged himself; another went off and lost himself in the world that did not know. And "Homebreaking Nell" laughed through it all and thought it would last forever.

Then, one night, she slew Ed Hines, her third husband. The jury acquitted her, of course, after a second trial, but the prosecutor had prosecuted hard and the six months in jail before the final disposition of her case brought out the hard, ugly seams in her face which before had been so light and had crept in so gradually that they were not noticed by her admirers. When she went back to her old job, the manager looked her over critically and shook his head. She had to go to a smaller cabaret and after a time to a still smaller one. Then, the patrons tired of her there and she had to descend another rung and so on continuously until she landed in a "joint" worse, if possible, than the one in which she had started.

It was here that Joe Nixon had found her. She wasn't much to love then. Heavy drinking and drugs, which she had resorted to to quiet her nerves after the ordeal of her two trials, had wrecked her quite thoroughly. But Joe seemed to think that she was still human and had a soul in her and she liked the gentle way in which he spoke to her and the tender look that was noticeable on his rough countenance when he gave her gifts. Nell had had five white husbands in her brief life (for two others had succeeded the ill-fated Ed Hines), but none of them had ever appeared so sincere and true blue as the Negro, Joe Nixon. After a time, Nell began to feel that she liked Joe.

And so it came about that Nell Bowen took up her residence on Dearborn Street among the people of Joe Nixon. She found them at the worst not unsociable, nor worse than those of the same class in her own race. There was a time when she didn't care much for Negroes— considered them rather uncouth animals. But now, she longed for companionship and the popularity that she used to enjoy in years past; and she dreamed of a return to power among black folk, when the name of "Homebreaking Nell" would once more make women sigh and men forget their vows.

And Joe Nixon, Negro though he was, was a man. Although he was of peaceful temperament, he had a compelling sort of personality that made him feared, respected and admired by his associates. At the institution of "Fast Black", on State Street, where he frequently went in search of amusement, he was known as the nerviest gambler that ever riffled a deck of cards. No matter how high the stakes, or how discouraging his run of luck, Joe Nixon never lost either his head or his nerve. Winning or losing, he was always the same Joe, making no boasts, asking no sympathy, displaying no emotion. They called him Iron Joe, for he had a soul of steel. He was born to rule. Perhaps if he had had a little education and social position, he would have long ago been in the Illinois Legislature.

II
SHUG LEWIS

It was something after three o'clock on Sunday morning when a creaking taxicab turned into Dearborn Street from Thirty-third and stopped with characteristic abruptness in the middle of the block before a wooden frame building, which from the outside appeared to consist of two flats and a basement. The two upper flats were without blinds and their broken windows were unpatched, indicating that they were vacant; but a dim light in the front of the basement hinted that somebody lived there.

The colored driver of the cab opened the door and examined the meter as a short, narrow-eyed, bullet-headed Negro hopped to the curb and reached into his pocket for the fare without making the slightest pretense at assisting the dilapidated, old-young white woman who stepped out after him. After paying the driver, however, he put his arm around her affectionately enough and as they walked slowly toward the rusty door of the basement flat, he talked softly to her. There was a pause while the woman turned a key in the lock and pushed the door open; then the two entered the flat, the man going in first. A moment later, the oil lamp on the table was turned up and filled the room with a sad yellow light.

There was pathetic disorder. A table in the center with a ragged cover; a bed in the corner with a ragged spread. The lace curtains were ancient, soiled and carelessly hung. The floor was covered with bits of old carpet, frayed at the edges and worn in the middle. The wall paper was stained and faded, where it was not entirely torn off. The atmosphere was damp and musty ... This was the home of Nell Bowen.

Her guest on this early morning occasion, however, was not Joe Nixon—that was certain. Joe was tall, broad-shouldered, square-jawed and light-brownskinned of complexion; not short and dark and bullet headed like this visitor. The years of reverse and decline, in fact, that had worked so much havoc with Nell's body, had not entirely crushed out her adventurous spirit. Joe Nixon, of course, was all that she could desire for a companion, but Nell Bowen had always considered a single lover woefully inadequate for herself. She liked to have men do battle over her. It gave her a strange sense of mastery to see two men become beasts because she had smiled at both. Ever since her coming to Dearborn Street, however, she had been known as Joe Nixon's girl and other men, knowing her to be such, hesitated to respond to her sly flirtations, whether they were interested in them or not. For Joe had the reputation of a man who played all games on the square—life, love, cards—and though he was peaceable enough most of the time, it was known that he stood for no "fooling" and had the wherewithal to make himself unpleasant in case any misguided person should succeed in ruffling his even temper.

Before long, therefore, Nell Bowen found that by virtue of the fact that she was Joe Nixon's girl, she would probably be left severely alone. The lack of competition for her hand irked her and consequently, when Shug Lewis, in utter defiance of the certain wrath of the mighty Joe, began to shower her with attentions, she welcomed him with both figurative and literal open arms. Unlike Joe, Shug Lewis did not work. However, by writing "policy" and playing whatever confidence games he could find victims for, with a little trick gambling on the side, he was able to realize an income sufficiently respectable to convince Nell that his friendship was worth cultivating. Nell knew that he was considered a low mean creature and that nobody really liked him, but he was a valuable source of income and she could easily overlook his little faults.

Shug dropped down beside Nell on the leaking red plush settee and yawned.

"Yes," he said with helpless resignation, "I might knowed we would be raided tonight. I thought something was going to happen no sooner'n I saw that jack of spades on the sidewalk when we was going out."

Nell looked slightly annoyed.

"You still worrying about that jack of spades?" she said in her dry husky voice. "Seems to me like a man of your age could get over all that superstition."

"Ain't no superstition," insisted Shug stubbornly as he mechanically put his arm about her and drew her closer to him. "That's just the truth. There's a conjure on that jack of spades for all my folks. I was playing whist this afternoon at Fast Black's, for two dollars a game and they turned up that jack of spades for trumps three times and damned if I had more than one little trump airy a one of the times they turned it. Commenced to play blackjack and it got after me again. Busted me out from twelve twice and every time I got a deal, some guy'd catch an ace with it and make blackjack on me. It don't mean me no good, I tell you."

Nell patted him tenderly on the cheek and kissed him.

"Maybe that'll take the Joner off you," she said teasingly.

Shug did not look reassured.

"At that," Nell went on soothingly, "you were luckier than the rest of the bunch. They couldn't make no bail and they've got to stay in jail till Monday."

"I know, but I'll have to see that judge down on Forty-eighth Street Monday morning right along with them," Shug retorted gloomily. "He'll just about give me about sixty days too, 'cause he ain't got no time for me."

Nell giggled.

"Tell him it's all the jack of spades' fault and maybe he'll let you go."

The seriousness of Shug's expression was pathetic.

"That ain't nothing to joke about, Nell. I tell you, that jack of spades don't mean me no good no time. Do you know what the jack of spades is?"

Nell didn't. She didn't appear to be much interested, but Shug went on to explain.

"It's a nigger that used to be in Mississippi about thirty years ago when I wasn't nothing but a kid. His name was Jack Spayd and folks all said he was a conjure man. My paw told the white folks something he did once and they got after him and lynched him for it and the last thing he did was to cuss paw out just when they was kicking the barrel out from under him."

Nell moved rather impatiently and sighed, but Shug continued persistently.

"Paw goes home right away and there is the jack of spades on the front step, with salt sprinkled over it and a knife stuck through it; and two weeks later, paw was dead with the appendicitis and while he was sick, he was always saying that he felt like a knife was sticking in his side."

"Do tell," observed Nell dryly; but Shug refused to take the hint.

"Ever since then, don't none of my folks see a jack of spades without we know there's some trouble on the way. There was my brother's kid. Got to eating a card and choked to death and what do you think the card was?"

Nell hazarded the queen of diamonds and laid her faded head on his shoulder. Shug was unmoved by her affection.

"It was that same jack of spades. And then, I was coming from Fast Black's two years ago and a card blew down from somewhere and landed face up right in front of me and it was the jack of spades and when I got home there was a special delivery there that ma was dead. And then I know one time when—"

"Aw, be still, Shug."

Nell had reached the limit of her endurance. It was little short of remarkable what a bore the sight of a jack of spades could make Shug Lewis. She essayed to touch his pride.

"Who ever heard of a big man being afraid of a little jack of spades," she chided. "The jack of spades ain't nothing but a card. You'd better be afraid of something that can do you some harm. I heard that Joe Nixon was looking for you to lay his hand against your head for running around here so much. You know Joe's a bad fellow when he gets mad."

This bit of strategy to divert Shug's mind from his sordid family history was successful. He gave a contemptuous grunt.

"What I want to be afraid of Joe Nixon for?" he retorted. "He's a meat man, ain't he? If he's concrete and eats nails, he can bluff me, but if he's made out of meat, I'll cut him down to my size."

Nell was pleased at this reaction. She led him on.

"Joe's a sweet papa," she observed slyly. "Don't you talk about hurting him. He's my man."

"Hell," commented Shug sullenly. "I'll bet he don't bring in these bucks like I do."

Nell stroked Shug's stiff, knotty hair lovingly.

"The only trouble with Joe," she said rather pensively, "is that he's always talking about holding myself up and making something out of me and a lot of damned movie stuff like that. I ain't never going to be anybody but Nell Bowen anyway. I can't get on to his line."

Shug took her and placed her on his lap. She twined her wrinkled arms about his neck as she had once, in her fresher days, twined them about the necks of millionaires.

"As long as you're Nell Bowen, you're bound to be all right with Shug Lewis," that gentleman declared. "If Joe Nixon wants a Grand Boulevard girl, let him go over on Grand Boulevard and get one. I come to Dearborn Street after mine."

"Tell mamma the truth, boy, tell mamma the truth," rejoined Nell.

Came a knocking at the door as of a powerful fist.

III
JOE NIXON

Nell leaped out of Shug's embrace.

"Who's there?" she called, a little startled.

"The law," replied a gruff voice from without.

Nell glanced at Shug.

"The law, hell," she retorted. "What's the game of coming around this early in the morning, Joe Nixon?"

"Open the door, woman, before I break it down."

The voice meant business. Shug felt for his revolver and swore. The police had taken it from him in the raid. Nell hesitated. The door received a mighty push from without. The rotting boards could not hold the lock. Another mightier push, and Joe Nixon stood before the abashed pair.

There was silence for possibly half a minute. Shug sprawled back on the settee, pushed his hands into his pockets and leered at the impromptu visitor. Nell appeared a little nervous. After a time she moved over to a shelf on the wall and drew a small automatic revolver from behind the clock. She felt safer with it. If Joe thought she was going to murder him in cold blood, he betrayed no anxiety. He stood motionless, looking from one to the other, a slight narrowing of the eyes the only expression on his face.

Shug finally drew a cigar out of his vest pocket, lighted it and crossed his legs with the air of one who is at his ease.

"Well, what of it?" he demanded insolently. "You see us here—now, what are you going to do about it?"

Joe was still silent. Nell moved close to him and put her hand on his shoulder. There was a little liquor on his breath.

"Come on, Joe," Nell said, "sit down—be yourself—don't start nothing in my house—you're drunk."

Joe looked down on her. She still had the revolver in her free hand. He stroked her faded hair tenderly.

"What's he to you?"

Nell ignored his question.

"You've done busted down my door, Joe. Now go on away—sit down—sober up."

Shug was still quietly smoking on the settee. Joe drew a deep sigh.

"I ain't drunk, hon. I've had a pint or two, maybe, but I've got plenty of sense."

Nell tried to smile in her old alluring way.

"Joe, honey, won't you—"

Joe suddenly took her hand from his shoulder and pushed her gently to one side.

"Sit down, kid," he said. "This thing's got to be settled." He walked around the table and stood directly before Shug.

"Well, Shug," he said, almost regretfully. "I guess it'll have to be either me or you tonight. I've been hearing a lot about you and letting you run on—but I guess it'll have to be either me or you tonight. I've been trying awful hard to make something out of this girl because I want her and you keep on running around behind my back making it hard on me. Of course, I know she ain't supposed to be much, but she's all I have ever loved and I ain't going to have her running around with any rat like you—while I'm alive."

Shug grunted.

"I ain't put no gun on her to make her go with me. She wouldn't run around with me if she didn't want to."

Joe knew Shug was speaking the truth, but he defended his love.

"You're putting temptation in her way, though, and you know she's weak and can't stand much temptation."

"I guess I've got to ask you about who I can have for a sweetie," challenged Shug sullenly.

Joe ignored him. He turned to the source of all the controversy.

"Nell, what is it that attracts you to fellows like this?"—he made a gesture toward the settee. "It wouldn't hurt me so much if you was more particular."

Nell looked at the floor.

"Of course," Joe went on, "if that's what you want, I guess—"

Nell arose and approached him again. She had laid the revolver on the table.

"Don't talk that way, daddy," she pleaded. "Can't you trust me?"

Joe did not resist her as she pulled him down on the settee, she herself sitting between him and Shug, with an arm around each.

"I love you both," continued the jaded siren. "Can't we be pals together?"

Both men arose, Shug scowling and sullen, Joe calm but firm.

"No, Nell," Joe said slowly. "We can't do it. It's got to be either him or me."

Nell was silent. They were all silent for a short space of time. Then Shug turned and faced his rival.

"I know what we'll do," he challenged. "You're supposed to be a hell of a gambler, ain't you? Well, we'll have a game of five-up right here and the winner gets the gal."

Joe thought seriously for a moment.

"The winner gets Nell," repeated Joe. "And the loser, what does he get?"

"He don't get anything—but a lot of air."

"You're trying to tell me that if you lose, you'll go away and let Nell alone?"

"Sure I will, if I lose."

Nell had gone to get the cards, but Joe was still dissatisfied.

"You expect me to trust you that way?" Joe said. "I'd take that up with a man, but with you, it's got to be either me or you."

Nell brought the deck and laid it on the table. Joe went on after a pause.

"It's your deal. The winner gets Nell. The loser—gets a bullet in his head. Deal."

Shug hesitated. Nell started and stared at Joe. He was not joking. He took a heavy revolver from his pocket.

"Give your gun to Nell."

Shug's composure was somewhat disturbed. This was an awful gamble. He had never played that way before.

"I ain't got no gun," he said a little nervously. "Do you think I'd of let you bust in here like you did if I had a gun? The law took it away from me."

"You ain't got none, have you?" Joe "fanned" him quickly. "Well, I'll unload mine. Now, listen—get this straight—the man that loses backs up against the wall and puts his hands up like a man. Here, Nell, you hold the gun and give it to the man that wins the game. Is that all right?"

Joe talked about the game with life for stakes as calmly as if it were penny ante. Shug hesitated. He seemed to realize that when he challenged Joe's gambling nerve, he had bitten off more than he could chew.

"How come the loser's got to be killed?" he wanted to know.

"Because that's the only way I can trust you—dead." Joe squared his jaw. "You began talking about gambling; now, deal."

Shug plainly did not like this sort of game at all. He gnawed his lower lip. If he had had his revolver, he probably would have shot it out with his cool, firm rival on the spot, but he was helpless. As he fingered the cards nervously, Nell whispered something to him. His brow wrinkled momentarily, then cleared up. He began to shuffle the deck.

"All right," he said, swallowing. "No backing out, now. These is your own stakes."

Joe folded his arms.

"Did you ever know *me* to back out of anything?"

Shug's hands trembled noticeably as he dealt six cards, three at a time to his calm opponent and himself. He turned a jack for the trump.

"Jack and one," he exclaimed. Then he sobered. It was the jack of spades.

"We ought to make this the best two out of three," he suggested uneasily.

"Sure, if you want it that way," agreed Joe.

"Yes," pursued Shug, "that jack of spades don't mean me no good. Bet I ain't got another trump."

Joe looked at his hand and "stood" on the queen and six spot. Shug made a ten and played the king and deuce for high, low and the game, bringing his score up to four, while Joe was without a point. Joe dealt and turned up a heart. Shug promptly showed him the ace for game.

"That damned jack of spades is bound to mess me up some way," he muttered in nervous exasperation.

Joe did not hear him, but guessed the substance of his complaint.

"You could've been shooting if you hadn't got scared," he observed placidly as Shug shuffled the deck for his second deal.

The second game went three hands, Joe getting out from three when he stood on the "dry" jack of diamonds and caught Shug without a trump. He displayed no emotion as he shuffled the deck for his deal.

"Yes, you could've been shooting," he remarked dryly.

Shug cursed the jack of spades again. The seriousness of the situation was coming home to him more strongly as the real showdown approached. Just the least bit of ill luck in this game and he was a dead man. The proposition was enough to make a stout heart flutter. Shug was getting markedly nervous.

"Damn it, Joe, I don't like this game! Take the damned gal, if you want her that bad."

"Not while you're walking around, Shug. I can't trust you. It's got to be either you or me."

Death-like stillness reigned. It was after four and nobody was abroad even on Dearborn Street. Shug felt extremely helpless and alone as he met the cold stare of the quiet man across the table from him. Sweat rose on his wrinkled forehead. His breathing became hard and audible. He looked appealingly at Nell, as if he thought she could do something.

Nell stood at the side of the table with her arms folded and the prospective death weapon in her right hand. She smiled at Shug.

"Come on, Shug, stand up," she encouraged. It was evident that this experience was giving her a sense of power not felt for many years. She whispered something else to Shug, Joe thought, but he did not question her about it.

"Well, what do you do?" he asked his opponent.

Shug picked up the six cards Joe had dealt him, and laughed aloud. A heart had been turned up, and he had the ace, king, jack and deuce.

Wildly joyful at this relief, he scored all four points and shuffled for the next deal eagerly.

"Now, I always could deal myself *one* point," he grinned confidently. "Put that gun close here, Nell, where that coon can't grab it when I win. You's a bad gambler, ain't you? Well, you don't need to think I won't shoot you. Looks to me like you're out on that limb."

Joe was indeed in a rather unenviable position. Just a single point stood between him and death. Just one more point on Shug's score and according to his own agreement, he would have to back up to the wall and let this lowest of humans across from him riddle him with bullets from the revolver of the girl he loved. Any ordinary man would have cracked under the strain—perhaps would have sought to escape through the door which was still partly open. But Iron Joe only held the edge of the table a little more tightly and swallowed.

"Five is the game," he said with no detectable emotion in his voice.

Nell moved over to Shug and patted him on the shoulder.

"Don't talk so much, Shug, you ain't won yet," she admonished.

Joe did not like the tender note in her voice nor the affectionate look which she gave Shug as she spoke, but he said nothing. Shug had the cards and turned up a spade for trumps. Joe stood on the ten and the five and played high, low and the game for three points. Shug swore violently as he threw his cards in for the next deal and remarked that he couldn't have any luck at all with spades. The score was now four and three. Shug was no longer boastful, but neither did he appear to be very fearful of the outcome. Joe had noticed that Shug had been rather strangely cool ever since Nell had seemed to whisper to him.

He shuffled the cards carefully. Somebody was going to go out on that hand. Shug needed one point and he needed two. Either the high trump or the low one by itself would put Shug out, while he needed both. Jack and game didn't count that hand. He handed the deck to Shug for the cut.

"Somebody's going to get shot after this hand," he said evenly.

Shug cut the cards silently. It was the zero hour. There was no sound audible as Joe carefully dealt the two hands. Nell stood again with her arms folded and the revolver in her right hand. She held her lower lip between her teeth and followed Joe's hand with mechanical interest. Shug was entirely composed. His cigar worked up and down and from side to side as he chewed on the end of it. Joe finished the deal, placed the deck on the table and turned the trump.

"Jack and four with you," he observed unexcitedly.

Shug swore violently. Joe had turned the jack of diamonds. In Shug's hand were the ace, four and deuce of spades, the king of clubs, the ace of hearts and the nine of diamonds. With anything but diamonds for the trump, Shug would have been almost sure to win on the high card. With spades and hearts, victory was certain. With clubs, it would take the ace to beat him. Shug surveyed his hand and the jack of diamonds turned up in disgust. He hesitated a moment, evidently waiting to see if he could get a hint of what Joe's hand contained. Joe was expressionless. He had not even looked at his hand. As he hesitated, Nell moved over to Joe's side.

"I'll give you the gun whether you win or not," she whispered.

Joe shook his head.

"Go on, kid, I don't play that way," he returned huskily.

Shug spread his hand out on the table.

"Run the cards man, and if you miss that hand, you're a good one."

Joe examined the hand and turned his own over. It revealed five small spades and the seven of clubs.

"Nary a diamond," he observed. "You could've been shooting on that nine spot if you hadn't got scared."

Shug couldn't understand how a man in the face of almost certain death could keep his composure so completely.

"You may as well give me the gun, Nell," he said. "He's bound to hit one of these aces or this king in the run—huh uh, he can't win now—turn it!"

Joe had dealt him the ace of clubs in the run. He had the high card in all three suits now for sure. Joe turned another diamond. Shug stood up.

"Come on, diamonds no more—run 'em on."

Joe ran the cards again, turning up diamonds once more. Nell was getting nervous. The gun was shaking violently in her hand. Shug ground his teeth in exasperation as Joe turned up another diamond and ran the cards on again.

"What's the use of keeping on?" he demanded. "You know you're beat no matter what you turn. Ain't I got high in every suit?"

Joe's chances did appear extremely slim, to tell the truth. There was only one remote possibility of his winning, with all the remaining aces in Shug's hand. He reminded Shug of the last hope.

"Suppose I turn another jack?"

Shug had entirely forgotten that possibility in his elation over his three aces. It sobered him somewhat, but he was still confident.

"Now, I know you ain't going to turn no two jacks on me in one deal."

Joe was not reassuring.

"It has been done," he remarked calmly as he turned over a diamond for the fifth time.

"Hell, man, ain't you never going to turn up a trump?" complained Shug. "Ain't there nothing but diamonds in that deck?"

Shug was getting a little worried. Diamonds were coming up so persistently that he feared it was a bad omen. Joe dealt quietly, three more cards to Shug, three more to himself. He set the deck on the table . . . turned over the trump. Shug started back, his face pale and ghastly.

"That damned jack of spades!"

Joe smiled very faintly.

"You could've been shooting if you hadn't got scared."

Shug, in the meantime, was looking at Nell. She had a hard smile on her face. Of a sudden he made a leap for her.

"Gi'me that damned gun, you double-crossing—"

Joe snatched the revolver from Nell's hand and pushed Shug back.

"Stand back, stand back! You can't pull off anything like that. I gamble fair with you and you'll gamble fair with me. Get back."

Shug backed up and collapsed on the settee.

"Don't shoot me, Joe, don't shoot," he begged. "You can have the gal—I don't want her—she's crooked—she said she wanted me and she'd give me the gun even if I lost—and then she went and double-crossed me. I'll let her alone, Joe. I'll get out of town—"

He paused, still shaking, but encouraged, for Joe had slowly lowered the weapon. Joe was looking searchingly at Nell, who was standing demurely at his side with her arm around his waist. He seemed suddenly to have forgotten Shug entirely.

"Did you tell *him* that too, Nell?" For the first time there was a slight tremor in his voice.

Nell was excited.

"No, no, of course not. What'd I want to tell him that for? You know what a powerful liar Shug Lewis is."

"She did say it," insisted Shug. "She told me that when she thought I was winning and then double-crossed me."

"Shug Lewis, you're just a lying hound!" Nell bared her stained and decaying teeth at him. "Don't believe him, Joe," she added in a gentler voice.

But Joe pushed her away.

"Nell, you ain't worth a damn," he sighed. "After all I've done for you and all I've tried to make out of you, you still ain't worth a damn. You never will be worth a damn, Nell, as long as your feet point frontwards. You've just made a sucker out of me and got me going to shoot a man over you.... I thought maybe you'd amount to something, sometime, but Nell—you ain't worth a damn."

He paused a moment. The man on the settee and the woman who was totally taken off her feet by the unexpected attack stared at Iron Joe, who for the first time appeared to be moved. Suddenly he made a gesture of despair. Nell dodged as if she thought he was going to hit her, but he hardly saw her.

"Go ahead and take the gal, Shug," Joe continued. "I don't want her. I wouldn't even kill a rat like you about her. Here."

And then Joe walked deliberately to Shug on the settee, gave him the loaded revolver and turned his back on Shug Lewis, the rat, the treacherous, the lowest of humans, his enemy, armed with a loaded revolver—Joe turned his back on Shug Lewis and walked out of the musty basement flat without the slightest suggestion of hurry. And Shug Lewis cowered on the settee, with murder in his eyes, but as powerless to shoot as if his fingers were paralyzed.

Outside the door, Joe Nixon crossed Dearborn Street and cast a farewell look back at Nell's squalid basement. Perhaps he had been a fool to take up with her from the first, but—well, he just thought there was something in her. He stood for a long time gazing at the pale light coming through the sieve-like curtains at the front windows. He was thinking of the past, when he used to have dreams that included Nell. Finally, he lit a cigarette, turned and started for Thirty-third Street....

A shot from Nell's flat arrested his footsteps, but did not startle him. He started back to the flat, but stopped.

"That damned fool's done gone and killed himself about that no 'count gal."

But a moment later, he saw the form of Shug Lewis dart out the front door and dodge into the gloom between the houses.

THE END

Unfinished Masterpieces

This short story was published in March 1927. Author Anita Scott Coleman writes about the end of a life in which so many opportunities have gone unmet.

There are days which stand out clearly like limpid pools beside the dusty road; when your thoughts, crystal clear as water, are pinioned in loveliness like star-points. Solitary days, which come often, if you are given to browsing in fields of past adventure; or rarely, if you are seldom retrospective; and not at all, if you are too greatly concerned with rushing onward to a nebulous future. Days whereupon your experiences glimmer before you waveringly like motion-pictures and the people you have known stroll through the lanes of memory, arrayed in vari-colored splendour or in amusing disarray. Days like these are to be revered, for they have their humors and their whimsicalities. Hurry your thoughts and the gathering imageries take flight. Perplexity but makes the lens of introspection blur. And of annoyance beware, for it is an evil vapour that disseminates and drowns the visions in the sea of grim realities. Such days must be cultivated. Scenes for their reception must be set. Cushions perhaps, and warmth of fire. Above all, the warmth of sweet content. Ease and comfort, comfort and ease and moods of receptivity. Then hither, come hither the places and the people we have known, the associations that withstand time's effacements. Backward ho, through the mazes of the past.

———

STOP! "Why howdy, Dora Johns." Darling playmate of my child-years. With wooly hair a length too short for even pigtails. Mud-spatters upon your funny black face. Mud-spatters all over your dress and your little black hands mud-spattered too.

Why? What? Come on and see. And lo! I am a child again.

Hand in hand, unmindful of her muddy ones, we skip around the old ramshackle house, back to the furthest corner of an unkempt yard, impervious to the tin cans, the ash-heap, the litter, the clutter that impedes our way, our eyes upon, our thoughts bent upon one small clean-swept corner, where there is mud. More mud and water in a battered tin can. And row after row of mud. No, not mud—not merely mud, but things made out of mud. Row on row, drying in the sun.

Carefully, I sit down, doubling up, to be as small as possible, for only this corner where mud things are drying is clean and corners are seldom, if ever, quite large enough. Besides, I must not touch the things made out of mud. If the dried ones fall, they break. If the moist ones are molested, be it with ever so gentle a finger, they lose their shape. Moreover, I must not disturb Dora.

Her little hands are busied with the mud. Little moulder's fingers are deftly playing their skill. Her child's face is alight. What has splashed her grave child's face with such a light? I wondered. I wonder now. The glitter of brittle talent, a gleam of sterling genius or the glow from artistic fires burning within the soul of a little black child?

———

Little Dora shaping figures out of mud. Vases and urns, dolls and toys, flying birds and trotting horses, frisking dogs and playing kittens, marvelous things out of mud. Crying aloud as though dealt a blow if one of the dried mud-figures is broken. Working in mud for endless hours, while the neighbor children play. Their hilarious merriment dropping like bombs into the quiet of our clean-swept corner. Deadly missiles seeking to find a mark. The insistent halloes of futile mirth forever bubbling on the other side of a high-board fence. The dividing fence and upon one side the clean-swept corner and the row on row of mud things drying in the sun. And Dora seeming not to heed the seething bubbles upon the other side, shaping, shaping marvelous things out of mud.

Yet, Oh Dora, now that the day is ours, will you not say, "When did the bombs of futile mirth strike their target? When did the tin-cans and the rags and the old ash-heap crowd you out from your clean-swept corner? What rude hand caused the dried mud shapes to fall and break? Who set a ruthless foot in the midst of your damp mud things?" Or were you too plastic, as plastic as your mud? You dare not tell. Only this you can whisper into the mists of our today. You are one of the Master's unfinished shapes which He will some day gather to mould anew into the finished masterpiece.

—

A lump of mud. Now, there is a sobriquet for you—you funny, funny man. Mr. William Williams. I saw you but once. We chanced to meet in the home of a mutual friend. I thought you so very funny then. Uncouth and very boorish, but ever, when these pageants of the past, these dumb shows of inarticulate folks arise before me upon retrospective days, you appear garbed in the tatters of pathos.

"I am fifty-one years old," you kept repeating. How pitiful those fifty-one years are. You wear a child's simplicity, the sort that is so sad to see upon a man. Fifty-one and penniless. Fifty-one and possessed of naught else but the clothing you wore. Fifty-one and no place on earth you might call home. You confessed to being a vagabond though "bum" was the term you used and you were very proud of your one accomplishment, an ability to avoid all labour.

"I've given no man a full day's honest work in all my fifty-one years," you boasted. "I gambles. I ain't no cotton-pickin' nigger." Your one and only boast after holding life, the fathomless fountain of eternal possibilities, in your possession for fifty-one priceless years.

Nevertheless you have lived and so intensely. You held us against our will. Clustered around you, listening to you talk. Relating clippings as it were from the scrap-book of your life.

Tales of the road, of the only places you knew. Roads leading away from plantations where the cotton waited to be picked by numberless "cotton-pickin' niggers". Roads leading to pool halls and gambling dens. Roads beginning and roads ending in "riding the roads", carrying backward and forward, here and yon through the weird goblin land of the South's black belt.

With a hardened casualness you told stories that revolted and at the same time cheered us with an all sufficing glow of thankfulness that life had spared us the sordidness of yours. Offhandily, you gave us humourous skits that tempered our laughter with wishes that we might know at least a bit of such a droll existence as had been yours. With magical words you painted pictures so sharply they cut scars upon our hearts. You drew others so filled with rollicking delight their gladsomeness was contagious. With the nonchalance of a player shuffling cards you flipped your characters before us, drawn directly from the cesspool of your contacts and spellbound we listened.

Someone remarked how wonderful you talked and you replied, "Once, I sorter wanted to write books. Once, I uster read a heaps. See times when I was broke and nobody would stake me for a game. I'd lay around and read. I've read the Bible through and through and every Police Gazette I could lay my hands on. Yes, suh, I've read a heap. And I've wished a lot'er times I'd sense enough to write a book."

Lump of mud. Containing the you, the splendid artist in you, the soul of you, the unfinished you in the ungainly lump of you, awaiting the gathering-up to be moulded anew into the finished masterpiece.

What a day! Here is my friend at whose fire-side I have lingered beholding Mr. William Williams, great lump of mud. To be sure, she also is an unfinished production. Though it is apparent that the Master had all but done when she slipped from his hands and dropped to earth to lie groping like the rest of us thereon.

Let us sit here together, friend, and enjoy this day.

I shall try to discover what recent gift you have given to the poor the while you are quietly stitching upon the garments, linens and scarlet, with which to clothe your household. Sit here and smile with the welcoming light in your eyes, knowing that your door is open to such as William Williams and Dora Johns, the Dora who is become as the mud beneath one's feet. Kind mistress of the widely opened door where white and black, rich and poor, of whatever caste or creed may enter and find comfort and ease and food and drink.

Nothing New

This short story by Marita O. Bonner was published in
November 1926. The story centers on Denny Jackson,
an African-American creative artist who enters a white
art school. A racial incident had occurred earlier that he
has not resolved. However, the earlier incident comes to
the fore when he is threatened by a white classmate. All
the rage he feels about race rises in him and jeopardizes
his future.

There was, once high on a hillside, a muddy brook. A brook full of yellow muddy water that foamed and churned over a rocky bed.

Halfway down the hillside the water pooled in the clearest pool. All
the people wondered how the muddy water cleared at that place. They
did not know. They did not understand. They only went to the pool
and drank. Sometimes they stooped over and looked into the water and
saw themselves.

If they had looked deeper they might have seen God.

People seldom look that deep, though. They do not always understand how to do things.

They are not God. He alone understands.

———

You have been down on Frye Street. You know how it runs from Grand
Avenue and the L to a river; from freckled-faced tow heads to yellow
Orientals; from broad Italy to broad Georgia; from hooked nose to
square black noses. How it lisps in French, how it babbles in Italian,
how it gurgles in German, how it drawls and crawls through Black Belt
dialects. Frye Street flows nicely together. It is like muddy water. Like
muddy water in a brook.

Reuben Jackson and his wife Bessie—late of Georgia—made a
home of three rooms at number thirteen Frye Street.

"Bad luck number", said the neighbors.

"Good luck number", said Reuben and Bessie.

Reuben did not know much. He knew only God, work, church, work and God. The only things Bessie knew were God, work, Denny, prayer, Reuben, prayer, Denny, work, work, work, God.

Denny was one thing they both knew beside God and work. Denny was their little son. He knew lots of things. He knew that when the sun shone across the room a cobwebby shaft appeared that you could not walk up. And when the water dripped on pans in the sink it sang a tune: "Hear the time! Feel the time! Beat with me! Tap-ty tap! T-ta-tap! Ta-ty-tap!" The water sang a tune that made your feet move.

"Stop that jigging, you Denny", Bessie always cried. "God! Don't let him be no dancing man". She would pray afterwards. "Don't let him be no toy-tin fool man"!

Reuben watched him once sitting in his sun shaft. Watched him drape his slender little body along the floor and lift his eyes toward the sunlight. Even then they were eyes that drew deep and told deeper. With his oval clear brown face and his crinkled shining hair, Denny looked too—well, as Reuben thought no boy should look. He spoke:

"Why don't you run and wrestle and race with the other boys? You must be a girl. Boys play rough and fight!"

Denny rolled over and looked up at his father. "I ain't a girl!" he declared deliberately.

He stared around the room for something to fight to prove his assertion. The cat lay peacefully sleeping by the stove. Denny snatched hold of the cat's tail to awaken it. The cat came up with all claws combing Denny.

"My God, ain't he cruel", screamed his mother. She slapped Denny and the cat apart.

Denny lay down under the iron board and considered the odd red patterns that the claws had made on his arms. . . . A red house and a red hill. Red trees around it; a red path running up the hill. . . .

"Make my child do what's right", prayed Bessie, ironing above him.

People are not God. He alone understands.

———

Denny was running full tilt down a hillside. Whooping, yelling, shouting. Flying after nothing. Young Frye Street, mixed as usual, raced with him.

There was no school out here. There were no street cars, no houses, no ash-cans and basement stairs to interfere with a run. Out here you could run straight, swift, in one direction with nothing to stop you but your own lack of foot power and breath. A picnic "out of town" pitched your spirits high and Young Frye Street could soar through all twelve heavens of enjoyment.

The racers reached the foot of the hill. Denny swerved to one side. A tiny colored girl was stooping over in the grass.

"Hey, Denny!" she called. Denny stopped to let the others sweep by.

"Hey, Margaret!" he answered, "What you doing?"

Margaret held up a handful of flowers. "I want that one." She pointed to a clump of dusky purple milkweeds bending behind a bush.

Denny hopped toward it.

He had almost reached it when the bush parted and a boy stepped out: "Don't come over here", he ordered. "This is the white kids' side!"

Denny looked at him. He was not of Frye Street. Other strange children appeared behind him. "This is a white picnic over here! Stay away from our side."

Denny continued toward his flower. Margaret squatted contentedly in the grass. She was going to get her flower.

"I said not to come over here", yelled the boy behind the bush.

Denny hopped around the bush.

"What you want over here?" the other bristled.

"That flower!" Denny pointed.

The other curved his body out in exaggerated childish sarcasm. "Sissy! Picking flowers." He turned to the boys behind him. "Sissy nigger! Picking flowers!"

Denny punched at the boy and snatched at the flower. The other stuck out his foot and Denny dragged him down as he fell. Young Frye Street rushed back up the hill at the primeval howl that set in.

Down on the ground, Denny and the white boy squirmed and kicked. They dug and pounded each other.

"You stay off the white kids' side, nigger!"

"I'm going to get that flower, I am!" Denny dragged his enemy along with him as he lunged toward the bush.

The flower beckoned and bent its stalk. On the white kids' side. Lovely, dusky, purple. Bending toward him. The milky perfume almost reached him. On the white kids' side. He wanted it. He would get it. Something ripped.

Denny left the collar of his blouse in the boy's hand and wrenched loose. He grabbed at the stem. On the white kids' side. Bending to him—slender, bending to him. On the white kids' side. He wanted it. He was going to have it—

The boy caught up to him as he had almost reached the flower. They fell again.—He was going to get that flower. He was going to. Tear the white kid off. Tear the white hands off his throat. Tear the white kid off his arms. Tear the white kid's weight off his chest. He'd move him—

Denny made a twist and slid low to the ground, the other boy beneath him, face downward. He pinned the boy's shoulders to the ground and clutching a handful of blonde hair in either hand, beat his head against the ground.

Young Frye Street sang the song of triumph. Sang it long and loud. Sang it loud enough for Mrs. Bessie Jackson—resting under a clump of trees with other mothers—to hear.

"I know them children is fighting!" she declared and started off in the direction of the yelling.

Halfway she met Margaret, a long milkweed flower dragging in one hand: "Denny", she explained, holding it up.

"I knew it", cried his mother and ran the rest of the way. "Stop killing that child", she screamed as soon as she had neared the mob. She dragged Denny off the boy. Dragged him through the crowd under a tree. Then she began:

"Look at them clothes. Where is your collar at? All I do is try to fix you up and now look at you! Look at you! Even your shirt torn!"

"Just as well him tear that for what he said", Denny offered.

This approximated "sauce" or the last straw or the point of overflow. His mother was staggered. Was there nothing she could do? Unconsciously she looked up to Heaven, then down to earth. A convenient bush flaunted nearby. She pulled it up—by the roots.

—On the white kids' side. The flower he wanted.—

God understands, doesn't He?

———

It had been a hard struggle. Reuben was still bitter and stubborn: "What reason Denny got to go to some art school? What he going to learn there?"

"Art! Painting!" Bessie defended. "The teachers at the high school say he know how to paint special like. He'd ought to go, they said."

"Yes, they said, but they ain't going to pay for him. He ought to go somewhere and do some real man's work. Ain't nothin' but women paddin' up and down, worryin' about paintin'."

"He's going all the same. Them teachers said he was better—!"

"Oh, all right. Let him go."

And Denny went to the Littler Art School. Carried his joyous six-foot, slender, brown self up on Grand Avenue, across, under, the elevated towers—up town. Up town to school.

"Bessie Jackson better put him on a truck like Annie Turner done her Jake", declared colored Frye Street. "Ain't no man got no business spendin' his life learnin' to paint."

"He should earn money! Money!" protested one portion of Frye Street through its hooked noses.

"Let him marry a wife", chuckled the Italians.

"He's going to learn art", said Denny's mother.

Denny went. The Littler School was filled with students of both sexes and of all races and degrees of life. Most of them were sufficiently gifted to be there. Days there when they showed promise. Days there when they doubted their own reasons for coming.

Denny did as well and as badly as the rest. Sometimes he even did things that attracted attention.

He himself always drew attention, for he was tall, straight and had features that were meant to go with the blondest hair and the bluest eyes. He was not blond, though. He was clear shaven and curly haired and brown as any Polynesian. His eyes were still deep drawing—deep telling. Eyes like a sea-going liner that could drift far without getting lost; that could draw deep without sinking.

Some women scrambled to make an impression on him. If they had looked at his mouth they would have withheld their efforts.

Anne Forest was one of the scramblers. She did not know she was scrambling, though. If anyone had told her that she was, she would have exploded, "Why! He is a nigger!"

Anne, you see, was white. She was the kind of girl who made you feel that she thrived on thirty-nine-cent chocolates, fifteen-dollar silk dress sales, twenty-five-cent love stories and much guilty smootchy kissing. If that does not make you sense her water-waved bob, her too carefully rouged face, her too perfumed person, I cannot bring her any nearer to you.

Anne scrambled unconsciously. Denny was an attractive man. Denny knew she was scrambling—so he went further within himself.

Went so far within himself that he did not notice Pauline Hammond who sat next to him.

One day he was mixing paint in a little white dish. Somehow the dish capsized and the paint flowed over the desk and spattered.

"Oh, my heavens!" said a girl's voice.

Denny stood up: "I beg your pardon." He looked across the desk.

Purple paint was splashed along the girl's smock and was even on her shoes.

"Oh, that's all right! No harm done at all", she said pleasantly.

Nice voice. Not jagged or dangling. Denny looked at her again. He dipped his handkerchief into the water and wiped off the shoes.

That done, they sat back and talked to each other. Talked to each other that day and the next day. Several days they talked.

Denny began to notice Pauline carefully. She did not talk to people as if they were strange hard shells she had to crack open to get inside. She talked as if she were already in the shell. In their very shell.

—Not many people can talk that soul-satisfying way. Why? I do not know. I am not God. I do not always understand—.

They talked about work; their life outside of school. Life. Life out in the world. With an artist's eye Denny noted her as she talked. Slender, more figure than heavy form, moulded. Poised. Head erect on neck, neck uplifted on shoulders, body held neither too stiff or too slack. Poised and slenderly moulded as an aristocrat.

They thought together and worked together. Saw things through each other's eyes. They loved each other.

One day they went to a Sargent exhibit—and saw Anne Forest. She gushed and mumbled and declared war on Pauline. She did not know she had declared war, though.

"Pauline Hammond goes out with that nigger Denny Jackson!" she informed all the girls in class next day.

"With a nigger!" The news seeped through the school. Seeped from the President's office on the third floor to the janitor down below the stairs.

Anne Forest only told one man the news. He was Allen Carter. He had taken Pauline to three dances and Anne to one. Maybe Anne was trying to even the ratio when she told him: "Pauline Hammond is rushing a nigger now."

Allen truly reeled. "Pauline! A nigger?"

Anne nodded. "Denny Jackson—or whatever his name is", she hastened to correct herself.

Allen cursed aloud. "Pauline! She's got too much sense for that! It's that nigger rushing after her! Poor little kid! I'll kill him!"

He tore off his smock with a cursing accompaniment. He cursed before Anne. She did not matter. She should have known that before.

Allen tore off the smock and tore along the hall. Tore into a group gathered in a corner bent over a glass case. Denny and Pauline were in the crowd, side by side. Allen walked up to Denny.

"Here you", he pushed his way in between the two. "Let this white girl alone." He struck Denny full in the face.

Denny struck back. All the women—except Pauline—fled to the far end of the room.

The two men fought. Two jungle beasts would have been kinder to each other. These two tore at each other with more than themselves behind every blow.

"Let that white woman alone, nigger! Stay on your own side!" Allen shouted once.—On your own side. On the white kids' side. That old fight—the flower, bending toward him. He'd move the white kid! Move him and get the flower! Move him and get what was his! He seized a white throat in his hands and moved his hands close together!

—

He did move the white kid. Moved him so completely that doctors and doctors and running and wailing could not cause his body to stir again. Moved him so far that Denny was moved to the County Jail.

Everything moved then. The judge moved the jury with pleas to see justice done for a man who had sacrificed his life for the beautiful and the true. The jury moved that the old law held: one life taken, take another.

Denny—they took Denny.

Up at the school the trustees moved. "Be it enacted this day—no Negro student shall enter within these doors—."

The newspapers moved their readers. Sent columns of description of the "hypnotized frail flower under the spell of Black Art". So completely under the spell she had to be taken from the stand for merely screaming in the judge's face: "I loved him! I loved him! I loved him!" until the court ran over with the cries.

Frye Street agreed on one thing only. Bessie and Reuben had tried to raise Denny right.

After that point, Frye Street unmixed itself. Flowed apart.

Frye street—black—was loud in its utterances. "Served Denny right for loving a white woman! Many white niggers as there is! Either Bessie or Reuben must have loved white themselves and was 'shamed to go out open with them. Shame to have that all come out in that child! Now he rottenin' in a murderer's grave!"

White Frye Street held it was the school that had ruined Denny. Had not Frye Street—black and white—played together, worked together, shot crap together, fought together without killing? When a nigger got in school he got crazy.

—

Up on the hillside the clear water pooled. Up on the hillside people came to drink at the pool. If they looked over, they saw themselves. If they had looked deeper—deeper than themselves—they might have seen God.

But they did not.

People do not do that—do they?

They do not always understand. Do they?

God alone—He understands.

DRAB RAMBLES

In the following short story, published in December 1927, Marita O. Bonner offers two portraits. In the first, she relates the tragic life of Peter Jackson, and in the second, she tells of the sad story of Madie Frye. Both Jackson and Frye are victims of racist working conditions that affect their safety and health. Their jobs are delineated as suitable only for what Jackson termed "ignorant black folk."

I am hurt. There is blood on me. You do not care. You do not know me. You do not know me. You do not care. There is blood on me. Sometimes it gets on you. You do not care I am hurt. Sometimes it gets on your hands—on your soul even. You do not care. You do not know me.

You do not care to know me, you say, because we are different. We are different you say.

You are white, you say. And I am black.

You are white and I am black and so we are different, you say. If I am whiter than you, you say I am black.

You do not know me.

I am all men tinged in brown. I am all men with a touch of black. I am you and I am myself.

You do not know me. You do not care, you say.

———

I am an inflow of God, tossing about in the bodies of all men: all men tinged and touched with black.

I am not pure Africa of five thousand years ago. I am you—all men tinged and touched. Not old Africa into somnolence by a jungle that blots out all traces of its antiquity.

I am all men. I am tinged and touched. I am colored. All men tinged and touched; colored in a brown body.

Close all men in a small space, tinge and touch the Space with one blood—you get a check-mated Hell.

A check-mated Hell, seething in a brown body, I am.

I am colored. A check-mated Hell seething in a brown body. You do not know me.

You do not care—you say.

But still, I am you—and all men.

I am colored. A check-mated Hell seething in a brown body.

Sometimes I wander up and down and look. Look at the tinged-in-black, the touched-in-brown. I wander and see how it is with them and wonder how long—how long Hell can seethe before it boils over.

How long can Hell be check-mated?

Or if check-mated can solidify, if this is all it is?

If this is all it is.

THE FIRST PORTRAIT

He was sitting in the corridor of the Out-Patients Department. He was sitting in a far corner well out of the way. When the doors opened at nine o'clock, he had been the first one in. His heart was beating fast. His heart beat faster than it should. No heart should beat so fast that you choke at the throat when you try to breathe. You should not feel it knocking—knocking—knocking—now against your ribs, now against something deep within you. Knocking against something deep, so deep that you cannot fall asleep without feeling a cutting, pressing weight laid against your throat, over your chest. A cutting, pressing weight that makes you struggle to spring from the midst of your sleep. Spring up.

It had beat like that now for months. At first he had tried to work it off. Swung the pick in his daily ditch digging—faster—harder. But that had not helped it at all. It had beaten harder and faster for the swinging. He had tried castor-oil to run it off of his system. Someone told him he ate too much meat and smoked too much. So he had given up his beloved ham and beef and chicken and tried to swing the pick on lighter things.

It would be better soon.

His breath had began to get short then. He had to stop oftener to rest between swings. The foreman, Mike Leary, had cursed at first and then moved him back to the last line of diggers. It hurt him to think he was not so strong as he had been.—But it would be better soon.

———

He would not tell his wife how badly his heart knocked. It would be better soon. He could not afford to lay off from work. He had to dig. Nobody is able to lay off work when there is a woman and children to feed and cover.

The castor oil had not helped. The meat had been given up, even his little pleasure in smoking. Still the heart beat too fast. Still the heart beat so he felt it up in the chords on each side of his neck below his ears.—But it would be better soon.

It would be better. He had asked to be let off half a day so he could be at the hospital at ten o'clock. Mike had growled his usual curses when he asked to get off.

"What the hell is wrong wit' you? All you need is a good dose of whiskey!"

He had gone off. When the doors of the Out-Patients Department opened, he was there. It took him a long time to get up the stairs. The knocking was in his throat so. Beads of perspiration stood grey on his black-brown forehead. He closed his eyes a moment and leaned his head back.

A sound of crying made him open them. On the seat beside him a woman held a baby in her arms. The baby was screaming itself red in the face, wriggling and twisting to get out of its mother's arms on the side where the man sat. The mother shifted the child from one side to the other and told him with her eyes, "You ought not to be here!"

———

He had tried to smile over the knocking at the baby. Now he rolled his hat over in his hands and looked down.

When he looked up, he turned his eyes away from the baby and its mother. The knocking pounded. Why should a little thing like that make his heart pound. He must be badly off to breathe so fast over nothing. The thought made his heart skip and pound the harder.

But he would be better soon.

Other patients began to file in. Soon the nurse at the desk began to read names aloud. He had put his card in first but she did not call him first. As she called each name, a patient stood up and went through some swinging doors.

Green lights—men in white coats—nurses in white caps and dresses filled the room it would seem, from the glimpses caught through the door. It seemed quiet and still, too, as if everyone were listening to hear something.

Once the door swung open wildly and an Italian came dashing

madly through—a doctor close behind him. The man threw himself on a bench: "Oh God! Oh God! I ain't that sick, I ain't so sick I gotta die! No! You don't really know. I ain't so sick!"

The doctor leaned over him and said something quietly. The nurse brought something cloudy in a glass. The man drank it. By and by he was led out—hiccuping but quieter.

———

Back in his corner, his heart beat smotheringly. Suppose that had been he? Sick enough to die! Was the dago crazy, trying to run away? Run as he would, the sickness would be always with him. For himself, he would be better soon.

"Peter Jackson! Peter Jackson. Peter Jackson. Five, Sawyer Avenue!" The nurse had to say it twice before he heard through his thoughts.

Thump. The beat of his heart knocked him to his feet. He had to stand still before he could move.

"Here! This way." The nurse said it so loudly—so harshly—that the entire room turned around to look at him.

She need not be so hateful. He only felt a little dizzy. Slowly he felt along the floor with his feet. Around the corner of the bench. Across the space beside the desk. The nurse pushed open the door and pressed it back. "Dr. Sibley?" she called.

The door swung shut behind him. Along each side of the room were desks. Behind each, sat a doctor. When the nurse called "Dr. Sibley", no one answered, so Jackson stood at the door. His heart rubbed his ribs unnecessarily.

"Say! Over here!"

The words and the voice made his heart race again.—But he would be better now. He turned toward the direction of the voice, met a cool pair of blue eyes boring through tortoise-rimmed glasses. He sat down.

The doctor took a sheet of paper. "What's your name?"

———

His heart had been going so that when he said "Peter Jackson", he could make no sound the first time.

"What's your name, I said."

"Peter Jackson."

"How old are you?"

"Fifty-four."

"Occupation? Where do you work?"

"Day laborer for the city."

"Can you afford to pay a doctor?"

Surprise took the rest of his breath away for a second. The question had to be repeated.

"I guess so. I never been sick."

"Well, if you can afford to pay a doctor, you ought not to come here. This clinic is for foreigners and people who cannot pay a doctor. Your people have some of your own doctors in this city."

The doctor wrote for such a long time on the paper then that he thought he was through with him and he started to get up.

"Sit down." The words caught him before he was on his feet. "I haven't told you to go anywhere."

"I thought—," Jackson hung on his words uncertain.

"You needn't! Don't think! Open your shirt." And the doctor fitted a pair of tubes in his ears and shut out his thoughts.

He fitted the tubes in his ears and laid a sieve-like piece of rubber against his patient's chest. Laid it up. Laid it down. Finally he said: "What have you been doing to this heart of yours? All to pieces. All gone."

Gone. His heart was all gone. He tried to say something but the doctor snatched the tube away and turned around to the desk and wrote again.

Again he turned around: "Push up your sleeve," he said this time.

The sleeve went up. A piece of rubber went around his arm above the elbow. Something began to squeeze—knot—drag on his arm.

"Pressure almost two hundred," the doctor shot at him this time. "You can't stand this much longer."

He turned around. He wrote again. He wrote and pushed the paper away. "Well," said the doctor, "you will have to stop working and lie down. You must keep your feet on a level with your body."

Jackson wanted to yell with laughter. Lie down. If he had had breath enough, he would have blown all the papers off the desk, he would have laughed so. He looked into the blue eyes. "I can't stop work," he said.

The doctor shrugged: "Then," he said, and said no more.

Then! Then what?

Neither one of them spoke.

Then what?

Jackson wet his lips: "You mean—you mean I got to stop work to get well?"

"I mean you have to stop if you want to stay here."

"You mean even if I stop you may not cure me?"

The blue eyes did go down toward the desk then. The answer was a question.

"You don't think I can make a new heart, do you? You only get one heart. You are born with that. You ought not to live so hard."

Live hard? Did this man think he had been a sport? Live hard. Liquor, wild sleepless nights—sleep-drugged, rag-worn, half-shoddy days? That instead of what it had been. Ditches and picks. Births and funerals. Stretching a dollar the length of ten. A job, no job; three children and a wife to feed; bread thirteen cents a loaf. For pleasure, church—where he was too tired to go sometimes. Tobacco that he had to consider twice before he bought.

"I ain't lived hard! I ain't lived hard!" he said suddenly. "I have worked harder than I should, that's all."

"Why didn't you get another job?" the doctor snapped. "Didn't need to dig ditches all your life."

Jackson drew himself up; "I had to dig ditches because I am an ignorant black man. If I was an ignorant white man, I could get easier jobs. I could even have worked in this hospital."

Color flooded the doctor's face. Whistles blew and shrieked suddenly outside.

Twelve o'clock. Mike would be looking for him.

He started for the door. Carefully. He must not waste his strength. Rent, food, clothes. He could not afford to lay off.

He had almost reached the door when a hand shook him suddenly. It was the doctor close behind him. He held out a white sheet of paper: "Your prescription," he explained, and seemed to hesitate. "Digitalis. It will help some. I am sorry."

Sorry for what? Jackson found the side-walk and lit his pipe to steady himself. He had almost reached the ditches when he remembered the paper. He could not find it. He went on.

THE SECOND PORTRAIT

By twelve o'clock, noon, the washroom of Kale's Fine Family Laundry held enough steam to take the shell off of a turtle's back. Fill tubs with steaming water at six o'clock, set thirty colored women to rubbing and shouting and singing at the tubs and by twelve o'clock noon the room is over full of steam. The steam is thick—warm—and it settles on your flesh like a damp fur rug. Every pore sits agape in your body; agape—dripping.

Kale's Fine Family Laundry did a good business. Mr. Kale believed in this running on oiled cogs. Cogs that slip easily—oiled from the lowest to the highest.

Now the cogs lowest in his smooth machinery were these thirty tubs and the thirty women at the tubs. I put the tubs first, because they were always there. The women came and went. Sometimes they merely went. Most all of them were dark brown and were that soft bulgy fat that no amount of hard work can rub off of some colored women. All day long they rubbed and scrubbed and sang or shouted and cursed or were silent according to their thirty natures.

Madie Frye never sang or shouted or cursed aloud. Madie was silent. She sang and shouted and cursed within. She sang the first day she came there to work. Sang songs of thanksgiving within her. She had needed that job. She had not worked for ten months until she came there. She had washed dishes in a boarding house before that. That was when she first came from Georgia. She had liked things then. Liked the job, liked the church she joined, liked Tom Nolan, the man for whom she washed dishes.

———

One day his wife asked Madie if she had a husband. She told her no. She was paid off. Madie, the second, was born soon after. Madie named her unquestioningly Madie Frye. It never occurred to her to name her Nolan, which would have been proper.

Madie bore her pain in silence, bore her baby in a charity ward, thanked God for the kindness of a North and thanked God that she was not back in Culvert when Madie was born, for she would have been turned out of church.

Madie stopped singing aloud then. She tried to get jobs—dishwashing—cleaning—washing clothes—but you cannot keep a job washing someone's clothes or cleaning their house and nurse a baby and keep it from yelling the lady of the house into yelling tantrums.

Madie, second, lost for her mother exactly two dozen jobs between her advent and her tenth month in her mother's arms.

Madie had not had time to feel sorry for herself at first. She was too busy wondering how long she could hold each job. Could she keep Madie quiet until she paid her room rent? Could she keep Mrs. Jones from knowing that Madie was down under the cellar stairs in a basket every day while she was upstairs cleaning, until she got a pair of shoes?

By the time she went to work in Kale's Fine Family Laundry, she had found the baby a too great handicap to take to work. She began to leave Madie with her next door neighbor, Mrs. Sundell, who went to church three times every Sunday and once in the week. She must be good enough to keep Madie while her mother worked. She was. She kept Madie for two dollars a week and Madie kept quiet for her and slept all night long when she reached home with her mother. Her mother marvelled and asked Mrs. Sundell how she did it.

"Every time she cries, I give her paregoric. Good for her stomach."

———

So the baby grew calmer and calmer each day. Calmer and quieter. Her mother worked and steamed silently down in Kale's tub-room. Worked, shouting songs of thanksgiving within her for steady money and peaceful nights.

June set in, and with it, scorching days. Days that made the thick steam full of lye and washing-powder eat the lining out of your lungs. There was a set of rules tacked up inside the big door that led into the checking-room that plainly said: "This door is never to be opened between the hours of six in the morning and twelve noon. Nor between the hours of one and six p.m."

That was to keep the steam from the checkers. They were all white and could read and write so they were checkers.

One day Madie put too much lye in some boiling water. It choked her. When she drew her next breath, she was holding her head in the clean cool air of the checking-room. She drew in a deep breath and coughed. A man spun across the floor and a white hand shot to the door. "Why the hell don't you obey rules?" He slammed the door and Madie stumbled back down the stairs.

A girl at the end tub looked around. "Was that Mr. Payne?" she asked.

Madie was still dazed; "Mr. Payne?" she asked.

"Yah. The man what closed the door."

"I don't know who he was."

The other laughed and drew closer to her. "Better know who he is," she said.

Madie blinked up at her. "Why?"

The girl cocked an eye: "Good to know him. You can stay off sometimes—if he likes you." That was all that day.

———

Another day Madie was going home. Her blank brown face was freshly powdered and she went quietly across the checking-room. The room was empty it seemed at first. All the girls were gone. When Madie was half across the room she saw a man sitting in the corner behind a desk. He looked at her as soon as she looked at him. It was the man who had yanked the door out of her hand, she thought. Fear took hold of her. She began to rush.

Someone called. It was the man at the desk. "Hey, what's your rush?" The voice was not loud and bloody this time. It was soft—soft—soft—like a cat's foot. Madie stood still afraid to go forward—afraid to turn around.

"What, are you afraid of me?" Soft like a cat's foot. "Come here."

—Good to know him—

Madie made the space to the outer door in one stride. The door opened in. She pushed against it.

"Aw, what's the matter with you?" Foot-steps brought the voice nearer. A white hand fitted over the doorknob as she slid hers quickly away.

———

Madie could not breathe. Neither could she lift her eyes. The door opened slowly. She had to move backwards to give it space. Another white hand brushed the softness of her body.

She stumbled out into the alley. Cold sweat stood out on her.

Madie second had cost her jobs and jobs. She came by Madie keeping that first job.

Madie was black brown. The baby was yellow. Was she now going to go job hunting or have a sister or brother to keep with Madie second?

Cold perspiration sent her shivering in the alley.

And Madie cursed aloud.

———

Not in my day or your tomorrow—perhaps—but somewhere in God's day of meting—somewhere in God's day of measuring full measures overflowing—the blood will flow back to you—and you will care.

THE MAN WHO WANTED TO BE RED

In this short story, Frank Horne writes about a young man named Juda. His people are "Greeners." The "great red men" consider the Greeners beasts without souls. Juda works on an experiment hoping to change the Greeners to red so that there will be one race. But as he progresses, he begins to wonder if once the Greeners become red they will possess the same hard-heartedness and cruel nature as the reds. This story was published in July 1928.

Once upon a time in the far away Kingdom of Ur there lived a young man called Juda. Juda lived in an age when science ruled the world. Men who had gone before him had wrestled with the problems of the universe, torn from nature her innermost secrets, solved her deepest mysteries, harnessed her to earthly machines to do their work. It was a golden age; riches flowed throughout the land, great buildings thrust climbing towers into the sky. The streets were filled with busy people rearing fresh columns to the gods they worshipped; great schools rose at every hand where the young learned from the old how to fill their pockets with gold, how to become worshippers in the Temples of the Golden Calf. But these things meant little to Juda; for Juda's people were Greeners, and the Greeners were like the earth under foot and the dogs in the alley.

Now it so happened that the kings and princes of the land, and all their busy followers were people of great beauty, tall and straight with long hair, golden as the sky at the break of day, and their skins a gorgeous red, like the heart of a flame, and a blazing ruby and the western sky when the sun goes down. And they owned the land, and possessed all that was in it, and far back in their history, the councilors and the elders realized that some one was needed in the kingdom to till the fields, and hew the wood and draw the water. So the traders manned their ships and sailed across the seas to a far country where they found a peculiar people roaming the forests. These people wore no clothes, and lived in huts and had no money, but their bodies were strong and their muscles glistened in the sun and their skin was green, green as an emerald is green and the leaves of a laughing tree and water in deep places. The great red men looked upon them and shook their heads wisely and said one to the other:

"These people cannot talk as we talk; they worship no gods like ours; they do not live in beautiful houses as we do."

And others said, "Yes, and they roam the woods like beasts, and they laugh and make merry, but have no clothes, nor books, nor churches. Surely they have no souls, but their bodies are strong and we can use them."

And they all agreed, "Yes, they have no souls and we can use them."

So they fell upon these people, who were Juda's people, and took them from their homes, and the forests they seemed to love and tied them up like cattle and threw them into the dark holds of the ships and set sail for home. All the way back, these green women moaned, and searched for their children, and made sounds very much like red people in agony, and the big green men, bound and tied, sat and stared like children lost in a wood, grown tired with futile running. And sometimes down in the dark bowels of the ships they sang, and their singing was like the breaking of many hearts. But the great red men on the decks stopped up their ears and said one to the other, "They are beasts and have no souls," and went their way.

And so Juda's people came to the Kingdom of Ur and were locked in hovels away from their forests and great red men with whips and lashes were put over them; they were driven into the fields before the sun had risen, and all the long day till darkness came, the green people worked in the teeming sun; and sometimes, when the sun was too hot and the labors hard, they would pause in their work, and the beaters would fall upon them with whips and lashes, and curses and drive them back to their labors. Throughout the length and breadth of the land, these slaves became known as "Greeners," and were regarded like beasts of the field.

Juda's people had lost their freedom, and their homes, and their families and the comradeship of the forests, and instead they were bound into slavery, crowded into dirty huts, beaten at the least provocation, and still their laughter ran like the rippling waters of their far country and they sang their songs to their own gods. In the deep still nights the red men awakened to hear sad, beautiful melodies rising out of the huts and some of them tossed in their beds and wondered at this thing. And soon, too, other red men looked upon these green women and found their bodies fair, and took them, so that there gradually arose a race of people neither red nor green, but shading from the paleness of a summer sky before the dawning to the soft whiteness of new fallen snow. These people became known as the "whites" and they were hated on all sides. The red men saw some of their blood in them and hated them for it; the Greeners, while these were their own children, were uncomfortable in their presence, so in the Kingdom of Ur, the "whites" became the outcasts and the scourged of both races.

—

Juda was a "white". His father was a red man called Moda from a far country. He was a scientist and a chemist of great renown. Juda's mother was a Greener who had slaved in Moda's house. Moda had been a kind man. He studied long in old mysterious books; sometimes he worked for days in his laboratory at the top of the house, days in which he neither slept nor paused for eating. And Juda's mother administered to him, and cared for him and fed him. As Juda grew, Moda took him into his work room; slowly disclosed to him his discoveries, taught him to analyze, to create, to understand. Juda's mind was keen and his hand nimble. As Moda aged, he leaned more and more upon Juda, till one dark night, after three uninterrupted days on one experiment, even while he was calling off to Juda the readings on the thermometer, he crumpled and fell before the apparatus. Juda jumped to his side. Moda looked into his eyes, whispered "Juda," softly, like a dying wind in a strong tree, and spoke no more.

And Juda worked on in the days to follow. When Moda had died, they were in the midst of an awesome discovery. Together they had built a vacuum tube, larger, more powerful than had ever been made. They had liberated a flying stream of electrons catapulting through space with the velocity of light. In the path of this terrific bombardment, they had placed many objects and noted many wondrous changes. Placed in a lead chamber at the end of the tube, he had seen the electronic stream change rabbit's hair snow white after an exposure of one-tenth of a second, seen it change white salt to brown, and the pure white glass of his apparatus to a deep royal purple.

—

One night many months after Moda's death, Juda lay in bed and as was his custom before he fell asleep, he thought of his experiments of the day. That very morning he had subjected three blades of grass to the mysterious reagent he had discovered. When he turned off the current and opened the lead chamber, where the three green blades had lain, were three red streaks, red like the heart of a flame and a blazing ruby and the western sky when the sun goes down. Now as he thought of it, a sudden tremendous thought fired his brain. He shivered with the audacity of the idea. It startled him so that he rose quickly, drew on his robe, and climbed quietly to his laboratory. The moon flooded the room with a silver flood; the glassware and metal of his complex apparatus gleamed at him like some grinning, twisted gargoyle. He pressed the switch and awakened the room with light. He stepped hurriedly to the apparatus, opened the door of the chamber and there, as if to clear his doubt, lay the three red wisps, just as he had left them. His hands trembled as he held them and an ecstatic joyousness pervaded his being. He shut off the light, ran down the stairs to the door of his mother's room. He opened it quietly and looked in. She was sleeping peacefully, and his eyes looked long upon the gorgeous green of her arm, which had slipped from under the cover. He hesitated for a moment, then closed the door softly and returned to his room. He threw himself upon his bed but the wildness of his vision would not let him sleep. He tossed and turned and his thoughts ran riot till the first grayness crept up into the sky. He heard his mother stirring down below. He drew on his clothes and hurried to her room. As she sat upon the side of her bed and he at her knees, Juda, in a flood of eager language, told her of his experiment . . . of his discovery . . . of his own vision. She listened closely, her eyes growing tender as her son breathlessly unfolded his plan. He told her of his hope and his desire. He asked that she help him. With calm resignation, she answered him:

"Yes, my Juda."

He left her and rushing aloft to his laboratory returned in a trice with a bottle, some gauze and cotton and a thin sharp scalpel in his hands. His mother had meanwhile bared her body to the waist, and at his request she lay at full length upon the bed, with the broad expanse of her back uppermost. Juda had become again the eager scientist, like a full-bred hound upon a scent. He knelt over his mother and swabbed a space in the small of her back, and then very carefully, painstakingly with the little blade, he peeled off a two-inch square of her emerald skin. Every now and then a slight quiver of the flesh was the mother's only response. He deftly dressed the open place, placed the precious green square between two thin glass plates, kissed his mother silently upon the cheek, and ran again for the stairs, leaving the door swinging open in his haste.

———

Into his laboratory again, and now all his fervor and haste seemed to have left him. Slowly and carefully, with continual reference to his notes he remounted his apparatus; made sure of all the connections, all the supports, all the glassware; made new parts, tested out old ones, checked the electric circuit, modulated its force, tried auxiliary experiments to be sure his apparatus was ready and correct in every detail.

At last all was ready. The sun was already sinking like a flaming ball, when he slowly opened the heavy leaden door of the exposure chamber, and placed in position the glass plates, containing between them the little square of his mother's skin. He closed the door firmly, took one final look at the vacuum tube, then with a last audible intake of breath, he threw the switch which sent the current leaping across the electrodes of the gigantic tube. A low, ominous hum filled the air, and slowly a glowing aura surrounded the end of the tube and he seemed to see the flying ions catapulting into the leaden chamber with the speed of a ray of light. His chronometer lay upon the stone table and his eyes were glued upon its crawling hand . . . one minute . . . two minutes . . . 25 seconds . . . With a quick motion, he threw back the switch. The humming ceased, the aura gradually faded and after waiting an eternal space, he threw open the door of the chamber, reached in and drew forth the two glass plates, and between them he saw a square of gorgeous red . . . red like the heart of a flame, and a blazing ruby and the western sky where the sun was even now setting like a fiery ball. A cry of ecstatic joy arose in his heart. He wanted to shriek from his windows into the streets below, "Eureka! Eureka!" Then suddenly there seemed to wail through the recesses of his mind, the sorrow of his beloved people . . . the sorrow song of the Greeners . . .

Go down
Moses
Way down in Egypt's Land
Tell old Pharaoh
To let ma' people go—

His heart swelled in his breast. He would be a prophet to his people, he would strike off from their hearts the chains of slavery, he would bring joy and peace to the down-trodden. A golden, spilling cry seemed to fill the sky, darkening before the dying rays of the sinking sun.

———

Juda ran to his mother; shared with her his precious secret, but she, though she wept in joy at his triumph, said no word, soothing his throbbing head against her breast. How long he lay there, he did not know, but night had fallen and he left the house to walk into the streets. He felt the impulse to feast his eyes upon the things he would change. His path carried him past the dirty hovels of the Greeners, the children rolling and playing in the filthy streets; the big green men, drunk with bodily fatigue, sprawled upon the floors, asleep or hopelessly staring into space; the green women futilely striving for some order in the chaos. These things had saddened Juda, but tonight a wild joy was his; those people too, would have the beauties and the joys of life; they too, would inherit the riches of the Kingdom of Ur; they, too, would bear red children!

Farther up he went into the rich city past the glorious houses of the red men, past their temples of worship and their buildings of trade and Juda was thrilled with the joy of it; these, things, too, would be shared by his people. He paused in front of a beautiful bazaar, gay with lights and color. He heard sharp words and stepped closer to the door. There stood a Greener, who seemed to be attempting to buy something. The red men snarled at him like angry dogs, and when he quietly replied, they struck him in the mouth and the blood came. Another hit him from behind, then several set upon him and threw him from the place, his body falling at Juda's feet with a sickening thud. The red men turned, not even looking to see whether he lived or not. The joy died suddenly in Juda's heart. He lifted the Greener to his feet; the man looked sadly into Juda's eyes, and saying nothing, dragged his broken body off into the night. Juda looked back and the red men had forgotten and gone their ways; he looked off in the dark and he seemed to hear a voice, saying

> Forgive them
> They know not what they do ...

———

A strange feeling arose in Juda, and as he turned his steps for home, an ever growing doubt seemed to be tearing at the glory of his dream. Would his discovery make his people's heart like that? Would it make them beasts too ... would it make their hearts hard like these buildings? ... these torturous doubts swamped his mind and filled him with a great fear. Back he went through the streets of the Greeners and he heard the deep, joyous laughter of his people, the abandon and hope of their singing, the ecstatic cries of the children as they played in the streets. From far down the road, he heard them chanting:

> My Lord's
> Gonna move this wicked race
> O Lord
> This wicked race
> Gonna raise up a nation
> Shall obey ...

He stood listening for a long space at his doorway. He turned and climbed the steps like a man grown suddenly old and weary of his heavy burden. At the door of his mother's room, he paused. It was late but he could hear her and he went in. She looked into his face, and saw the sadness written there. She again said no word, but drew his head again upon her breast, and as he sobbed as though his heart had broken, she held him tightly, and in her eyes a strange light burned. After a long space, he left her silently, and this time his step upon the stairs was firmer and his eyes again flashed brightly. He stepped into his beloved laboratory which he had left so triumphantly but a short space before. He pressed the light button and walked up to the gleaming apparatus. He looked at it long and lovingly. His gaze travelled along the stone-topped table, and stopped suddenly upon the thick book of notes that still lay open where he had left it. There lay all of the heart-aches, all the successes, all the milestones along the weary march of his discovery. There lay the liberation of a race, the freedom of a people. For but a moment he paused, then with a quick movement, closed the book, lifted it from the table and carried it to the side of the room where his bunsen flame was still burning. He thrust its pages into the flame, and as the thin smoke arose, he felt as though his dreams, and Moda's too, were dying there. He held it in his fingers till the flames licked too close. Then he pitched it under the hood, and watched it long till the embers died in the ashes. With the last spark, something seemed to fade in his brain, and he stood dazed and weakened at the thing he had done. He turned back to his table and his apparatus. His fingers toyed absently with some colored bits of cloth, remnants of some past experiment. Something he saw aroused him. A new thought, a fresh question awoke in his brain. He hurriedly made a few adjustments, mounted a piece of colored cloth and threw his switch. He reached down into a drawer of the table, took out a clean, fresh notebook, and after reading the thermometer, began writing . . .

"It is noticed that at a temperature of 40 degrees C and at a pressure of three atmospheres, the electronic stream increases . . ."

PART THREE

PLAYS

ON THE FIELDS OF FRANCE

This one-act play was written by Joseph Seamon Cotter, Jr., who died in 1919. This play was published posthumously in June 1920.

PERSONS REPRESENTED

A WHITE AMERICAN OFFICER

A COLORED AMERICAN OFFICER

TIME—PRESENT

PLACE—BATTLEFIELD OF NORTHERN FRANCE

(Curtain rises on White American Officer and Colored American Officer, both mortally wounded.)

WHITE OFFICER *(Rises on elbow and sees someone across field. Speaks slowly as if in pain)*—I say there, my good fellow, have you a drop of water to spare? The Boches have about done for me, I fear.

COLORED OFFICER *(Turns over)*—Who calls?

WHITE OFFICER *(Sees that he is a fellow-officer)*—It is I, a fellow-officer, my friend. A shell has gone through my body and the fever has parched my lips. Have you a drop to spare?

COLORED OFFICER *(Speaks in catches)*—I am—about done for— myself. They've got me—through the lung. I've enough water—to moisten our—lips about as long—as either of—us will be here. *(They drag themselves across toward each other. They get close enough to touch hands.*

COLORED OFFICER *hands his canteen to* WHITE OFFICER, *who moistens his lips and hands it back.)*

WHITE OFFICER—That is much better, my friend. I have been lying here for several hours, it seems, waiting for someone. We went over the Boches' trenches in a bombing squad and they got me coming back.

COLORED OFFICER—I was range-finding—and the snipers—got me. I have been dragging—myself towards our trenches—for an hour or so. I got this—far and decided to—stop and close my eyes—and wait for the—end here. It won't be—far off anywhere. (WHITE OFFICER'S *strength begins to fail and he slips back.* COLORED OFFICER *takes his hand and he raises himself up with an effort and speaks.)*

WHITE OFFICER—I thought I was gone then. My strength is going fast. Hold my hand. It won't feel so lonesome dying way over here in France.

COLORED OFFICER *(Takes his hand)*—I feel much better—myself. After all—it isn't so hard—to die when—you are dying—for Liberty.

WHITE OFFICER—Do you feel that way too? I've often wondered how your people felt. We've treated you so bally mean over home that I've wondered if you could feel that way. I've been as guilty as the rest, maybe more so than some. But that was yesterday—What is that I see? *(Rises with unbelievable strength and points toward the heavens.)* Do you see it? It is a white-haired figure clad in the Old Continentals, standing there within the gates of heaven. And he is beckoning for me. It is Washington.

COLORED OFFICER—*(Speaks excitedly and rapidly.)* I see him, I see him. And who is that beside him with his swarthy chest bare and torn? It is Attucks—Crispus Attucks, and he beckons to me. *(He gasps for breath, fatigued with his rapid talk.)*

WHITE OFFICER—They stand hand in hand. And there is Lee. He beckons to me. Those serried hosts behind him,—they're Forrest and his men. They call to me to join them.

COLORED OFFICER—*(Speaks slowly now, gasping for breath all the while.)* And there is—Carney with the Old Flag—still in the air. And back of—him, those swarthy—hosts, they're Shaw—and his black—heroes. And they—beckon to me.

WHITE OFFICER—*(Slips back on elbow.)* They stand hand in hand over there and we die hand in hand here on the fields of France. Why couldn't we have lived like this at home? They beckon to us, to you and to me. It is one country she will some day be, in truth as well as in spirit—the country of Washington and Attucks, *(speaks slowly and painfully)* of Lee and Carney. The country of the whites and the country of the blacks. *Our* country!

WHITE OFFICER AND COLORED OFFICER—*(together)* America! *(They fall back hand in hand as their life blood ebbs away.)*

THE BROKEN BANJO

This prize-winning play, written by Willis Richardson, was published in the March and April 1926 issues of *The Crisis*. Richardson also offers a brief biography of his life.

"I was born in Wilmington, N. C., November 5, 1889, and lived there until the riot of 1898, after which my parents came to Washington where I obtained whatever school education I have in the secondary and high schools. After being graduated from the M St. High School in 1910 I began working in the government service and began a serious study of Poetry, Drama and the Novel.

"When I considered myself sufficiently well prepared I began to write plays, the first of which, besides four children's plays for THE BROWNIES' BOOK, was 'The Deacon's Awakening', brought to public view in THE CRISIS of November, 1920, and staged the following year at St. Paul, Minn. This was not much of a success and I remained unheard of until The Ethiopian Art Players under Raymond O'Neil very successfully produced 'The Chip Woman's Fortune' in Chicago, Washington and on Broadway in 1923. The following year my third play, 'Mortgaged', was staged by the Howard Players of Howard University under Montgomery Gregory and Alain Locke; and in May, 1925, the same play was staged by the Dunbar Dramatic Club in a Drama Tournament at Plainfield, N. J. The rare thing about this occasion was that out of the eight or ten clubs producing plays, one Negro club produced a Negro play by a Negro author. The play, which I consider one of my poorest, gained fourth place among some of the best American one-acters.

"Besides the production of 'The Broken Banjo' under the auspices of THE CRISIS in August, 1925, 'The Chip Woman's Fortune' is promised a production in November by The Negro Art Players, and 'Rooms For Rent', a new play, is promised production by the same group in December. This is all save that 'The New Negro' contains a new play, 'Compromise', in which I have some confidence. My disappointment is that up to the present time none of my three-act plays has had an opportunity to be made visible."

CHARACTERS

Matt Turner.
Emma, his wife.
Sam, her brother.
Adam, her cousin.
A policeman.

The dining room of Matt and Emma Turner is still and dark-looking, with a door at the right leading to the outside and at the left leading through the kitchen. There is a square table in the center of the room with two chairs, the only ones in the room, near it. A cupboard is at the rear and at the right of this is a window. At the left side below the door is a small closet concealed by curtains. When the play begins Matt, a short strongly-built man of thirty, is sitting at the left of the table picking a banjo. He is not by any means a good player, but his desire to play well is his religion. He plays on for a few minutes until his wife, Emma, a woman of twenty-seven, appears at the kitchen door.

EMMA. *(In disagreeable tone.)*—Matt, for Gawd's sake stop that noise.

MATT. *(Looking up and stopping for a moment.)*—What the devil's the matter with you?

EMMA.— Ah got a headache and Ah'm tired o' hearin' that bum music. It's a wonder you wouldn' find somethin' else to do. You c'n come out in the back yard and split me some wood if you want to.

MATT.— Didn' Ah work all night? You think Ah'm goin' to work all night then come home and split wood in the day time? If you don't like this music put your head in a bag, then you won't hear it.

EMMA.—You ain't got no feelin's for nobody but yourself. You just got that old job, and before you got it Ah had to work ma hands almost off to keep things going; this is the thanks Ah get for what Ah done.

MATT.— You needn' throw that in ma face; you didn' have to work if you didn' want to.

EMMA.— If Ah hadn' a' worked we'd a' gone to the poorhouse.

MATT.— Maybe we would a' been better off.

EMMA.— If you wasn' so selfish you'd get along better; but you don't care a thing about nobody or nothin' but that old banjo.

MATT.— Is Ah got any cause to care about anything else?

EMMA.— How about me?

MATT.— Well, that's diff'ent. If Ah didn' care nothin' about you Ah would 'a' been gone long ago. But what about me? Don't eve'ybody in town hate me? Don't your whole family despise the very ground Ah walk on?

EMMA.— It ain't their fault.

MATT.— It is their fault. Didn' they all try to stop me from comin' to see you? Didn't Ah have to beat the devil out o' that black brother and cousin o' yours before they'd let me alone? And don't they hate me for it?

EMMA. *(Defending her family.)*—Now, don't start to callin' nobody black, 'cause you ain't got no room to call nobody black. Sam and Adam is just as light as you is.

MATT.— Maybe they is, but they ain't as honest, and they ain't nothin' but loafin' jail-birds.

EMMA.— Ah don't see where you get nothin' by throwin' that at me.

MATT.—You know it's the truth; and you know Ah ain't never been to jail.

EMMA.—It ain't too late; don't be braggin'.

MATT.—You talk like you'd like to see me go to jail.

EMMA.—You ought to have better sense than that.

MATT.—Well, here's somethin' Ah want to tell you about Sam and Adam before Ah forget.

EMMA.—What?

MATT.—Ah want you to keep 'em out o' here. They don't do nothin' but loaf around all the time and come here to eat eve'ything they c'n get.

EMMA.—Sam and Adam ain't doin' nobody no harm.

MATT.—Yes, they is; they're doin' me harm.

EMMA.—How's they doin' you harm?

MATT.—They come here and eat up ma grub, then go round talkin' about me. Ah wouldn' mind givin' 'em a bite now and then if they was friends o' mine.

EMMA.—Is you got any friends at all?

MATT.—No, Ah ain't got no friends. Ain't anybody likes me but you, and you ain't crazy about me.

EMMA.—Well, you oughtn' to be so disagreeable, then you would have some friends.

MATT.—Ah don't know, Ah recken Ah gets along just as well without 'em.

EMMA.—No, you don't. Ain't nobody gets along just as well without friends.

MATT.—When you ain't got so many friends you ain't got so many people to come around and eat you up.

EMMA.—Ain't nothin' in bein' so stingy.

MATT.—Ah ain't givin' nobody nothin'; that's why Ah'm tellin' you to tell them two fools to keep out o' here.

EMMA.—Ah ain't goin' to insult nobody.

MATT.—If you don't tell 'em Ah will; cause Ah don't want 'em in here. That settles it.

EMMA.—Ah ain't makin' no more enemies. We got enemies enough.

MATT.—You don't look out for ma int'rest much.

EMMA.—Yes, Ah do; Ah'm thinkin' for you eve'y minute o' ma life, but you don't know it. You never will know it till you get in a big pinch.

MATT.—There ain't no use of us quarrelin'. We quarrel too much anyhow, Ah reckon.

EMMA.—Ah reckon so too.

(He begins to pick his banjo again and after looking at him for a moment half fondly she goes back to the kitchen. There are a few minutes of silence save the picking of the banjo. Presently Emma reappears at the door and addresses Matt in kinder tones.)

EMMA.—Matt!

MATT.—Huh?

EMMA.—Is you got any money?

MATT.—No.

EMMA.—That's mighty funny.

MATT.—Funny how?

EMMA.—You workin' eve'y night makin' good wages, and you don't give me nothin' but the money to run the house. What does you do with the rest of it?

(Matt is silent.)

　　—You mean you ain't got a cent, Matt?

MATT.—Ah ain't got no spare money.

EMMA.—No spare money?

MATT.—No.

EMMA.—Well, what is you got?

MATT.—Ah got five dollars Ah was savin' to buy some music with.

EMMA.—You wouldn't buy music when Ah need the money for somethin' else, would you, Matt?

MATT.—What you need money for?

EMMA.—Ah need shoes for one thing.

MATT.—Ah need shoes too.

EMMA. *(Coming forward and showing her worn shoes.)*—Look at mine.

MATT. *(Looking at them.)*—They is pretty bad.

EMMA.—There ain't nothin' to 'em but uppers.

MATT.—How much your shoes goin' to cost?

EMMA.—Ah don't know. You c'n get 'em second handed if you want to. You ought to get a good second handed pair for two or three dollars.

MATT.—Ah tell you what Ah'll do.

EMMA.—What?

MATT.—Ah'll get you them shoes if you'll tell Sam and Adam to keep out o' here.

EMMA.—Why don't you tell 'em, Matt?

MATT.—Ah tell you the truth, Emma, Ah don't want to tell 'em cause Ah don't want to have no more trouble. Time Ah tell 'em to stay out Ah know they'll start a argument, then Ah'll have to beat 'em up like Ah done once before. And Ah get tired fightin' sometime, deed Ah do.

EMMA.—Ah'll tell 'em then.

MATT. *(Rising.)*—All right, Ah'll go get the shoes.

EMMA.—Go out the alley through the back way to that Jew store. Ah seen some second handed ones in the window.

MATT.—What size you want?

EMMA.—Sevens.

MATT.—What kind?

EMMA.—Black. That's the only kind Ah ever wear.

MATT.—A pair o' black sevens. All right, if Ah can't get 'em there Ah'll get 'em somewhere else.

(He goes out through the kitchen leaving his banjo on the table. Emma picks up the banjo, looks at it and shakes her head. As she puts it down and starts back to the kitchen Sam and Adam enter from the other door. Sam is 33, taller than Matt, but not so sturdily built. Adam is 30, about Matt's height, but not so stout as Matt is. Both are careless loafers; the former is gruff with a mean temper; the latter is lively and playful.)

ADAM. *(As they enter.)*—Hi, Emma.

EMMA. *(Stopping in the doorway and speaking in unwelcoming tones.)*—Hi.

SAM. *(Roughly.)*—What's the matter with you?

EMMA.—Nothin'.

SAM.—Got anything to eat?

EMMA.—No.

ADAM.—That's mighty funny. You used to always have somethin' to eat round here.

EMMA.—Don't you all never think about nothin' but eatin'?

(Sam and Adam look at each other puzzled.)

SAM. *(Sitting at the left of the table.)*—Is you and Matt been fussin' this mornin'?

EMMA.—No.

ADAM. *(Sitting on the table.)*—Somethin' must be wrong; you never did act like this before.

EMMA.—Ain't nothin' wrong with me.

SAM. *(Looking towards the kitchen.)*—Seems like Ah smell cabbage. Ain't you cookin' cabbage?

EMMA.—Yes.

SAM.—Thought you didn't have nothin' to eat.

EMMA.—Them cabbage is for Matt's dinner.

SAM.—Can't we have some?

EMMA.—No, Ah ain't goin' to let you all eat up his dinner.

ADAM.—Ah know what's the matter now, Sam.

SAM. *(Turning to him.)*—What?

ADAM. —Matt's been spoonin' with huh and turned huh against us.

EMMA. *(Angrily.)*—You go to the devil.

(She goes quickly into the kitchen.)

SAM.—Ah'll bet that damned bully's been talkin' about us.

ADAM.—Ah'll bet so too. Lend me your knife.

SAM. *(Handing Adam the knife.)*— Ah'd like to run this between his ribs.

ADAM. *(Taking the knife and taking a match from his pocket.)*—Don't let him see you first.

SAM.—He ain't as bad as you think he is.

ADAM. *(Making a tooth-pick with the match.)*—Ah'll always remember how he beat us up once.

SAM.—He won't never beat us up again. Ah got him in the palm o' ma hand.

ADAM. *(Putting the knife into his pocket.)*—How you goin' to stop him from beatin' us up?

SAM. *(Holding out his hand.)*—Wait a minute, gimme that knife.

ADAM.—Lemme keep it a day or two.

SAM.—No, give it right back here now.

ADAM.—Ah'll give it back to you tomorrow.

SAM. *(Catching him by the pocket.)*—No, give it right here now.

ADAM. —What's the use o' bein' so mean?

SAM. *(Looking him in the eye and speaking more firmly.)*—Gimme that knife! Give it here!

ADAM. *(Putting the knife on the table.)*—Don't be such a sorehead.

SAM.—You better stop kiddin' with me. Ah don't feel like kiddin' today. Ah feel like runnin' this thing in a certain feller's ribs.

ADAM. —Don't cut at him and miss him, cause if you do you know what'll happen.

SAM.—Ain't nothin' goin' to happen. Didn' Ah say Ah had him in the palm o' ma hand.

ADAM. *(Laughing).*—You tryin' to kid me.

SAM.—No, Ah ain't kiddin'. Ah don't kid when Ah talk about him. Ah could tell you a thing or two if Ah wanted to. You know they ain't caught the one that killed old man Shelton yet.

ADAM. *(Interested.)*—You talk like you know somethin'.

SAM.—You c'n bet your life Ah know somethin'.

ADAM.—What is it?

SAM.—That's all right, Ah'll talk at the right time. Watch me call huh in here and bawl huh out. *(Calling.)* Emma! Emma!

EMMA.—What?

SAM.—Come here.

(Emma comes to the kitchen door.)

EMMA.—What you want?

SAM.—Is Matt been talkin' about me?

EMMA.—What would Matt be talkin' about you for?

SAM.—Ain't no use o' lying, Ah know somethin's been goin' on. Now, what is it?

EMMA.—If you want to be told, Ah'll tell you, all right. Matt don't want you and Adam hangin' round here eatin' up his grub.

SAM.—Oh, he don't, don't he?

EMMA.—No.

SAM.—Ah reckon you don't neither.

EMMA.—That ain't for me to say. Matt rents the house and buys the grub and it's up to him to say who he wants round and who he don't.

ADAM.—Ah told you Matt had been lovin' with huh.

SAM.—Well, Matt better be careful; Ah know a thing or two about him.

EMMA.—Now there ain't no use o' you goin' and makin' up nothin' on Matt.

SAM.—Ah ain't makin' nothin'; this is the truth. Ah seen it with ma own eyes.

EMMA. *(Interested.)*—You seen what?

SAM.—Ah know it'll knock you bald-headed when Ah tell you.

EMMA.—You better be careful when you talk about Matt; that's all Ah got to say.

SAM.—Careful or not careful, Matt killed old man Shelton and Ah seen him do it.

EMMA. *(Excitedly.)*—It's a lie! you know it's a lie!

SAM.—No, it ain't no lie. Ah seen him do it, and if he ain't careful how he acts with me Ah'll get him strung up by his neck.

EMMA.—Don't eve'ybody know that the one that killed old man Shelton got away and ain't never been caught.

SAM.—Matt's the one that got away and ain't never been caught.

EMMA.—You can't make nobody believe that. If you had a knowed that about Matt you'd a told it long ago much as you hate him.

SAM.—Ah didn't tell it 'cause he's your husband and Ah didn't want to put you in a hole; but now you turned against me and Ah don't care.

EMMA.—Ah ain't turned against you.

SAM.—Yes, you is. You don't even believe what Ah'm sayin' now.

EMMA.—Ain't no way for you to make me believe that.

SAM.—It ain't, ain't it? Well, Ah'll tell you just how it happened.

EMMA.—You gettin' ready to make up somethin' now.

SAM.—Ah was standin' right in the bushes when Ah seen Matt comin' along pickin' his banjo and not watchin' where he was walkin'. He walked right in old man Shelton's potato patch. Then old man Shelton runned out and started to beatin' Matt over the head with his stick. He hit Matt once or twice, but the next time he hit Matt put up his banjo to knock off the lick, and the lick broke the banjo. That made Matt so mad that before he knowed it he had picked up a rock and hit the old man right in the head with it and the old feller fell like a log. Matt grabbed his banjo and beat it and they ain't caught him yet.

EMMA.—Ah know you don't think Ah'm believin' that.

SAM.—That's all right, Ah'll prove it when he comes in here.

EMMA.—You sure is got to prove it to me. Ah don't believe a word you say. You all let me alone and let me cook ma husband's dinner.

(She goes into the kitchen.)

ADAM.—It's mighty funny you ain't said nothin' to me about that before now.

SAM.—Didn't Ah tell you Ah was holdin' ma tongue 'cause Ah didn't want to get Emma in bad. You wouldn't want me to hurt ma own sister, would you?

ADAM.—Seems like you might a told me anyhow long as we been runnin' together. You didn't think Ah'd pimp, did you?

SAM. *(Closing the whole matter.)*—Ain't no use to argue about it now.

(He takes the banjo up and looks at it.)

SAM.—This old thing's give that guy a lot o trouble.

(He tries to pick the banjo, but is not successful.)

ADAM. *(Taking hold of the banjo.)*—Lemme show you how to pick it.

SAM. *(Still holding on to it.)*—No, you can't pick it.

EMMA. *(Appearing at the kitchen door.)*—You all better put that banjo down before you break it.

SAM.—Let go the thing, Adam, and quit your playin'.

(He pulls the banjo suddenly from Adam's hand and it accidentally strikes the table and is broken.)

EMMA. *(Coming forward.)*—Now, look what you done. You all broke that banjo and Matt's goin' to raise the devil.

SAM. *(To Adam.)*—Ah told you to quit your kiddin'.

ADAM.—If you had a let me have the thing—

EMMA. *(Snatching the banjo from Sam.)*—Ain't no use o' makin' excuses now. The thing's broke. What you goin' to do about it?

SAM.—Ah ain't goin' to do nothing about it.

EMMA.—Both of you better get out o' here before Matt comes back.

SAM.—We ain't scared o' Matt as long as we know what we know.

EMMA.—Ah'm goin' to hide this thing 'cause Ah don't want to see nobody hurt.

(She puts the banjo into the closet.)

SAM.—Don't worry, ain't nobody goin' to get hurt.

EMMA. *(Listening.)*—Ah believe Ah hear him comin' now.

SAM.—Let him come.

(They are silent until Matt enters from the kitchen with a package under his arm.)

ADAM.—Hi, Matt.

MATT. *(Shortly.)*—Hi.

    (To Emma in a different tone.)—Here's the shoes, Emma.
(He takes the shoes to the table and as he puts them down he notices that the banjo is not there.)

MATT.—Where's ma banjo?

EMMA.—You don't want no banjo now. Lemme see the shoes.

MATT.—Yes, Ah do want ma banjo. Who moved it?

EMMA.—Ah moved it. Wait till you get your dinner, then get it.

MATT. *(Striking the table with his open hand.)*—Ah want it now, right now.

EMMA.—Matt, for Gawd's sake don't be thinkin' about that old banjo all the time.

MATT. *(Beginning to look around.)*—Ah'll find it myself.

(He goes to the cupboard, and in his eagerness pulls the drawer and all its contents out on the floor.)

EMMA. *(Beginning to untie the package.)*—Ah'm goin' to look at these shoes.

MATT. *(Turning to her.)*—Don't touch them shoes till Ah find ma banjo. Now, where is it?

EMMA. *(After a pause, pointing to the curtains.)*—In there.

(Matt reaches behind the curtains and brings out the banjo.)

MATT. *(In consternation.)*—Broke! Who the devil broke this banjo? Emma, who broke ma banjo?

(The others are silent.)

EMMA. *(Pleading with him.)*—Don't make no trouble, Matt; please don't make no trouble.

MATT. *(Taking the shoes from the table.)*—If you don't tell me who broke ma banjo Ah'm goin' to take these shoes right back.

(Emma is silent.)—All right, back they go.

EMMA. *(As he starts out.)*—Don't take 'em, Matt; don't take 'em back!

MATT.—Who broke it, then?

EMMA.—Sam broke it! Sam and Adam!

MATT. *(Throwing the shoes on the table and starting for Sam.)*—Ah'll fix you, you black dawg!

(Sam leaves the chair quickly and jumps behind the table. Matt takes the chair up to throw it at him.)

SAM.—Don't hit me with that chair. Ah know who killed old man Shelton!

(Matt holds the chair in the air as if he is fastened in that position and stares at Sam in wonder.)

SAM.—Ain't no use o' lookin' at me like that. Ah seen you when you hit him with that rock.

(Matt lets the chair come slowly to the floor.)

SAM. *(Coming around the table and snapping his fingers in Matt's face.)*—You ain't so smart now, is you? You ain't so anxious to smash that chair over ma head now, is you? Ah got you where Ah want you now. Ah got you in the palm o' ma hand.

(Matt does not speak but goes quietly to the hall door and locks it, putting the key into his pocket. He comes back to the table.)

SAM.—Who the devil you think you scarin' by lockin' that door?

(Matt goes over and locks the kitchen door before he speaks.)

MATT. *(Coming to the table again.)*—You might have me in the palm o' your hand, but you won't have me there long.

EMMA.—For Gawd's sake, Matt, what you goin' to do?

MATT.—You keep out o' this.

SAM.—You can't scare me now.

ADAM. *(At last finding his voice.)*—No, you can't scare us now with what we know on you.

MATT.—What you all know on me ain't goin' to do you no good, 'cause ain't neither one of you goin' out o' this house till you swear by the Gawd that made you you won't never say no more about me and old man Shelton.

SAM.—How you think you goin' to make us swear?

MATT. *(More determined and angry.)*—Ah'm goin' to beat you till you do, or keep you right here and starve you to death.

(To Emma.)—Bring that Bible out here, Emma.

(Emma gets the Bible from behind the curtains and puts it on the table.)

MATT.—Ah know you both believe in Gawd and the devil and heaven and hell, 'cause you ain't got the guts not to; and you goin' to raise your right hands and swear on this book.

SAM. *(Taking his knife from his pocket.)*—If you lay your hands on me Ah'll stick this knife in you.

MATT. *(Reaching behind the curtains and bringing out an axe handle.)*—Ain't no use for you to start that 'cause Ah e'n settle you with one lick on the head.

ADAM. *(Who has lost his nerve.)*—Aw, we'll swear; what's the use o' fightin' about it?

MATT. —Come on, then, and be quick about it.

SAM.—Don't you do it, Adam.

ADAM.—Ah ain't goin' to stay in here all day.

(Adam comes around and puts his left hand on the Bible.)

MATT.—Lift your right hand.

(Adam raises his right hand.)

MATT.—Do you swear by the Gawd that made you you won't never say nothin' about me and old man Shelton?

ADAM.—Yes.

MATT.—Don't say that. Say 'Ah do'.

ADAM.—Ah do.

MATT *(To Sam who stands away.)*—Now it's your turn.

SAM.—You'll have a nice time makin' me swear.

MATT.—If you don't swear Ah'll keep you right here and beat the devil out o' you till you change your mind.

ADAM *(Winking at Sam while Matt is glaring at him.)*—Come on and do it, Sam; Ah want to get out o' here.

MATT.—If he don't come on he'll be sorry for it.

SAM. *(After looking steadily at Adam for a moment.)*—All right, Ah swear not to tell.

MATT.—No, you don't. You can't play that with me. Come on round here to this Bible.

(Sam goes to the table and puts his left hand on the Bible, raising his right hand.)—Do you swear by the Gawd that made you you won't never say nothin' about me and old man Shelton?

SAM.—Ah do.

MATT.—Now both of you e'n go; and don't never put your foot in here no more.

(He throws the key over on the floor.)

ADAM. *(As he picks up the key.)*—We'll go, all right.

SAM. *(After the door is unlocked.)*—We'll go, but Ah'll get even with you one way or the other.

MATT. *(Starting towards them angrily.)*—Get out a' here!

(They hasten out, closing the door behind them.)

MATT. *(Coming back to the table after unlocking the kitchen door.)*—Ah didn' think that would ever get out about old man Shelton; but you never e'n tell.

EMMA.—Ah didn' know you had done that, Matt.

MATT.—Ah didn' believe nobody did. Ah didn' mean to kill him. When he broke ma banjo Ah hit him harder than Ah thought.

EMMA.—What you goin' to do now?

MATT.—Nothin' but keep quiet about it.

EMMA.—Yes, you is goin' to do somethin', too. You goin' to make your getaway.

MATT.—Get away for what? Didn' they swear not to tell?

EMMA.—And when they was swearin' Ah seen Adam winkin' at Sam. Swearin' with them don't amount to a row o' pins.

MATT.—They'd be scared to tell after swearin' on the Bible.

EMMA.—Don't you believe it. Soon as Sam gets full o' moonshine whiskey he'll tell everything he knows and that he don't know too. He'll forget he ever seen a Bible.

MATT.—Ah don't feel like runnin' from nobody.

EMMA.—Sam's mad now; and Sam mad is just like Sam drunk, he'll do anything.

(There is a pause while Emma awaits Matt's decision.)

Well, if you won't get ready Ah'll get you ready.

(She hurries out through the hall door. Matt sits resting his head on his hands. Presently Emma returns with a bundle of clothes which she puts on the table as she hurries to the kitchen. In a few moments she returns, wrapping some bread in a paper. She puts the bread in with the clothes.)

MATT.—Ah reckin you right about goin', Emma.

EMMA.—Ah know Ah'm right. They're gettin' ready to play some trick on you. Ah seen it in their eyes.

MATT.—Where must Ah go? Ah ain't got a cent.

EMMA.—That's all right, you go out the back way cross the fields to Uncle Silas' and get him to row you cross the river. When you get over beat it to A'nt Linda's and tell huh to hide you till Ah come.

MATT.—You reckon Uncle Silas 'll take me over? He don't like me. Nobody never did like me.

EMMA.—Tell him Ah said so. He'll do it for me.

MATT.—When you comin'?

EMMA.—Ah'll start out in the mornin'.

MATT.—But how about the money? We'll need money if we're goin' anywhere.

EMMA.—That's all right about the money. Ah got a hundred and forty dollars sewed up in ma mattress. Ah been denyin' maself things that Ah wanted and needed and savin' a little at a time, 'cause Ah knowed with that temper o' yours you'd get in trouble one time or nother.

MATT. *(Taking the bundle in one hand and the banjo in the other and going to the kitchen door.)*—Ah reckon Ah been a mighty poor husband to you, but you been a mighty good wife to me, Emma; if we ever get out o' this trouble, Ah'm goin' to turn over a new leaf. Ah'm goin' now and don't you be long comin'.

EMMA.—Ah'll be there first thing in the mornin'.

MATT.—All right, so long.

EMMA. *(Starting towards him.)*—So long, Matt.

(While Matt is hesitating at the kitchen door Sam and Adam enter hurriedly through the other door followed by an officer.)

SAM. *(Pointing to Matt.)*—There he is!

THE OFFICER.—Wait a minute, Matt; Ah want you.

MATT. *(Still standing in the doorway.)*—What do you want with me?

THE OFFICER.—Sam told me all about old man Shelton.

SAM.—Ah told you Ah'd fix you, you bully.

MATT. *(Dropping his banjo and bundle and quickly getting his club.)*—All right, if you want me, take me!

THE OFFICER. *(Pointing a warning finger at Matt.)*—There ain't no use for you to try that, you can't get away with it.

EMMA. *(Catching Matt's arm and holding him.)*—Don't do that, Matt! Don't do it! You'll just get in more trouble.

MATT.—Ah'm in all the trouble Ah c'n get in. It can't be no worse.

EMMA.—Yes, it can be worse. They won't give you but ten or fifteen years for old man Shelton 'cause you didn't mean to do that, but if you kill this man they'll hang you.

MATT.—Ah reckon you right, Emma; You always been right and Ah always been wrong. If Ah ever get out o' this Ah'll have enough sense to mind what you say.

(Allowing her to take the stick from him he goes over to the officer.)

SAM.—Better put the irons on him.

THE OFFICER.—That's all right, he'll go.

MATT. *(Turning to Emma as they are about to go.)*—Good bye, Emma.

EMMA. *(Standing at the left of the table her whole body trembling.)*—Good bye,—Matt.

(As they close the door Emma raises her hands to her eyes as if to hold back the tears.)

(THE END.)

EXIT, AN ILLUSION

This play, written by Marita O. Bonner, was published in October 1928.

FOREWORD

(Which presents the setting, the characters, and the argument)

The room you are in is mixed.

It is mixed.

There are ragged chairs with sorry sagging, ragged bottoms.— There are lace curtains with sorry ragged holes—but all over the chairs are scattered clothes, mostly lingerie of the creamiest, laciest, richest, pastel-crepe variety.

Everything is mixed.

Dishes are pushed back on the table. They may be yesterday's dishes or they may be today's. But dishes are pushed back and the table cloth is rumpled back. A pair of red kid pumps are on the edge of the table. Your eyes skip from the scarlet omen of their owner's hasty death— omen, if the bottom still holds in superstition—

Shoes mixed with dishes on the table.

Newspapers, pillows, shoes and stockings are scattered across the floor, making a path straight to an exquisite dressing-table of the variety type. This stands at the extreme right of the stage.

There is a window at right back—nearly at the centre—through which you see snow falling. Directly beside the window there is a door which must lead into an inner hall. It is not stout enough to be an outer door. It is the brownish sort of non-de-script door that shuts a cheap flat off from the rest of the world.

On the left side of the room is an open couch-bed. The sheets and blankets depend almost to the floor in uneven jags. Easily, then, you can see the figure of a woman lying there. Her hair which is a light brown—lies with a thick waving around her head. Her face—thin—is almost as pale as the sheets. She is sleeping with an arm hung over the side of the bed. Even though she keeps tossing and twitching as if she would come awake, she holds her arm over the side.

Down on the floor on the same side, lying so that her arm falls across him—there is a man. A part of his face shows against the bed-clothes and you can see he is blackly brown with the thin high-poised features that mark a "keen black man."

You can see at a glance that his slender body is caste for high things. High things. High things of the soul if the soul is fully living—high things of the flesh if the soul is fully dead.

He is Buddy.

The girl is Dot.

You are in their flat.

They are most assuredly not brother and sister.

Neither are they man and wife.

The room is mixed.

—Dot suddenly leans over the side toward Buddy. You wonder how she awakens so easily.

DOT—"Well Buddy I got a date. I got to get gone. Buddy! Buddy!" *(She leans over further and shakes him.)*

BUDDY—"Hunh—hunh? What say, Dot?" *(He wakes up).* "What say Dot?" *(He yawns).* "Uh-uh! Guess I was asleep. What say?"

DOT—"I say I got a date, Buddy."

BUDDY *(fully awake at once)*—"Date? Where you think you're going keeping a date sick as a dog and with the snow on the ground! *(He looks toward the window.)* Snowing now! Where you think you're going?"

DOT—"I got a date I tell you!"

BUDDY—"An' I tell you you ain't go-going to keep it!"

DOT—"Aw cut that stuff! How long since you thought you could tell me when to go and when to come! Store that stuff!"

BUDDY—I ain't storing nothing! You ain't going, I say."

DOT—"Aw Buddy I been knowing the guy all my life! Played with him when I's a kid! Been on parties with him since I been going around!"

BUDDY—"Aw don't try that old friend stuff! What's his name?"

DOT—"Exit."

BUDDY—"Exit? Exit! Where'd he get that ! off the inside of a theayter door? Exit! Exit! What's his other name or is that the onliest one he got?"

DOT—"Mann. Exit Mann. That's his name. Yeah—" *(She hesitates and seems to be uncertain.)*

BUDDY—"Well it sure is a rotten name! Must be hiding from the cops behind it!"

(Dot takes this opportunity to rise from her couch. The filmy night garment clings to her almost as closely as her flesh. You see she is not curved. You see she is flat where she should curve, sunken where she should be flat. You wish she would lie down again but she gets up—almost falls back—takes hold of the back of the chair and passes across the room to the dressing table.)

BUDDY—"Look at you! 'Bout to fall down! You better lay down again." *(Dot has begun to brush her hair before the dressing table. She brushes rapidly with strokes that grow vigorous as if each one made some new strength start up in her.)*

DOT—"Aw let me alone! I'm going out!"

(Buddy sits on the floor and watches her. She rouges her cheeks and paints her lips and begins to powder heavily with white powder.)

BUDDY—"You ain't fixin' to go out passing are you?"

DOT—"Aw don't ask so many fool questions!"

BUDDY *(growing angry)*—"Don't get too smart! Guess there's something after all in what the fellers been saying 'bout you anyhow."

DOT —"What your nigger friends been saying now?"

BUDDY—"Nigger friends? You're a nigger yourself for all your white hide!"

DOT *(shrugging)*—"I may not be—You'd never know!"

BUDDY —"Aw shut up! You'd like to think ya was white! You'd have never lived with niggers if you'd a been all white and had a crack at a white man!"

(Dot starts to speak—changes her mind—and paints her lips again.)

BUDDY *(after a second's silence)*—"Take some of that stuff off!"

DOT—"I can't! Mann likes a woman like me to paint up so I'll flash out above the crowd."

BUDDY—"Mann! what's Mann got to do with the way you look! Look here you! You been running 'round with this fellow Mann? *(He plunges to his feet and lunges toward her.)* Is he the white feller they been seeing you out with for the past three months?"

DOT—"They? What they? Some more of your—!"

BUDDY—"Don't call them niggers again you half-white—"

(Dot catches him by the shoulder and pushes him away.—She selects a piece of clothes out of a drawer.)

DOT—"I told you in the beginning I been knowing this guy all my life! Been out with him!"

BUDDY—"Is he white?"

DOT—"I don't know!"

BUDDY—"You don't know! Where'd you meet him?"

DOT—"Aw for God sake shut up and let me alone! I never met him! This is the last time I'm going to tell you I been knowing him all my life!"

BUDDY—"Naw I ain't lettin' you alone! Naw I ain't letting you alone! This is the guy the fellers been telling me about! This is the guy! Ol' lop-sided lanky white thing! Been hanging around you at all the cafes and dances and on the streets all the time I'm out of the city! I'm out of the city—working to keep you—you hanging around with some no 'count white trash! So no 'count he got to come in nigger places, to nigger parties and then when he gets there—can't even speak to none of them. Ain't said a word to nobody the fellers say! Ain't said a word! Just settin' 'round—settin' 'round—looking at you—hanging around you—dancin' with you! He better not show hisself 'round here while I'm here!"

DOT—"He can't never come when you're here."

BUDDY—"You right he can't come here. Can't never come! He better be afraid of me."

DOT—"He ain't afraid of you. He's afraid of your love for me."

BUDDY—*(laughing shortly).* "Aw for crap sake! My love! He ain't afraid of my love! He's afraid of my fist!"

(Dot does not seem to hear him now. She talks to herself—"It's almost time! It's almost time!")

Buddy hears her the second she speaks—"Almost time for what?"

DOT—"Him to come!"

BUDDY—"Who?"

DOT—"Exit!"

BUDDY—*(cursing).* "He ain't coming here! He ain't coming here! I'll knock his head clean off his shoulders if he comes here!"

DOT—"He's coming!"

BUDDY—"I'll kill you 'fore he gets here and then kill him when he comes!"

DOT—"Aw Buddy—don't take on so! If you love me he can't come in between your love and come to me!"

(Buddy curses until his veins are swollen—packed full of the poison of the curses.)

BUDDY—"Damn you! Damn you!! Trying to throw this 'your love' stuff out to cam'flage and hide behind. I tol' you when we were fussing before you went to sleep that I didn't believe you when you said everybody was lying on you! You said everybody was lying and you was tellin' the truth! Say you ain't never been with other men! Naw I don't love you!"

(He breaks off and rushes to a drawer and snatches out a mean, ugly, blue-black, short pistol.)

DOT—*(screaming and overturning her chair)* "Aw Buddy—Buddy don't! You love me!"

BUDDY—"Shut up!!" *(He lifts the gun as if he were going to bring it down—raking her with fire the length of her body. He stops—)* "Naw I don't love you! Half-white rat!"

DOT—*(crawling to her knees away from him)* "Then he's got to come! I got to go with him!"

BUDDY—"Yas he's got to come! And when he comes I'll fix you both! Get up!" *(He prods her with his foot.)* Get up! Get up and dress to go out before your Exit is here! Exit! Exit! I'll Exit him when I get through with you!"

(Dot completes her powdering then she suddenly reaches her hat down from a hook above the table. It is a smart black turban. It is black crepe and is wound and wound around. She snatches up a sealskin coat that has been lying on another chair and begins to put it on.)

BUDDY—"You must be foolish! What you putting the coat on over the night-clothes for?"

DOT—"I ain't got time to put no more on."

BUDDY—"Aw yes you got time, sister! Put on all you want! I ain't going to run you off before he gets here! You ain't going 'til your Exit comes!"

DOT—"This is all I need—all I need! I'm ready."

BUDDY—"You're ready—where's your friend? Can't go without him!"

DOT—"He's here! *(she points.)* "There he is." *(And close behind Buddy you see a man standing. He is half in the shadow. All you can see is a dark over-coat, a dark felt hat. You cannot see his face for his back is turned. You wonder how he came there. You wonder if perhaps he has not been there all the while.)*

BUDDY—*(starting back as he sees the man.)* "You're a regular sneak, ain't you! Ain't enough to sneak in and take a man's girl while he's out workin! Got to sneak in his house! Sneak in on him when he's minding his business!"

(The man does not move or answer. Dot's color is bright. Her eyes glow in the semi-shadow. The lights in the room seem dimmer somehow. Dot is breathing so that the fur mounts and slides—mounts and slides on her bosom. She keeps wetting her lips as if they were drying out. She starts across the floor toward him but pauses and draws back almost at once.)

BUDDY—*(still talking to the man.)* "Turn around and say something! Turn around and say something! They say all you do is hang around niggers' places and keep a still tongue!" *(To Dot)* "Go on over! Go on up to your Exit. Go on so you can go off the way I am sending you off. Go off like you lived! Lying in some man's arms—then lying to me *(as if to himself)*—That's the way to die anyhow; jus' like you lived!"

DOT—*(rubbing a hand across her face.)* "Buddy!" *(gasping)* "Buddy! Say you love me! I don't want to go! I don't want to go with him!"

(Buddy's answer is an inarticulate wild roar.—"Get on to him! Get on over to him!")

(With a scream and a quick run Dot crosses the little space and as quickly the man opens his arms and draws her to him without turning around.)

DOT—*(crying smothered against the coat as if she were far away)* "Buddy— Buddy—Buddy! Do you love me? Say you love me before I go!"

(As she cries out the man begins to walk toward the back door. Buddy curses and fires at the same time. A stray shot strikes the light. It goes out. Buddy scratches a match and you see the man standing in the doorway—about to cross the threshold. His back is still turned but as you look he slowly begins to turn around.)

BUDDY—"Mann? Mann! Dot! Dot!

(At that the man turns fully and you see Dot laid limp—hung limp—silent. Above her, showing in the match light between the overcoat and the felt hat are the hollow eyes and fleshless cheeks of Death.

But almost at once the light flares back. You see the room as it was at first. Dot on her couch with her arms hanging over the side—Buddy lying beside the couch. The red shoes on the table.)

DOT—*(struggling awake)*—"Buddy! *(You can hear a rattling in her throat. A loud rattling. The rattling of breath soon to cease).* "Buddy!!! Buddy!! Aw God, he can't hear me!—Buddy, do you love me? Say you love me 'fore I go! Ah—ah—ah—!" *(The rattling is loud—loud. It stops on a high note. She stretches rigid and is still.)*

(The room is quiet an instant. You think you hear the rattling, though.)

BUDDY—*(striving in his sleep)* "Exit!! Mann!! Exit! *(He pauses—then cries aloud)* You lied! Naw I don't love you! *(He cries so loudly that he comes fully awake and sits up swiftly)*—"Say Dot—I had a—! Dot! Dot!! Oh my God *(he touches her)* My Dot! *(and he leans over her and begins to cry like a small boy).* Oh Dot!—! I love you! I love you!"

PART FOUR

ESSAYS

TWILIGHT: AN IMPRESSION

Author William Stanley Braithwaite offers a philosoph-
ical view of the feeling and symbols of twilight in the
following essay, which was published in April 1912.

The road followed part of the way between rows of stone walls on either side that enclosed meadows and fields, and groups of little woods
straggling along, until they began to border the road with tall trees
when the stone walls stopped. The trees stood bare in the crisp, still air
at the top of the hill where the road began to descend, their branches
tracing the lemon and orange of the western sky as I left them behind
me; a low murmur of sighing winds mingled with the cracking of dry
bark which sounded fainter and fainter as I descended where the
woods abruptly ended. Before me lay the sea to the southeast, and cir-
cling the southern shore jagged cliffs fortified the sloping land against
centuries of assaulting and angry foam. The sandy beach formed a
crescent eastward, along which the road separated it from the alternate
swamp, meadow and field, stretching to the outskirts of the town in the
distance that lay south and west, meeting the open uplands and valleys
to the north.

Going down where the ocean lay at my feet, I inhaled a full breath
of its pungent odors, and turned around to look upon the scene that
silhouetted itself against the vivid western sky. On the crest of the hill
the naked tree trunks cut their dark shadows into the infinitude of the
heavens, and seemed not terrestrial things that had very firm roots in
this earth. Already the rosy tinge reflected from the departed sun was
filling the spaces between the trees, contrasting its delicate, immater-

ial color against the sombre hilltop. I turned from the miracle of the west to the mystery of the east; to the earth and sea and sky, melting their outlines, their definite and sharp formations of wave and rock and cloud, into the obliterating dusk creeping insistently from the east. A white sail stood against the obscurity bravely for a while, just above the horizon, where the green wall of the sea was fast changing to dark purple. First, its reflection of a slant of crimson from the west faded, then the gleaming sail itself became dimmer and dimmer until it melted into the afterglow. The meadows and fields kept their character longer than the sea. When the sun or moon is shining on the sea at any angle it is full of wonderful changes; atmosphere, clouds and winds give it color and motion and mood; twilight gathers all these effects into one modulation of tone and feeling, full of suggestion and spiritual symbolism, before passing into the monotone of night's darkness. It is different with the land. The slant of meadow and field, the delicate, shimmering outlines of distant hills against the sky, the pointed tops of trees, hollows and rocks, and winding roads, reflect by some inexplicable magic their shadowy presences against the soft suffusion of the dusk. The atmosphere becomes a woven veil of shadows; the wind undulates it as if the spirit of nature breathed meditatively through the changing hour, that was conscious in itself of that deeper change beneath appearances from which the seasons are born. And so I looked upon the land and saw Nature, as it were, in her private chamber of dreams, and felt vaguely the sea, passionate in its tranquil unrest, its innumerable and unending waves like a silent army of soldiery stealing upon the sleeping shores of the world.

It was neither day nor night; it was the pause between, the suspension of twilight. There was no sound, for the murmur of the waves upon the sands and the sigh of low winds that ran over the sere grass, mingled and became silence to that tense and physical passivity when all the senses become but one sense of spiritual feeling and vision. I walked on over the hardening road where neither man nor beast broke upon my solitude. I was conscious of no motion; I seemed to have fallen in with the rhythm of silence that bore me in perfect harmony with earth. There was the realization of not being alone, of having companions that the sound of my lips could not reach, nor my hands touch, but who crowded my memory with images and filled my imagination with voices. I paused often and turned, as if to answer some questions, just to catch a shadow settling along the ridge beside the road, and nothing beyond but the dim gray-blue silence for miles. I had kept my eyes leveling the landscape, discerning the contour of the road, defining against the distance a track of foam that marked the rim of the sea, but now, lifting them to the sky, I discovered a point of light breaking through the atmosphere; it twinkled and vanished, but gazing steadily, I saw it burst a white flame, the first star burning against the shadow of the sky. I watched a cluster bloom and shoot their javelin points of radiance into an infinity of silence. Turning my eyes to earth again, everything had drawn closer; the sea seemed to wash its liquid presence around my feet, my hands felt the hilltops pressing their vague strength through the gloom, and the roadside fields rose in the foreground to shut out the rumblings of humanity. The light waned and the dusk began to menace. I had been lifted for one minute above time and eternity; I had felt the foregathering of all existence in the visible delay of night and day. The passage of the ivory gates had been traversed, and I saw the meaning of many things that had puzzled and escaped me in the crowded streets of cities. For I read clear in the twilight pause that was now a swift surrender, the secret at the heart of humanity. I had gone upon that twilight walk the messenger of man's mystery, his inexplicable relationship to nature, his still more subtle and inexplicable relationships with his kind. His very existence seemed to me symbolized in that scene of earth and sea. The presence of man exiled from it, nothing could be realized without his memory or the memory of him. Brain and will and spirit, he dominated the solitude and silence, the inviolable regularity of earth's rhythm, the law of wind and wave, all these worked according to his necessity, harnessed themselves to his perpetuation.

There was no more day. The darkness completely swallowed the hills; now and then a dull washing of waves upon the sands told me where the sea heaved its naked breast to the stars that spangled the wide heavens. The earth was in secret, hiding her memories in the silence and obscurity of night. I stood with no questioning spirit. I was satisfied to be, assured and confident of what was to be. The twilight I had known was the womb of time that conceived to-morrow, and I knew that man's life was the womb that carried the seed of immortality.

ALL GOD'S CHILLUN GOT EYES

This essay, written by E. Franklin Frazier and published in April 1924, relates a personal account of his eyes being repaired by a white doctor. Frazier endures fear of further harm to his eyes and the possibility of damage to his spirit because of the color of his skin.

Being one of God's "chillun", I have eyes. Moreover, being one of his "chillun", I am subject to the ills that befall his children. So, when my eyes which I depend upon constantly indicated strain, I inquired for a specialist in the city. I found that the best specialist was a Scotchman who had come to this country and established himself in the South. His office was on the thirteenth floor of one of those structures to which this city points as a sign of its progress.

Now, in this monument of progress, they have arranged for the preservation of the purity of God's white chillun by having special elevators for God's chillun of my complexion. White people, of course, can ride in the colored elevator, if they are willing to risk momentary contamination, for the sake of dispatch in their business. In short, white people can ride with colored people but colored people are forbidden to ride with white people. Therefore, I was confronted by the problem of having my eyes repaired without damaging my spirit.

Immediately, some white reader will ask the eternal question: "Do you want to be with white people?" My answer is simple. I wanted to get to the thirteenth floor. At that moment, I did not want to be with white people or colored people, tall people or short people, bow-legged people or straight-legged people. I did not even want to go to heaven, while that desire was unfulfilled. There were many things that I did not want, when I attempted to engage in the simple process of getting from one floor to another. I did not want to be reminded my skin was brown. I did not want to hear a lot of foolishness about social equality and racial purity. Above all, I did not want to be marked off as unfit for human association. Enough!

Mount the stairs with me. I am still young and can use my legs and save my self-respect.

The doctor received me cordially, for he soon learned that I was a professor in a college for which he does some work. Immediately, he began to address me by my last name, as if I were his bootblack or office boy, or life-long friend. (I learned afterwards that he had been a very apt student of Southern incivilities). Resentment leaped up within me. Should I protest and let him know that I was simply there on a professional visit and expected the same courtesies accorded other patients? A voice within me reasoned thus: "Be calm, you young fool. Don't you realize that this is the only specialist in the city to take care of you and it is more important that your eyes are treated than that you should teach him a lesson in politeness?" Then the voice whispered: "If you resent, he might put them. . . . No! No! no civilized man could do that. But they have even burned out Negroes' eyes in the South." Realizing the truth of this, I decided to rationalize the situation. This man was simply an ill-bred coward with a veneer of civilization who was afraid to be a gentleman. I was his superior in manners and humanity.

He led me into a room rather dimly lighted by a court and told me to tell the girl who would come in that I was waiting to have drops put into my eyes. Soon, a thin ghostly girl, clothed in black, glided into the room. Evidently a descendant of the noble Anglo-Saxons of the clay hills of Georgia, she had a pallid face, sunken eyes and lips painted a gaudy red. When she filled the eye dropper from one of the three bottles on the shelf, and approached me, I almost shrank from her. Was she sure from which bottle she had taken the fluid? Did she care? I was only a "nigger". Perhaps, she did not want to wait on colored people. I had refrained from antagonizing the doctor. Should I not propitiate this white apparition gliding towards me?

A sign of propitiation among human beings is a smile. A voice spoke out: "You fool, don't you dare smile. It would be all right, if an humble ante-bellum *darky* did so; but you are a young Negro college professor. Don't you know that you are out of the place God fitted you for? Already, you have shown your rebellious spirit by walking up thirteen flights, rather than ride with 'your people'. This is dangerously near a desire for social equality. Have you forgotten that in a town where you taught, white people kicked one of your students unmercifully, because he was accused of smiling at a white girl on the street? In a room with a white woman in the South, a Negro's smile would be equal to an attack." She dropped the fluid into my eyes and left the room triumphantly. Suspense. Uncertainty... Yes, I can still see, and it does not hurt.... Do not rejoice too soon.... In five minutes, she entered again. She dropped the fluid into my eyes a second time and left the room.... The suspense lessens.... After repeating this several times, she said in a voice not unkind: "I put it in five times. Didn't I?"

With this ordeal passed, I returned to the doctor, who resumed the examination. Again, he showed the same disregard for common courtesy. As I descended the democratic stairs (white and colored people can walk down the same stairs) I wondered if going up on a Jim Crow elevator were any worse than letting an ill-bred coward insult you. Well, I suppose as long as all God's chillun got eyes that need attention in this land of white supremacy, in the absence of colored specialists, it will be a choice between blindness and insult and discomfiture.

ON BEING YOUNG—A WOMAN—
AND COLORED

This 1925 prize essay was written by Marita O. Bonner,
who was at the time a recent graduate of Radcliffe College. Bonner here raises personal issues that are relevant for contemporary college-educated black women.

You start out after you have gone from kindergarten to sheepskin covered with sundry Latin phrases.

At least you know what you want life to give you. A career as fixed
and as calmly brilliant as the North Star. The one real thing that money
buys. Time. Time to do things. A house that can be as delectably out
of order and as easily put in order as the doll-house of "playing-house"
days. And of course, a husband you can look up to without looking
down on yourself.

Somehow you feel like a kitten in a sunny catnip field that sees sleek,
plump brown field mice and yellow baby chicks sitting coyly, side by
side, under each leaf. A desire to dash three or four ways seizes you.

That's Youth.

But you know that things learned need testing—acid testing—to
see if they are really, after all, an interwoven part of you. All your life
you have heard of the debt you owe "Your People" because you have
managed to have the things they have not largely had.

So you find a spot where there are hordes of them—of course
below the Line—to be your catnip field while you close your eyes to
mice and chickens alike.

If you have never lived among your own, you feel prodigal. Some
warm untouched current flows through them—through you—and
drags you out into the deep waters of a new sea of human foibles and

mannerisms; of a peculiar psychology and prejudices. And one day you find yourself entangled—enmeshed—pinioned in the seaweed of a Black Ghetto.

Not a Ghetto, placid like the Strasse that flows, outwardly unperturbed and calm in a stream of religious belief, but a peculiar group. Cut off, flung together, shoved aside in a bundle because of color and with no more in common.

Unless color is, after all, the real bond.

Milling around like live fish in a basket. Those at the bottom crushed into a sort of stupid apathy by the weight of those on top. Those on top leaping, leaping; leaping to scale the sides; to get out.

There are two "colored" movies, innumerable parties—and cards. Cards played so intensely that it fascinates and repulses at once.

Movies.

Movies worthy and worthless—but not even a low-caste spoken stage.

Parties, plentiful. Music and dancing and much that is wit and color and gaiety. But they are like the richest chocolate; stuffed costly chocolates that make the taste go stale if you have too many of them. That make plain whole bread taste like ashes.

There are all the earmarks of a group within a group. Cut off all around from ingress from or egress to other groups. A sameness of type. The smug self-satisfaction of an inner measurement; a measurement by standards known within a limited group and not those of an unlimited, seeing, world. . . . Like the blind, blind mice. Mice whose eyes have been blinded.

Strange longing seizes hold of you. You wish yourself back where you can lay your dollar down and sit in a dollar seat to hear voices, strings, reeds that have lifted the World out, up, beyond things that have bodies and walls. Where you can marvel at new marbles and bronzes and flat colors that will make men forget that things exist in a flesh more often than in spirit. Where you can sink your body in a cushioned seat and sink your soul at the same time into a section of life set before you on the boards for a few hours.

You hear that up at New York this is to be seen; that, to be heard.

You decide the next train will take you there.

You decide the next second that that train will not take you, nor the next—nor the next for some time to come.

For you know that—being a woman—you cannot twice a month or twice a year, for that matter, break away to see or hear anything in a city that is supposed to see and hear too much.

That's being a woman. A woman of any color.

You decide that something is wrong with a world that stifles and chokes; that cuts off and stunts; hedging in, pressing down on eyes, ears and throat. Somehow all wrong.

You wonder how it happens there that—say five hundred miles from the Bay State—Anglo Saxon intelligence is so warped and stunted.

How judgment and discernment are bred out of the race. And what has become of discrimination? Discrimination of the right sort. Discrimination that the best minds have told you weighs shadows and nuances and spiritual differences before it catalogues. The kind they have taught you all of your life was best: that looks clearly past generalization and past appearance to dissect, to dig down to the real heart of matters. That casts aside rapid summary conclusions, drawn from primary inference, as Daniel did the spiced meats.

Why can't they then perceive that there is a difference in the glance from a pair of eyes that look, mildly docile, at "white ladies" and those that, impersonally and perceptively—aware of distinctions—see only women who happen to be white?

Why do they see a colored woman only as a gross collection of desires, all uncontrolled, reaching out for their Apollos and the Quasimodos with avid indiscrimination?

Why unless you talk in staccato squawks—brittle as sea-shells—unless you "champ" gum—unless you cover two yards square when you laugh—unless your taste runs to violent colors—impossible perfumes and more impossible clothes—are you a feminine Caliban craving to pass for Ariel?

An empty imitation of an empty invitation. A mime; a sham; a copy-cat. A hollow re-echo. A froth, a foam. A fleck of the ashes of superficiality?

Everything you touch or taste now is like the flesh of an unripe persimmon.

. . . Do you need to be told what that is being . . . ?

Old ideas, old fundamentals seem worm-eaten, out-grown, worthless, bitter; fit for the scrap-heap of Wisdom.

What you had thought tangible and practical has turned out to be a collection of "blue-flower" theories.

If they have not discovered how to use their accumulation of facts, they are useless to you in Their world.

Every part of you becomes bitter.

But—"In Heaven's name, do not grow bitter. Be bigger than they are",—exhort white friends who have never had to draw breath in a Jim-Crow train. Who have never had petty putrid insult dragged over them—drawing blood—like pebbled sand on your body where the skin is tenderest. On your body where the skin is thinnest and tenderest.

You long to explode and hurt everything white; friendly; unfriendly. But you know that you cannot live with a chip on your shoulder even if you can manage a smile around your eyes—without getting steely and brittle and losing the softness that makes you a woman.

For chips make you bend your body to balance them. And once you bend, you lose your poise, your balance, and the chip gets into you. The real you. You get hard.

. . . And many things in you can ossify . . .

And you know, being a woman, you have to go about it gently and quietly, to find out and to discover just what is wrong. Just what can be done.

You see clearly that they have acquired things.

Money; money. Money to build with, money to destroy. Money to swim in. Money to drown in. Money.

An ascendancy of wisdom. An incalculable hoard of wisdom in all fields, in all things collected from all quarters of humanity.

A stupendous mass of things.

Things.

So, too, the Greeks . . . Things.

And the Romans. . . .

And you wonder and wonder why they have not discovered how to handle deftly and skillfully, Wisdom, stored up for them—like the honey for the Gods on Olympus—since time unknown.

You wonder and you wonder until you wander out into Infinity, where—if it is to be found anywhere—Truth really exists.

The Greeks had possessions, culture. They were lost because they did not understand.

The Romans owned more than anyone else. Trampled under the heel of Vandals and Civilization, because they would not understand.

Greeks. Did not understand.

Romans. Would not understand.

"They." Will not understand.

So you find, they have shut Wisdom up and have forgotten to find the key that will let her out. They have trapped, trammeled, lashed her to themselves with thews and thongs and theories. They have ransacked sea and earth and air to bring every treasure to her. But she sulks and will not work for a world with a whitish hue because it has snubbed her twin sister, Understanding.

You see clearly—off there is Infinity—Understanding. Standing alone, waiting for someone to really want her.

But she is so far out there is no way to snatch at her and drag her in.

So—being a woman—you can wait.

You must sit quietly without a chip. Not sodden—and weighted as if your feet were cast in the iron of your soul. Not wasting strength in enervating gestures as if two hundred years of bonds and whips had really tricked you into nervous uncertainty.

But quiet; quiet. Like Buddha who—brown like I am—sat entirely at ease, entirely sure of himself; motionless and knowing, a thousand years before the white man knew there was so very much difference between feet and hands.

Motionless on the outside. But inside?

Silent.

Still . . . "Perhaps Buddha is a woman."

So you too. Still; quiet; with a smile, ever so slight, at the eyes so that Life will flow into and not by you. And you can gather, as it passes, the essences, the overtones, the tints, the shadows; draw understanding to your self.

And then you can, when Time is ripe, swoop to your feet—at your full height—at a single gesture.

Ready to go where?

Why . . . Wherever God motions.

The Young Blood Hungers

Published in May 1928 by Marita O. Bonner, this essay is about the confusion of youth and the hunger for plain truths.

The Young Blood sits—back to an Eternity—face toward an Eternity. Hands full of the things ancestry has given—thriving on the things today can give—guided vocationally—inducted spiritually—fed on vitamins—defended against diseases unthinkable—hungry.

The Young Blood hungers.

It's an old hunger. The gnawing world hunger. The hunger after righteousness.

—I speak not for myself alone.

Do not swiftly look and think you see and swiftly say, "It is not, most certainly, a hunger for righteousness this Young Blood feels!"

But it is. It is the Hunger.

Some Young Blood feels it—and then they see if they can out-strip it—if they can get rid of the gnawing—try to dance it off as a man smokes off a trouble—try to float it off on a drunken sea—try to cast a spell on it. Daze it off.

Sometimes the Old Blood perceives the hunger and offers food: "It's the World Hunger," the Old Blood says. "It's the Hunger-After-Righteousness. Take God. Take Him as we have taken Him."

That is what the Old Blood says: "Take God—Take Him as we have taken Him."

And the Young Blood sits still hungry and answers: "Not your God as you had Him."

The Young Blood sits. The Young Blood hungers yet. They cannot take God as the Old Blood takes Him.

Not God sitting at the top of a million worn orthodox steps. God in the old removed far-off Heaven. Not God showering thunder-wrath and stripping man of all Life's compensations to prove him righteous. Not God always offering a heavenly reward for an earthly Hell. Not God poured out in buttered sentences from the pulpit four or five times a month. Not the Old Blood's God demanding incessant supplication—calling for constant fear.

Not the Old Blood's God—but the God His own Son said that He really is. His own Son, Jesus, who knew Him better than any earth-born creature knew Him. Jesus who said that He was a friendly father who wanted respectful fear and confidential chats and obedience to principle and cooperation and thanksgiving as much as He wanted supplication.—I speak not for myself alone, Lord. The Young Blood hungers.—

The Old Blood argues: "You don't seek God in too-brief garments and too-tinted cheeks—too fancy-free dance steps—too fancy-free Thoughts-about-Things."

Perhaps not—but how?

Up the million steps? Removed? Far? How? How?

The Young does not know. The Young hungers.

The Young Blood hungers and searches somehow. The Young Blood knows well that Life is built high on a crystal of tears. A crystal of tears filled with Illusory Veils of Blind Misunderstandings and Blunderings. Enough filmy veils wet with tears, stamped down hard beneath your feet to let you rise up—out—above—beyond.

Just think of the number of veils cast down! Just think of the tears to pack them down hard so you can stand on them.

Yet that is growing.

The Young Blood knows that growing means a constant tearing down of Illusory Veils that lift themselves thin—filmy—deceptive—between you and truth. Veils that flutter breath-thin across things and make you mistake the touch of Heaven for the touch of Hell.

Veils—breath-thin—so thin you feel them rather than see them.

Tearing down Illusory Veils. Jesus called it watching. Such watching that I of myself and you of yourself cannot do it alone. Veils lift themselves sometimes in the still of the night when even the soul is asleep. Eyes that kept Israel and did not slumber nor yet sleep are needed to help with the tearing down.

I speak not for myself alone, Lord. The Young Blood hungers for Eyes to watch.—

All this the Young Blood knows. All this and more.

Young Blood knows that some Truths solidified in Eternity will not rot until Eternity crumbles. Solidified in Eternity. One love perhaps is to be pure and clean or it is not love. When the mists of Half-Lies play around the face of a truth—Lord—the Young Blood hungers.

Solidified in Eternity—Rooted and tipping in Eternity. Young Blood knows this. And yet if you fumble through the mists of Half-Lies-About-Things to feel the Truth-About-Real-Things safe—sound—solid—behind you—are you a crab—a prude—out of step with your age?

Are there no regular drum-beats? Can't you mark your step to one drum that beats from the rim of Eternity up through the Dark Ages—through the Middle Ages—through Renaissances—through Wars and Remakings-of-Worlds—to the same rhythm?

Is there not a pulse-beat you can feel—beating—steady—Bloody Reigns and Terrors and Inquisitions and Torments—up to Hells-of-Republics and back?

Or is it, after all, a new gait for every new day?

A new drum?

A new rhythm?

A new pulse-beat?

A new step?

A new Heaven?

A new Hell?

Today, a Truth. Tomorrow, a Lie.

Everything new. Raw and new. No time to root before the sun sets its first rays of a new day dawning.

The Young Blood hungers for Truth for God. For the God they called Jehovah when Christ was yet to come. Where is Jehovah?—

A brief breath of a paper-weight-dress—slippers—perfumed—curled—rouged even. Can't you toss your soul out—up—beyond the mere room-full of brief breaths of dresses—perfumes—curls—rouge—and walk and talk to God?

Must you come—eyes down-cast—to an altar four or five times a month to meet God of a Sabbath morn? Can you only commune with Him when you take Christ's body and blood on an appointed day from hands not always too free from blood—before eyes that seem to lick out and eat up—lusting for Young Blood? Isn't it the call for God thrilling in the voice of Young Blood when it is lifted in song—no matter the song? Isn't it God seeking God in the question of Young Blood when it asks: "Do you understand things? Sometimes I am afraid? Do you understand?"

—

If Young Blood knew how to converse with God—would so many Young feet stumble in the drunken mazes of seeking to find Self—seeking to find Truth—seeking to drown cries within—seeking enchantments to fill hollows within—seeking to catch up with something greater than yourself in a swift mad consuming fire-flash of living?

—It's the gnawing pains.—

Gnawing pains make you toss your body around. Make you toss your body now this way—now that. Young Blood hungers. Young Blood feels the gnawing pains of hunger—you do not know where your body will come—where it will go. All you wish is to toss your self away from the pain gnawing within.

—It's the gnawing pains.—

Can a mote appear to lay blindness across the vision?

Isn't there a part of Young Blood that leapt into being at Eternity and goes on through all Eternity? Isn't there something that sees beyond curls and rouge?

—I speak not for myself alone, Lord.—

Something winding and winding in the rhythmic inanities of a dance, Young Blood hears things beside the music—the feet—the talk—the chaff of laughter.

Sometimes when you teeter to a jazz-band's play voices speak within you and seem to say:

Oh dance, fool! Dance!

You may prance, fool, prance

You may skim, you may slide,

You may dip, you may glide,

But you've lied to yourself,

Oh you've lied—lied—lied.

—Gave a damn for the night—

—Chanced your all upon Today—

But you've lied! Yes you've lied!

—I'm the Voice that never died.

Voices and Hunger. Searchings and Seekings. Stumbling—falling—rising again. —I speak not for myself alone, Lord! The Young Blood hungers. —Back toward an Eternity. Facing Eternity. Perhaps that is the way in which Young Blood is to sit—back toward an Eternity—face toward an Eternity—hungering.

Perhaps it must be that God must be sought in new ways—new

ways—fewer steps—fewer steps—each time there comes Young Blood—each time there comes Young Blood—until they find Him.

A few less steps each time. A few less steps each time.

Soon the top.

Then—no longer Hunger.

Then no longer—Hunger.

—I speak not for myself alone, Lord! The Young Blood hungers.—

COLLEGE

This essay by Loren R. Miller received the first prize in the 1926 *Crisis* contest. Miller reevaluates his idealism about college and his future in this essay. He attempts to come to terms with the harsh realities of life for a black professional in America.

At last you have come to college. You are going to be a lawyer. You tell that so proudly now. You are bewildered by what you have found at college. Somehow you feel a vague disappointment. You can't tell just where your disappointment lies, yet you feel it. Perhaps you expected too much. You thought that college would be different. You have not found it so. You had always thought that college was a place where they had Ideals. Of course you never had any clear perception of what Ideals were. You just supposed that Ideals made college different.

You decide that if you understood college, you might find those things which you expected. You hasten to adapt yourself. You join the proper things; the college Y. M. C. A., Forums, Groups, the most prosperous church, colored of course. Perhaps you pledge to a frat (colored, too), go through Hell week and gain a coveted pin, which you prize so highly at first and later on bestow on any coed who strikes your fancy.

You feel a little sense of importance. You are becoming part of your school. You are caught in the whirl. You shout at pep meetings. You attend convocation. You hear Great Educators glibly talk Democracy; Noted Divines urge Find God; Successful Business Men Shout Success. You can't quite understand all this gibberish, but these men must know whereof they speak. They were all once poor undergrads like you; now they are worshipped. You swallow the whole sickening mess. These things, you say, must be the Ideals which I sought at college.

You are swept along with the crowd. You fear to stop and reason. You feel more and more uncomfortable. "Here," you say, "are the same prejudices that I have always met." That bothers you. You didn't expect prejudice and Ideals to dwell side by side.

You appeal to the older students. They answer evasively. They say, "Well, we can't expect too much." You have met the inferiority complex that permeates your race-thinking; you don't know it, but you have.

You reason that if you become like the other students they will have to accept you. You affect cigarettes, liquor, wild parties, all collegiate things. You catch the school spirit. You root wildly for the team. You boast of your school prowess. Of course you can never hope to play on the team. You cannot belong to literary societies or pep organizations or any other extra curricula activities. You accept such discriminations as your place. Inferiority is fast becoming a part of your thinking process.

A year or two passes thus. You have become a leader in your various activities. You have not found what you sought at college despite your mad efforts. That vague something which you called Ideals still eludes you. You try to lose yourself and your uneasiness in your activities. You are not very successful in that.

A dozen little discriminations annoy you, discriminations that you have known all your life, it is true, but you hoped to escape them at college. You are urged to support the school and always denied any part in it. You become discontented.

You still hear learned discourses on Democracy. You begin to suspect the speakers of a little hypocrisy. You think that the Noted Divines are perhaps not as much engaged in God's work as they would pretend.

You become a little critical of the activities. Nothing ever comes of them. You sense that they, too, are hollow gestures. They are but playthings from which ambitious students gain honor.

The students as a whole are disappointing. They shun you except when they want something. That hurts; after you have made such an effort to be like them, then you can't be accepted. They can never refer to you in the singular. You are always addressed as one of "you fellows". You can't understand why you can never be an individual.

Your own groups are far from satisfactory. For the most part they are engaged in a mad effort to conform, to be collegiate. Underneath this outward show you find them cynical enough. They give public lip ser-vice to success and Democracy, but they sneer at it privately. However they are in the grip of a terrible inferiority complex and hope for a chance to be allowed to achieve a small success. That's all they ask.

You begin to look more critically at the social order. You soon de-termine that all is not as well with the scheme of things as you have been told. In fact you think it is not well at all. You have been misled.

You turn your attention to your own leaders. On close inspection you find them leading a double existence much the same as you lead in college. They must shout platitudes of Democracy with leaders of the other race, but must never hope for too much for themselves. They cringe and cower before the others. They fear to strike out boldly lest they lose the miserable status assigned to them. You shudder to think that this must be your lot. You see now that it is part of your inheri-tance along with a dark skin.

The whole thing palls on you. Activities, groups, parties, being col-legiate all fail you. You try to escape. You withdraw within yourself. You turn to literature.

You discover Poetry, Philosophy; you knew hazily that such things existed but you never had time to enjoy them. A new world opens to you, a magnificent world of the arts, Poetry, Painting, Music, Sculp-ture.

You are captivated. You push further. You find you must rid your-self of old prejudices and values to enjoy this strange new world. You do so gladly. Even your old God must go. You regret that about God. He was such a convenient old chap on which to blame everything, but he must go.

You go further. You have discovered Life!

Life, there it is, Life! This is what you sought when you came to College. This is the Ideal of which you dreamed.

You dream anew, wonderful rose-hued dreams; dreams of Oxford, of Paris, of Rome, of Life. Dreams which you sense intuitively will never come true. That is why they are so dear to you.

You decide secretly, almost shame-facedly that you will not be a lawyer. You have found yourself. You have found how to live. You will not barter living for money or for success. You will cling to it at any cost.

You will not be forced to live a terrible, double existence cringing before the crowd. Leaders, you think, are like the college cheer-leader shouting with the masses. He who yells the college yell louder than anyone else becomes the yell leader. In life he who shouts Democracy louder than the other is made a Senator. You don't want that. You want the right to think, to live your own way.

You dream like that for a while, then you become uneasy again. You know you can't be in college forever. You are faced with the necessity of making a living. What career will you choose? You examine yourself. You may write a little; short sketchy things, or half baked verse. You know that you need time and training to develop in that respect.

There are many things from which your color will forever bar you. Oh, if you were a genius you might break down those barriers, but you aren't. You wonder, you think of men of your race who have succeeded: Dunbar, Tanner, Hayes, Cullen, Hughes, you realize that they are what the world terms genius. You are not. What will you do? How will you find time and opportunity to develop yourself?

You become panicky, frightened. It is as though you wandered in a dark house, alone and afraid and could see the bright light outside. Then suddenly you found the door locked and barred and couldn't get out.

The race above, refusing you; your own race below unable to help you and you, caught between them. The one thrusting you down, the other helpless to shove you up.

You are helpless. You become frantic.

Then you are caught as in a terrible storm. A storm that grips you, tears at you, beats you down and casts you aside beaten.

The storm clears; no it doesn't clear. It settles! That's it; it settles into a heavy fog! A terrible blighting fog to blind you, always.

You must go on with that fog forever in your face. On and on fighting a battle that is forever lost. No battle is so bitter as the one you must fight knowing that defeat awaits inevitably at the end. And defeat exists only in the mind! Now if your inferiority complex would let you go, you might rise, but it won't; it grips you more tightly.

You know that you will be crushed and crammed into a preconceived mold, your place, then sneered at and hated because you are there. That is reality. You must be a sacrifice to superior White Gods; to inferior Black Gods.

You are hopeless, dejected. You cast about for some thing on which to cling. Not God, you have lost him, bartered him for reality, then lost them both. You will never find him again. You will pretend to, but you won't. Not the Church; you know it is hollow, empty. Not your old values; you know now that they were but illusions. Not your own race to any great extent; it too is hopeless and helpless.

Then, because it is the path of least resistance, you hate and curse. You curse yourself, your race, all races, the Gods, all things.

You hate blindly and with a holy hatred; it is holy like the hatred of the Crusaders for Moslems; holy like the hatred of America for her enemies when she went forth to make a world safe for Democracy; holy like the hatred of missionaries for heathen Gods as they go to plant the Cross of Jesus Christ. You lose sight of everything but hating for a while.

Your career. Oh yes, your career; you must have a career. You were right in the first place. You will be a lawyer after all; a lawyer to confound these fools with their own laws giving life, liberty and the pursuit of happiness. Ha, that will be sweet, to see them choke on their own mouthings! You will show them just how far you will rise in spite of them. You will be ruthless and make them give you a place.

You plunge into law. You secretly loathe it. You still find yourself writing bitter little sketches, tragic bits of verse but you repress them; then you find your superlative emotions slowly receding. They were too high to sustain themselves. You aren't so bitter now, neither do you dream anymore. You return to commonplace things and become passively interested in them. You become more tolerant of your fellow students' attitude. You understand now why they accepted their place so readily. They had gone through the struggle before you. You see your leaders in a new light. You understand the terrible burden that they must carry. They must live a double life; their only escape is in their hypocritical attitude of acceptance of things they know are false.

You realize fully now what you will be in the end. You must be but little more than a shyster lawyer. You will be pushed down to preying on police court characters, loose women and gamblers, with perhaps a small share of legitimate business. You will have to become a pillar of the church, a respectable, God-fearing citizen. You will, in time, even prate of honesty and success as those before you have done. You may even inspire some one to follow your example.

Secretly you hope that you will be able to keep a part of you sacred to your dreams. It will be a small part, you know. You are beaten now and thankful with Swinburne

"That even the weariest river,
Winds some where safe to sea."

You hope, against hope, that the winding will not be too long.

COUNTEE CULLEN TO HIS FRIENDS

Poet Countee Cullen, at the time of writing this letter in 1929, was the son-in-law of the editor of *The Crisis,* W. E. B. Du Bois. He wrote from Paris, where he was spending a year on a Guggenheim fellowship. As he traveled throughout Europe, he wrote to his friends via *The Crisis* to offer his thoughts and impressions.

Paris, January 18, 1929.

Dear Friends: You to whom I have owed letters so long; certainly it is an inspired editor who suggests a series of open correspondence to you as a means of retaining a friendship that has perhaps begun to wane under ill-treatment. Tactfully the editor adds that what I say may at scattered intervals interest you.... I am not psychologist enough to attempt an interpretation of the soul of Europe, nor physician enough to diagnose its maladies for comparison with American ailments; for it is only the scientific mind that is discriminating enough not to measure by its own temperament the mores of a foreign people. Europe with America for its yardstick may be disappointing, but Europe measured in its own terms is like an inspirational tonic.... Thinking back with no attempt at an orderly survey, this new life at first assumes the aspect of a kaleidoscopic view of cities: Le Havre, Paris, Marseilles, Algiers, Berlin, Vienna, Etaples, Geneva, and again Paris. The memory of each city is illumined by some incident or series of happenings, mostly personal, some trivial, but each a guarded souvenir.... Le Havre unique because it marked the Seven League Boot stride from continent to continent; a seaport town, rife with sailors and scurrying, perspiring tourists, a town with which to pass the time of day but not to engage in lengthy conversation; a town to remember for an exhibition of Americanism overseas: the three ladies were evidently of German extraction, for the two elderly ones seemed to find it less of an effort to converse in that language than in a broken English. The youngest, however, a woman about forty, had been thoroughly Americanized and it pained her terribly to use her ancestral tongue even when conversing with her mother. Poor, excited lady; she had misplaced her baggage, or rather an irresponsible porter had misplaced it for her; and the boat train was about to leave for Paris. The lady knew no French; it never occurred to her that perhaps her train companions might be able to stumble through a sentence or two. Therefore she attempted to make the train conductor understand English by bawling it into his ear very loud and very fast. When this novel method of teaching a foreign language in one lesson failed, she remarked with real feeling and disgust, "Why I thought everybody over here spoke two languages." The conductor surely spoke French and it is not past belief that he may have been well versed in Chinese. But to the Lords of the Earth two languages mean your own and English.... Then Paris en route to Algiers. It was July 13th; tomorrow Paris would celebrate her Independence Day and the Fall of the Bastille. We must stay over for the parade. We had missed it two years ago, and we hankered for a sight of the strapping black French colonial who, we had been told, led the parade with twirling baton, glistening face, and the gayest of martial strides. But, alas, though in Paris, we fell asleep as New Yorkers; consequently we arose at eleven to view a parade that had already passed at nine.... Then off to Algiers by way of Marseilles to rest there for a day or two in the hope of meeting and exchanging a word with Claude McKay, but he was too deep in the beauties of Seville to get to Marseilles before we sailed for Algiers.... Algiers, a deceptive hussy of a town, a sort of whited sepulchre, beautiful with its white, sunkindled roofs glimpsed from the deck of a slowly incoming steamer, but squalid and sickly under closer inspection.... Berlin, an orderly, clean, regimented city, as if on dress parade; the Germans shaped for joviality but in the main serious-miened. Remembered incidents: Crab-soup at Kempinsky's; a chance encounter on the street with the Marcus Garveys; a similar encounter with J. Francis Mores, a former luminary of the old Lafayette Stock Company. He played Valentine when we saw our first opera; it was Faust and given by the Lafayette Players, and Abbie Mitchell was a heavenly voiced Marguerite. Drinking coffee in a Berlin cafe and suddenly hearing the strains of "*Nobody Knows the Trouble I've Seen*" being softly wafted to us from a distant corner of the room; looking up gratefully to see the pianist watching us, his expression conveying the wish to make a stranger welcome with some remembrance from his own people. . . . Vienna, where we were shown about by a group of Socialist friends who displayed with pride the city government's efforts to meet the housing needs of a highly impoverished people. Cooperative apartment houses that covered blocks and squares; simple, unpretentious dwellings of little beauty but built for endurance and service. "We have no money," our friends explained, "for ornamentation. We must expend all for utility." We visited one of the apartments, a one-room kitchenette and bathroom arrangement for which the occupant pays less than one dollar per week. Vienna and the Socialist watchword: *Freundschaft* . . . Etaples a southern summer village in France noted for at least one luminous distinction as being the summer home of Henry Ossawa Tanner. *"And did you once see Shelley plain?"* We have slept in Tanner's house, have watched him cut and mix salad at his table, seasoning it with the meticulousness of the conscientious artist; and we have witnessed in him one more instance that the coming of years and the accumulation of honors need not dull a man's human sympathies and his wit, nor make him unduly vexed at youngsters who stand in his studio and ask him witless questions about his easel and his oils. A drive with Tanner to Paris Plage and to Le Touquet of the famous Casino where evening regalia is required for permission to enter and stake your money on little red and black balls. But gaming tables are not for poor poets; a peep into the halls of chance must suffice. . . . Geneva and a happy week there as the guest of the Quaker Hostel, all arranged through Mabel Byrd formerly of the Brooklyn and New York Y. W. C. A.'s. . . . international gatherings where every conceivable race and country were represented; the air shot through with intense hopes and prophecies for world peace, the brotherhood of the races, the millennium. And always and everywhere a keen interest in the Negro, in many instances a livelier knowledge of what he is doing than is found in his own purlieus. . . . Geneva and a mountain drive on a brisk October morning; the summit reached, and fronting one in the distance the cold, austere, majesty of Mount Blanc, a moment to remember as long as the mind can remember beauty. Leaving Geneva with a sort of welcoming farewell ringing in our ears, "Come back to Geneva and read your new poems to us when they are finished. . . ." Then Paris again, and well, Paris needs another letter.

COUNTEE CULLEN.

Augusta Savage: An Autobiography

Augusta Savage, educator and sculptor, relates her early life as a child of an impoverished family in Florida, and her rise to become one of America's most celebrated sculptors. This essay was published in August 1929.

I was born in Florida of poor parents. I am the seventh child in a family of fourteen. Nine of us reached maturity. My father, who was burned to death in January this year, was a minister and very fond of good books. At the mud pie age, I began to make "things" instead of mud pies. I had very little schooling and most of my school hours were spent in playing hookey in order to go to the clay pit—we had a brick yard in our town—and make ducks out of clay.

Our family moved to West Palm Beach in 1915, and as there was no clay soil down there, my clay modeling was at a standstill, until I chanced to pass a pottery on the outskirts of the town and having begged a bit of clay from the potter, I resumed my modelling. The objects created from this clay were brought to the attention of the superintendent of the county fair which was due to open within three weeks. This man, the late Mr. George Graham Currie, persuaded me to enter my models in the fair, which I did. Being the only work of its kind on exhibit, it created a small sensation. A special prize of $25 was awarded me, and this together with public contributions donated by the tourists with the admonition to go to New York and study art, netted me $175.

I persuaded my family to let me go to Jacksonville, Florida, where I hoped to "do" the busts of all of our rich colored people there and so make enough money to finance my art career. I am thankful to say that the said rich folks refused to be "done" and I was soon almost stranded.

I managed to pay my fare to New York and arrived with a balance of $4.60 and a determination to learn sculpturing in six months. I was directed to Cooper Union by the late Solon Borglum and was accepted on the merits of my work. After three months, I was forced to quit school and go to work, but was recalled and offered a working scholarship, which provided for my room and board and carfare, 1921–1922.

In 1923, I applied for and was granted a scholarship which entitled me to study at Fontainebleau, France. [On the American Committee were Whitney Warren, Ernest C. Peixotto, Edwin Blashfield, Howard Greenley, Thomas Hastings, Herman MacNeil and James Gamble Rogers.] When it was discovered that I was black, the Committee withdrew the scholarship.

In 1925, through the efforts of Dr. W. E. B. Du Bois, I was granted a working scholarship which entitled me to study at the Royal Academy of Fine Arts at Rome, Italy; but as I had to pay my travelling expenses and as that was impossible to me, I was unable to take it.

In 1929, through the efforts of Mr. John E. Nail and Mr. Eugene Kinckle Jones of the National Urban League, I have been granted the Julius Rosenwald Fellowship for two years' study abroad. The Fellowship was originally for $1,500 per year, but has been raised to $1,800.

I have exhibited at the 135th Street Branch Library, New York; Douglas High School, Baltimore, Maryland; and at the Sesqui-Centennial, Philadelphia.

New Literature on the Negro

In the following essay, Jessie Fauset discusses recent books published by African Americans. Fauset contends that these books can be viewed in two distinct categories. The first concerns how African Americans are viewed by their own race; the second concerns the status of African Americans as they move in the white world in a homeland that both races share. This essay was published in the June 1920 issue.

That the Negro has come into Literature to stay is evidenced by the increasing number of books issued each year in which the Negro, or his condition, form the main discussion. It is impossible adequately to take up the great matters of the day—economics, social welfare, labor, the whole question of national readjustment of post-war times,—without including his shadowed but persistent figure. The books which we have listed here fall easily into two classes, one in which the Negro is seen among his own distinct activities, and the other in which he moves in contradistinction to the whites with whom he shares his home in America.

It is interesting to note the incongruities which arise from taking two sets of facts, in themselves absolutely true to reality, and mingling them into an inharmonious jumble. This is the sort of thing done by Paul Reboux in his amazingly inconsistent book *Romulus Coucou.* M. Reboux is, I suspect, trying to make clear two pictures, the reaction of the early African immigrant to occidental civilization, and the intolerance of the white American with regard to his black compatriot.

Briefly the story concerns the picturesque Coucou family of New Orleans which numbers among its members one Romulus Coucou, whose mother (Madame Coucou) is black, but whose father was white. Romulus is described as being a decided cut above his half relatives, including his step-father and his own mother. He is a druggist's clerk with every prospect of advance, and although his life in the home of his step-father, who runs a laundry, does not apparently irk him, he aspires undoubtedly to something higher. He chances to spy one day at the theatre a young French girl, Jacqueline Béliard, with whom he falls violently in love. Thence all his misfortunes. He contrives to meet her, wins her affection and holds it too despite his admission of black blood. She becomes his fiancée—she has not been long enough in America to realize what all this entails. Romulus makes an honorable request of the girl's brother for his sister's hand, is spurned, takes to cocaine and whiskey, loses his position, wanders off to Jamaica to assist a forlorn revolutionist, returns and finds Jacqueline the wife of a white American. Consumed by love and jealousy he persists in a course of debasement and debauchery, and finally, to assist in a performance of voodoo rites, kidnaps Jacqueline's baby so that there may be white human blood at the orgy. At the last moment, overwhelmed with remorse, he returns the child unharmed to the garden of its stricken parents' home. Concealed he watches Jacqueline rush toward her child thus miraculously restored, sees her about to faint, and darting forth catches her in his arms. At this moment he is discovered, his motives misinterpreted and he meets the popular American death for Negroes.

The story is told with a delicately malicious style and with absolutely no attempt at exposition. It is pure narrative and description and one finishes it without the least idea where M. Reboux "gets off at". His inconsistencies are amazing. Thus Romulus shown on the cover picture, supposedly with M. Reboux's consent, as a creature with overhanging thick lips, bulbous chin, broad retreating nose, and a very tiny, but undeniable pigtail peeping from his hatbrim, is described by the author as being "one of those men who through the influence of his white blood, possessed beautiful eyes, well-matched (harmonieux) features, a mouth and nose of the European type, a clear, creamy skin, and delicately modelled limbs. His hair alone proclaimed his race." It is the possession of equally frizzy hair on the part of Jacqueline which first calls his attention to her. One thinks that perhaps she too has a drop of dark blood, but this mystery is never explained. Romulus in writing to Jacqueline displays an intimate knowledge of Plutarch and Voltaire. His style is very elevated. When he pleads his suit before Jacqueline's brother he says, "I speak French, as you see ... English too naturally, a little Italian and Spanish. M. Beaugé has helped me with my literature." Does it seem that such a man could be induced to assist at the practice of voodooism, even supposing that such rites are carried on in New Orleans in these days?

The times are evidently of today, for M. Reboux speaks once of "German propaganda". Yet in the very next breath, on the very next line he speaks of "old Negroes still unoriented to America's customs, nursing in the depths of their hearts an agony of homesickness for the jungles of the Congo"! A remarkable atavism there! With the same malice he says of Jacqueline's sister-in-law, "Her native pride filled her with an indulgent scorn with respect to Mother Europe and induced her to believe that the products of the United States are always the finest, the most beautiful, the most extraordinary in the entire world. In a word she was an American." Just at the end his delicate malice becomes terrific irony. "What's the trouble?" asks one. "They're burning a Negro," is the reply. "Oh, yes, it's New Year's Day," shrugs the first.

The book, as far as I know, has not yet been translated, but it is written in language simple enough for the most casual student of French.

———

In *Unwritten History,* Bishop Levi J. Coppin deals with his own life in an account which when one comes to think of it is more wonderful than any fairy tale that ever was written. For his is the story of a man who though actually free-born was none the less under the influence of slavery conditions, and yet rose to a Bishopric. The book is written in a pleasant, discursive style which makes the too frequent bad spelling, passed over by some careless proofreader, all the more lamentable. Incidentally Bishop Coppin touches on the history of that amazing institution, the A. M. E. Church. He says:

"One of the things connected with the history of our people, not generally known or considered, and which seems mysterious even to those who consider it, is the fact that in 1866, one year after the surrender, the A. M. E. Church was fifty years old in its organic form, and seventy-nine years old counting from the date, 1787, when the revolt against segregation at St. George took place. Just how this handful of people, without social, political and civil prestige; poor and unlearned, and hemmed in from every side by slavery, and the spirit and influence of slavery, could organize and maintain itself so long and so well, is, indeed, a mystery. One would not imagine, until his attention is called to the fact, that at the dawn of freedom, there was a regularly organized religious denomination; with Bishops, a Book Repository, a weekly newspaper, hymn book and discipline and a church school, and with seven annual conferences operating in different states, as follows: the New England States, New York, Pennsylvania, Maryland, Ohio, Indiana and Missouri."

Unwritten History will have more than an ordinary interest, I suspect, for colored Philadelphians, since in it the Bishop pays tribute to Mrs. Fanny Jackson Coppin of I. C. Y. fame. Tracing as it does the author's career from the condition of a poor boy through that of storekeeper, teacher, minister, journalist and Bishop in the field of South Africa, this narrative is bound to prove an inspiration to the youth of any nation.

———

Miss Delilah L. Beasley has adopted an interesting and unusual method in her remarkable volume *The Negro Trail-Blazers of California*. First she shows through indisputable evidence that a Negro was in the original party which left Spain in 1526 in "an exploring overland expedition from Florida to the Pacific coast". Then from this point she gives an account of Negro pioneers in all forward movements in California down to the Great War. Miss Beasley's book is a compilation showing much painstaking research, since she supplies sources and statistics for almost every statement of importance. Of course its greatest value lies in its contribution to our far too little knowledge of Negro explorers. Cabeza de Vaca, a Spanish explorer and historian of the early 16th century, gives the names of those who after nine years of exploring were fortunate enough to reach the Pacific coast. He says:

"And now that I have given an account of the ship, it may be well to record also who those are and where from, whom it pleased God to rescue from all those dangers and hardships. The first is: Alonzo de Castillo Maldonado, a native of Salamanca. The second is Andrew Dorantes, born of Benjar, but a resident of Gilraleon. The third is Alvar Nuñez Cabeza de Vaca, son of Frances de Vera and grandson of Pedro de Vera, who conquered the Canary Islands. The fourth is Estevanico, an Arab Negro from Azamore on the Atlantic Coast of Morocco."

The book is profusely illustrated.

———

In a discussion somewhat too sententious and insufficiently constructive Dr. A. B. Jackson does in his *Man Next Door* emphasize three very important factors in the Negro's development. It is impossible to overlook the vast influence which the Negro Church exerts over its members. Here is really the forcing-house of three-fourths of the race's leaders. "While the church is not a commercial institution—" he says, "as a matter of self preservation it is beginning to develop a veiled and crafty acumen, which if carefully noted reveals a generalship more erudite than it is usually credited with. Virtually it is saying today: 'We are specialists, we are teaching religion, we appreciate our grasp upon the people, yet if other worthy interests desire a clientele we shall gladly help you.'" Dr. Jackson defines well the Negro's love of learning when he writes, "His desire for education is no mere fanciful hysteria, but the expression of a determination to earn a place in a world that demands intelligence". The most significant passage in this book is one in which the need of race consciousness and first aids to its attainment are stressed. The author continues: "The hopes of evolving a distinctive racial culture which will in turn give birth to a fine sense of race consciousness, lies in the education of the young by educators who experience and express an exalted perception of racial patriotism. Every Negro teacher should know and with a supreme patriotic pleasure feel the urge to teach the true history of ancient Africa and the part black men have played in giving culture and civilization to our world. Every Negro school should have a supplementary graded course for carrying this message of hope to the minds of black boys and girls. Every Negro college should have a chair devoted to the history of black men."

The Sword of Nemesis by R. Archer Tracy, and *The Immediate Jewel of His Soul* by Herman Dreer, do not by any means represent the highest type of novel. They are too long drawn out, the language is often stilted and the plot in each instance shows some improbabilities. *The Sword of Nemesis* is a tale of mystery, murder and love in the West Indies. *The Immediate Jewel of His Soul* treats of the adventures both in social reform and in love of a young Negro minister in a small southern town. But in spite of their shortcomings both these books are of some value, in as much as they mark—in the first-named book particularly,—the launching of an essay by Negro writers into the realm of pure romantic fiction. This is a relief when one considers that nearly all writing on the part of colored Americans seeks to set forth propaganda. Dr. Tracy and Mr. Dreer have both contrived to establish a colored background against which an occasional white figure moves. The reverse of this is too often the case in stories about colored people.

Most colored Americans and a good many white know of cases where people with a strain of Negro blood have gone over to the white world. But the really white girl who for some reason has been consigned to the black world and then comes back to the white, presents a new aspect. In Miss Ovington's *Shadow* Hertha Ogilvie has been placed among colored people to hide her mother's disgrace. She grows up with these people, loves them genuinely and when the indisputable evidence comes that she is white, hates to leave them. But according to the code of her town she must. She comes to New York, to get away, as much as anything else, from her torturing love for Lee Merryvale, a young white man, who had been attracted to her while she was colored, but whose motives based on our queer color codes could not be honorable. Her life in New York and Brooklyn is interesting and varied. She learns something of the Labor Problem—discussed at somewhat too great length—and still more of America's persistent prejudice toward her Negro citizens. Hertha often longs for the sheer human kindness of her foster relatives, but for a long time she is glad that she belongs to the white world. Then comes the crash. Her foster brother Tom, colored of course, crosses her path. At her behest he comes to see her, meets her by accident in a Brooklyn park, and of course speaks to her. Hertha's unworthy lover, Dick Brown, resents this; an assault which bids fair to become a lynching ensues. But Hertha saves the day by pretending that she is colored and that Tom is her brother. Dick Brown turns away in disgust. Hertha gets Tom to a hospital and afterwards to their first home in Georgia, glad to return to that humble but sincere haven. However, Lee Merryvale is still there. It seems he has never ceased to love her, or she him. And the two are left evidently about to embark on the great romance.

Miss Ovington has written with much insight. Hertha is a fine, sensitive character, with a keen sense of gratitude. Kathleen, the Irish woman, is splendid and so also is the dimly-portrayed Ellen, Hertha's foster sister, who in my mind is the most typical figure of latter day colored people in the book. The possibilities which open up to Hertha, and the change of attitude toward her on the part of her white neighbors, when she finds that she too is white, is very illuminating. But the really important effect of the story is to leave one keenly alive to the need of a new set of values. What are the things that really count,— pride of race, prestige, or loyalty and kindness? Hertha grows to dread the change which seems to be coming over her. Her contact with her own people had played havoc with her best principles. "The white world's phantoms were clouding her spirit, turning her affectionate gratitude into shrinking fear. They were standing between her and a past that she loved." She senses the silliness of the whole color question. What was it all about? Clearly only an aspect of mind. "How glad I am to be white," she thinks once. "And yet how queer it is to be glad, for I've always been just the same." And again, "Looking into Tom's face, his good face with its serious forehead, its kindly mouth, she believed that even Dick, were he there, must cease his nasty screeching about niggers and see that boys were boys, black or white, and that here was a young American of whom to be proud". But finally "I'm tired of the white world", she cries desperately. Well, she comes into her own at last. Colored readers, I am inclined to think, will wince a bit at the thought that Hertha, when white, is willing to marry Lee Merryvale, who certainly would not have married her as long as he thought she was colored. But perhaps this is an extension of the double standard. And then too in her readjustment of her own values, Hertha may have stumbled across the necessity for the eternal compromise between ideals and things as they are.

———

In *Darkwater* Dr. Du Bois has bestowed on the world a triple gift. He has made the most significant single contribution to the "Negro Problem" of the age; he has added to the storehouse of outstanding and noble literature; and he has served as a mouthpiece and inspiration for the oppressed peoples of both hemispheres. Indeed so much has been said about this book both in the newspapers and magazines and in these pages that the only excuse for further mention could be some attempt to explain the reaction to it of the people whom Dr. Du Bois represents.

The psychology of the hunted, the hurt, the broken, the oppressed, is a hard thing to get at. It is obscured sometimes by fear, sometimes by pride. Dr. Du Bois with a fearlessness and a pride too real to fear pity or misinterpretation gives the world an account of what millions of people suffer, not because they are black, but because of the construction which a dominant white world has put on that color. And as he writes dark people become free; they put away false shame, they are glad that they have instincts which permit them to feel, to pity, to sicken before ruthlessness and cruelty. They realize new rights and privileges and the blessings of the power of choice. This terrible, grasping, raging white world of which Dr. Du Bois too truly writes,— is it then the tremendous, glorious thing with the marvellous ideals of which they learn in the mixed schools and colleges of America, where all teachers and all precepts are white? In this darker world which they inhabit, there is ignorance and poverty and misery, but at least there are not hands dripping with another people's blood, hearts filled with hypocrisy, homes gorgeously outfitted but reared over the graves of helpless slaves. And so though they dare not become complacent, these dark folk are suddenly content to be black.

With the contentment comes fresh knowledge of fundamentals, a glimpse of possibilities. When a dark man comes to realize that much of the world's injustice toward him is based on an attitude, not on a verity, he begins to vision hope. In the chapter called "The Souls of White Folk"—which together with the "Damnation of Women" and the

"Litany of Atlanta" are the favorites for colored readers,—in this chapter Dr. Du Bois says: "The degrading of men by men is as old as mankind and the invention of no one race or people. Ever have men striven to conceive of their victims as different from the victors, endlessly different, in soul and blood, strength and cunning, race and lineage. It has been left, however, to Europe and to modern days to discover the eternal world-wide mark of meanness,—color!" So after all there is nothing really in the theory that color means inferiority, it is merely a convenient assumption. But assumptions, attitudes are variable, things which may be changed. And so the dark world falls a thinking. Thinking what? Dr. Du Bois answers with only too prophetic frankness. "It is thinking that as wild and awful as this shameful war was, it is nothing to compare with that fight for freedom which black and brown and yellow men must and will make unless their oppression and humiliation and insult at the hands of the White World cease. The Dark World is going to submit to its present treatment just as long as it must and not one moment longer."

Finally colored people like to think that this book is indicative. After all Dr. Du Bois is theirs. The genius which he evinces is, of course, not racial but individual, as all genius must be. But the training, the breadth of outlook, the ability to marshal facts and to interpret them, the exercise of judgment the wide-range of treatment as shown in the use of both poetry and prose, lastly the large patience—these are qualities which men are not born with; they are the prizes offered by life and so are among the attainable and a colored man has attained them. "Here are the things for which we shall strive," cries colored America.

THE SYMBOLISM OF BERT WILLIAMS

Bert Williams (1874–1922), entertainer and comedian, was born in Antigua, British West Indies. Williams moved with his family first to New York and then to California. In 1895, he met George Nash Walker, and they formed a vaudeville team, Williams and Walker. Following the death of Bert Williams, Jessie Fauset wrote about his unique art form. This essay was published in May 1922.

To say that the average Negro is the Negro artist's harshest critic would be undoubtedly to state a truism whose deepest meaning would not be immediately apparent. Thus among many colored theatregoers Charles Gilpin's rendition of The Emperor Jones caused a deep sense of irritation. They could not distinguish between the artistic interpretation of a type and the deliberate travestying of a race, and so their appreciation was clouded. Our great fault is our inability to distinguish between a horizontal or class and a vertical or racial section of life. I need hardly add that the character of Emperor Jones is a class type.

No such irritation bemused our understanding of Bert Williams, for he was to us the racial type itself. That is why he is symbolic.

By a strange and amazing contradiction this *Comedian* symbolized that deep, ineluctable strain of melancholy, which no Negro in a mixed civilization ever lacks. He was supposed to make the world laugh and so he did but not by the welling over of his own spontaneous subjective joy, but by the humorously objective presentation of his personal woes and sorrows. His *rôle* was always that of the poor, shunted, cheated, out-of-luck Negro and he fostered and deliberately trained his genius toward the delineation of this type because his mental as well as his artistic sense told him that here was a true racial vein.

This does not mean that he leaped by inspiration into the portrayal of the black roustabout. Mr. Williams first took stock of his own limitations. He was used to considering these as a boy in the High School in California whence he had been brought some years after leaving his home in Nassau in the Bahamas. His first glance at those limitations revealed that he could not afford to attend Leland Stanford University as he had dreamed; his second revealed that though he had a decided liking for the stage and even a slight possibility of gratifying his liking, color would probably keep him from ever making "the legitimate."

The field that lay open to him then and in which he started was that of minstrelsy. During those first few months with his troupe it fell to his lot to brush shoes and press dress-suits, to polish the nickel on the banjos, to arrange the chairs in a semi-circle and finally to take his place in that same semi-circle. How his youthful eyes would have stared if he could have looked forward to the setting of a Ziegfeld production! Could he but have foreseen the weariness of the way!

One day he took in as partner George Walker and the two appeared in vaudeville at the Midway Plaisance in San Francisco where they tasted the beginning of a fame destined to spread the world over. At first Williams was the clever man and Walker the fool, but very shortly they reversed their positions: "I'm funnier along this line than you," Williams said to his partner and so he proved himself. From that day on he never forsook the character of the shambling, stupid, wholly pathetic dupe.

As his success grew, his ambitions soared, but always they brought him up against his boundaries, the wall of prejudice. Subjectively his power was limitless; objectively it had to soar up but not outwards. With that most fundamental characteristic of true genius he took up the task of making the most of his restricted opportunities. Without the slightest knowledge of the dialect of the American Negro, he set to work to acquire it. He watched, he listened, he visited various Negro districts North and South, he studied phonetics. He could make his listener distinguish between variations of different localities. He affected, his admirers will remember, a shambling, shuffling gait which at intervals in his act would change into a grotesque sliding and gliding—the essence of awkward naturalness. But awkward or graceful, it was not natural to him, but simply the evolution of a walk and dance which he had worked out by long and patient observation of Negro prototypes.

It took him years of practice and constant watchfulness to be able to portray to its fullest the shiftlessness, the dolefulness, the "easiness" of the type of Negro whose persistent ill-luck somehow endeared him to our hearts. He was so real, so simple, so credulous. His colored auditors laughed but often with a touch of rue,—this characterization was too near to us; his hard luck was our own universal fate.

Everyone knows of the dramatic triumphs of the Williams and Walker troupe, from California to Chicago, then to New York where they played a thirty weeks' engagement with Koster and Bials (a record-breaker for those days) and finally an appearance before King Edward VII at Buckingham Palace. This triumph would have meant to another the zenith of a career, not only would he have failed to go beyond, he would have thought there was no beyond. To Mr. Williams it was only the stepping-stone to the attainment of greater perfection. While in London he studied with Pietro the art of pantomime and from him he evolved those curiously short-ranged, awkward but sure gestures which supplemented so well the workings of his face. That wonderful face mobile and expressive even under its black paint!

Painstakingly, bit by bit, he made himself a great artist; what power of mimicry he possessed natively he used; what he lacked he picked up by careful study until that, too, was his own; at last constructively and spontaneously he became a great luminary in the world of comic art. Ziegfeld realized this and after the death of Walker took him on in the "Follies" where for a long time he struck the truest artistic note in that medley of banality, rich costumes and shining flesh. His marriage was unusually happy, his coffers were sufficiently full, his friends were many, his love of books for which he possessed an unusually nice appreciation was gratified. He found pleasure in his music. But something irked.

He could not forget his color and the limitations it imposed on him in his chosen field. In spite of his greatness he was unusually modest. He did not push himself, he was tolerant in the presence of intolerance, but he simply could not understand "what it was all about. I breathe like other people," he said, "I eat like them—put me at a dinner and I'll use the right fork. I think like other people. In London I am presented to the King, in France I have sat at dinner with the president of the republic, while here in the United States I am often treated with an air of personal and social condescension by the gentleman who sweeps out my dressing room or by the gentleman whose duty it is to turn the spotlight on me.

"And yet it was here in the United States that a war was fought in the sixties about a certain principle. It seems strange, doesn't it?"

Others of us find it strange, too.

At last, this very year, he was billed to feature in a play written especially for him, in which he was the star, in which all the action centered about him. "Under the Bamboo Tree" was a charming farce and admirably suited to the quiet drollery of the man whom Al Weeks styled our "gentlest comedian". And in the midst of it after he had sung for a few nights his song called "Puppy Dog" in which he likened his own loneliness in the play to that of a homeless, friendless mutt to whom he said "when you die no one will care because they'll say 'only a puppy dog has gone' "—after all this he collapsed one night quite suddenly in the theatre and came back to New York to die.

But everybody cared!

The press was instant with expressions of sympathy, regret and appreciation. He was called our greatest comedian and compared, as indeed he deserved to be, with those other great wits of the world, Shakespeare and Molière and Mark Twain. In the bitter bleakness of a March day fifteen thousand people throned the streets to his funeral; there were two services, one at St. Philip's in Harlem, another at the Temple of the Grand Lodge of the Order of Masons. We were all proud to know of his plaudits, we knew he merited them, but with our pride was mingled a passionate strain of resentment. If the world knew of his great possibilities why had it doomed this stalwart, handsome creature, to hide his golden skin, his silken hair, his beautiful, sensitive hands under the hideousness of the eternal black make-up. Why should he and we obscure our talents forever under the bushel of prejudice, jealousy, stupidity—whatever it is that makes the white world say: "No genuine colored artist; coons, clowns, end-men, clap-trap, but no undisguisedly beautiful presentation of Negro ability."

The irony of it has made us all a little sadder so much so that when this morning I, who unfortunately did not know him, read in the *Tribune:* "Eddie Cantor gets a clean face", my eyelids stung with the prick of sudden tears.

That is a fine concept which Oliver Wendell Holmes gave to mankind from his contemplation of "The Chambered Nautilus". He bids us rear for life one stately mansion after another, each embracing and overtowering the preceding one:

"Let each new temple nobler than the last
Shut thee from heaven with a dome more vast,
Till thou at length art free."

It is pleasant to think of Mr. Williams thus building the structures of his life: first his little profession of minstrelsy, then his partnership and success with Mr. Walker; his appearance before nobility and royalty; his entré as a feature-artist into the Follies—an unprecedented stride that for the colored man;—and finally his triumphant emergence as a star—still in black-face. And beyond and around all these structures he reared the unfailing quality and precision of style which was the impress of his art. But greater than any of these towered the temple of his character, of that disposition which left him for all his greatness gentle, modest, unenvious; which for all his heartbreak left him without bitterness, able to oppose to intolerance a mild and thoughtful kindliness, and to offer an intense appreciation to those who without prejudice recognized and loved him. The dome of this temple grew so vast that it touched the sky—and he "at length is free."

His resignation to suffering took the sting out of the malevolence of fate.

I have tried jealously to keep Bert Williams with his struggles, his triumphs, his heartbreaks and his consolations as the symbol of our own struggling race. But is not the part he played as the helpless creature,—always beaten, always conquered,—symbolic of all poor human flesh which is ever worsted by life or the things of life, by love or the lack of love, by poverty or riches, by loneliness or a satiety of companionship? Yet does not this same poor human flesh meet all this with a tear, a sigh, a shrug, a brave smile and the realization that this is life? All that the most unfortunate can do—provided he wills to live—is to buckle down to life and try it again.

In one of the plays which Mr. Williams shared with Mr. Walker, the latter in the *rôle* of the haughty, ungrateful sharper orders his victim from his doors. Bert can not believe that he means this but Walker assures him that he does.

"All right," says Bert sadly, shambling, stumbling inimitably across the stage, "I'll go." But as he reaches the exit he straightens up and thunders in that wonderful voice of his: "But I shall return."

It was pitiful, it was funny, it was life.

Without hope we could not live. And so we hope that Bert has found the answer to his song "somewhere the sun is shining—but where?"— and that he is basking in the warmth and glow of unstinted artistic comradeship and appreciation. But more than that we hope that his death and the stream of appreciation which it evoked—alas too tardily—will teach this silly, suffering old world to lay aside its prejudices, its traditions, its petty reserves and to bestow honor where it is due—when it is due.

Thus at length shall we all be free.

PLÁCIDO

James Weldon Johnson considered Plácido in some respects the greatest of all the Cuban poets. Johnson discusses Plácido as a poet and reviews the many tragic elements of his birth, life, and death. This essay was published in January 1922.

Among the greatest poets of Latin-America are men of Negro blood. There are Plácido and Manzano in Cuba; Vieux and Durand in Haiti, Machado de Assis in Brazil; Léon Laviaux in Martinique, and others still that might be mentioned. Plácido and Machado de Assis rank as great in the literatures of their respective countries without any qualifications whatever. They are world figures in the literature of the Latin languages. Machado de Assis is somewhat handicapped in this respect by having as his tongue and medium the lesser known Portuguese, but Plácido, writing in the language of Spain, Mexico, Cuba and of almost the whole of South America, is universally known. His works have been republished in the original in Spain, Mexico and in most of the Latin-American countries; several editions have been published in the United States; translations of his works have been made into French and German.

Plácido is in some respects the greatest of all the Cuban poets. In sheer genius and the fire of inspiration he surpasses even the more finished Hérédia. Then, too, his birth, his life and his death ideally contained the tragic elements that go into the making of a halo about a poet's head. Plácido was born in Habana in 1809. The first months of his life were passed in a foundling asylum; indeed, his real name, Gabriel de la Concepcion Valdes, was in honor of its founder. His father took him out of the asylum, but shortly afterwards went to Mexico and died there. His early life was a struggle against poverty; his youth and manhood was a struggle for Cuban independence. His death placed him in the list of Cuban martyrs. On the 27th of June, 1844, he was lined up against a wall with ten others and shot by order of the Spanish authorities on a charge of conspiracy. In his short but eventful life he turned out work which bulks more than six hundred pages. During the few hours preceding his execution he wrote three of his best known poems, among them his famous sonnet, "Mother, Farewell!"

Plácido's sonnet to his mother has been translated into every important language—William Cullen Bryant did it in English—but in spite of its wide popularity, it is, perhaps, outside of Cuba, the least understood of all Plácido's poems. It is curious to note how Bryant's translation totally misses the intimate sense of the delicate subtility of the poem. The American poet makes it a tender and loving farewell of a son who is about to die to a heart-broken mother; but that is not the kind of a farewell that Plácido intended to write or did write.

The key to the poem is in the first word, and the first word is the Spanish conjunction *Si* (if). The central idea, then, of the sonnet is, *"If the sad fate which now overwhelms me should bring a pang to your heart, weep no more, for I die a glorious death and sound the last note of my lyre to you."* Bryant either failed to understand or ignored the opening word, "If", because he was not familiar with the poet's history.

While Plácido's father was a Negro, his mother was a Spanish white woman, a dancer in one of the Habana theatres. At his birth she abandoned him to a foundling asylum, and perhaps never saw him again, although it is known that she outlived her son. When the poet came down to his last hours he remembered that somewhere there lived a woman who was his mother; that although she had heartlessly abandoned him; that although he owed her no filial duty, still she might, perhaps, on hearing of his sad end feel some pang of grief or sadness; so he tells her in his last words that he dies happy and bids her not to weep. This he does with nobility and dignity, but absolutely without affection. Taking into account these facts, and especially their humiliating and embittering effect upon a soul so sensitive as Plácido's, this sonnet, in spite of the obvious weakness of the sestet as compared with the octave, is a remarkable piece of work.

In considering the Aframerican poets of the Latin languages I am impelled to think that, as up to this time the colored poets of greater universality have come out of the Latin-American countries rather than out of the United States, they will continue to do so for a good many years. The reason for this I hinted at in the first part of this preface. The colored poet in the United States labors within limitations which he cannot easily pass over. He is always on the defensive or the offensive. The pressure upon him to be propagandic is well nigh irresistible. These conditions are suffocating to breadth and to real art in poetry. In addition he labors under the handicap of finding culture not entirely colorless in the United States. On the other hand, the colored poet of Latin-America can voice the national spirit without any reservations. And he will be rewarded without any reservations, whether it be to place him among the great or declare him the greatest.

So I think it probable that the first world-acknowledged Aframerican poet will come out of Latin-America. Over against this probability, of course, is the great advantage possessed by the colored poet in the United States of writing in the world-conquering English language.

Negro Authors and

White Publishers

James Weldon Johnson writes here that certain African-
American writers complain that white publishers have
set a standard in which they choose the writings of
black authors—a standard that depicts the race in a
wrongful and distasteful manner. These black authors
further contend that white publishers refuse to consider
their work because it portrays black life on too high a
level. This essay, published in 1929, refutes this claim by
discussing recently published fiction and nonfiction
works by black authors.

Negro writers, like all writing folks, have many things to complain
about. Writers have always felt and many of them have plainly said that
the world did not fully appreciate their work. This attitude has seldom
been justified. The great or good writers who have not been acknowledged as such by the generation in which they lived are rare. And
where such acknowledgment has not been accorded by the generations
which touched an author's life, posterity has hardly ever revoked the
unfavorable judgment.

Nevertheless, writers have many good reasons for complaining; for
their lot is a hard one. And it may be that Negro writers have some special good reasons for complaining; I am not sure that at the present
time this is so. However that may be, there is one complaint that some
younger Negro writers are uttering with greater and greater insistence
which I do not think is based on the facts and which reacts to the injury of the writers uttering it. This complaint is: that the leading white
publishers have set a standard which Negro writers must conform to
or go unpublished; that this standard calls only for books depicting the
Negro in a manner which tends to degrade him in the eyes of the
world; that only books about the so-called lower types of Negroes and
lower phases of Negro life find consideration and acceptance.

Now, in the first place, there is a certain snobbishness in terming
the less literate and less sophisticated, the more simple and more

primitive classes of Negroes as "lower". At least as literary material, they are higher. They have greater dramatic and artistic potentialities for the writer than the so-called higher classes, who so closely resemble the bourgeois white classes. The vicious and criminal elements—and we must admit that even in our own race there are such elements—are rightly termed "lower", but even they have more accessible dramatic values than the ordinary, respectable middle-class element. It takes nothing less than supreme genius to make middle-class society, black or white, interesting—to say nothing of making it dramatic.

But I am jotting down this brief essay with the prime purpose of pointing out the dangers, especially to young writers, in complaining that publishers refuse to consider their work because it portrays Negro life on too high a level. When a writer begins to say and then believe that the reason why he cannot get published is because his work is *too good* he is in a bad way. This is the way that leads to making a fetish of failure. It is a too easy explanation of the lack of accomplishment. It is this "superior work—sordid publishers—low brow public" complex that gives rise to the numerous small coteries of unsuccessful writers, white as well as colored; the chief function of the members of these coteries being the mutual admiration of each other's unpublished manuscripts. This attitude brings its adherents to a position of pathetic futility or ludicrous superiority.

Within these seven or eight years of literary florescence I doubt that any first class publisher has turned down first rate work by any Negro writer on the ground that it was *not on a low enough level.* Now, suppose we look at the actual facts as shown by the books published in these recent years by leading publishers. Let us first take fiction and list the books depicting Negro life on the "upper" levels or shedding a favorable light on the race that have been published:

There Is Confusion	Jessie Fauset
Fire in the Flint	Walter White
Flight	Walter White
The Prince of Washington Square	Harry F. Liscomb
Quicksand	Nella Larsen
Dark Princess	W. E. B. Du Bois
Plum Bun	Jessie Fauset
Passing	Nella Larsen

Now, those depicting Negro life on the "lower" levels:

Cane...Jean Toomer
Tropic Death...Eric Walrond
Home to Harlem..Claude McKay
Walls of Jericho...Rudolph Fisher
The Blacker the Berry ....Wallace Thurman
Banjo..Claude McKay

The score is eight to six—with "Tropic Death", "Walls of Jericho" and "Cane" on the border line. In non fiction the "upper level" literature scores still higher. In that class we have:

A Social History of the American Negro ....Benjamin Brawley
Negro Folk Rhymes..Thomas W. Talley
The Book of American Negro Poetry ....Ed. James Weldon Johnson
The New Negro ....Ed. Alain Locke
The Book of American Negro Spirituals..
....Ed. James Weldon Johnson
The Second Book of
American Negro Spirituals ....Ed. James Weldon Johnson
Color ....Countée Cullen
Caroling Dusk ....Ed. Countée Cullen
Darkwater ....W. E. B. Du Bois
Gift of Black Folk...W. E. B. Du Bois
Plays of Negro Life.......................................Ed. Locke and Gregory
God's Trombones..James Weldon Johnson
Copper Sun ....Countée Cullen
Negro Labor in the United States....................................Charles H. Wesley
A Bibliography of the Negro in
Africa and America ....Monroe N. Work
What the Negro Thinks ....R. R. Moton
Rope and Faggot ....Walter White
An Autumn Love Cycle.........................Georgia Douglas Johnson

In the other column, in non fiction, we have only:

The Weary Blues...Langston Hughes
Fine Clothes to the Jew ....Langston Hughes

And it must be said that although Mr. Hughes shows a predilection for singing the "lower" and "humbler" classes of Negroes, these two volumes contain many poems that are highly inspirational.

In non fiction the score is nineteen to two. I do not see how any one who looks at these figures can fail to see that the complaint against the publishers is not in consonance with the facts. I believe that Negro writers who have something worth while to say and the power and skill to say it have as fair a chance today of being published as any other writers.

STEPS TOWARD THE NEGRO THEATRE

In this essay, Alain Locke contends that African Americans have produced sufficient talent and credible plays. However, he contends that the time has come for an endowed artistic center where all phases of critical art are taught and cultivated. This essay was published in December 1922.

Culturally we are abloom in a new field, but it is yet decidedly a question as to what we shall reap—a few flowers or a harvest. That depends upon how we cultivate this art of the drama in the next few years. We can have a Gilpin, as we have had an Aldridge—and this time a few more—a spectacular bouquet of talent, fading eventually as all isolated talent must; or we can have a granary of art, stocked and stored for season after season. It is a question of interests, of preferences:—are we reaping the present merely or sowing the future? For the one, the Negro actor will suffice; the other requires the Negro drama and the Negro theatre.

The Negro actor without the Negro drama is a sporadic phenomenon, a chance wayside flower, at mercy of wind and weed. He is precariously planted and still more precariously propagated. We have just recently learned the artistic husbandry of race drama, and have already found that to till the native soil of the race life and the race experience multiplies the dramatic yield both in quality and quantity. Not that we would confine the dramatic talent of the race to the fence-fields and plant-rooms of race drama, but the vehicle of all sound art must be native to the group—our actors need their own soil, at least for sprouting. But there is another step beyond this which must be taken. Our art in this field must not only be rescued from the chance opportunity and the haphazard growth of native talent, the stock must be cultivated beyond the demands and standards of the market-place, or must be safe somewhere from the exploitation and ruthlessness of the commercial theatre and in the protected housing of the art-theatre flower to the utmost perfection of the species. Conditions favorable to this ultimate development, the established Negro Theatre will alone provide.

In the past, and even the present, the Negro actor has waited to be born; in the future he must be made. Up till now, our art has been patronized; for the future it must be endowed. This is, I take it, what we mean by distinguishing between the movement toward race drama and the quite distinguishable movement toward the Negro Theatre. In the idea of its sponsors, the latter includes the former, but goes further and means more; it contemplates an endowed artistic center where all phases vital to the art of the theatre are cultivated and taught—acting, playwriting, scenic design and construction, scenic production and staging. A center with this purpose and function must ultimately be founded. It is only a question of when, how and where. Certainly the time has come; everyone will admit that at this stage of our race development it has become socially and artistically imperative. Sufficient plays and sufficing talent are already available; and the awakened race consciousness awaits what will probably be its best vehicle of expansion and expression in the near future.

Ten years ago it was the theory of the matter that was at issue; now it is only the practicabilities that concern us. Then one had constantly to be justifying the idea, citing the precedents of the Irish and the Yiddish theatres. Now even over diversity of opinion as to ways and means, the project receives the unanimous sanction of our hearts. But as to means and auspices, there are two seriously diverse views; one strenuously favoring professional auspices and a greater metropolitan center like New York or Chicago for the Negro Theatre; another quite as strenuously advocating a university center, amateur auspices and an essentially educational basis. Whoever cares to be doctrinaire on this issue may be: it is a question to be decided by deed and accomplishment—and let us hope a question, not of hostility and counter-purpose, but of rivalry and common end.

As intended and established in the work of the Department of Drama at Howard University, however, the path and fortunes of the latter program have been unequivocally chosen. We believe a university foundation will assure a greater continuity of effort and insure accordingly a greater permanence of result. We believe further that the development of the newer forms of drama has proved most successful where laboratory and experimental conditions have obtained and that the development of race drama is by those very circumstances the opportunity and responsibility of our educational centers. Indeed, to maintain this relation to dramatic interests is now an indispensable item in the program of the progressive American college. Through the pioneer work of Professor Baker, of Harvard, the acting and writing of plays has become the natural and inevitable sequence, in a college community, of the more formal study of the drama. Partly through the same channels, and partly as a result of the pioneer work of Wisconsin, college production has come to the rescue of the art drama, which would otherwise rarely get immediate recognition from the commercial theatre. And finally in its new affiliation with the drama, the American college under the leadership of Professor Koch, formerly of North Dakota, now of the University of North Carolina, has become a vital agency in community drama, and has actively promoted the dramatization of local life and tradition. By a threefold sponsorship, then, race drama becomes peculiarly the ward of our colleges, as new drama, as art-drama, and as folk-drama.

Though concurrent with the best efforts and most significant achievements of the new drama, the movement toward Negro drama has had its own way to make. In addition to the common handicap of commercialism, there has been the singular and insistent depreciation to stereotyped caricature and superficially representative but spiritually misrepresentative force. It has been the struggle of an artistic giant in art-engulfing quicksands; a struggle with its critical period just lately safely passed. Much of this has been desperate effort of the "bootstrap-lifting kind," from the pioneer advances of Williams, Cole, Cook, and Walker, to the latest achievements of "Shuffle Along." But the dramatic side has usually sagged, as might be expected, below the art level under the imposed handicap. Then there has been that gradual investment of the legitimate stage through the backdoor of the character rôle; the hard way by which Gilpin came, breaking triumphantly through at last to the major rôle and legitimate stardom. But it is the inauguration of the Negro art drama which is the vital matter, and the honor divides itself between Burghardt Du Bois, with his "Star of Ethiopia", staged, costumed, and manned by students, and Ridgeley Torrence, with his "Three Plays for a Negro Theatre." In the interim between the significant first performances and the still more significant attempts to incorporate them in the Horizon Guild and Mrs. Hapgood's Players, there was organized in Washington a Drama Committee of the N. A. A. C. P. which sponsored and produced Miss

Grimké's admirable pioneer problem-play, "Rachael," in 1917. Between the divided elements of this committee, with a questionable pa-
ternity of minority radicalism, the idea of the Negro Theatre as
distinguished from the idea of race drama was born. If ever the history
of the Negro drama is written without the scene of a committee wran-
gle, with its rhetorical climaxes after midnight—the conservatives
with their wraps on protesting the hour; the radicals, more hoarse with
emotion than effort, alternately wheedling and threatening—it will
not be well-written. The majority wanted a performance; the minority,
a program. One play no more makes a theatre than one swallow, a summer.

The pariah of the committee by the accident of its parentage became the foundling and subsequently the ward of Howard University.
In its orphan days, it struggled up on the crumbs of the University
Dramatic Club. One recalls the lean and patient years it took to pass
from faculty advice to faculty supervision and finally to faculty control; from rented costumes and hired properties to self-designed and
self-executed settings; from hackneyed "stage successes" to modern
and finally original plays; and hardest of all progressions, strange to relate, that from distant and alien themes to the intimate, native and
racial. The organization, under the directorship of Professor Montgomery Gregory of a Department of Dramatics, with academic credit
for its courses, the practical as well as the theoretical, and the fullest
administrative recognition and backing of the work have marked in the
last two years the eventual vindication of the idea. But from an intimacy of association second only to that of the director, and with better grace than he, may I be permitted to record what we consider to be
the movement's real coming of age? It was when simultaneously with
the production of two original plays on race themes written in course
by students, staged, costumed, and manned by students, in the case of
one play with the authoress in rôle, there was launched the campaign
for an endowed theatre, the successful completion of which would not
only give the Howard Players a home, but the Negro Theatre its first
tangible realization.

As will already have been surmised from the story, the movement
has, of course, had its critics and detractors. Happily, most of them are
covered by that forgiveness which goes out spontaneously to the opposition of the short-sighted. Not they, but their eyes, so to speak, are
to blame. Rather it has been amazing, on the other hand, the proportion of responsiveness and help that has come, especially from the
most prominent proponents of the art drama in this country; names

too numerous to mention, but representing every possible section of opinion—academic, non-academic; northern, southern, western; conservative, ultra-modern; professional, amateur; technical, literary; from within the university, from the community of Washington; white, black. Of especial mention because of special service, Gilpin, O'Neil, Torrence, Percy Mackaye, Du Bois, Weldon Johnson, and the administrative officers of the University; and most especially the valuable technical assistance for three years of Clem Throckmorton, technical director of the Provincetown Players, and for an equal time the constant and often self-sacrificing services of Miss Marie Forrest in stage training and directing, services recently fitly rewarded by appointment to a professorship in the department. But despite the catholic appeal, interest and cooperation it is essentially as a race representative and race-supported movement that we must think of it and that it must ultimately become, the best possible self-expression in an art where we have a peculiar natural endowment, undertaken as an integral part of our higher education and pursuit of culture.

The program and repertoire of the Howard Players, therefore, scarcely represent the full achievement of the movement; it is the workshop and the eventual theatre and the ever-increasing supply of plays and players that must hatch out of the idea. The record of the last two years shows in performances:

1920–21—

"Tents of the Arabs"—Lord Dunsany.

"Simon the Cyrenean"—Ridgeley Torrence.

"The Emperor Jones"—Guest performance with Charles Gilpin at the Belasco; student performance at the Belasco.

Commencement Play, 1921–22—

"The Canterbury Pilgrims"—Percy Mackaye. Repetition of first bill in compliment of the delegates to the Washington conference on Limitation of Armaments.

"Strong as the Hills" (a Persian play)—Matalee Lake.

Original Student Plays—

"Genefrede,"—a play of the Life of Toussaint L'Ouverture—Helen Webb.

"The Yellow Tree"—DeReath Irene Busey.

Commencement Play—

"Aria de Capo"—Edna St. Vincent Millay.

"The Danse Calinda"—a Creole Pantomime Ms. Performance—Ridgeley Torrence.

A movement of this kind and magnitude is, can be, the monopoly of no one group, no one institution, no paltry decade. But within a significant span, this is the record. The immediately important steps must be the production of original plays as rapidly as is consistent with good workmanship and adequate production, and the speedy endowment of the theatre, which fortunately, with the amateur talent of the university, means only funds for building and equipment. I am writing this article at Stratford-on-Avon. I know that when stripped to the last desperate defense of himself, the Englishman with warrant will boast of Shakespeare, and that this modest Memorial Theatre is at one and the same time a Gibraltar of national pride and self-respect and a Mecca of human civilization and culture. Music in which we have so trusted may sing itself around the world, but it does not carry ideas, the vehicle of human understanding and respect; it may pierce the heart, but does not penetrate the mind. But here in the glass of this incomparable art there is, for ourselves and for the world, that which shall reveal us beyond all propaganda on the one side, and libel on the other, more subtly and deeply than self-praise and to the confusion of subsidized self-caricature and ridicule. "I saw Othello's visage in his mind," says Desdemona explaining her love and respect; so might, so must the world of Othello's mind be put artistically to speech and action.

THE NATIONAL ASSOCIATION OF
NEGRO MUSICIANS

In the period around the Great War, there was an effort
by African Americans to organize a national association
of musicians. The story of their effort and objectives is
recorded in the following essay by Carl Diton, which
was published in May 1923.

When a score or more of prominent musicians and artists hailing from
different parts of the United States met at the national capital during
the latter part of the spring of 1919, little did they surmise that they
were taking an initial step toward a national association that would, in
less than four years, grow to a membership of over one thousand with
34 branches.

To the association's first presiding officer, Henry Grant, an unusually well-schooled musician and educator, should go the honor of having made the launching of such an invaluable association possible, for
it was he who called the first conference and who laid before it a solid,
constructive working plan which subsequently became the structural
foundation of the present national organization.

In connection with the idea of forming a national association, however, it is fair to record that there were two other prominent men who
were ambitious to perform a similar service for the race. In 1914,
Clarence Cameron White, violinist-composer and educator, issued a
call from Boston for a national meeting, but was compelled to call it off
because of the excitement attending the outbreak of the World War. In
1918, Nathaniel Dett, well-known composer, issued a similar sum-
mons, only to be frustrated by the memorable influenza epidemic. It is
interesting to note though, that the association, young as it is, has
shown fine political wisdom in choosing for its second president the

former of these two men in recognition of his pioneer effort to bring about closer union among Negro-American musicians.

At present, the most brilliant achievement of the National Association of Negro Musicians is its conventions. This fact should not be under-estimated, for in point of constructive thought, to say nothing of the vast crowds of people attendant upon its evening concert sessions when the standing room of the largest procurable auditoriums is at a premium, these conventions go far towards rivaling those of older and more experienced national associations. Every year brings forth an amazing wealth of the noblest kind of talent which is, even to the older and more seasoned members, vividly startling.

The 1919 convention was held in Chicago. In 1920, the association convened at New York City, the guest of St. Philip's Protestant Episcopal Parish. Nashville received the convention in 1921, the Baptist group and Fisk University co-operating in the entertainment and comfort of the delegates. It is, however, the consensus of opinion that the Columbus, Ohio, convention of 1922, characterized by the absolute satisfaction of the delegates as to their personal comfort, the total absence of anything that savored of graft, and the absolute punctuality of the sessions, was the masterpiece of them all. The character of this year's convention, which will be held at Chicago, July 24 to 26 inclusive, remains to be seen.

The present usefulness of the association then, is assured through its annual meetings. No young Negro musician could possibly make this annual pilgrimage without getting sufficient inspiration to last a twelvemonth. As to its future usefulness, much more must be anticipated. To be fully effective, it must link itself with other large important groups, the School and the Church, for the reasons that it must not suffer for want of intellectual appreciation nor for economic assurance.

Every school devoted to the education of Negro youth including the subject of music in its curriculum, should have a branch of the National Association of Negro Musicians, provided there is not already a branch organization in the respective municipality, for the association will need for its future constituent membership educated musicians to carry on the work of skilled, scientific organization, which is becoming more and more complex every day. Its members must have vision, capacity for creative thought, even more so than now, and appreciation for aggressive propaganda for the future.

With the co-operation of the Church, the National Association of Negro Musicians might well do wonders. It should work toward the improvement of church music by urging the clergy to procure always the best trained organists and to do all in their power to keep them under the instruction of good teachers; to encourage their choir members to follow the Azalia Hackley doctrine of cultivating the voice no matter how beautiful it may be in its natural state; to invite artists of national prominence to their churches for recitals, thus affording the community moments of musical inspiration; and last, but by no means least, to incorporate the spiritual in the order of worship. These are only a few of the myriad possibilities which might well be attempted with some degree of success. Let us hope that the members of the National Association of Negro Musicians will start this movement by assuming a friendly attitude toward some of these reforms.

Soviet Russia and the Negro

Published in two parts, this essay was written by Claude McKay. He examines an international view of African Americans. McKay also relates his own views on Russia and its people's attitudes on race. This article appeared in the December 1923 and January 1924 issues of *The Crisis.*

The label of propaganda will be affixed to what I say here. I shall not mind; propaganda has now come into its respectable rights and I am proud of being a propagandist. The difference between propaganda and art was impressed on my boyhood mind by a literary mentor, Milton's poetry and his political prose set side by side as the supreme examples. So too, my teacher,—splendid and broadminded though he was, yet unconsciously biased against what he felt was propaganda— thought that that gilt-washed artificiality, "The Picture of Dorian Gray", would outlive "Arms and the Man" and "John Bull's Other Island". But inevitably as I grew older I had perforce to revise and change my mind about propaganda. I lighted on one of Milton's greatest sonnets that was pure propaganda and a widening horizon revealed that some of the finest spirits of modern literature—Voltaire, Hugo, Heine, Swift, Shelley, Byron, Tolstoy, Isben—had carried the taint of propaganda. The broader view did not merely include propaganda literature in my literary outlook; it also swung me away from the childish age of the enjoyment of creative work for pleasurable curiosity to another extreme where I have always sought for the motivating force or propaganda intent that underlies all literature of interest. My birthright, and the historical background of the race that gave it to me, made me very respectful and receptive of propaganda and world events since the year 1914 have proved that it is no mean science of convincing information.

American Negroes are not as yet deeply permeated with the mass movement spirit and so fail to realize the importance of organized propaganda. It was Marcus Garvey's greatest contribution to the Negro movement; his pioneer work in that field is a feat that the men of broader understanding and sounder ideas who will follow him must continue. It was not until I first came to Europe in 1919 that I came to a full realization and understanding of the effectiveness of the insidious propaganda in general that is maintained against the Negro race. And it was not by the occasional affront of the minority of civilized fiends—mainly those Europeans who had been abroad, engaged in the business of robbing colored peoples in their native land—that I gained my knowledge, but rather through the questions about the Negro that were put to me by genuinely sympathetic and cultured persons.

The average Europeans who read the newspapers, the popular books and journals, and go to see the average play and a Mary Pickford movie, are very dense about the problem of the Negro; and they are the most important section of the general public that the Negro propagandists would reach. For them the tragedy of the American Negro ended with "Uncle Tom's Cabin" and Emancipation. And since then they have been aware only of the comedy—the Negro minstrel and vaudevillian, the boxer, the black mammy and butler of the cinematograph, the caricatures of the romances and the lynched savage who has violated a beautiful white girl.

A very few ask if Booker T. Washington is doing well or if the "Black Star Line" is running; perhaps some one less discreet than sagacious will wonder how colored men can hanker so much after white women in face of the lynching penalty. Misinformation, indifference and levity sum up the attitude of western Europe towards the Negro. There is the superior but very fractional intellectual minority that knows better, but whose influence on public opinion is infinitesimal, and so it may be comparatively easy for white American propagandists—whose interests behoove them to misrepresent the Negro—to turn the general indifference into hostile antagonism if American Negroes who have the intellectual guardianship of racial interests do not organize effectively, and on a world scale, to combat their white exploiters and traducers.

The world war has fundamentally altered the status of Negroes in Europe. It brought thousands of them from America and the British and French colonies to participate in the struggle against the Central Powers. Since then serious clashes have come about in England between the blacks that later settled down in the seaport towns and the natives. France has brought in her black troops to do police duty in the occupied districts in Germany. The color of these troops, and their customs too, are different and strange and the nature of their work would naturally make their presence irritating and unbearable to the inhabitants whose previous knowledge of Negroes has been based, perhaps, on their prowess as cannibals. And besides, the presence of these troops provides rare food for the chauvinists of a once proud and overbearing race, now beaten down and drinking the dirtiest dregs of humiliation under the bayonets of the victor.

However splendid the gesture of Republican France towards colored people, her use of black troops in Germany to further her imperial purpose should meet with nothing less than condemnation from the advanced section of Negroes. The propaganda that Negroes need to put over in Germany is not black troops with bayonets in that unhappy country. As conscript-slave soldiers of Imperial France they can in no wise help the movement of Negroes nor gain the sympathy of the broad-visioned international white groups whose international opponents are also the intransigent enemies of Negro progress. In considering the situation of the black troops in Germany, intelligent Negroes should compare it with that of the white troops in India, San Domingo and Haiti. What might not the Haitian propagandists have done with the marines if they had been black instead of white Americans! The world upheaval having brought the three greatest European nations—England, France and Germany—into closer relationship with Negroes, colored Americans should seize the opportunity to promote finer inter-racial understanding. As white Americans in Europe are taking advantage of the situation to intensify their propaganda against the blacks, so must Negroes meet that with a strong countermovement. Negroes should realize that the supremacy of American capital today proportionately increases American influence in the politics and social life of the world. Every American official abroad, every smug tourist, is a protagonist of dollar culture and a propagandist against the Negro. Besides brandishing the Rooseveltian stick in the face of the lesser new world natives, America holds an economic club over the heads of all the great European nations, excepting Russia, and so those bold individuals in Western Europe who formerly sneered at dollar culture may yet find it necessary and worth while to be discreetly silent. As American influence increases in the world, and especially in Europe, through the extension of American capital, the more necessary it becomes for all struggling minorities of the United States to organize extensively for the world wide propagation of their grievances. Such propaganda efforts, besides strengthening the cause at home, will certainly enlist the sympathy and help of those foreign groups that are carrying on a life and death struggle to escape the octuple arms of American business interests. And the Negro, as the most suppressed and persecuted minority, should use this period of ferment in international affairs to lift his cause out of his national obscurity and force it forward as a prime international issue.

Though Western Europe can be reported as being quite ignorant and apathetic of the Negro in world affairs, there is one great nation with an arm in Europe that is thinking intelligently on the Negro as it does about all international problems. When the Russian workers overturned their infamous government in 1917, one of the first acts of the new Premier, Lenin, was a proclamation greeting all the oppressed peoples throughout the world, exhorting them to organize and unite against the common international oppressor—Private Capitalism. Later on in Moscow, Lenin himself grappled with the question of the American Negroes and spoke on the subject before the Second Congress of the Third International. He consulted with John Reed, the American journalist, and dwelt on the urgent necessity of propaganda and organizational work among the Negroes of the South. The subject was not allowed to drop. When Sen Katayama of Japan, the veteran revolutionist, went from the United States to Russia in 1921 he placed the American Negro problem first upon his full agenda. And ever since he has been working unceasingly and unselfishly to promote the cause of the exploited American Negro among the Soviet councils of Russia.

With the mammoth country securely under their control, and despite the great energy and thought that are being poured into the revival of the national industry, the vanguard of the Russian workers and the national minorities, now set free from imperial oppression, are thinking seriously about the fate of the oppressed classes, the suppressed national and racial minorities in the rest of Europe, Asia, Africa and America. They feel themselves kin in spirit to these people. They want to help make them free. And not the least of the oppressed that fill the thoughts of the new Russia are the Negroes of America and Africa. If we look back two decades to recall how the Czarist persecution of the Russian Jews agitated Democratic America, we will get some idea of the mind of Liberated Russia towards the Negroes of America. The Russian people are reading the terrible history of their own recent past in the tragic position of the American Negro to-day. Indeed, the Southern States can well serve the purpose of showing what has happened in Russia. For if the exploited poor whites of the South could ever transform themselves into making common cause with the persecuted and plundered Negroes, overcome the oppressive oligarchy—the political crackers and robber landlords—and deprive it of all political privileges, the situation would be very similar to that of Soviet Russia to-day.

In Moscow I met an old Jewish revolutionist who had done time in Siberia, now young again and filled with the spirit of the triumphant Revolution. We talked about American affairs and touched naturally on the subject of the Negro. I told him of the difficulties of the problem, that the best of the liberal white elements were also working for a better status for the Negro, and he remarked: "When the democratic bourgeoisie of the United States were execrating Czardom for the Jewish pogroms they were meting out to your people a treatment more savage and barbarous than the Jews ever experienced in the old Russia. America", he said religiously, "had to make some sort of expiatory gesture for her sins. There is no surfeited bourgeoisie here in Russia to make a hobby of ugly social problems, but the Russian workers, who have won through the ordeal of persecution and revolution, extend the hand of international brotherhood to all the suppressed Negro millions of America".

I met with this spirit of sympathetic appreciation and response prevailing in all circles in Moscow and Petrograd. I never guessed what was awaiting me in Russia. I had left America in September of 1922 determined to get there, to see into the new revolutionary life of the people and report on it. I was not a little dismayed when, congenitally averse to notoriety as I am, I found that on stepping upon Russian soil I forthwith became a notorious character. And strangely enough there was nothing unpleasant about my being swept into the surge of revolutionary Russia. For better or for worse every person in Russia is vitally affected by the revolution. No one but a soulless body can live there without being stirred to the depths by it.

I reached Russia in November—the month of the Fourth Congress of the Communist International and the Fifth Anniversary of the Russian Revolution. The whole revolutionary nation was mobilized to honor the occasion, Petrograd was magnificent in red flags and streamers. Red flags fluttered against the snow from all the great granite buildings. Railroad trains, street cars, factories, stores, hotels, schools—all wore decorations. It was a festive month of celebration in which I, as a member of the Negro race, was a very active participant. I was received as though the people had been apprised of, and were prepared for, my coming. When Max Eastman and I tried to bore our way through the dense crowds that jammed the Tverskaya Street in Moscow on the 7th of November, I was caught, tossed up into the air, and passed along by dozens of stalwart youths.

"How warmly excited they get over a strange face!" said Eastman. A young Russian Communist remarked: "But where is the difference? Some of the Indians are as dark as you." To which another replied: "The lines of the face are different, the Indians have been with us long. The people instinctively see the difference." And so always the conversation revolved around me until my face flamed. The Moscow press printed long articles about the Negroes in America, a poet was inspired to rhyme about the Africans looking to Soviet Russia and soon I was in demand everywhere—at the lectures of poets and journalists, the meetings of soldiers and factory workers. Slowly I began losing self-consciousness with the realization that I was welcomed thus as a symbol, as a member of the great American Negro group—kin to the unhappy black slaves of European Imperialism in Africa—that the workers of Soviet Russia, rejoicing in their freedom, were greeting through me.

Russia, in broad terms, is a country where all the races of Europe and of Asia meet and mix. The fact is that under the repressive power of the Czarist bureaucracy the different races preserved a degree of kindly tolerance towards each other. The fierce racial hatreds that flame in the Balkans never existed in Russia. Where in the South no Negro might approach a *"cracker"* as a man for friendly offices, a Jewish pilgrim in old Russia could find rest and sustenance in the home of an orthodox peasant. It is a problem to define the Russian type by features. The Hindu, the Mongolian, the Persian, the Arab, the West European—all these types may be traced woven into the distinctive polyglot population of Moscow. And so, to the Russian, I was merely another type, but stranger, with which they were not yet familiar. They were curious with me, all and sundry, young and old, in a friendly, refreshing manner. Their curiosity had none of the intolerable impertinence and often downright affront that any very dark colored man, be he Negro, Indian or Arab, would experience in Germany and England.

In 1920, while I was trying to get out a volume of my poems in London, I had a visit with Bernard Shaw who remarked that it must be tragic for a sensitive Negro to be an artist. Shaw was right. Some of the English reviews of my book touched the very bottom of journalistic muck. The English reviewer outdid his American cousin (except the South, of course, which could not surprise any white person much less a black) in sprinkling criticism with racial prejudice. The sedate, copperhead "Spectator" as much as said: no "cultured" white man could read a Negro's poetry without prejudice, that instinctively he must search for that "something" that must make him antagonistic to it. But fortunately Mr. McKay did not offend our susceptibilities! The English people, from the lowest to the highest, cannot think of a black man as being anything but an entertainer, boxer, a Baptist preacher or a menial. The Germans are just a little worse. Any healthy looking black coon of an adventurous streak can have a wonderful time palming himself off as another Siki or a buck dancer. When an American writer introduced me as a poet to a very cultured German, a lover of all the arts, he could not believe it, and I don't think he does yet. An American student tells his middle class landlady that he is having a black friend to lunch: "But are you sure that he is not a cannibal?" she asks without a flicker of a humorous smile!

But in Petrograd and Moscow, I could not detect a trace of this ignorant snobbishness among the educated classes, and the attitude of the common workers, the soldiers and sailors was still more remarkable. It was so beautifully naive; for them I was only a black member of the world of humanity. It may be urged that the fine feelings of the Russians towards a Negro was the effect of Bolshevist pressure and propaganda. The fact is that I spent most of my leisure time in nonpartisan and anti-Bolshevist circles. In Moscow I found the Luxe Hotel where I put up extremely depressing, the dining room was anathema to me and I grew tired to death of meeting the proletarian ambassadors from foreign lands, some of whom bore themselves as if they were the holy messengers of Jesus, Prince of Heaven, instead of working class representatives. And so I spent many of my free evenings at the Domino Café, a notorious den of the dilettante poets and writers. There came the young anarchists and Menshevists and all the young aspiring fry to read and discuss their poetry and prose. Sometimes a group of the older men came too. One evening I noticed Pilnyak the novelist, Okonoff the critic, Feodor the translator of Poe, an editor, a theatre manager and their young disciples, beer-drinking through a very interesting literary discussion. There was always music, good folk-singing and bad fiddling, the place was more like a second rate cabaret than a poets' club, but nevertheless much to be enjoyed, with amiable chats and light banter through which the evening wore pleasantly away. This was the meeting place of the frivolous set with whom I eased my mind after writing all day.

The evenings of the proletarian poets held in the Arbat were much more serious affairs. The leadership was Communist, the audience working class and attentive like diligent, elementary school children. To these meetings also came some of the keener intellects from the Domino Café. One of these young women told me that she wanted to keep in touch with all the phases of the new culture. In Petrograd the meetings of the intelligentzia seemed more formal and inclusive. There were such notable men there as Chukovsky the critic, Eugene Zamiatan the celebrated novelist and Maishack the poet and translator of Kipling. The artist and theatre world were also represented. There was no Communist spirit in evidence at these intelligentzia gatherings. Frankly there was an undercurrent of hostility to the Bolshevists. But I was invited to speak and read my poems whenever I appeared at any of them and treated with every courtesy and consideration as a writer. Among those sophisticated and cultured Russians, many of them speaking from two to four languages, there was no overdoing of the correct thing, no vulgar wonderment and bounderish superiority over a Negro's being a poet. I was a poet, that was all, and their keen questions showed that they were much more interested in the technique of my poetry, my views on and my position regarding the modern literary movements than in the difference of my color. Although I will not presume that there was no attraction at all in that little difference!

On my last visit to Petrograd I stayed in the Palace of the Grand Duke Vladimir Alexander, the brother of Czar Nicholas the Second. His old, kindly steward who looked after my comfort wanders round like a ghost through the great rooms. The house is now the headquarters of the Petrograd intellectuals. A fine painting of the Duke stands curtained in the dining room. I was told that he was liberal minded, a patron of the arts, and much liked by the Russian intelligentzia. The atmosphere of the house was theoretically non-political, but I quickly scented a strong hostility to Bolshevist authority. But even here I had only pleasant encounters and illuminating conversations with the inmates and visitors, who freely expressed their views against the Soviet Government, although they knew me to be very sympathetic to it.

During the first days of my visit I felt that the great demonstration of friendliness was somehow expressive of the enthusiastic spirit of the glad anniversary days, that after the month was ended I could calmly settle down to finish the book about the American Negro that the State Publishing Department of Moscow had commissioned me to write, and in the meantime quietly go about making interesting contacts. But my days in Russia were a progression of affectionate enthusiasm of the people towards me. Among the factory workers, the red-starred and chevroned soldiers and sailors, the proletarian students and children, I could not get off as lightly as I did with the intelligentzia. At every meeting I was received with boisterous acclaim, mobbed with friendly demonstration. The women workers of the great bank in Moscow insisted on hearing about the working conditions of the colored women of America and after a brief outline I was asked the most exacting questions concerning the positions that were most available to colored women, their wages and general relationship with the white women workers. The details I could not give; but when I got through, the Russian women passed a resolution sending greetings to the colored women workers of America, exhorting them to organize their forces and send a woman representative to Russia. I received a similar message from the Propaganda Department of the Petrograd Soviet which is managed by Nicoleva, a very energetic woman. There I was shown the new status of the Russian women gained through the revolution of 1917. Capable women can fit themselves for any position; equal pay with men for equal work; full pay during the period of pregnancy and no work for the mother two months before and two months after the confinement. Getting a divorce is comparatively easy and not influenced by money power, detective chicanery and wire pulling. A special department looks into the problems of joint personal property and the guardianship and support of the children. There is no penalty for legal abortion and no legal stigma of illegitimacy attaching to children born out of wedlock.

There were no problems of the submerged lower classes and the suppressed national minorities of the old Russia that could not bear comparison with the grievous position of the millions of Negroes in the United States to-day. Just as Negroes are barred from the American Navy and the higher ranks of the Army, so were the Jews and the sons of the peasantry and proletariat discriminated against in the Russian Empire. It is needless repetition of the obvious to say that Soviet Russia does not tolerate such discriminations, for the actual government of the country is now in the hands of the combined national minorities, the peasantry and the proletariat. By the permission of Leon Trotsky, Commissar-in-chief of the military and naval forces of Soviet Russia, I visited the highest military schools in the Kremlin and environs of Moscow. And there I saw the new material, the sons of the working people in training as cadets by the old officers of the upper classes. For two weeks I was a guest of the Red navy in Petrograd with the same eager proletarian youth of new Russia, who conducted me through the intricate machinery of submarines, took me over aeroplanes captured from the British during the counter-revolutionary war around Petrograd and showed me the making of a warship ready for action. And even of greater interest was the life of the men and the officers, the simplified discipline that was strictly enforced, the food that was served for each and all alike, the extra political educational classes and the extreme tactfulness and elasticity of the political commissars, all Communists, who act as advisers and arbitrators between the men and students and the officers. Twice or thrice I was given some of the *kasha* which is sometimes served with the meals. In Moscow I grew to like this food very much, but it was always difficult to get. I had always imagined that it was quite unwholesome and unpalatable and eaten by the Russian peasant only on account of extreme poverty. But on the contrary I found it very rare and sustaining when cooked right with a bit of meat and served with butter—a grain food very much like the common but very delicious West Indian rice-and-peas.

The red cadets are seen in the best light at their gymnasium exercises and at the political assemblies when discipline is set aside. Especially at the latter where a visitor feels that he is in the midst of the early revolutionary days, so hortatory are the speeches, so intense the enthusiasm of the men. At all these meetings I had to speak and the students asked me general questions about the Negro in the American Army and Navy, and when I gave them the common information, known to all American Negroes, students, officers and commissars were unanimous in wishing that a group of young American Negroes would take up training to become officers in the Army and Navy of Soviet Russia.

The proletarian students of Moscow were eager to learn of the life and work of Negro students. They sent messages of encouragement and good will to the Negro students of America and, with a fine gesture of fellowship, elected the Negro delegate of the American Communist Party and myself to honorary membership in the Moscow Soviet.

Those Russian days remain the most memorable of my life. The intellectual Communists and the intelligentzia were interested to know that America had produced a formidable body of Negro intelligentzia and professionals, possessing a distinctive literature and cultural and business interests alien to the white man's. And they think naturally, that the militant leaders of the intelligentzia must feel and express the spirit of revolt that is slumbering in the inarticulate Negro masses, precisely as the emancipation movement of the Russian masses had passed through similar phases.

Russia is prepared and waiting to receive couriers and heralds of good will and interracial understanding from the Negro race. Her demonstration of friendliness and equality for Negroes may not conduce to promote healthy relations between Soviet Russia and democratic America, the anthropologists of 100 per cent pure white Americanism may soon invoke Science to prove that the Russians are not at all God's white people. I even caught a little of American anti-Negro propaganda in Russia. A friend of mine, a member of the Moscow intelligentzia, repeated to me the remarks of the lady correspondent of a Danish newspaper: that I should not be taken as a representative Negro for she had lived in America and found all Negroes lazy, bad and vicious, a terror to white women. In Petrograd I got a like story from Chukovsky, the critic, who was on intimate terms with a high worker of the American Relief Administration and his southern wife. Chukovsky is himself an intellectual "westerner", the term applied to those Russians who put Western-European civilization before Russian culture and believe that Russia's salvation lies in becoming completely westernized. He had spent an impressionable part of his youth in London and adores all things English, and during the world war was very pro-English. For the American democracy, also, he expresses unfeigned admiration. He has more Anglo-American books than Russian in his fine library and considers the literary section of the New York *Times* a journal of a very high standard. He is really a maniac of Anglo-Saxon American culture. Chukovsky was quite incredulous when I gave him the facts of the Negro's status in American civilization.

"The Americans are a people of such great energy and ability," he said, "how could they act so petty towards a racial minority?" And then he related an experience of his in London that bore a strong smell of *cracker* breath. However, I record it here in the belief that it is authentic for Chukovsky is a man of integrity: About the beginning of the century, he was sent to England as correspondent of a newspaper in Odessa, but in London he was more given to poetic dreaming and studying English literature in the British Museum and rarely sent any news home. So he lost his job and had to find cheap, furnished rooms. A few weeks later, after he had taken up his residence in new quarters, a black guest arrived, an American gentleman of the cloth. The preacher procured a room on the top floor and used the dining and sitting room with the other guests, among whom was a white American family. The latter protested the presence of the Negro in the house and especially in the guest room. The landlady was in a dilemma, she could not lose her American boarders and the clergyman's money was not to be despised. At last she compromised by getting the white Americans to agree to the Negro's staying without being allowed the privilege of the guest room, and Chukovsky was asked to tell the Negro the truth. Chukovsky strode upstairs to give the unpleasant facts to the preacher and to offer a little consolation, but the black man was not unduly offended:

"The white guests have the right to object to me," he explained, anticipating Garvey, "they belong to a superior race."

"But," said Chukovsky, "*I* do not object to you, *I* don't feel any difference; we don't understand color prejudice in Russia."

"Well," philosophized the preacher, "you are very kind, but taking the scriptures as authority, I don't consider the Russians to be white people."

THE YOUNGER LITERARY MOVEMENT

Many African Americans concerned about the progress of black literature in the early 1920s believed that those writers who sought to pass along the literature of the race were diminishing and that there were not enough younger writers coming along to fill the void. W. E. B. Du Bois and Alain Locke, in the following, discuss Jean Toomer's novel, *Cane,* and Jessie Fauset's novel *There Is Confusion.* Du Bois and Locke conclude that Toomer and Fauset are two great novelists with promising futures. This essay was published in January 1924.

I

There have been times when we writers of the older set have been afraid that the procession of those who seek to express the life of the American Negro was thinning and that none were coming forward to fill the footsteps of the fathers. Dunbar is dead; Chesnutt is silent; and Kelly Miller is mooning after false gods while Brawley and Woodson are writing history rather than literature. But even as we ask "Where are the young Negro artists to mold and weld this mighty material about us?"—even as we ask, they come.

There are two books before me, which, if I mistake not, will mark an epoch: a novel by Jessie Fauset and a book of stories and poems by Jean Toomer. There are besides these, five poets writing: Langston Hughes, Countée Cullen, Georgia Johnson, Gwendolyn Bennett and Claude McKay. Finally, Negro men are appearing as essayists and reviewers, like Walter White and Eric Walrond. (And even as I write comes the news that a novel by Mr. White has just found a publisher.) Here then is promise sufficient to attract us.

We recognize the exquisite abandon of a new day in Langston Hughes' "Song For a Banjo". He sings:

Shake your brown feet, Liza,
Shake 'em Liza, chile,

Shake your brown feet, Liza,
(The music's soft and wile).
Shake your brown feet, Liza,
(The Banjo's sobbin' low),
The sun's goin' down this very night—
Might never rise no mo'.

Countée Cullen in his "Ballad of the Brown Girl" achieves eight lyric lines that are as true as life itself. There is in Claude McKay's "If We Must Die" a strain martial and mutinous. There are other echoes— two from dead poets Jamison and Cotter who achieved in their young years long life if not immortality. But this essay is of two books.

The world of black folk will some day arise and point to Jean Toomer as a writer who first dared to emancipate the colored world from the conventions of sex. It is quite impossible for most Americans to realize how straight-laced and conventional thought is within the Negro World, despite the very unconventional acts of the group. Yet this contradiction is true. And Jean Toomer is the first of our writers to hurl his pen across the very face of our sex conventionality. In "Cane", one has only to take his women characters *seriatim* to realize this: Here is Karintha, an innocent prostitute; Becky, a fallen white woman; Carma, a tender Amazon of unbridled desire; Fern, an unconscious wanton; Esther, a woman who looks age and bastardy in the face and flees in despair; Louise, with a white and a black lover; Avey, unfeeling and unmoral; and Doris, the cheap chorus girl. These are his women, painted with a frankness that is going to make his black readers shrink and criticize; and yet they are done with a certain splendid, careless truth.

Toomer does not impress me as one who knows his Georgia but he does know human beings; and, from the background which he has seen slightly and heard of all his life through the lips of others, he paints things that are true, not with Dutch exactness, but rather with an impressionist's sweep of color. He is an artist with words but a conscious artist who offends often by his apparently undue striving for effect. On the other hand his powerful book is filled with felicitous phrases— Karintha, "carrying beauty perfect as the dusk when the sun goes down",—

"Hair—
Silver-grey
Like streams of stars"

Or again, "face flowed into her eyes—flowed in soft creamy foam and plaintive ripples". His emotion is for the most part entirely objective. One does not feel that he feels much and yet the fervor of his descriptions shows that he has felt or knows what feeling is. His art carries much that is difficult or even impossible to understand. The artist, of course, has a right deliberately to make his art a puzzle to the interpreter (the whole world is a puzzle) but on the other hand I am myself unduly irritated by this sort of thing. I cannot, for the life of me, for instance see why Toomer could not have made the tragedy of Carma something that I could understand instead of vaguely guess at; "Box Seat" muddles me to the last degree and I am not sure that I know what "Kabnis" is about. All of these essays and stories, even when I do not understand them, have their strange flashes of power, their numerous messages and numberless reasons for being. But still for me they are partially spoiled. Toomer strikes me as a man who has written a powerful book but who is still watching for the fullness of his strength and for that calm certainty of his art which will undoubtedly come with years.

It had been my intention when I began this essay to discuss also Miss Fauset's novel. But Mr. Locke has sent us such an admirable and discriminating disquisition on this book that I gladly yield to him.

—W. E. B. D.

II

The novel that the Negro intelligentzia have been clamoring for has arrived with Jessie Fauset's first novel, "There Is Confusion". What they have been wanting, if I interpret rightly, is not merely a race story told from the inside, but a cross section of the race life higher up the social pyramid and further from the base-line of the peasant and the soil than is usually taken. We scarcely realize how by reaction to social prejudice we have closed our better circles physically and psychologically: it is not always the fault of the novelist that he can depict only the peasant type and his urban analogue, the Negro of the slums. But here in refreshing contrast with the bulk of fiction about the Negro, we have a novel of the educated and aspiring classes. Miss Fauset has, however, not made the error of growing rootless flowers or exploring detached levels. Indeed she has sketched a Negro group against a wide social background of four generations—almost as much perspective as can be gotten on any social group in America, and moreover has not glossed over the slave régime, its ugly facts and its uglier consequences, though she has treated it incidentally as part of the genealogy and heredity of her characters. It is essentially a novel of blood and ancestry such as might be expected to come from the Philadelphia tradition which the author shares, and the Philadelphia scene which is part of her story. Yet it is too contemporary, not merely in incident, but in the phase of the race problem which it reflects, to be a period novel, a resurrection of the past. On the contrary it throbs with some of the latest reactions of the race situation in this country upon the psychology and relations of colored and white Americans of the more intelligent classes. It is this delineation of the problem as seen from the heights of respectability and from at least a plateau of culture that sharply differentiates Miss Fauset's novel from others.

Joanna Marshall—more a heroine than most heroines, since she actually focusses and dominates in turn the life of her family, the estrangements and marriages of her brother and of her lover—is a strange character at war against herself. One part stoic, one part artistic, one part human with an emotional intensity and sincerity that is not Caucasian, she achieves success in her art at the very instant of her greatest disillusionment; but not before she had played unconscious havoc with several lives by her ambition and unswerving devotion to the ideals of success.

Complicated as these lives are at almost every turn by the peculiar handicaps and confusions of color, it is well for the artistry and the worth of the book that the *primary confusions are those more universal ones of human nature and its type-psychologies.* The atmosphere of the book is that of Quaker faith and sober optimism, and its constructive suggestion is that of an eventual mutual understanding and coöperation through the discipline of experience. It is as though two antithetic sides of life, male and female, white and black, had each to work out its own chastening and enlargement through sorrow and disillusionment to find itself, late but not always too tragically late, able to rise from the level of confusion to the level of coöperation and understanding.

The book has what I maintain is the prime essential for novels with such subject matter—social perspective, social sanity. A problem novel without this is either a raw and brutal cross-sectioning or medicated and unpalatable propaganda. From these two evils, the book happily and skillfully escapes. Of the style, one may say, that it fits the subject—and in this day of the confusion and compounding of styles, what can be better said? Certainly it sustains with interest a story that is more heavily ballasted with truth than two or three of the usual run of social novels that sail on a breezy style to the heavens of "six best sellers". So that it can be confidently commended to that increasing band who, thank God, want truth with their fiction, and who will welcome especially upon the race question and its reactions on the best types and classes of colored folk, a social document of sterling and intimate character.

—A. L.

III

These, then, are the two books of the younger Negro Movement; read them and enjoy them as I have done and spread the glad tidings.

ANTAR, NEGRO POET OF ARABIA

Written by Maud Cuney Hare for the June and July 1924 issues of *The Crisis*. This essay tells of Antar, the "Negro" poet of Arabia, who is the son of a black mother and Arab father. This essay reveals Antar's great talent as a poet as well as his deep and abiding love for his cousin. It also tells of his adventures and persecution.

The increasing recognition in song and speech now being won by talented men of Negro birth in the New World brings to mind certain great names of the earliest centuries that won and held undying fame and bequeathed to the Old World and the New World joy in their romance and achievement. Foremost among these is the poet-warrior, Antar.

One of his famous poems has been preserved. It is found as the sixth poem of the "Moallacat"—the "golden verses"—which are considered in Arabia the greatest poems ever written and which were hung on the Caaba at the Holy Temple at Mecca that all the pilgrims who came there might know them and do obeisance to them. The "Moallacat" belongs to the first school of Arabian poetry—to the "Gahilieh",—"time of ignorance".

A second school of poetry is said to have entered with the advent of Islam. As Mohammedanism did not foster poetry or music at the beginning, much of the poetry of the first period was lost. Later, however, poetry was set to music and the love song became the favorite song of the people.

The Antar poem belongs to the time of the war of Dahis, and, like the five poems which preceded it in the epic, it lauds the victors of the battle-field, describes the beauties of nature and praises the camel of the desert. The main theme however, is love.

The poem of Antar begins:

"Have the bards who preceded me left any theme unsung?

What therefore shall be my subject? Love alone must supply my lay. Dost thou then recollect, after long consideration, the mansion of thy beloved?" ......

"O bower of Abla, in the valley of Jiwaa, give me tidings of my love—

O bower of Abla, may the morning rise on thee with prosperity and health!"

In some versions of the romance of Antar, the beloved is called "Ibla".

The author of the poem is not a legendary character, but one Antar Bin Shaddad who was born about the year 498 A.D., the son of a slave girl, Zebeeba, and Shedad, a nobleman of the tribe of Abs. Antar, who became one of Arabia's most noted poets, has been taken as a subject for an opera written by the composer, the late Gabriel Dupont, and the work produced some time ago at the Opera in Paris. It was not that the theme of Antar had been unsung, for the spell of the desert and the romance of the Red Sea have before had their fascination for composer and dramatist.

Rimsky-Korsakoff's symphony, "Antar", with its wealth of barbaric color and oriental fire has been deservedly popular, while a lyrical drama entitled "Antar", written by M. Chékri-Ganem, was first produced at the Odéon, Paris, in 1910 and met with great favor. Rimsky-Korsakoff's symphony as absolute music does not follow the traditional stories of the poet's life as does the opera which Dupont wrote to Chékri-Ganem's play.

The libretto is drawn from that voluminous work known as "The Romance of Antar", which was published in Cairo in 32 volumes and has been translated from the Arabic in sections by various scholars. There are two editions of the work—one known as the Syrian Antar, the other as the Arabian Antar. The abridged work was first introduced to European readers in 1802, the translation made and issued in four books by Terrick Hamilton in 1819.

The "Romance" is a companion piece to the Arabian Nights and is the standard work of Arabia. The seemingly numberless tales that are incorporated in "The Romance of Antar" are those of the desert that were traditional and were retold and preserved by Asmai during the reign of Harun-al-Rashid.

The importance of the work lies in the fact that it gives the manners and customs of the real Arabs and Bedouins who existed before the time of Mohammed. They lived in tents and cities, were proud of their lineage, and possessed many fine traits of character. They cultivated oratory and excelled in poetry. Even in the early centuries they recognized a kinship between poetry and music. The discovery of talent in a young poet was the occasion of great rejoicing and worthy poets were honored at an annual Assembly which was held at Ocaah, at which time there was general rejoicing by the tribe and singing by the women to the accompaniment of the timbrels.

It was the exceptional talent of Antar, as well as his bravery in battle that made his song to Ibla prophetic:

"Shall we meet in the land of Shuraba and Hima and shall we live in joy and happiness?

"I am the well-known Antar, the chief of his tribe, but when I am gone, history shall tell of me."

Marvelous and fabulous are the adventures told in "The Romance of Antar", and from them come the most important incidents of his life as told in the opera. The scene is the desert; the tribe is that of Abs, one of the most fearless of Arabia, and the chief is the noble Jazeemah. Among their number, Shedad, the son of Carad, goes forth with members of his family to seek their fortune. They journey to the land of Shurebah and while on their marauding expedition they attack the wealthy tribe of Jezeela and take many camels together with a woman of ebony hue who was found tending them.

Halting beside a stream to divide the spoils, Shedad notices the woman whom he saw to be "uncommonly beautiful and well-shaped, her appearance elegant and striking." Fascinated, he soliloquizes: "In blackness there is some virtue if you observe its beauty well; the eyes do not regard the white or red. Were it not for the black of the mole on the fair cheek how would lovers feel the value of its brilliancy? Were not musk black it would not be precious. Were it not for the black of night, the dawn would not rise. Were it not for the black of the eye, where would be its beauty? And thus it is that the black ambergris has the purest fragrance."

Shedad takes the woman, Zebeeba, and her two children, Jereer and Shiboob, and renounces all claim to any further share of the booty. After their return home to the tribe, a child was born to them and Shedad overjoyed named him Antar. Early accompanying his mother to the pastures, the child soon learned to tend the cattle. He grew exceedingly strong and was of great courage. Fearing neither beast nor man, he sought out wild animals that he might conquer and slay them.

Killing cruel Daji whom he found mistreating an old woman, he is brought to trial before King Zoheir. He is befriended by Prince Malik and thus begins a life-long friendship with both the King and his son. The King, exonerating the boy, addresses Shedad:

"Your son's conduct reflects credit on you—his behavior will remain as a memorial to all generations—he has loathed oppression and violence and has followed the path of propriety and virtue."

Among those who gather about him is Ibla, the beautiful daughter of Malik, his father's brother. Quickly love overtakes him. One day upon beholding her flowing tresses, he becomes enraptured:

"That fair maid lets down her ringlets and she is completely hid in her hair, which appears like the dark shades of night. It is as if she were the brilliant day, and as if the night had enveloped her in obscurity. It is as if the full moon was shining in its splendor and all the stars were concealed by its lustre—her charms bewitch all around her, and all are anxious to offer their services; they live in her beauties and loveliness, and they are imbued with sweetness from her perfections, and receive new spirit from her graces."

"Revile me not for my love of her, for I am distracted for her, and live but as the victim of my love. I will conceal my affection in my soul till I can see that I am sufficiently fortunate one day to serve her."

The warriors and chiefs go on a pilgrimage to the holy shrine while the women and children who remain at home amuse themselves at a social gathering. Antar sees Ibla singing and playing amongst them and recites verses in her praise. She is greatly pleased, but Antar is despised because of his birth. He becomes the victim of many forms of persecution, but in spite of all he determines to become worthy of his love. Of her charms, he sings:

"She moves; I should say it was the branch of the Tamarisk that waves its branches to the southern breeze. She approaches; I should say it was the frightened fawn, when a calamity alarms it in the waste. She walks away; I should say her face was truly the sun when its lustre dazzles the beholders. She gazes; I should say it was the full moon of the night when Orion girds it with its stars. She smiles, and the pearls of her teeth sparkle, in which there is the cure for the sickness of lovers. She prostrates herself in reverence towards her God; and the greatest of men bow down to her beauties. O Ibla! when I most despair, love for thee and all its weaknesses are my only hope."

When Shedad and his followers go to attack the tribe of Temeem, the women make a holiday at the lake of Zatool Israd. The girls carry their instruments and there is music and song. Antar, who is left to protect the women, is entranced at the sight of Ibla. To the beating of the cymbals the girls sing:

"The boughs dance in the groves, among the trees, in the graceful movement: the dew drops fall, and the flowers and the trees are studded with its pearls. The season is delightful; let it pass in enjoyment, and misfortunes begone! The opportunity is delicious, let us grasp in haste its sweets".

In the midst of the singing and dancing, they are suddenly attacked by a troop of seventy Bedouins, "armed with cuirasses and coats of mail, and Aadite helmets". The horsemen seize the women and children—Antar overpowers one of the warriors, mounts his steed and disperses the men. He lunges at the chief and kills him with his spear.

Modestly refraining to tell of the incident, he falls under suspicion and is punished, but the King learns of his heroism and invites him to a feast. He is asked to recite some of his poems that have now caused attention. His poetic gift procures him honor but arouses envy, as well. In spite of their treachery, he comes again and again to the rescue of Shas and Rebia and members of the tribe.

King Zoheir makes him a gift of a fine Arab horse, clothes him in fine robes and removes him from the servants' quarters and from the care of the flocks.

Ibla's mother learns of his laudatory verses and she and Ibla ask Antar to recite them. Modestly he speaks:

"O Ibla, my description cannot portray thee, for thou comprehendest every perfection. Were I to say thy face is like the full moon of heaven, where in that full moon is the eye of the antelope? Were I to say thy shape is like the branch of the Erak tree; O thou shamest it in the grace of thy form. In thy forehead is my guide to truth; and in the night of thy tresses I wander astray. Thy teeth resemble stringed jewels; but how can I liken them to lifeless pearls? Thy bosom is created as an enchantment. O may God protect it ever in that perfection! To be connected with thee is to be connected with every joy, but separated from all my world is the bond of thy connexion. Under thy veil is the rosebud of my life, and thine eyes are guarded with a multitude of arrows; round thy tent is a lion warrior, the sword's edge, and the spear's point. O thy face is like the full moon of heaven, allied to light, but far from my hopes."

The mother of Ibla praises him for his high qualities and offers to marry him to Ibla's servant, Khemisa! Antar exclaims: "Never will I be united but with her my soul adores." It is a determination approved by

Ibla, who cries: "May God accomplish thy wishes; and may He grant thee the woman thou lovest, and mayest thou live in peace and happiness!" The poems of Antar are now published for the tribe and they are sung and recited.

Now at this time, Ibla and many of Shedad's relatives are invited to a marriage feast of one of the Ghiftan tribe. While journeying on, they are attacked by foes; Antar puts to flight the tribe of Moostalik, protects Ibla and slays the Chief. In gratitude she cries: "God protect thee, thou black in face, but fair in deeds—thou ornament of men."

Shedad's pride and affection increase for Antar, but he is reluctant to give him the honor and rank of an Arabian son. Antar beseeches him but is refused the dignity due an Arab of nobility. In great sorrow he decides to leave the tribe of Abs and journey alone over the desert.

Wandering across the plains, he meets Chief Ghegadh, who greatly admires him, and he is asked to join the tribe as one of their warriors. He becomes the possessor of a noble horse, Abjer, and takes part in terrific raids. Alone he is annihilating a band of horsemen, when his good friend, Prince Malik, who is in search of him, comes upon him and persuades him to return home.

His father affectionately greets him with the kiss between the eyes, and the surname of "Aboolfawaris" is bestowed upon him. The King has his poetry recorded in order that the tribe may have the honor of being rated amongst the most eloquent Arabians. However, Antar is deeply wounded by the opposition to his love. True to her sex, Ibla sees his sorrow, pities him and loves him.

Malik, the father, finds it expedient to betroth her to Amarah, a nobleman of light character. Prince Malik arrives just in time to prevent the consummation of the marriage plans, and pitying Antar he begs Shedad to honor his son.

Shedad, divided by pride in Antar and fear of the scorn of the tribe, refuses to brave their displeasure and declares that the tribe of Abs, proud of their lineage, would hate him for doing that which had never been done before.

In anger Antar attacks Amarah and as a punishment he is demoted to the care of the sheep and camels. His heavy heart is cheered by a message from Ibla—"Tell him that if my father even makes my grave my resting-place, none but him do I desire, none but him will I choose."

The Absians are attacked by the Teyans. They relied always on the prowess of Antar, but now he deliberately holds aloof. About to be defeated, they appeal to him. He replies: "What dost wish me to do? I am indeed grieved at thy distress. O that I could rescue thee from destruction and defeat, but I am a slave."

They become hard pressed and again seek his aid. At last the wife of the King and other women of the Court, together with Ibla, are taken prisoners. Malik, her father, promises her hand to Antar if he will rescue her. On he rushes, riding his horse Abjer, and crying: "My sword is my father and the spear in my hand is my father's brother, and I am the son of my day in the heights of the desert!"

In the fray, he rescues Ibla and her companions and puts the enemy to flight. He is welcomed with gratitude by the King, and his wife Temadhur pleads his cause. Malik, Shas and Rebia are outwardly grateful but inwardly they rage and together they plot against him.

Shas declares that Shedad will shame the tribe of Abs should he honor Antar with the rank of a noble son, and Antar, crushed in spirit, yet still of great pride, offers to leave and join another tribe. The King entreats him to remain, but he replies:

"Enjoyment is ever desired after absence and friendship is wished for after separation. I have been merciful to those who are not aware of the value of my mercy and my friendship has not been properly appreciated.

"But had I not a chief who commands me, liberal in speech and exalted in power I would do myself justice with my sword and soon would I show the difference between virtue and outrage."

When the King reproaches Malik for his broken promise to Antar, he devises another method of ridding the tribe of the importunate lover. He demands of Antar the gift of one thousand Asafeer camels as a dowry for Ibla. Now Asafeer camels are found only in the kingdom of Monzar, a most powerful tribe, the possessor of untold armies. Antar does not know of the perils besetting him nor that Malik believes he has asked the unobtainable of him, so blithely goes forth on his quest.

"He pitches his tent near a spring and behold there was an old Sheikh with bent back—his face almost touched his knees. So I said to him, 'why art thou thus stooping?' He said, as he waved his hands towards me, 'my youth is lost somewhere on the ground, and I am stooping in search of it' ".

Offering him hospitality, the old man listens to his mission, after which he warns him that he is sent forth with the hope that he might be destroyed. Antar, disillusioned, sad and lonely, though still determined and unafraid, speaks:

"In the land of Shurebah are defiles and valleys; I have quitted them and its inhabitants live in my heart. Fixed are they therein, and in my eyes; and even when they are absent from me, they dwell in the black of mine eye; and when the lightning flashes from their land, I shed tears of blood and pass the night leagued with sleeplessness. The breeze of the fragrant plants makes me remember the luscious balmy airs of the Zatool-irsad. O Ibla, let thy visionary phantom appear to me, and infuse soft slumbers over my distracted heart! O Ibla, were it not for my love of thee, I would not be with so few friends and so many enemies! I am departing and the back of my horse shall be my resting place; and my sword and mail my pillow, till I trample down the lands of Irak, and destroy their deserts and their cities. . . . The eyes of the envious shall watch; but the eyes of the pure and the faithful shall sleep; and I will return with numerous Asafeer camels that my love shall procure, and Shiboob be my guide."

After many desperate encounters, Antar succeeds in capturing one thousand Asafeer camels from the slaves of the King of Arab chiefs, but Nuan, the son, captures him and he is bound upon the back of his horse Abjer. Taken before the King, he is asked whether he is a warrior or a slave:

"My Lord, I am of the tribe of the noble Abs. Nobility amongst liberal men is the thrust of the spear, the blow of the sword, and patience beneath the battle dust. I am the physician of the tribe of Abs when they are in sickness, their protector in disgrace, the defender of their wives when they are in trouble and their horseman when they are in glory and their sword when they rush to arms."

Monzar is astonished at his fluency of speech and questions him of his love: "Hast thou then", Monzar asks, "with all this fortitude and eloquence exposed thy life to the sea of death for the sake of an Arab girl?"

"Yes, my Lord, it is love that emboldens man to encounter dangers and horrors. There is no peril to be apprehended but from a look from beneath the corner of a veil . . . . The eyelashes of the songstress from the corner of the veil are more cutting than the edge of the cleaving scimitars; and when they wound the brave are humbled, and the corners of their eyes are flooded with tears.

"O lightnings! waft my salutations to her, and to all the places and pastures where she dwells. O ye dwellers in the forest of Tamarisks, if I die, mourn for me when my eyes are plucked out by the hungry fowls of the air. O ye steeds, mourn for a knight who could engage the lions of death in the field of battle. Alas, I am an outcast and in sorrow!"

Monzar, who also possesses the gift of eloquence, admires Antar and has him unbound. He proves his prodigious strength by performing remarkable feats, conquers the Persians in battle and brings about a reconciliation between the Persian, Chosroe, and Monzar who had been estranged.

Refusing to listen to Monzar's pleading to remain as one of them, he is given magnificent gifts and added to his share of the plunders of war, Arab horses, jewels and many slaves, he is given a tiara from the head of the King and a canopy of silver to sit under on his wedding night. In spite of the offer of priceless treasures, he turns homeward.

Meanwhile, his devoted brother Shiboob takes refuge in the cave of a shepherd, who befriends him and allows him to escape. Escaping from the land of Shiban, and believing Antar to have been slain, he reaches home bewailing his death. Knowing that Antar has been wantonly sacrificed, the tribe of Abs is greatly grieved and Ibla, broken of heart, swears fealty to his memory. Her father is weighted down by the hatred and scorn of all who believe him to be responsible for Antar's death and he decides to emigrate and to wed Ibla secretly to the conqueror Vachid.

Learning of the plot, Ibla is greatly distressed, and although cruelly treated by her brother and father, she persists in her refusal to wed. But they journey on. In the midst of an attack by marauders, they are, to their great surprise, met by Antar, who is on his way home with his great riches. He rescues the party and Ibla is overjoyed.

Malik rides on ahead to announce to King Zoheir and all the tribe that Antar is safe and returning to his tribe. In the midst of the rejoicing, Antar gives his wealth to Ibla, but Malik, thwarted in his plans, forbids the lovers to meet.

Antar in sorrow resolves to go to Mecca, mounts his steed and again goes forth with Shiboob to the sacred valley, where he seeks consolation in Nature. He has marvelous adventures, rescues his enemies, Shas and Malik, who have wandered from home, and is again sent on a difficult errand, ostensibly to seek a more suitable marriage gift for Ibla.

With no intention of keeping his promise, Malik spirits Ibla away. Upon Antar's return, he is aghast at the sight of her abandoned home. The lovers succeed in exchanging messages and Antar sends his brother to comfort Ibla while he enters a battle with the hostile tribe which has imprisoned Ibla.

He puts the tribe of Temeem to flight, protects the women and children, rescues Ibla and wins the admiration of Ghayadh.

"Hail! I greet thee, branch of the tamarisk! Welcome to the new moon of the desert and the city! O Ibla! thy form during my absence was ever in the core of my heart and my eye. Since thou hast been absent, all my joys have been absent, all my pleasures closed and my bloodshot eyes have passed the night in sleeplessness."

The final artifice of Malik is frustrated. Repeatedly he is thrown into difficult situations in which he is forced to rely upon Antar's kindness and intrepidity, and at last he speaks honestly: "God is with thee. Thou hast revived me after extinction. Thou hast exerted thyself and the tribe has been annihilated. Let us swear by thy generosity."

Great sorrow comes to Antar by the death of his good friends, King Zoheir and his dearly beloved protector, Prince Malik. Cais now reigns as king, and in great admiration of Antar's exploits in battle with King Numan's army, he demands that Malik keep his promise and give Ibla in immediate marriage to Antar.

Antar, his love now won, is gloriously happy, but he wishes his joy to be shared by his many friends and so he delays the ceremonies for ten days, in order that he might reach the Kings of the various tribes of the plains. The land of Shurebah and Mt. Saadi is a land of feasting and joy for seven days and nights.

The kings and their warriors bring magnificent gifts. The pavilion of burnished gold and jewels, the gift of Chosroe, is made ready and the tiara and coronet from the land of Shiban is placed on Ibla's head and forehead. The consummation of the marriage of Antar and Ibla is honored by a splendid feast given by King Cais.

The sumptuous wedding scene closes the fourth book, the last, of Terrick Hamilton's translation. The superb closing scene of the opera is taken from Asmai's "Romance of Antar", in which is told the remarkable, heroic death of the poet.

In reality, the poet's death occurs at an advanced age and sons survive him. Meanwhile the discovery is made that Zebeeba, the Abyssinian mother of Antar, was herself of royal blood, enslaved through warfare, the victim of one of the frequent invasions, perhaps, of the Abyssinians who succeeded in placing a number of Governors in southern Arabia during the early centuries.

In the last act of the opera, Antar is slowly dying from the wound received by a poisoned arrow. Ibla is ignorant of his fate. Barring the way that she may escape from a warring band, he dies seated upright on his noble horse.

Amarat, who treacherously instigated his murder, believes Antar to be alive and with his band he flees in terror from the greatly feared warrior. But Antar is no more. Seated on his steed, with sword in hand, victorious even in death, he wins the praise of friend and foe:

"God bless thee, brave Antar, thou protectest the weak even though thou art dead."

THE NEGRO IN LITERATURE

William Stanley Braithwaite analyzes the history of
African Americans in American literature in this essay.
Braithwaite asserts that African-American literature
may be classified into three main divisions: poetry, fiction, and the essay. This essay was published in September 1924.

True of his origin on this continent, the Negro was projected into literature by his neighbor. He was *in* American literature long before he
was a part of it as a creator. I ought to qualify this last, perhaps, by saying that as a racial unit during more than two centuries of an enslaved
peasantry, the Negro's creative qualities were affirmed in the *Spirituals.*
In these, as was true of the European folk-stock, the race gave evidence
of an artistic psychology; without this artistic psychology no race can
develop vision which becomes articulate in the sophisticated forms
and symbols of cultivated expression. Expressing itself with poignancy
and a symbolic imagery unsurpassed, indeed, often unmatched, by any
folk-group, the race in servitude was at the same time both the finished
shaping of emotion and imagination, and also the most precious mass
of raw material for literature America was producing. Quoting the
first, third and fifth stanzas of James Weldon Johnson's *"O Black and Unknown Bards,"* I want you to take it as the point in the assertion of the
Negro's way into literature:

> O Black and unknown bards of long ago,
> How came your lips to touch the sacred fire?
> How, in your darkness, did you come to know
> The power and beauty of the minstrel's lyre?
> Who first from midst his bonds lifted his eyes?

Who first from out the still watch, lone and long?
Feeling the ancient faith of prophets rise
Within his dark-kept soul, burst into song?

What merely living clod, what captive thing,
Could up toward God through all its darkness grope,
And find within its deadened heart to sing
These songs of sorrow, love, and faith and hope?
How did it catch that subtle undertone,
That note in music heard not with the ears?
How sound the elusive reed so seldom blown,
Which stirs the soul or melts the heart to tears?
There is a wide, wide wonder in it all,
That from degraded rest and servile toil
The fiery spirit of the seer should call
These simple children of the sun and soil.
O black slave singers, gone, forgot, unfamed,
You—you, alone, of all the long, long line
Of those who've sung untaught, unknown, unnamed,
Have stretched out upward, seeking the divine.

Because it was possible to sing thus of a race: of a race oppressed, il-
literate, and toil-ridden, it became also by some divine paradox irre-
sistibly urgent to make literary material out of the imagination and
emotion it possessed in such abundance.

I can do no more than outline the Negro in literature as he has been
treated by American writers of mixed nationalities. I present this word
nationalities because, though American by a declaration of a unity, one
must not overlook the deep and subtle atavistic impulses and energies
which have directed, or misdirected, the imagination, in creating character and experience, atmosphere and traits, in the use of the Negro as
literary material.

The first conspicuous example, and one which has more profoundly
influenced the world than any other, of the Negro in literature was
"Uncle Tom's Cabin." Here was a sentimentalized sympathy for a
downtrodden Race, but one in which was projected a character, in
Uncle Tom himself, which has been unequalled to this day. The Negro
in literature had its starting point with this book. Published in 1852, it
foreran for many years the body of literature which began during Reconstruction and lasted until the publication of Thomas Dixon's "The
Leopard's Spots," which began, and was the exponent, of an era of riot

and lawlessness in literary expression. Between the Civil War and the end of the century the subject of the Negro in literature is one that will some day inspire the literary historian with a magnificent theme. It will be magnificent not because there is any sharp emergence of character or incidents, but because of the immense paradox of racial life which came up thunderingly against the principles and doctrines of Democracy and put them to the severest test that they had known. It was a period when, in literature, Negro life was a shuttlecock between the two extremes of humor and pathos. The Negro was free, and was not free. The writers who dealt with him for the most part, refused to see the tragedy of his situation and capitalized his traits of humor. These writers did not see that his humor was a mask for the tragedies which were constantly a turbulent factor in his consciousness. If any of the authors who dealt with the Negro during this period had possessed gifts anywhere near approaching to genius, they would have penetrated this deceiving exterior of Negro life, sounded the depths of tragedy in it, and have produced a masterpiece. Irwin Russell was the first to versify the superficial humor of this Race, and, though all but forgotten today by the reading world, is given the characteristic credit by literary historians for discovering and recording the phantasies of Negro humor. Thomas Nelson Page, a kindly gentleman with a purely local imagination, painted an ante-bellum Negro in his fiction which was infinitely more truthful to the type contemporaneous with his own manhood during the restitution of the overlordship of the defeated slave owners in the Eighties. Another writer, who of all Americans made the most permanent contribution in dealing with the Negro, was Joel Chandler Harris. Much as we admire this lovable personality, the arts of his achievements were not in himself, but in the Race who supplied his servile pen with a store of fertile folk material. Indeed, the Race was its own artist, and only in its illiteracy lacked the power to record its speech. Joel Chandler Harris was the divinely appointed amanuensis to preserve the oral tales and legends of a Race in the "B'rer Rabbit" cycle.

The three writers I have mentioned do not by any means exhaust the list of writers who put the Negro into literature during the last half of the Nineteenth century. Mr. Howells added a shadowy note to his social record of American life with "An Imperative Duty" and prophesied the Fiction of the "Color Line". But his moral scruples—the persistent, artistic vice in all his novels—prevented him from consummating a just union between his heroine with a touch of Negro blood and his hero. It is useless to consider any others because there were none who succeeded in creating either a great story or a great character out of Negro life. Two writers of greater importance than the three I have named dealing with Negro life, are themselves Negroes, and I am reserving discussion of them for the group of Race writers I shall name presently. One ought to say, in justice to the writers I have mentioned, that as white Americans it was incompatible with their conception of the inequalities between the races to glorify the Negro into the serious and leading position of hero or heroine in fiction. Only one man, that I recall, had both the moral and artistic courage to do this and that was Stephen Crane in a short story called "The Monster". But Stephen Crane was a man of genius and, therefore, could not besmirch the integrity of an artist.

With Thomas Dixon, "The Leopard's Spots", we reach a distinct stage in the treatment of the Negro in fiction. In this book the Color Line type of fiction is, frankly and viciously, used for purposes of propaganda. This Southern author foresaw an inevitable consequence of the intimate contact and intercourse between the two races, in this country. He had good evidence upon which to base his fears. He was, however, too late with his cry for race purity—which meant, of course, Anglo-Saxon purity. The cry itself ought to have shamed all those critics who approved it; whose consciences must have taken a twinge in recollecting how the Saxon passion had found so sweetly desirable the black body of Africa. Had Dixon been a thinker, had his mind been stored with the complex social history of mankind, he would have saved himself a futile and ridiculous literary gesture. Thomas Dixon, of a quarter of a century ago, and Lothrop Stoddard of to-day, are a pair of literary twins whom nature has made sport of, and who will ultimately submerge in a typhoon of Truth. For Truth is devastating to all who would pervert the ways of nature.

Following "The Leopard's Spots", it was only occasionally during the next twenty years that the Negro was sincerely treated in fiction by white authors. There were two or three tentative efforts to dramatize him. Sheldon's "The Nigger" was the one notable early effort. And in fiction Paul Kester's "His Own Country" is, from a purely literary point of view, its outstanding performance. This type of novel failed, however, to awaken any general interest. This failure was due, I believe, to the illogical ideas and experiences presented, for there is, however indifferent and negative it may seem, a desire on the part of self-respecting readers, to have honesty of purpose, and a full vision in the artist.

The first hint that the American artist was looking at this subject with full vision was in Torrence's "Granny Maumee". It was drama, conceived and executed for performance on the stage, and therefore had a restricted appeal. But even here the artist was concerned with the primitive instincts of the Race, and, though faithful and honest in his portrayal, the note was still low in the scale of racial life. It was only a short time, however, before a distinctly new development took place in the treatment of Negro life by white authors. This new class of work honestly strove to endow the Negro with many virtues that were still, with one or two exceptions, treating the lower or primitive strata of his existence. With one or two exceptions referred to, the author could only see the Negro as an inferior, superstitious, half-ignorant and servile class of people. They did recognize, however, in a few isolated characters an ambitious impulse,—an impulse, nevertheless, always defeated in the force of the story. Again in only one or two instances did these authors categorically admit a cultured, independent layer of society that was leavening the Race with individuals who had won absolute equality of place and privilege with the best among the civilized group of to-day.

George Madden Martin, with her pretentious foreword to a group of short stories, called "The Children of the Mist,"—and this is an extraordinary volume in many ways—quite believed herself, as a Southern woman, to have elevated the Negro to a higher plane of fictional treatment and interest. In succession, followed Mary White Ovington's "The Shadow," in which Miss Ovington daringly created the kinship of brother and sister between a black boy and white girl, had it brought to disaster by prejudice, out of which the white girl rose to a sacrifice no white girl in a novel had hitherto accepted and endured; Shands' "White and Black", as honest a piece of fiction with the Negro as a subject as was ever produced by a Southern pen—and in this story, also, the hero, Robinson, making an equally glorious sacrifice for truth and justice, as Miss Ovington's heroine; Clement Wood's "Nigger", with defects of treatment, but admirable in purpose, wasted though, I think, in the effort to prove its thesis on wholly illogical material; and lastly, T. S. Stribling's "Birthright", more significant than any of these other books, in fact, the most significant novel on the Negro written by a white American, and this in spite of its totally false conception of the character of Peter Siner. Mr. Stribling's book broke new ground for a white author in giving us a Negro hero and heroine. He found in the Race a material for artistic treatment which was worthy of an artist's respect. His failure was in limiting, unconscious as it was on the part of the author, the capacity of the hero to assimilate culture, and in forcing his rapid reversion to the level of his origin after a perfect Harvard training. On the other hand, no author has presented so severe an indictment as Mr. Stribling in his painting of the Southern conditions which brought about the disintegration of his hero's dreams and ideals.

Three recent plays should here be mentioned, of the Negro put into literature by white authors: I refer to O'Neill's "Emperor Jones," and "All God's Chillun Got Wings," and "Goat Alley". In all these plays, disregarding the artistic quality of achievement, they are the sordid aspects of life and undesirable types of character which are dramatized. The best and highest class of racial life has not yet been discovered for literary treatment by white American authors; that's a task left for Negro writers to perform, and the start has been made.

In closing this phase of my paper let me quote in extenuation of much that I have said in the foregoing a passage from an article in a recent number of *The Independent,* which reads:

"During the past few years stories about Negroes have been extremely popular. A Magazine without a Negro story is hardly living up to its opportunities. But almost every one of these stories is written in a tone of condescension. The artists have caught the contagion from the writers and the illustrations are ninety-nine times out of a hundred purely slapstick stuff. Stories and pictures make a Roman holiday for the millions who are convinced that the most important fact about the Negro is that his skin is black. Many of these writers live in the South or are from the South. Presumably they are well acquainted with the Negro, but it is a remarkable fact that they almost never tell us anything vital about him, about the real human being in the black man's skin. Their most frequent method is to laugh at the colored man and woman, to catalogue their idiosyncrasies, their departure from the norm, that is, from the ways of the whites. There seems to be no suspicion in the minds of the writers that there may be a fascinating thought life in the minds of the Negroes, whether of the cultivated or of the most ignorant type. Always the Negro is interpreted in the terms of the white man. White-man psychology is applied and it is no wonder that the result often shows the Negro in a ludicrous light.'

I shall have to run back over the years to where I began to survey the achievement of Negro authorship. The Negro as a creator in American literature is of comparatively recent importance. All that was accomplished between Phyllis Wheatley and Paul Lawrence Dunbar, considered by critical standards, is negligible, and of historical interest only. Historically it is a great tribute to the Race to have produced in Phyllis Wheatly not only the slave poetess in 18th century Colonial

America, but to know she was as good, if not a better poetess, than Ann Bradstreet whom literary historians give the honor of being the first person of her sex to win fame as a poet in America.

Negro authorship may, for clearer statement, be classified into three main activities: Poetry, Fiction, and the Essay, with an occasional excursion into other branches. In the drama, practically nothing has been achieved, with the exception of Angelina Grimké's "Rachel," which is notable for its sombre craftsmanship. Biography has given us a notable life story, told by himself, of Booker T. Washington. Frederick Douglass's story of his life is eloquent as a human document, but not in the graces of narration and psychologic portraiture which has definitely put this form of literature in the domain of the fine arts. In philosophic speculation the Negro has made a valuable contribution to American thought; indeed, with Einstein endeavored to solve the complicated secrets of infinity, in Robert Brown's "The Mystery of Space," a work, which, but for the discernment of a few perceptive critics, has failed to win the recognition it deserves. In aesthetic theory and criticism the Negro has not yet made any worth-while contribution though a Negro scholar, Professor W. S. Scarborough, has published a Greek grammar which was adopted as a standard text book. In history and the historical monograph there has been in recent years a growing distinction of performance. It is now almost a half century since Williams's history of the Negro Race was published, and Trotter's volume on the Negro in music. The historical studies of to-day by Dr. Carter Woodson are of inestimable service in the documenting of the obscure past character and activity of Negro life; and Benjamin Brawley, who, beside his social history of the Negro, has written a study of the Negro in art and literature and a valuable "History of the English Drama." The literary contributions of the Negro have only begun, but the beginning is significant. His accomplishment has been chiefly in imaginative literature, with poetry, by far, the prominent practice. Next to poetry, comes fiction; and though his preoccupation runs back nearly a century, he gives promise in the future of a greater accomplishment in prose fiction. In the third field of the Negro's literary endeavor, the essay, and discursive article, dealing chiefly with racial problems, there has been produced a group of able writers assaulting and clearing the impeded pathway of racial progress.

Let us survey briefly the advance of the Negro in poetry. Behind Dunbar, there is nothing that can stand the critical test. We shall always have a sentimental and historical interest in those forlorn and pathetic figures who cried in the wilderness of their ignorance and oppression.

With Dunbar we have our first authentic lyric utterance, an utterance more authentic, I should say, for its faithful rendition of Negro life and character than for any rare or subtle artistry of expression. When Mr. Howells, in his famous introduction to the "Lyrics of Lowly Life," remarked that Dunbar was the first black man to express the life of his people lyrically, he summed up Dunbar's achievement and transported him to a place beside the peasant poet of Scotland, not for his art, but precisely because he made a people articulate in verse. The two chief qualities in Dunbar's work are humour and pathos, and in these with an inimitable portrayal, he expressed that era of conscious indecision disturbing the Race between the Civil War and the nineteenth century. No agitated visions of prophecy burn and surge in his poems. His dreams were anchored to the minor whimsies, to the ineffectual tears of his people deluded by the Torch of a Liberty that was leading them back into abstract bondage. He expressed what he felt and knew to be the temper and condition of his people. Into his dialect work he poured a spirit, which, for the first time, was the soul of a people. By his dialect work he will survive, not so much because out of this broken English speech he shaped the symbols of beauty or the haunting strains of melody, but because into it he poured the plaintive, poignant tears and laughter of the soul of a Race.

After Dunbar many versifiers appeared all largely dominated by his successful dialect work; I cannot parade them here for tag or comment. Not until James W. Johnson published his Fiftieth Anniversary Ode on the emancipation in 1913, did a poet of the Race disengage himself from the background of mediocrity. Mr. Johnson's work is based upon a broader contemplation of life, life that was not wholly confined within any racial experience, but through the racial he made articulate that universality of the emotions felt by all mankind. His verse possesses a vigor which definitely breaks away from the brooding minor undercurrents of feeling which has previously characterized the verse of Race poets. Mr. Johnson brought, indeed, the first intellectual substance to the content of poetry and a craftsmanship which, less spontaneous than that of Dunbar's, was more balanced and precise.

Two other poets have distinguished themselves, though not to the same degree as Mr. Johnson. Fenton Johnson is one of those who began with a very uncertain measure of gifts, but made a brief and sudden development, only to retire as suddenly into the silence; the other poet, Leslie Pinckney Hill, has published one creditable book which has won for him a place among Negro poets, but which is the result of an intellectual determination to versemaking rather than the outpouring of a spontaneous poetic spirit.

Let me here pay tribute to a woman who has proven herself the foremost of all women poets the Race has so far produced: Georgia Douglas Johnson is a lyricist who has achieved much and who ought to achieve a great deal more. She has the equipment which nature gives in endowing the poetic spirit; her art is adequate but to say this is not to be satisfied with the best use of her gifts. A capture by her of some of the illusive secrets of form would often transmute her substance into the golden miracle of art.

I come now to Claude McKay, who unquestionably is a poet whose potentialities would place him supreme above all poets of the Negro Race. But I am afraid he will never justify that high distinction. His work may be easily divided into two classes: first, when he is the pure dreamer, contemplating life and nature, with a wistful and sympathetic passion, giving expression with subtle and figurative music to his dreams; secondly, when he is the violent and angry propagandist, using his natural poetic gifts to clothe arrogant and defiant thoughts. When the mood of "Spring in New Hampshire" or the sonnet "The Harlem Dancer" possesses him, he is full of that desire, of those flames of beauty which flower above any or all men's harming; in these are the white dreams which shine over the Promised Land of the Race's conquest over its enemies; it is the literature of those magnificent Psalms against which all the assaults of time dissolve, and whose music and whose vision wash clean with the radiance of beauty. How different, in spite of the admirable spirit of courage and defiance, are his poems of which the sonnet "If We Must Die" is a typical example. Passion is not a thing of words,—it is an essence of the spirit! He who slaves and burns with beauty is a more triumphant conqueror than he who slaves with a sword that the victim might break.

> Too green the springing April grass,
> Too blue the silver speckled sky,
> For me to linger here, alas,
> While happy winds go laughing by,
> Wasting the golden hours indoors.
> Washing windows and scrubbing floors.
>
> Too wonderful the April night,
> Too faintly sweet the first May flowers,
> The stars too gloriously bright,

For me to spend the evening hours,
When fields are fresh and streams are leaping,
Weary, exhausted, dully sleeping.

Let me refer briefly to a type of literature in which there have been many pens with all the glory going to one man. Dr. Du Bois is the most variously gifted writer which the Race has produced. Poet, novelist, sociologist, historian and essayist, he has produced books in all these branches of literature—with the exception I believe, of a formal book of poems,—and being a man of indomitable courage I have often wondered why,—and gave to each the distinction of his clear and exact thinking, and of his sensitive imagination and passionate vision. "The Souls of Black Folk" was the book of an era; it was a painful book, a book of tortured dreams woven into the fabric of the sociologist's document. In this book, as well as in many of Dr. Du Bois's essays, is often my personal feeling that I am witnessing the birth of a poet, phoenix-like, out of a scholar. Between "The Souls of Black Folk" and "Darkwater," published three years ago, Dr. Du Bois has written a number of books, none more notable, in my opinion, than his novel "The Quest of the Silver Fleece" in which he made *cotton* the great protagonist of fate in the lives of the Southern people, both white and black. In European literature nature and her minions have long been represented in literature as dominating the destinies of man; but in America I know of only two conspicuous accomplishments of this kind,—one, Frank Norris in his dramatization of the influence of *wheat* and the other, Dr. Du Bois's in his dramatization of the influence of *cotton*.

Let me again quote a passage from the afore-mentioned article from *The Independent:*

"The white writer seems to stand baffled before the enigma and so he expends all his energies on dialect and in general on the Negro's minstrel characteristics. . . . We shall have to look to the Negro himself to go all the way. It is quite likely that no white man can do it. It is reasonable to suppose that his white psychology will always be in his way. I am not thinking at all about a Negro novelist who shall arouse the world to the horror of the deliberate killings by white mobs, to the wrongs that condemn a free people to political serfdom. I am not thinking at all of the propaganda novel, although there is enough horror and enough drama in the bald statistics of each one of the annual Moton letters to keep the whole army of writers busy. But the Negro novelist, if he ever comes, must reveal to us much more than what a Negro thinks about when he is being tied to a stake and the torch is being applied to his living flesh; much more than what he feels when he is being crowded off the sidewalk by a drunken rowdy who may be his intellectual inferior by a thousand leagues. Such a writer, to succeed in a big sense, would have to forget that there are white readers; he would have to lose self-consciousness and forget that his work would be placed before a white jury. He would have to be careless as to what the white critic might think of it; he would need the self-assurance to be his own critic. He would have to forget for the time being, at least, that any white man ever attempted to dissect the soul of a Negro."

What I here quote is both an inquiry and a challenge! Well informed as the writer is, he does not seem to detect the forces which are surely gathering to produce what he longs for.

The development of fiction among Negro authors has been, I might almost say, one of the repressed activities of his literary life. A fair start was made the last decade of the Nineteenth century when Chesnutt and Dunbar were turning out both short stories and novels. In Dunbar's case, had he lived, I think his literary growth would have been in the evolution of the Race novel as indicated in "The Uncalled" and the "Sport of the Gods." The former was, I think, the most ambitious literary effort of Dunbar; the latter was his most significant; significant because, thrown against the background of New York City, it displayed the life of the Race as a unit, swayed by the currents of existence, of which it was and was not a part. The story was touched with that shadow of destiny which gave to it a purpose more important than the mere racial machinery of its plot. In all his fiction, Dunbar dealt with the same world which gave him the inspiration for his dialect poems. It was a world he knew and loved and became the historian of without any revising influence from the world which was its political and social enemies. His contemporary, Charles W. Chesnutt, was to supply the conflict between the two worlds and establish with the precision of a true artist, the fiction of the Color Line.

Charles W. Chesnutt is one of the enigmas in American literature. There are five volumes to his credit, not including his life of Frederick Douglass for the Beacon Biography Series. From first to last, he revealed himself as a fictional artist of a very high order. The two volumes of short stories, "The Wife of His Youth and Other Stories," and "The Conjure Woman," are exquisite examples of the short story form equal to the best in American literature. Primarily a short story writer, Mr. Chesnutt showed defects in his long novels which made them a joy to read. I recall the shock a certain incident in "The House Behind the Cedars" gave me when I first read the book at the time it was published, puzzled that human nature should betray its own most passionate instincts at a moment of the intensest crisis. I realized later, or at least my admiration for Mr. Chesnutt's art, led me to believe that the fault was not so much his art as the problem of the Color Line. This problem, in its most acute details, was woven into the best novel Mr. Chesnutt has written called "The Marrow of Tradition." Certainly he did in that work an epic of riot and lawlessness which has served for mere pictorial detail as a standard example. In 1905, Mr. Chesnutt published "The Colonel's Dream," and thereafter silence fell upon him. I have heard it said that disappointment because his stories failed to win popularity was the cause of his following the classic example of Thomas Hardy by refusing to publish another novel. The cases are not exactly parallel because, while Hardy had refused to write another novel following the publication of "Jude the Obscure," I have heard it rumored that Mr. Chesnutt has written other stories but will not permit their publication.

From the publication of Chesnutt's last novel until the present year there has been no fiction by the Race of any importance, with the exception of Dr. Du Bois's "The Quest of the Silver Fleece," which was published in 1911. This year of 1924 will have given four new books by writers, which seem to promise the inauguration of an era that is like to produce the major novelists. Joshua Hen Jones's "By Sanction of Law," is a book that will hold the attention of readers who demand a thrilling story; it designs no new pattern of fiction, produces no new texture of expression. A vigorous narrative, it piles incident upon incident, with dialogue, love and violence.

Mr. Walter White's novel "The Fire in the Flint," is a swift moving story built upon the authentic experience of the author, with the terrors and pities of racial conflict.

Two outstanding achievements in the entire range of fiction are the books by Jessie Redmon Fauset and Jean Toomer. Miss Fauset in her novel "There Is Confusion," has created an entirely new milieu in the treatment of the Race in fiction. She has taken a class within the Race, given it an established social standing, tradition, culture, and shown that its predilections are very much like those of any civilized group of human beings. In her story Race fiction emerges from the Color Line and is incorporated into that general and universal art which detaches itself from prejudice of propaganda and stands out the objective vision of artistic creation. Her beginning is conspicuous; her development may well be surprising.

These rambling remarks on the Negro in literature I may well bring to a close with this public confession that I believe that of all the writers I have mentioned, the one who is most surely touched with genius is Jean Toomer the author of "Cane." I believe this, not only on account of what he has actually accomplished in "Cane," but for something which is partly in the accomplishment and partly in the half articulate sense and impression of his powers. This young man is an artist; the very first artist in his Race who, with all an artist's passion and sympathy for life, its hurts, its sympathies, its desires, its joys, its defeats, and strange yearnings can write about the Negro without the surrender or compromise of the artist's vision. It's a mere accident that birth of association has thrown him into contact with the life that he has written about. He would write just as poignantly, just as transmutingly, about the peasants of Russia, or the peasants of Ireland, had experience but given him the knowledge of their existence. "Cane" is a book of gold and bronze, of dusk and flame, of ecstasy and pain, and Jean Toomer a bright morning star of a new day of the Race in literature!

—

Still . . . "Perhaps Buddha is a woman."

CRITERIA OF NEGRO ART

In the following piece, W. E. B. Du Bois raises some issues regarding the negative judgments of black art. He asserts that African Americans must review and acclaim their own art with free and unfettered judgment. He further contends that blacks should not wait for white America to say that black art is great before saying so, too. "Criteria of Negro Art" was published in October 1926.

So many persons have asked for the complete text of the address delivered by Dr. Du Bois at the Chicago Conference of the National Association for the Advancement of Colored People that we are publishing the address here.

———

I do not doubt but there are some in this audience who are a little disturbed at the subject of this meeting, and particularly at the subject I have chosen. Such people are thinking something like this: "How is it that an organization like this, a group of radicals trying to bring new things into the world, a fighting organization which has come up out of the blood and dust of battle, struggling for the right of black men to be ordinary human beings—how is it that an organization of this kind can turn aside to talk about Art? After all, what have we who are slaves and black to do with Art?"

Or perhaps there are others who feel a certain relief and are saying, "After all it is rather satisfactory after all this talk about rights and fighting to sit and dream of something which leaves a nice taste in the mouth".

Let me tell you that neither of these groups is right. The thing we are talking about tonight is part of the great fight we are carrying on and it represents a forward and an upward look—a pushing onward. You and I have been breasting hills; we have been climbing upward; there has been progress and we can see it day by day looking back along blood-filled paths. But as you go through the valleys and over the foothills, so long as you are climbing, the direction,—north, south, east or west,—is of less importance. But when gradually the vista widens and you begin to see the world at your feet and the far horizon, then it is time to know more precisely whither you are going and what you really want.

What do we want? What is the thing we are after? As it was phrased last night it had a certain truth: We want to be Americans, full-fledged Americans, with all the rights of other American citizens. But is that all? Do we want simply to be Americans? Once in a while through all of us there flashes some clairvoyance, some clear idea, of what America really is. We who are dark can see America in a way that white Americans can not. And seeing our country thus, are we satisfied with its present goals and ideals?

In the high school where I studied we learned most of Scott's "Lady of the Lake" by heart. In after life once it was my privilege to see the lake. It was Sunday. It was quiet. You could glimpse the deer wandering in unbroken forests; you could hear the soft ripple of romance on the waters. Around me fell the cadence of that poetry of my youth. I fell asleep full of the enchantment of the Scottish border. A new day broke and with it came a sudden rush of excursionists. They were mostly Americans and they were loud and strident. They poured upon the little pleasure boat,—men with their hats a little on one side and drooping cigars in the wet corners of their mouths; women who shared their conversation with the world. They all tried to get everywhere first. They pushed other people out of the way. They made all sorts of incoherent noises and gestures so that the quiet home folk and the visitors from other lands silently and half-wonderingly gave way before them. They struck a note not evil but wrong. They carried, perhaps, a sense of strength and accomplishment, but their hearts had no conception of the beauty which pervaded this holy place.

If you tonight suddenly should become full-fledged Americans; if your color faded, or the color line here in Chicago was miraculously forgotten; suppose, too, you became at the same time rich and powerful;—what is it that you would want? What would you immediately seek? Would you buy the most powerful of motor cars and outrace Cook County? Would you buy the most elaborate estate on the North Shore? Would you be a Rotarian or a Lion or a What-not of the very last degree? Would you wear the most striking clothes, give the richest dinners and buy the longest press notices?

Even as you visualize such ideals you know in your hearts that these are not the things you really want. You realize this sooner than the average white American because, pushed aside as we have been in America, there has come to us not only a certain distaste for the tawdry and flamboyant but a vision of what the world could be if it were really a beautiful world; if we had the true spirit; if we had the Seeing Eye, the Cunning Hand, the Feeling Heart; if we had, to be sure, not perfect happiness, but plenty of good hard work, the inevitable suffering that always comes with life; sacrifice and waiting, all that—but, nevertheless, lived in a world where men know, where men create, where they realize themselves and where they enjoy life. It is that sort of a world we want to create for ourselves and for all America.

After all, who shall describe Beauty? What is it? I remember tonight four beautiful things: The Cathedral at Cologne, a forest in stone, set in light and changing shadow, echoing with sunlight and solemn song; a village of the Veys in West Africa, a little thing of mauve and purple, quiet, lying content and shining in the sun; a black and velvet room where on a throne rests, in old and yellowing marble, the broken curves of the Venus of Milo; a single phrase of music in the Southern South—utter melody, haunting and appealing, suddenly arising out of night and eternity, beneath the moon.

Such is Beauty. Its variety is infinite, its possibility is endless. In normal life all may have it and have it yet again. The world is full of it; and yet today the mass of human beings are choked away from it, and their lives distorted and made ugly. This is not only wrong, it is silly. Who shall right this well-nigh universal failing? Who shall let this world be beautiful? Who shall restore to men the glory of sunsets and the peace of quiet sleep?

We black folk may help for we have within us as a race new stirrings; stirrings of the beginning of a new appreciation of joy, of a new desire to create, of a new will to be; as though in this morning of group life we had awakened from some sleep that at once dimly mourns the past and dreams a splendid future; and there has come the conviction that the Youth that is here today, the Negro Youth, is a different kind of Youth, because in some new way it bears this mighty prophecy on its breast, with a new realization of itself, with new determination for all mankind.

What has this Beauty to do with the world? What has Beauty to do with Truth and Goodness—with the facts of the world and the right actions of men? "Nothing", the artists rush to answer. They may be right. I am but an humble disciple of art and cannot presume to say. I am one who tells the truth and exposes evil and seeks with Beauty and for Beauty to set the world right. That somehow, somewhere eternal and perfect Beauty sits above Truth and Right I can conceive, but here and now and in the world in which I work they are for me unseparated and inseparable.

This is brought to us peculiarly when as artists we face our own past as a people. There has come to us—and it has come especially through the man we are going to honor tonight*—a realization of that past, of which for long years we have been ashamed, for which we have apologized. We thought nothing could come out of that past which we wanted to remember; which we wanted to hand down to our children. Suddenly, this same past is taking on form, color and reality, and in a half shame-faced way we are beginning to be proud of it. We are remembering that the romance of the world did not die and lie forgotten in the Middle Age; that if you want romance to deal with you must have it here and now and in your own hands.

I once knew a man and woman. They had two children, a daughter who was white and a daughter who was brown; the daughter who was white married a white man; and when her wedding was preparing the daughter who was brown prepared to go and celebrate. But the mother said, "No!" and the brown daughter went into her room and turned on the gas and died. Do you want Greek tragedy swifter than that?

Or again, here is a little Southern town and you are in the public square. On one side of the square is the office of a colored lawyer and on all the other sides are men who do not like colored lawyers. A white woman goes into the black man's office and points to the white-filled square and says, "I want five hundred dollars now and if I do not get it I am going to scream."

Have you heard the story of the conquest of German East Africa? Listen to the untold tale: There were 40,000 black men and 4,000 white men who talked German. There were 20,000 black men and 12,000 white men who talked English. There were 10,000 black men and 400 white men who talked French. In Africa then where the Mountains of the Moon raised their white and snow-capped heads into the mouth of the tropic sun, where Nile and Congo rise and the Great Lakes swim, these men fought; they struggled on mountain, hill and valley, in river, lake and swamp, until in masses they sickened, crawled and died; until the 4,000 white Germans had become mostly bleached bones; until nearly all the 12,000 white Englishmen had returned to South Africa, and the 400 Frenchmen to Belgium and

*Carter Godwin Woodson, 12th Spingarn Medalist.

Heaven; all except a mere handful of the white men died; but thousands of black men from East, West and South Africa, from Nigeria and the Valley of the Nile, and from the West Indies still struggled, fought and died. For four years they fought and won and lost German East Africa; and all you hear about it is that England and Belgium conquered German Africa for the allies!

Such is the true and stirring stuff of which Romance is born and from this stuff come the stirrings of men who are beginning to remember that this kind of material is theirs; and this vital life of their own kind is beckoning them on.

The question comes next as to the interpretation of these new stirrings, of this new spirit: Of what is the colored artist capable? We have had on the part of both colored and white people singular unanimity of judgment in the past. Colored people have said: "This work must be inferior because it comes from colored people." White people have said: "It is inferior because it is done by colored people." But today there is coming to both the realization that the work of the black man is not always inferior. Interesting stories come to us. A professor in the University of Chicago read to a class that had studied literature a passage of poetry and asked them to guess the author. They guessed a goodly company from Shelley and Robert Browning down to Tennyson and Masefield. The author was Countée Cullen. Or again the English critic John Drinkwater went down to a Southern seminary, one of the sort which "finishes" young white women of the South. The students sat with their wooden faces while he tried to get some response out of them. Finally he said, "Name me some of your Southern poets". They hesitated. He said finally, "I'll start out with your best: Paul Laurence Dunbar"!

With the growing recognition of Negro artists in spite of the severe handicaps, one comforting thing is occurring to both white and black. They are whispering, "Here is a way out. Here is the real solution of the color problem. The recognition accorded Cullen, Hughes, Fauset, White and others shows there is no real color line. "Keep quiet! Don't complain! Work! All will be well!"

I will not say that already this chorus amounts to a conspiracy. Perhaps I am naturally too suspicious. But I will say that there are today a surprising number of white people who are getting great satisfaction out of these younger Negro writers because they think it is going to stop agitation of the Negro question. They say, "What is the use of your fighting and complaining; do the great thing and the reward is there." And many colored people are all too eager to follow this advice;

especially those who weary of the eternal struggle along the color line, who are afraid to fight and to whom the money of philanthropists and the alluring publicity are subtle and deadly bribes. They say, "What is the use of fighting? Why not show simply what we deserve and let the reward come to us?"

And it is right here that the National Association for the Advancement of Colored People comes upon the field, comes with its great call to a new battle, a new fight and new things to fight before the old things are wholly won; and to say that the beauty of truth and freedom which shall some day be our heritage and the heritage of all civilized men is not in our hands yet and that we ourselves must not fail to realize.

Here there is in New York tonight a black woman molding clay by herself in a little bare room, because there is not a single school of sculpture in New York where she is welcome. Surely there are doors she might burst through, but when God makes a sculptor He does not always make the pushing sort of person who beats his way through doors thrust in his face. This girl is working her hands off to get out of this country so that she can get some sort of training.

There was Richard Brown. If he had been white he would have been alive today instead of dead of neglect. Many helped him when he asked but he was not the kind of boy that always asks. He was simply one who made colors sing.

There is a colored woman in Chicago who is a great musician. She thought she would like to study at Fontainebleau this summer where Walter Damrosch and a score of leaders of art have an American school of music. But the application blank of this school says: "I am a white American and I apply for admission to the school."

We can go on the stage; we can be just as funny as white Americans wish us to be; we can play all the sordid parts that America likes to assign to Negroes; but for anything else there is still small place for us.

And so I might go on. But let me sum up with this: Suppose the only Negro who survived some centuries hence was the Negro painted by white Americans in the novels and essays they have written. What would people in a hundred years say of black Americans? Now turn it around. Suppose you were to write a story and put in it the kind of people you know and like and imagine. You might get it published and you might not. And the "might not" is still far bigger than the "might." The white publishers catering to white folk would say, "It is not interesting"—to white folk, naturally not. They want Uncle Toms, Topsies, good "darkies" and clowns. I have in my office a story with all the earmarks of truth. A young man says that he started out to write and had his stories accepted. Then he began to write about the things he knew best about, that is, about his own people. He submitted a story to a magazine which said, "We are sorry, but we cannot take it." "I sat down and revised my story, changing the color of the characters and the locale and sent it under an assumed name with a change of address and it was accepted by the same magazine that had refused it, the editor promising to take anything else I might send in providing it was good enough."

We have, to be sure, a few recognized and successful Negro artists; but they are not all those fit to survive or even a good minority. They are but the remnants of that ability and genius among us whom the accidents of education and opportunity have raised on the tidal waves of chance. We black folk are not altogether peculiar in this. After all, in the world at large, it is only the accident, the remnant, that gets the chance to make the most of itself; but if this is true of the white world it is infinitely more true of the colored world. It is not simply the great clear tenor of Roland Hayes that opened the ears of America. We have had many voices of all kinds as fine as his and America was as deaf as she was for years to him Then a foreign land heard Hayes and put its imprint on him and immediately America with all its imitative snobbery woke up. We approved Hayes because London, Paris, and Berlin approved him and not simply because he was a great singer.

Thus it is the bounden duty of black America to begin this great work of the creation of beauty, of the preservation of beauty, of the realization of beauty, and we must use in this work all the methods that men have used before. And what have been the tools of the artist in times gone by? First of all, he has used the truth—not for the sake of truth, not as a scientist seeking truth, but as one upon whom truth eternally thrust itself as the highest handmaid of imagination, as the one great vehicle of universal understanding. Again artists have used goodness—goodness in all its aspects of justice, honor, and right—not for sake of an ethical sanction but as the one true method of gaining sympathy and human interest.

The apostle of beauty thus becomes the apostle of truth and right not by choice but by inner and outer compulsion. Free he is but his freedom is ever bounded by truth and justice; and slavery only dogs him when he is denied the right to tell the truth or recognize an ideal of justice.

Thus all art is propaganda and ever must be, despite the wailing of the purists. I stand in utter shamelessness and say that whatever art I have for writing has been used always for propaganda for gaining the right of black folk to love and enjoy. I do not care a damn for any art that is not used for propaganda. But I do care when propaganda is confined to one side while the other is stripped and silent.

In New York we have two plays: "White Cargo" and "Congo." In "White Cargo" there is a fallen woman. She is black. In "Congo" the fallen woman is white. In "White Cargo" the black woman goes down further and further and in "Congo" the white woman begins with degradation but in the end is one of the angels of the Lord.

You know the current magazine story: a young white man goes down to Central America and the most beautiful colored woman there falls in love with him. She crawls across the whole isthmus to get to him. The white man says nobly, "No." He goes back to his white sweetheart in New York.

In such cases, it is not the positive propaganda of people who believe white blood divine, infallible, and holy to which I object. It is the denial of a similar right of propaganda to those who believe black blood human, lovable, and inspired with new ideals for the world. White artists themselves suffer from this narrowing of their field. They cry for freedom in dealing with Negroes because they have so little freedom in dealing with whites. DuBose Heywood writes "Porgy" and writes beautifully of the black Charleston underworld. But why does he do this? Because he cannot do a similar thing for the white people of Charleston, or they would drum him out of town. The only chance he had to tell the truth of pitiful human degradation was to tell it of colored people. I should not be surprised if Octavius Roy Cohen had approached the *Saturday Evening Post* and asked permission to write about a different kind of colored folk than the monstrosities he has created; but if he has, the *Post* has replied, "No. You are getting paid to write about the kind of colored people you are writing about."

In other words, the white public today demands from its artists, literary and pictorial, racial prejudgment which deliberately distorts truth and justice, as far as colored races are concerned, and it will pay for no other.

On the other hand, the young and slowly growing black public still wants its prophets almost equally unfree. We are bound by all sorts of customs that have come down as second-hand soul clothes of white patrons. We are ashamed of sex and we lower our eyes when people will talk of it. Our religion holds us in superstition. Our worst side has been so shamelessly emphasized that we are denying we have or ever had a worst side. In all sorts of ways we are hemmed in and our new young artists have got to fight their way to freedom.

The ultimate judge has got to be you and you have got to build yourselves up into that wide judgment, that catholicity of temper which is going to enable the artist to have his widest chance for freedom. We can afford the truth. White folk today cannot. As it is now we are handing everything over to a white jury. If a colored man wants to publish a book, he has got to get a white publisher and a white newspaper to say it is great; and then you and I say so. We must come to the place where the work of art when it appears is reviewed and acclaimed by our own free and unfettered judgment. And we are going to have a real and valuable and eternal judgment only as we make ourselves free of mind, proud of body and just of soul to all men.

And then do you know what will be said? It is already saying. Just as soon as true art emerges; just as soon as the black artist appears, someone touches the race on the shoulder and says, "He did that because he was an American, not because he was a Negro; he was born here; he was trained here; he is not a Negro—what is a Negro anyhow? He is just human; it is the kind of thing you ought to expect."

I do not doubt that the ultimate art coming from black folk is going to be just as beautiful, and beautiful largely in the same ways, as the art that comes from white folk, or yellow, or red; but the point today is that until the art of the black folk compels recognition they will not be rated as human. And when through art they compel recognition then let the world discover if it will that their art is as new as it is old and as old as new.

I had a classmate once who did three beautiful things and died. One of them was a story of a folk who found fire and then went wandering in the gloom of night seeking again the stars they had once known and lost; suddenly out of blackness they looked up and there loomed the heavens; and what was it that they said? They raised a might cry: "it is the stars, it is the ancient stars, it is the young everlasting stars!"

Our Negro "Intellectuals"

Allison Davis offers a critical analysis of black intellectuals. Davis believes that critical analysis is essential to understanding the place of blacks in America. This essay was published in August 1928.

For nearly ten years, our Negro writers have been "confessing" the distinctive sordidness and triviality of Negro life, and making an exhibition of their own unhealthy imagination, in the name of frankness and sincerity. Frankness is no virtue in itself, however, as any father will tell his son, nor is sincerity. A dog or savage is "sincere" about his bestialities, but he is not therefore raised above them. The modern novel has been frankly and sincerely preoccupied with sex, but has not escaped an insane naturalism. It is a question, then, of the purpose for which one is being sincere. It is quite evident that the sincerity of Milton, of Fielding, and of Dr. Johnson is different in kind from the sincerity of Mr. D. H. Lawrence and Mr. James Joyce. If sincerity is to justify one in exploiting the lowest traits of human nature; and in ignoring that sense in man which Cicero says differentiates him from other animals,—his sense for what is decent—then sincerity is a pander to a torpid animalism.

The plea of sincerity, of war against hypocrisy and sham, therefore, is no defence for the exhibitionism of Mr. George S. Schuyler and Mr. Eugene Gordon, nor for the sensationalism of such works as Dr. Rudolph Fisher's HIGH YALLER or Mr. Langston Hughes' FINE CLOTHES TO THE JEW. The first two writers by their coarse frivolousness and scandalmongering falsely represent that the Negro has no self-respect. A bawling confession from the house-tops is a poor substitute for honest and discriminating self-examination, in race criticism as in religion. Mr. Schuyler and Mr. Gordon may be clever intellectual gymnasts; as such they belong with the vaudeville, and not with the men who set new currents of thought moving in Negro life. Of our Menckenites, however, more later; let us first include in our view those who ought to be termed our Van Vechtenites. Mr. Van Vechten is not responsible for the beginning of our literary effort to appear primitive, but he brought the movement to its complete fruition, and gave it the distinction of his patronage.

———

Our writers started almost ten years ago to capitalize the sensational and sordid in Negro life, notably in Harlem, by making it appear that Negro life is distinctive for its flaming "color", its crude and primitive emotion. This facile acceptance of the old, romantic delusion of "racial literatures", which goes back beyond Taine all the way to Mme. de Stael, was a convenient mould for the energies of writers who had no tradition to guide them in treating Negro themes. What was more to the point, it interested the sophisticated reading public, at the height of the "jazz age" following the war, because it seemed to bring fresh and primitive forces to a jaded age.

These young writers hit upon two means of injecting primitivistic color in their work; one, the use of the Harlem cabaret and night life, and the other, a return to the African jungles. Since Mr. MacKay's HARLEM DANCER, the cabaret has been an unhealthy obsession with these youths, who in their relative naïveté imagine that there is something profoundly stirring about the degradation of its habitués. Even the best writers, Mr. McKay, Mr. Cullen, Mr. Hughes, and Dr. Fisher, as well as many of their less gifted imitators, have exploited the cabaret. The jazz band became the model which the Negro poet sought to imitate. It is particularly unfortunate that Mr. James Weldon Johnson should yield to this jazzy primitivism in choosing the title GOD'S TROMBONES for a work purporting to represent the Negro's religious fervor. Of course here, as always, the Negro movement must be seen in relation to the broader current of American literature. Mr. Waldo Frank, Mr. Scott Fitzgerald, and a host of other white authors were at the same time popularizing the jazz complex. In illustration, moreover, Mr. Miguel Covarrubias and Mr. Winold Reiss did more than Mr. Aaron Douglas and Mr. Richard Bruce to represent the Negro as essentially bestialized by jazz and the cabaret.

In this mad rush to make the Negro exhibit his sensational and primitivistic qualities, our young writers did not lack white support. Mr. Carl Van Doren encouraged them in this fashion: "But if the reality of Negro life is itself dramatic, there are of course still other elements, particularly the emotional power with which Negroes live—or at least to me seem to live. What American literature decidedly needs at the moment is color, music, gusto, the free expression of gay or desperate moods. If the Negroes are not in a position to contribute these items, I do not know what Americans are." Mr. Max Rheinhardt spoke of the necessity for the Negro dramatist's remaining true to the original spontaneity of his race by portraying "pure emotion, almost independent of words or setting". This myth of the spiritual and artistic virtue of spontaneous emotion in the Negro was enthusiastically supported by Mr. Carl Van Vechten. I think that the severest charge one can make against Mr. Van Vechten is that he misdirected a genuine poet, who gave promise of a power and technique exceptional in any poetry,—Mr. Hughes. Mr. Van Vechten disclaims any influence upon Mr. Hughes' first book, THE WEARY BLUES, for which he wrote a preface expressing undiluted primitivism. The evident reply is that the drop from the best poems of this first book to any of those in FINE CLOTHES TO THE JEW, which Mr. Van Vechten undoubtedly *did* influence, is the real proof of his having finally misdirected Mr. Hughes.

———

Now came the devastating result of the primitivism which our Negro writers had concocted and made a holy cause. NIGGER HEAVEN was the telos, the perfect flowering of the "cabaret school". By means of the same sensational primitivism and the creation of half a dozen cabarets which Harlem could never boast, Mr. Van Vechten warped Negro life into a fantastic barbarism. What was most pernicious in NIGGER HEAVEN was the representation that the Negro upper class is identical with the pleasure-seekers and cabaret-rounders. NIGGER HEAVEN was the logical outcome of the forces our "intellectuals" had championed for five years, and in a very real sense these "intellectuals" were responsible for its writing and its success. With its appearance there arose in the minds of many Negro writers and readers some doubt concerning the whole movement toward "color" and exhibitionism. The most prominent writers, however, could not evade the natural result of their own practice, and defended Mr. Van Vechten on the ground of artistic sincerity, for which they found proof chiefly in his mixing socially with Negroes. Here again the pretense of sincerity justified the most unalleviated sensationalism. In fact, the total effect of the whole movement was that Negroes are sincerely bestial.

An atavistic yearning for the African jungles, which was entirely simulated, was the second device of these poets for adding "color" to the Negro. The desire of young poets to "dance naked under palm trees", and to express themselves in jungle loves has been the favorite device for making poetry authentically Negroid. Tom-toms, love-dances, strange passions and savage urges have been the paraphernalia of almost every budding poetaster. Even Mr. Cullen made especial use of the jungle urge in his early and best known poems, HERITAGE and THE SHROUD OF COLOR. This whole primitivistic interpretation of the Negro is the white man's facile point of view, and our Negro "intellectuals" wanted to appear as the white man would have them. The most important assertion of the related primitivism of cabaret and jungle is the work of a white poet, Mr. Lindsay's CONGO. There is nothing more foreign to the Negro's imagination than this yearning for savage Africa, and it is a false note every time it is struck by a Negro poet. The African tradition which we want to uncover and make fruitful is certainly not that of savagery, but of self-containment, fortitude, and culture.

At times the poets achieved something beautiful and significant in spite of their material and creed. Mr. McKay's poem, HARLEM SHADOWS touches on nobility and a higher imaginative view than most American realistic poetry ever reaches. The title poem of Mr. Hughes' THE WEARY BLUES created a representative symbol for the frustration and inertia into which Negro life is penned. There were poems in McKay, Cullen, and Hughes which gave evidence of a higher understanding of Negro life, but this quality of their imagination was not developed. Mr. Hughes especially chose to exploit the meretricious themes of jazz, instead of developing the powers shown in such poems as AUNT SUE'S STORIES and WHEN SUE WEARS RED. The indubitable gift of Mr. Hughes and of one or two other poets was sacrificed to a dogma, which necessitated their being atavistic and "colorful" at the expense of a full and experimental development of their imagination. The untrammeled self-expression which the supporters of the movement claimed for it was actually freedom only to be as *primitivistic* as one liked. There was no freedom from the creed that a Negro poet ought to be barbaric.

II

Our primitivistic poets and story-tellers have been ousted from the stage lately by a rising group of young critics, writing for magazines and Negro newspapers. They are Menckenites, largely inspired by their master's attack upon Negro preachers and "misleaders", and his heralding of the self-critical Negro. Now the genuine critic is the individual who can fix upon the excellent and significant in the welter of all that is obvious and passing, and who can reveal how this seed may be made fruitful. Even though he must expose what is trivial or pernicious, he moves from a perception of what is true. Such a critic will illustrate his higher standards by the point from which he attacks false standards. His criticism, then, is vital, even in the act of denying. We do not look to him for reform and solutions, but we do expect him to give currency to real and high principles. In applying these standards with an *esprit de finesse* to the ever shifting flux of the energies which make for chaos, he will give perspective to the so-called "men of action".

A vital grasp upon standards, then, and the ability to apply them flexibly to the "gushing forth of novelties" which is the other side of life are the qualifications of the critic. Our Negro "intellectuals" have tried to substitute a display of their own and the race's eccentricities for these virtues. Mr. Schuyler and Mr. Gordon are likely to become the forerunners of a line of young critics, who will pose as the thoughtful and emancipated Negro. They will pretend to represent a positivistic and experimental attitude toward the Negro's situation, to replace the religious fatalism and inferiority complex of our older leaders. It is precisely this specious liberalism in our little Menckenites, which makes them dangerous. The Negro to-day is at a critical and strategic point of transition, where the cry of intellectual emancipation will lead him after false lights, unless he is willing to be thoroughly critical. We must avoid the recurrent, human tendency to exchange one extreme for another. Complete trust of all that parades as intelligence, and an effort to be hypercritical are not the proper cure for an inferiority complex. Smartness and a superficial cynicism are not substitutes for reflection and vision.

Mr. Schuyler and Mr. Gordon are interested only in expressing themselves, their cleverness without taste, their radicalism without intelligence, their contempt for Negro leaders and our upper class, uninformed by serious principles. The most obvious fact concerning Mr. Schuyler's articles is their coarse flippancy which he no doubt means to be a protective hardening for the sensitiveness and race-consciousness of Negroes. But to become hardened to such terms as "smoke", "Ziggaboo", "crow", "dinge", "shine", or to take refuge in thumbing one's nose by hurling back "cracker", "peckerwood", and "hill-billy", is not to gain stoical strength, but to lose self-respect. The qualities which have kept the Negro's spirit unbroken are a gift for irony of a broader kind, and an everlasting fortitude.

Reflection and contemplation, alone, can insure the critic's virtues of perspective and balance. Reflection is made evident by one's discrimination, one's power of making vital distinctions. What Mr. Schuyler, Mr. Gordon, and their school, as well as Mr. Mencken, lack, is just this faculty of discriminating judgment. Mr. Schuyler especially reveals his lack of all standards in his frivolous and universal cynicism. In his indiscriminate jeering at all efforts to ameliorate white animosity and injustice, and at the efforts of such men as "Dr. Lampblack of the Federal Society for the Exploitation of Lynching, who will eloquently hold forth for the better part of an hour on the blackamoor's gifts to the Great Republic, and why, therefore, he should not be kept down", Mr. Schuyler betrays his own intellectual muddle.

Mr. Gordon's innocence of any standards and his intellectual confusion are illustrated by his naive theory that the tradition which the Negro wants to preserve is that of the black-face minstrel and the Stephen Foster folk. THE NEGRO'S INHIBITIONS, so far as it is at all honest and serious, is an unconscious *reductio ad absurdum* of the primitivistic creed. The Negro is to treasure his eccentricities simply because they are spontaneous and differentiate him from the white man! If Mr. Gordon had any real perception he would have found ideals based upon the character of the Negro which distinguish him from the white man in a more fundamental sense. The qualities which have moulded the Negro are not emotional crudeness and colorful spontaneity; they are fortitude, an oriental spirituality and unworldliness, and a faculty of laughing at any tendency towards self-pity, which more than anything human approaches the laughter of Mr. O'Neil's Lazarus!

Without intelligent standards, then, our Menckenites still insist upon expressing themselves. What they really set up for our improvement, in the place of standards, is their own personality. The virtue of their writing they believe to lie in the brilliance and iconoclastic smartness with which they demolish what is obviously ignorant and mean. Every man or movement treated is warped and caricatured by the necessity for displaying their own temperament. Mr. Schuyler expresses his fantastic misconception of the affluence recently acquired by Negro writers, in this fashion: "the black scribblers, along with the race orators, are now wallowing in the luxury of four-room apartments, expensive radios, Chickering pianos, Bond Street habiliments, canvas-back duck, pre-war Scotch, and high yellow mistresses". And Mr. Schuyler is "wallowing" in his own temperament! Similarly Mr. Gordon's representation that most Negroes are blind apes of everything in the white world is only a reflection of his individual desire to pose before the white public. So long as we have had romantic confessionalists, we have been acquainted with those who desire "to publish themselves", in Emerson's phrase; but when they set themselves up as serious critics, they become public dangers.

III

Our "intellectuals", then, both those in literature and those in race criticism, have capitalized the sensational aspects of Negro life, at the expense of general truth and sound judgment. Primitivism has carried the imagination of our poets and storytellers into the unhealthy and abnormal. A sterile cynicism has driven our Menckenized critics into smart coarseness. With regard to the primitivists, the first thing to be settled is whether our lives are to be interpreted with relation to the Negro race or the human race. Are there any traits peculiar to Negro character, and if so, are those traits especially crude emotions? It will appear, I think, that the qualities of fortitude, irony, and a relative absence of self-pity are the most important influences in the lives of Negroes, and that these qualities are the secret strength of that part of us which is one with a universal human nature. Our poets and writers of fiction have failed to interpret this broader human nature in Negroes, and found it relatively easy to disguise their lack of a higher imagination by concentrating upon immediate and crude emotions.

Our critic "intellectuals" also lack this quality of elevation. Mr. Schuyler, Mr. Gordon, and their imitators, (at two removes from Mr. Mencken!) are preoccupied with the sordid and trivial aspects of Negro life. On the whole, the facts of Negro life are sordid; they have been so for three hundred years, as a result of slavery, and will very likely remain so for sometime to come. *We are going on our grit,* and it is these higher secret powers which I have indicated, (call them spiritual or chemical, as you like) which we must preserve and apply intelligently to our future development. Self-respect is vital if we are to retain our courage, and self-respect is precisely the quality which these critics lack. "Such conceits as clownage keeps in pay" are their qualifications, and the Negro has had enough clowning,—from his leaders down. I have already defined the true critic as the individual who holds fast to his perception of what is excellent and real, in the midst of appearances, and who applies his standards with discrimination to the flux of actual life. The genuinely qualified critics of Negro life will fix upon the inner strength of Negro character as illustrated in the last three hundred years, and, discounting the trivial and irrelevant, will reinterpret these persistent characteristics for the new Negro to whom he will be as an eye.

A MUSICAL INVASION OF EUROPE

R. Nathaniel Dett was music director of the Hampton
Institute Choir when this essay was published in 1930.
During the choir's international touring, Dett realized
the virus held by many regarding African American
stereotypes had infected people around the world.

The discovery of the presence of forty young Negroes accompanied
by five older ones among the "tourist third" passengers of the French
steamer, *De Grasse,* which sailed from New York, Wednesday morning,
April 23, was the cause of much conjecture.

"Islanders," was one comment; "A Negro show," was another; "Entertainers," was still another. But as the dress of the party was quiet,
and none drank wine, spoke dialect, or indulged in gambling, these
conjectures did not seem to be substantiated, and the mystery deep-
ened. When it was further noted that these young people were reserved in their dancing, orderly at games, unobstrusive at meals, and
friendly to strangers without making advances, curiosity over-rode
convention, and inquiries, amounting almost to demands, were made
that we tell who and what we were, and wherefore and whither we
were bound.

"A choir from a Negro school?" "Then surely we would sing; perhaps someone would sing a solo. Let's see—'I'll Always Be in Love
With You'—that's a pretty song, but 'Ole Man River' is better, don't you
think—has more snap, and well, you know, it's more characteristic."

When it became known that the choir's repertoire contained only
classic music and that most of this was of a religious nature, wonder
gave place to a sort of amused surprise, and it seemed for a while that
by their refusal to sing jazz, the members of the Hampton Choir would

ostracise themselves. But youth has its own appeal, and quite soon after sailing, the Negro student choristers were the center of a warm and kindly interest, making many friends. Meanwhile, requests for a demonstration became more and more insistent.

On Sunday, April 27, a beautifully decorated folder proclaimed that on the same evening the Hampton Institute A Capella Choir of forty mixed voices, Dr. R. Nathaniel Dett, Director, would give a "Concert de Bienfaisance," the purpose apparently being to help the Marine Welfare Society. In truth, this was only a remote reason for the concert, for chiefly, the recital was the choir's tribute to the feeling of fine fellowship which had characterized all "tourist third" on the passage over. This, the first of our two concerts aboard the *De Grasse*, was given in the tourist salon, with a hundred per cent attendance of our fellow travelers and a sprinkle of those from the first class deck. The program was enthusiastically received with ovations for chorus, soloists, and conductor at its conclusion. But the most striking feature of the evening was the amazement of the audience at what was heard and the resulting increased interest amounting almost to excitement over the influences which had made such things possible.

Everyone was interested in knowing that this was a student choir of forty voices conscripted from the various schools of the college which go to make up Hampton Institute. The choir's success was the result of frequent and diligent practice on the part of the students not in the School of Music—five o'clock in the morning rehearsals not being uncommon especially in the men's section; only thirteen were regularly enrolled in the School of Music; five were from the School of Business; ten from the School of Education; three from the School of Home Economics, and one was an agriculturist. The Trade School was represented by two tailors, one tinsmith, one bricklayer, and two auto mechanics; there were only two Academy students. The prime mover of the enterprise was Mr. George Foster Peabody, a distinguished trustee of Hampton, far-famed for his philanthropy.

Although the Choir had sung professionally for over five years in such places as Carnegie Hall, New York; Symphony Hall, Boston; Academy of Music, Philadelphia; Temple of Music, Library of Congress, Washington, there were many who felt a considerable doubt as to the advisability of a European tour. It had been reported that some of the American Boy Scouts, the year before, had made themselves ridiculous by carousing in Paris, and that the Ocean College of American students had given Europe a false opinion of the average American student by their indiscreet behavior.

The retarding influence of these objections was so strong that for a while it seemed as if nothing else could result. However, after the regular church service Easter Sunday morning, upon invitation of the director of the choir, those singers who constituted the "chosen" met with the president and chaplain and a few friends of the school for a final consecration and prayer service. At six-thirty, the same evening, what seemed to be the whole of Hampton Institute, and a goodly number of citizens of the nearby towns of Newport News, Hampton, and Phoebus, gathered at Old Point Comfort docks, and amid cheering, the waving of handkerchiefs, crying, and singing, the Hampton Institute Choir set sail.

Receptions in honor of the Hampton Institute Choir overseas began May 1, when the Lord Mayor of Plymouth, accompanied by the Deputy-Mayor and four mace-bearers, all in scarlet robes, met the forty singers as the party landed at the docks at Plymouth.

The Lord Mayor made a thrilling welcoming address, to which Dr. Dett responded. The choir sang the beautiful choral, "Now Thank We All Our God," after which the party led by the Mayor moved in a procession to the railway station, where Mr. Douglas M. Durston, honorary director of the Plymouth Coleridge-Taylor Society, decorated Dr. Dett with the Society's pin.

At the second reception at No. 10 Downing Street, London, by Premier Ramsey MacDonald and his daughter Ishbel, attended by many of the nobility not only of England but also of other countries as well, the choir added "Were You There?" as recorded in *Religious Folk-Songs of the Negro,* to the program already given at the request of the Premier. Tea was served by Miss Ishbel MacDonald preceding the choir members' enjoying the rare privilege of being shown through the house and Executive Rooms.

Saturday morning, May 3, at nine-thirty o'clock, the Hampton Choir met the London Press Association and a number of their friends at the Y. M. C. A. This was a semi-formal and a very cosmopolitan gathering. The serving of refreshments was continuous, and consequently simultaneous with the conversation which was indulged in by small groups which moved at will from place to place. Accordingly, all present had an opportunity to talk with individual members of the Hampton Choir party, and so a more intimate idea of what we were like was made possible. However, the fact that the choir was made up entirely of students and not professionals did not seem to readily impress itself. Before the close of the morning, Mr. Hubert Peet, London journalist, introduced Dr. Dett who spoke on Negro Music and its development.

An occurrence which received almost world-wide notice was the tribute paid by the choir to the memory of Livingstone at his tomb in Westminster Abbey, concerning which Canon F. Lewis Donaldson of the Abbey wrote in the *Illustrated News* (London) as follows: "As they stood around the grave, and their hymn-song, now pathetic and plaintive, now thrilling and triumphant, rang through the great church, our memories were stirred to recall something of the tragic history of the race, which the white man for centuries had chained in cruel servitude."

The London audiences on both occasions of our formal concerts—Queen's Hall, May 3, and Royal Albert Hall, May 11—greeted us warmly and enthusiastically. The following is from an editorial which appeared in the London newspaper, *The Lady:* "In singing and especially in choral singing we find that amateurs are quite able to hold their own with professionals. Of the three foreign choirs heard in London last week, two, the Hampton Choir of colored singers from Virginia, and the Budapest Choir are composed of amateurs, and one, the Denmark Palestrina Choir of professionals drawn from the chorus of Opera at Copenhagen. Their performances could be judged by the same standard."

Between the two London concerts we were in Holland and Belgium. On the way the dikes, the windmills, the miles and miles of tulips, the wooden-shoe clad peasants, chiefly women, working on hands and knees in the fields, made a moving picture which fascinated the students and kept them continuously at the car windows.

Not having opportunity for previous rehearsal in the hall, the Salle du Cercle Artistique, in Antwerp, we were surprised to find that night that it had tricky acoustics, so that in spite of favorable newspaper criticism, we felt that we had not done our best. Next day we rehearsed early at the Beaux Arts in Brussels, and that concert proved to be one of our happiest. Moreover, occupying the royal box, was the Queen of Belgium, herself, to whom, by royal command, I was introduced. By request of the Queen, we sang again the Dett setting of "No More Auction Block for Me," which had moved the officials of the Congo Museum in the afternoon, at Tervurien, where Governor Louis Frank, former Minister of Colonies, had welcomed us, and Dr. Schoutenden, Director of the Museum, had showed us the world famous collection of African art. One very realistic carved and painted group portraying an African trying to protect his wife from a white trader had moved me to select the spiritual, "No More Auction Block for Me." Preceding the intermission, the members of the Belgian Band, whom the choir had entertained at Hampton, made a presentation of an enormous wreath of flowers tied with the Belgian and American colors with words of tribute printed in gold.

We sang at Amsterdam, Rotterdam, and the Hague, before going to France, where we were to appear at the Theatre Champs Elysees, Paris. The Elysees revealed itself a theatre elegant as the audience, which, under the patronage of Ambassador Edge, assembled to greet the Hampton Choir on the night of its Paris debut. A number of Americans were present, but contrary to the effect of a similar group at the Hague, they seemed to add to the enthusiasm of the audience. It was here that having been recalled a number of times, we sang the motet, "I'll Never Turn Back No More," on a Negro theme, hoping thereby to terminate the demonstration, but the result was an ovation which even continued after the fire curtain had been lowered. The success of our Paris debut was the more significant when it is recalled that the Hampton Choir was but one of three important concerts occurring the same evening.

Enesco, the violinist, a favorite in Europe, was at the Salle Gaveau; De Falla, the Spanish modernist, was giving a recital of his own compositions at the Salle Pleyel, probably the largest concert hall in Paris. Many of my personal friends in Paris who heard the Hampton Choir were also hosts to this great Spanish maestro. Of those who came back stage, I recall M. Pierre Schneider, editor of the *Magasin Musicale,* Paris; Madame Nadia Boulanger of the Fontainebleau School, whose pupil I had been the summer previous; Louis Schneider of the *Paris-New York Herald;* Madame Nordell, soprano and correspondent for the Martinique *News;* Professor Arthur Heacox, of the Oberlin Conservatory; John M. Lang, director of the Music League, Niagara Falls (my home town); Victor Dunbar, a young Negro who is achieving European success by giving solo recitals on the clarinet, and Madame Helen F. Burney. Many members of the Russian Ballet, who, in the afternoon had been waiting their turn while we were using the stage, returned that evening to express appreciation for our use of Russian numbers.

While in Paris we made two records for the Pathé Talking Picture Company which I hear have since been released in a number of Paris movie houses.

Our first concert on German soil was at Hamburg, a city which, on account of its many beautiful waterways, reminds one of the pictures of Venice. The audience was small but very enthusiastic. In Berlin we had our pictures taken in the gardens of the Embassy with the American Ambassador, Mr. Sackett, a former Tennesseean. The concert that evening was a great success.

Vienna is an Eastern Paris. It is every bit as beautiful with much the same care-free gayety, open-heartedness, and love of art. The tendency of many of its citizens it appears (not unlike that of some of our New Yorkers) is to estimate all things only in terms of their own city. Witness this graceful but rather left-hand compliment which appeared in one of the dailies following our concert. "We do not know whether or not the members of the Hampton Choir can blush, but if they can they would have no occasion to do so, were they compared with the best of our Viennese choirs."

I doubt if any group of people were ever more stared at by Europeans of all classes than was the Hampton Choir. Of course with the more cultured, there was an effort to cover the glance somewhat, but the universal curiosity was undisguisable, and, on taking thought, I would add, excuseable; for the glance of the continental European, when looking at Negroes, is of an entirely different nature generally from that of the average American, under the same circumstances.

In Salzburg, impressed by our impromptu exercises at the tomb of Mozart, a man who himself had been a choral conductor and a director of a symphony orchestra, volunteered his services as guide about the city. In the Cathedral of Salzburg, he remarked that the acoustics of the building were possibly the best in Europe, whereupon I said it would be pleasant to sing under such ideal circumstances. "It would be very nice if you would sing," our guide said. Noticing that there were a number of people praying, I hesitated. "You may sing," our guide urged, "but," he added, lowering his voice, "please don't sing any jazz." (Dear readers, please remember that we were in a cathedral!)

Signalling the choir into formation, we sang an "Ave Maria" in Latin. Our guide was astonished and greatly pleased. As we neared the exit he was full of praise and thanks. "That is a most beautiful Ave," he said, "but I don't believe I ever heard it before. Whose is it?" Not wishing to create a scene within sacred precincts nor to devastate by a single word one who had only shown us kindness, I waited until we were quite outside before saying as softly as I could: "Mine!"

We sang at Geneva, and were given a reception by the Students of the World Christian Federation which was the only direct contact we had with students abroad. Back in Paris, after a month of almost nightly appearances before different audiences, evidence that we had profited by our our experiences was indicated by the immediate and unvarying enthusiasm of the audiences.

The last concert abroad was one not scheduled but was given by request on the first-class deck of the *De Grasse*. To this, at the suggestion of the director of the choir, all the third-class passengers were invited.

The returning musicians of the Philharmonic orchestra and their wives were a large and important part of the audience. Mrs. Richard Copley, wife of our American manager, was also in attendance. The choir seemed to sense the presence of fellow musicians and sang with a will. It was an unforgettable night. The director of the Hampton Choir was presented to the audience by Mr. Van Praag. Led chiefly by the members of the Philharmonic there was a rousing ovation at the conclusion of the program. Of all successes, none was so precious to the Hampton Choir as this, for to have captured the musicians of our own country—that was achievement.

NEGRO AUTHORS' WEEK:
AN EXPERIMENT

The purpose of Negro Authors' Week was to encourage
young African Americans to greater aspirations in the
field of literature. C. Ruth Wright related the events of
the program in the April 1930 issue of *The Crisis*.

To have an entire week devoted to the study and promotion of Negro
literature and Negro writers seemed an excellent idea to Dr. R. R.
Wright, Jr., editor of *The Christian Recorder* and pastor of Jones Tabernacle A. M. E. Church in Philadelphia. He communicated this idea to
some of the younger members of his congregation and they seized
upon it enthusiastically.

The idea was to have an entire week devoted to a series of lectures
with a distinguished Negro author speaking each night and a compre-
hensive exhibit of books by and about Negroes. The members and
committee decided that the lecture and exhibit should be held at the
church and a nominal admission fee charged to cover expenses. The
purpose of the week should be "to encourage the young Negro to
greater aspiration in the field of literature; to acquaint the citizens of
Philadelphia with the achievements of Negroes in literature; and to
increase interest in the same".

That such an idea could be successfully put over caused a little
doubt in the minds of the promoters, as lectures are not exactly popular among Philadelphia colored people. Concerts, dramas, and the
purely social affairs, as dances, etc., are often successes, financially and
otherwise. But to have five lectures in nightly succession and *charge* for
them seemed, in advance, indicative of failure.

Preparations for a big Negro Authors' Week were started, however, and eight prominent authors were invited to appear during the week of December 7. A committee of young people was formed in the church, and a patrons' committee composed of Philadelphia citizens was organized. Each member of the latter committee sent to the secretary a list of from ten to twenty names of persons who would probably be interested in Negro Authors' Week to the extent of becoming a patron by purchasing two season tickets. A mailing list was compiled in this way, which, though not very extensive (numbering hardly five hundred names in all) was nevertheless valuable. A high percentage of persons responded with checks to the letters sent them. Through the contributions of patrons there was enough money to meet expenses the week before the first lecture was given.

Advertisement took the form largely of correspondence although the press provided advance notices. Announcements were sent through the churches and the public schools, and free admission tickets for the children were given to those schools whose principals asked for them. Some teachers had exhibits of colored authors' pictures in their classrooms.

The Week opened Monday night, December 7, with Mr. James Weldon Johnson as the speaker on "The Negro in Art and Literature", and Mr. Arthur Huff Fauset, a public school principal and author, presiding. A large and enthusiastic audience of white and colored people met Mr. Johnson, whose delightful manner, "charmingly nonchalant" as it was described by one enthusiastic youngster, completely won over his listeners.

Tuesday night, Dr. Kelly Miller, of Howard University, spoke on the subject of "The Negro Writing in His Own Defense". Dr. Miller gave an informing talk on the development of journalism among Negroes.

Wednesday night brought the largest audience of the week. Dr. W. E. B. Du Bois of THE CRISIS was the speaker on "The Opportunities for the Negro in the Field of Fiction". The speaker defended the failure of the Negro writer to measure up fully to standards of genuine artistry. "Publishers now refuse to publish books of Negro writers unless they are the type he feels will appeal to the white reader. The Negro writer, therefore, must produce a book in which the picture drawn of the Negro dovetails with the mental picture the whites have of the Negro". Mrs. Alice Dunbar Nelson presided.

On Thursday night the subject of "Negro History" was capably handled by Dr. Carter G. Woodson, the historian and director of the

Associated Publishers of Washington, D. C. Dr. Woodson reviewed for his hearers the various problems of Negro research.

Friday night was Poets' Night. A number of local poets read their compositions. The audience was disappointed at the absence of Langston Hughes, who was ill, but again became enthusiastic under the spell of Dr. Leslie P. Hill's introduction to the subject of Negro poetry. Mrs. Georgia Douglass Johnson, of Washington, charmed the audience with a delightfully intimate and personal sketch of various present day poets of her own acquaintance.

In addition to the lectures, a large exhibit of books was offered. About two dozen publishers cooperated by sending their publications by and about Negroes. The Library of Congress sent a collection of books for exhibit and the local colored newspapers lent files and old editions of their papers for exhibition.

These books were put on exhibit in the small lecture rooms surrounding the main auditorium and were classified as follows: Fiction, Poetry, Biography, History and Sociology, Religion, Music, Drama, Journalism, Philadelphia Authors, Government Exhibit, and Rare books, including Ph.D. theses and old books, some of the latter over 100 years old.

The sale of books, however, did not come up to the rather large expectation of the committee, and many had to be returned to the publishers. This may have been due, partly of course, to the general economic depression, but it was also indicative of what almost every speaker during the week had stated—that Negroes have not yet reached the stage where they will buy books in anything like large numbers. Nevertheless there is no reason to doubt that a very real and perhaps far-reaching interest was stimulated by this exhibit which gave hundreds of Negroes the chance to see the literary productions of their race.

The most popular authors, as far as sales went, were James Weldon Johnson, Carter G. Woodson, Arthur Fauset, and W. E. B. Du Bois. The publisher whose books proved most salable was the Associated Publishers, Inc., of Washington, D. C., a Negro concern. Sales in fiction were surprisingly low. Poetry was most popular, and history and sociology ranked next. This was probably due to the fact that many persons buying were making their first contacts with Negro literature and when they asked the sales people for recommendations of good books, they were usually directed to some anthology, or history of literature.

The attendance at the meetings averaged about 300 people a night.

Of the total attendance of 1500, the committee estimated that about 1200 of the number attended at least one lecture. Quite a few patrons, incidentally, attended three or four lectures and some were present every night.

We do not hesitate to say that if such a Negro Authors' Week under efficient management should be held every year in a hundred American cities, the outlook for Negro literature would be entirely revolutionized.

THE WORK OF A MOB

In the following essay, Walter White writes about several lynchings in Brooks and Lowndes Counties, Georgia, that had occurred in 1918, the same year White joined the staff of the N.A.A.C.P. He contributed to the N.A.A.C.P.'s fight against lynching in a very effective and dangerous way. Because of his Caucasian-like appearance, he could easily "pass." Taking advantage of his deceptive appearance, he was able to investigate lynching sites and secure data, which the Association publicized widely.

The recent strong letter of President Wilson on lynching was undoubtedly called forth by representations from colored people following the lynchings in Brooks and Lowndes Counties, Ga., May 17–24.

Hampton Smith, a white farmer, was killed, and newspaper dispatches report six persons as having been lynched for complicity. Investigation shows that at least eleven persons were killed.

Brooks and Lowndes Counties are situated in the southernmost part of the state of Georgia, near the Florida line. They are in the heart of the richest section of the state.

Hampton Smith, whose murder was the immediate cause of the holocaust of lynchings, was the owner of a large plantation in Brooks County. He bore a very poor reputation in the community because of ill treatment of his Negro employees.

Smith's reputation in this respect had become so wide-spread that he had the greatest difficulty in securing any help whatever. He, therefore, adopted the expedient of going into the courts and whenever a Negro was convicted and was unable to pay his fine or was sentenced to serve a period in the chaingang, Smith would secure his release and put him to work out his fine on his (Smith's) plantation. Sidney Johnson, the Negro who admitted before his death that he killed Smith, had been fined thirty dollars for gaming. Smith paid his fine and Johnson was put at work on the former's plantation until the thirty dollars had been worked out. Johnson had worked out the period and had put in considerable more time and had asked Smith to pay him for the additional time that he had served. Smith refused and a quarrel resulted. A few days later Johnson did not show up for work in the fields and Smith went to Johnson's cabin to discover the reason. Johnson told Smith that he was sick and unable to work. Smith thereupon began to beat him, in spite of the protestations of the victim. Johnson is said then to have threatened Smith and a few nights later, while sitting in his home, Smith was shot twice through the window near which he was sitting, dying instantly. His wife was also shot, the bullet passing through the center of her breast, miraculously missing both her heart and lungs. Her wound is not believed to be serious. The attending physician, Dr. McMichael, is said to have stated that she would recover.

There seems to be no evidence that Mrs. Smith was raped in addition to being shot.

As soon as news of the murder reached the community, great crowds of men and boys from the two counties hurried to the spot. Excitement ran high and posses were immediately formed to search for Johnson, as suspicion was immediately fastened on him because of the threats he had made against Smith's life. There was also talk of a conspiracy among a number of Negroes to kill Smith, and reports were circulated that the group involved had met at the home of Hayes Turner, another Negro who had suffered at the hands of Smith, and his wife, Mary Turner, whom Smith had beaten on several occasions. Hayes Turner, it is said, had previously served a term in the chaingang for threatening Smith, following Smith's beating of Turner's wife. Nevertheless, after his release, Turner had gone back to work for Smith again.

The first of the mob's victims to be captured was Will Head, a Negro of the community, who was caught on Friday morning, May 17, at 8:30, near Barney, Georgia; the second was Will Thompson, seized later on the same day. That night both were lynched near Troupeville, about five miles from Valdosta. Members of the mob stated to the investigator that over seven hundred bullets were fired into the bodies of the two men. The investigator learned from a man who admitted being in the mob, but who stated that he had no part in the lynching, the names of the two leaders of the Friday night mob and of fifteen of the other members of the mob. These names were given to the investigator on his promise that he would not divulge the name of the informant, as to do so would mean that he would undoubtedly be subjected to bodily violence and perhaps death, for having given the information.

These names were furnished to Governor Hugh M. Dorsey, of Georgia, on July 10, by the investigator in person.

In addition to those named to the Governor there were many more from Quitman and a large number from Valdosta and the surrounding country whose names were not learned.

On Saturday morning Hayes Turner was captured and lynched near the fork of the Morven and Barney roads. On being captured he was placed in the Quitman jail and for some reason unknown to the investigator was taken later in the day by Sheriff Wade and Roland Knight, the clerk of the county court, ostensibly to be carried to Moultrie for safekeeping. Turner was taken from these men *en route* to Moultrie, at the fork of the roads about three and a half miles from town. He was lynched with his hands fastened behind him with handcuffs and was allowed to hang there until Monday when he was cut down by county convicts and buried about half a hundred feet from the foot of the tree on which he was lynched. During Sunday following the lynching, hundreds of automobiles, buggies and wagons bore sightseers to the spot while many more tramped there on foot.

Another Negro was lynched on Saturday afternoon near Morven at a spot known as the Old Camp Ground. This person may have been Eugene Rice whose name appeared in the Georgia press among the identified and acknowledged victims, but who was never even remotely connected with Hampton Smith's killing.

About a week after the tragedy, or tragedies, started, the bodies of three unidentified Negroes were taken from the Little River, below Barney. It is not known whether these bodies were those of some already accounted for or whether these were additional victims of the mob. At the last accounts the bodies themselves had disappeared and could not be located.

The murder of the Negro men was deplorable enough in itself, but the method by which Mrs. Mary Turner was put to death was so revolting and the details are so horrible that it is with reluctance that the account is given. It might be mentioned that each detail given is not the statement of a single person but each phase is related only after careful investigation and corroboration. Mrs. Turner made the remark that the killing of her husband on Saturday was unjust and that if she knew the names of the persons who were in the mob that lynched her husband, she would have warrants sworn out against them and have them punished in the courts.

This news determined the mob to "teach her a lesson," and although she attempted to flee when she heard that they were after her, she was captured at noon on Sunday. The grief-stricken and terrified woman was taken to a lonely and secluded spot, down a narrow road over which the trees touch at their tops, which with the thick undergrowth on either side of the road, made a gloomy and appropriate spot for the lynching. Near Folsom's Bridge over the Little River a tree was selected for her execution—a small oak tree extending over the road.

At the time she was lynched, Mary Turner was in her eighth month of pregnancy. The delicate state of her health, one month or less previous to delivery, may be imagined, but this fact had no effect on the tender feelings of the mob. Her ankles were tied together and she was hung to the tree, head downward. Gasoline and oil from the automobiles were thrown on her clothing and while she writhed in agony and the mob howled in glee, a match was applied and her clothes burned from her person. When this had been done and while she was yet alive, a knife, evidently one such as is used in splitting hogs, was taken and the woman's abdomen was cut open, the unborn babe falling from her womb to the ground. The infant, prematurely born, gave two feeble cries and then its head was crushed by a member of the mob with his heel. Hundreds of bullets were then fired into the body of the woman, now mercifully dead, and the work was over.

Chime Riley, another Negro who was supposed to have left the community, was found by the investigator to have been lynched instead. By the time that he was killed, the mob evidently had begun to become fearful of too many outrages and determined to conceal his body. Although no one seems to have even remotely connected him with the murder of Smith, he was lynched, his hands and feet tied together and turpentine cups, made of clay and used to catch the gum from the pine trees when "chipped," thus becoming very heavy, were tied to his body and he was thrown into the Little River near Barney. The informant in this case, seen on the spot where Mary Turner was lynched, stated that when the river was low he had gone down to see if the body had come up. Finding no trace of the body, he assumed that it had become lodged in a sand bar. He stated that he found one of the cups, however, which he was keeping as a "souvenir."

During the outbreak, another Negro by the name of Simon Schuman, who lived on the Moultrie Road near Berlin, was called to the door of his home one night between eight and nine o'clock. He was seized and had not been seen since up to the time (seven weeks later) that the investigator was in the section. The interior of his house was demolished, his family being driven out, and the furniture was hacked to pieces. His family, at the time of the investigator's visit, was living on the Bryce Plantation, near Berlin. The offense alleged against Schuman is unknown.

Contrary to press reports, Sidney Johnson was not hiding in the swamps near Valdosta, but was in Valdosta from the time of the murder of Smith to the time that he was killed. During this time, he is said to have made the statement to several persons that he alone was implicated in the killing of Smith and that he alone killed him. There was no suspicion of Johnson's presence in Valdosta until Johnson went to another Negro, John Henry Bryant by name, and asked for food and aid in making good his escape. Apparently it was Johnson's intention to wait until the vigilance of the mobs was relaxed and the roads no longer watched and then flee from the country. Bryant gave Johnson the food and then hastened to town to tell where Johnson was. The house was immediately surrounded by a posse headed by Chief of Police Dampier. This was done with caution as Johnson was known to be armed and had sworn that he would never be taken alive. Johnson had only a shot-gun and a revolver, while the posse was armed with high-powered rifles. The firing began and the Chief was wounded in the hand and one of his men in the neck.

After the firing had gone on for a few minutes, Johnson's firing ceased. A few more bullets were fired into the house for good measure as it was thought that the cessation of firing might be a ruse on Johnson's part. When it did not resume, still acting cautiously, the house was rushed and Johnson's body was found, dead. Cheated out of its prey, the crowd took the body, unsexed it with a sharp knife, threw the amputated parts into the street in front of the house, and then tied an end of a rope around Johnson's neck. The other end was tied to the back of an automobile and the body dragged in open daylight down Patterson Street, one of Valdosta's business thoroughfares, and out to a place near Barney and near the scene of the crime. There the dead body was fastened to a tree and burned to a crisp.

Very careful attention was given by the investigator to the accounts given at the outbreak of the affair that it was caused by the circulation of pro-German propaganda in the section prior to the outbreak in the hope of stirring up racial disturbances. Absolutely no evidence was found.

Since the lynchings, more than five hundred Negroes have left the immediate vicinity of Valdosta alone and many more have expressed the determination that they too were going to leave as soon as they could dispose of their lands and gather their crops. This wholesale migration occurred in spite of threats made that any Negro who attempted to leave the section would thus show that he was implicated in the murder of Smith and would be dealt with accordingly. Hundreds of acres of untilled land flourishing with weeds and dozens of deserted farm-houses give their own mute testimony of the Negroes' attitude toward a community in which lynching mobs are allowed to visit vengeance upon members of their race.

All of the facts outlined above, including the names of mob leaders and participants, were given in a memorandum presented by the investigator on July 10 to Governor Hugh M. Dorsey. Governor Dorsey received the information gladly and has promised to take action on the evidence submitted. In a message addressed to the Georgia legislature on July 3, 1918, Governor Dorsey denounced mob violence in strong terms, saying:

"Mob violence should be suppressed, and by State authorities.

"If this is not done, it is very probable that Federal intervention will not be long delayed."

Documents of the War

This is the controversial essay published in May 1919, that W. E. B. Du Bois refers to in "Editing *The Crisis*" (above).

The following documents have come into the hands of the Editor. He has absolute proof of their authenticity. The first document was sent out last August at the request of the American Army by the French Committee which is the official means of communication between the American forces and the French. It represents American and not French opinion and we have been informed that when the French Ministry heard of the distribution of this document among the Prefects and Sous-Prefects of France, they ordered such copies to be collected and burned.

Mission Militaire Française

PRÈS L'ARMÉE AMÉRICAINE.
Le 7 août 1918.

Confidentiel

AU SUJET DES TROUPES NOIRES AMERICAINES

1°. *Il importe que les Officiers Français appelés à exercer un commandement sur les troupes noires américaines, ou à vivre à leur contact, aient une notion exacte de la situation des nègres aux ETATS-UNIS. Les considérations exposées dans le note suivante devraient donc leur être communiquées, et il y a un intérèt*

considérable, à ce qu'elles soient connues et largement diffuses. Il appartiendra
mémo aux Autorités Militaires Françaises, de renseigner à ce sujet par l'inter-
médiaire des Autorités civiles, les populations françaises des cantonnemonts de
troupes américaines de couleur.

2°. Le point de vue américain sur la "question nègre" peut paraitre discutable
à bien des esprits français. Mais il ne nous appartient pas, à nous Français, de
discuter ce que certains appellent un "préjudice." L'opinion Américaine est
unanime sur la "question noire," et n'admettrait pas la discussion.

Le nombre élevé de nègres aux ETATS-UNIS (15 millions environ) créérait
pour la race blanche de la République un danger de dégénérescence si une sépa-
ration inexorable n'était faite entre noirs et blancs.

Comme ce danger n'existe pas pour la race française, le public français s'est
habitué à traiter familièrement le "noir" et à être très indulgent à son égard.

Cette indulgence et cette familiarité blessent profondément les Américains. Ils
les considèrent comme une attente à leurs dogmes nationaux. Ils craignent que le
contact des Français n'inspirent aux noirs américaine des prétentions qu'ils con-
siderent comme intolérables. Il est indispensable que tous les efforts soient faits
pour éviter d'indisposer profondément l'opinion américaine.

Bien que citoyen des ETATS UNIS, l'homme de couleur est considéré par
l'Américain Blanc comme un être inférieur avec lequel on ne peut avoir que des
relations d'affaires ou de service. On lui reproche une certaine inintelligence, son
indiscrétion, son manque de conscience civique ou professionnelle, sa familiarité.

Les vices du nègre sont un danger constant pour l'Américain, qui doit les
réprimer sévèrement. Par exemple, les troupes noires Américaines en France ont
donné lieu, à elles seules, à autant de plaintes pour tentatives de viol, que tout le
reste de l'Armée, et cependant, on ne nous a envoyé comme soldats qu'une élite au
point de vue physique et moral, car le déchet, à l'incorporation a été énorme.

CONCLUSION

1°. Il faut éviter touts intimaté trop grande d'officiers français avec des officiers noirs, avec lesquels, on peut être correct et aimable, mais qu'on ne peu traiter
sur le même pied que des officier blancs Américains sans blesser profondément ces
derniers. Il ne faut pas partager leur table et éviter le serrement de mains et les
conversations ou fréquentations en dehors de service.

2°. Il ne faut pas vanier d'une manière exagérée les troupes noires américains,
surtout devant des Américains. Reconnaitre leurs qualités et leurs services, mais
en termes modérés conformes à la stricte réalité.

3°. Tâcher d'obtenir des populations des cantonnements qu'elle no gâtent pas
les nègres. Les Américains sont indignés de toute intimité PUBLIQUE de

*femme blanche avec des noirs. Ils ont élevé récemment des véhémentes protesta-
tions contre une grasure de la "Vie Parisienne" intitulée "l'Enfant du Dessert"
représentant une femme en cabinet particulier avec un nègre. Les familiarités
des blanches avec les noirs sont, du reste, profondément regrettées de nos coloni-
aux expérimentés qui y voient une perte considérable du prestige de la race
blanche.*

*L'autorité militaire no peut intervenir directement dans cette question, mais
elle peut influer sur les populations par les Autorités civiles.*

(Signé) Linard.

FRENCH MILITARY MISSION

STATIONED WITH THE AMERICAN ARMY
August 7, 1918.

SECRET INFORMATION

CONCERNING BLACK AMERICAN TROOPS

1. *It is important for French officers who have been called upon to exercise
command over black American troops, or to live in close contact with them, to have
an exact idea of the position occupied by Negroes in the United States. The information set forth in the following communication ought to be given to these officers and it is to their interest to have these matters known and widely
disseminated. It will devolve likewise on the French Military Authorities,
through the medium of the Civil Authorities, to give information on this subject
to the French population residing in the cantonments occupied by American colored troops.*

2. *The American attitude upon the Negro question may seem a matter for discussion to many French minds. But we French are not in our province if we undertake to discuss what some call "prejudice." American opinion is unanimous on
the "color question" and does not admit of any discussion.*

*The increasing number of Negroes in the United States (about 15,000,000)
would create for the white race in the Republic a menace of degeneracy were it
not that an impassable gulf has been made between them.*

*As this danger does not exist for the French race, the French public has become
accustomed to treating the Negro with familiarity and indulgence.*

*This indulgence and this familiarity are matters of grievous concern to the
Americans. They consider them an affront to their national policy. They are
afraid that contact with the French will inspire in black Americans aspirations*

which to them [the whites] appear intolerable. It is of the utmost importance that every effort be made to avoid profoundly estranging American opinion.

Although a citizen of the United States, the black man is regarded by the white American as an inferior being with whom relations of business or service only are possible. The black is constantly being censured for his want of intelligence and discretion, his lack of civic and professional conscience and for his tendency toward undue familiarity.

The vices of the Negro are a constant menace to the American who has to repress them sternly. For instance, the black American troops in France have, by themselves, given rise to as many complaints for attempted rape as all the rest of the army. And yet the [black American] soldiers sent us have been the choicest with respect to physique and morals, for the number disqualified at the time of mobilization was enormous.

CONCLUSION

1. *We must prevent the rise of any pronounced degree of intimacy between French officers and black officers. We may be courteous and amiable with these last, but we cannot deal with them on the same plane as with the white American officers without deeply wounding the latter. We must not eat with them, must not shake hands or seek to talk or meet with them outside of the requirements of military service.*

2. *We must not commend too highly the black American troops, particularly in the presence of [white] Americans. It is all right to recognize their good qualities and their services, but only in moderate terms, strictly in keeping with the truth.*

3. *Make a point of keeping the native cantonment population from "spoiling" the Negroes. [White] Americans become greatly incensed at any public expression of intimacy between white women with black men. They have recently uttered violent protests against a picture in the "Vie Parisienne" entitled "The Child of the Desert" which shows a [white] woman in a "cabinet particulier" with a Negro. Familiarity on the part of white women with black men is furthermore a source of profound regret to our experienced colonials who see in it an over-weening menace to the prestige of the white race.*

Military authority cannot intervene directly in this question, but it can through the civil authorities exercise some influence on the population.

(Signed) Linard

—

The following document is a specimen of the numerous and continuous requests made by white commanders of colored regiments to get rid of colored officers. It will be noted that at the date this document was sent Colored officers had had very little chance to prove their efficiency.

G. H. G., A. E. F.
8/25/1918

11440-A124

Headquarters 372nd Infantry
S. P. 179, France
August 24, 1918.

From: The Commanding Officer, 372nd Infantry,
To: The Commanding General, American E. F.
Subject: Replacement of Colored Officers by White Officers.

1. Request that colored officers of this regiment be replaced by white officers for the following reasons:

First: The racial distinctions which are recognized in civilian life naturally continue to be recognized in the military life and present a formidable barrier to the existence of that feeling of comradeship which is essential to mutual confidence and *esprit de corp.*

Second: With a few exceptions there is a characteristic tendency among the colored officers to neglect the welfare of their men and to perform their duties in a perfunctory manner. They are lacking in initiative. These defects entail a constant supervision and attention to petty details by battalion commanders and other senior officers which distract their attention from their wider duties; with harmful results.

2. To facilitate the desired readjustment of officer personnel it is recommended,

A. That no colored officers be forwarded to this regiment as replacements or otherwise.

B. That officers removed upon recommendation of efficiency boards be promptly replaced by white officers of like grade. But, if white officers are not available as replacements; white officers of lower grades be forwarded instead.

C. That the opportunity be afforded to transfer the remaining colored combat officer personnel to labor organizations or to replacement units for other colored combat organizations according to their suitability.

3. Reference letter No. 616-3s written by Commanding General 157th D. I. on the subject August 21, 1918, and forwarded to your office through military channels.

(Signed) Herschel Tupes,
Colonel, 372nd Infantry.

Received A. G. O.
  26th Aug., 1918,
    G. H. Q., A. E. F.
      1st Ind. [Endorsement.]
G. H. Q., A. E. F., France, August 28, 1918
—To Commanding Officer, 372nd Infantry, A. E. F.
1. Returned.
2. Paragraph two is approved.
3. You will submit by special courier requisition for white officers to replace officers relieved upon the recommendation of efficiency board.
4. You will submit list of names of officers that you recommend to be transferred to labor organization or to replacement units for other colored combat organizations; stating in each case the qualifications of the officers recommended.
By command of General Pershing:

(Signed) W. P. Bennett,
Adjutant General.

2nd Ind. [Endorsement.]
Hg. 372nd Infantry, S. P. 179, France, September 4, 1918—To Commanding General, A. E. F., France.
1. Requisition in compliance with par. 3, 1st. Ind. is enclosed herewith. Special attention is invited to the filling of two original vacancies by app.

———

The following letter was sent contrary to military regulations to a U. S. Senator by the man who was Chief of Staff of the colored Ninety-second Division; in other words, by the man who more than any other single person was responsible for the morale and efficiency of this Division. We shall prove later that every essential statement made in this letter against Negro troops is either false or misleading.

HEADQUARTERS VI ARMY CORPS

AMERICAN EXPEDITIONARY FORCES
Dec. 6, 1918.

My Dear Senator:
    Now that a reorganization of the army is in prospect, and as all officers of the temporary forces have been asked if they desire to remain in the regular army, I think I ought to bring a matter to your attention that is of vital importance not only from a military point of view but

from that which all Southerners have. I refer to the question of Negro officers and Negro troops.

I have been Chief of Staff of the 92nd (Colored) Division since its organization and shall remain on such duty until it starts its movement in a few days back to the United States, when I go to the 6th Corps as the Chief of the Operation Section of that unit. My position has been such that I can speak from intimate knowledge and what I have to say is based on facts which I know fully and not from secondhand information.

To start with: all company officers of infantry, machine guns and engineers were Negroes; as were also most of the artillery lieutenants and many of the doctors. Gradually as their incompetence became perfectly evident to all, the engineers and artillerymen, were replaced by white officers. They remained with the infantry until the end, and also with a few exceptions with the machine guns.

The record of the division is one which will probably never be given full publicity, but the bare facts are about as follows. We came to France in June, were given seven weeks in training area instead of the four weeks in training area usually allotted, then went to a quiet sector of the front. From there we went to the Argonne and in the offensive starting there on September 26, had one regiment in the line, attached to the 38th French Corps. They failed there in all their missions, laid down and sneaked to the rear, until they were withdrawn. Thirty of the officers of this regiment alone were reported either for cowardice or failure to prevent their men from retreating—and this against very little opposition. The French and our white field officers did all that could possibly have been done; but the troops were impossible. One of our majors commanding a battalion said "The men are rank cowards there is no other word for it."

Next we were withdrawn to another defensive sector where we remained until the armistice; having some minor engagements against any enemy who had no offensive intentions.

During our career, counting the time in America, we have had about thirty cases of rape, among which was one where twenty-two men at Camp Grant raped one woman, and we have had eight (I believe) reported in France with about fifteen attempts besides. There have been any number of self-inflicted wounds, among others one captain.

There have been numerous accidental shootings, several murders, and also several cases of patrols or sentinels shooting at each other. And at the same time, so strict had been the supervision and training that many officers passing through our areas would remark that our men actually had the outer marks of better discipline than the other divisions. They were punctillious about saluting, their appearance was excellent. They kept their animals and equipment in good condition. General Bullard, commanding our Second Army, asked me my estimate and I said they could do anything but fight. They have in fact been dangerous to no one except themselves and women.

In these organizations where we have white company officers, namely the artillery and engineers, we have had only one case of rape. The undoubted truth is that the Colored officers neither control nor care to control the men. They themselves have been engaged very largely in the pursuit of French women, it being their first opportunity to meet white women who did not treat them as servants.

During the entire time we have been operating there has never been a single operation conducted by a colored officer where his report did not have to be investigated by some field officer to find out what the real facts were. Accuracy and ability to describe facts is lacking in all, and most of them are just plain liars in addition.

The foregoing is just to give you an insight into the facts. Should any effort be made to have Negro officers, or for that matter Negro troops, the career of this division should be asked for; and every officer who has been a field officer of the 92nd Division should be summoned before the Committee to give his experience and opinions. Their statements, based on a year's experience should certainly carry a great deal of weight, and all of them state the same thing, only varying in extremes.

> With best wishes, I am
> Sincerely yours,
> (Signed) Allen J. Greer,
> Colonel, General Staff, U. S. A.
> Hon. Kenneth D. McKellar,
> United States Senate,
> Washington, D. C.

The following letter written by a Negro officer to an American friend illustrates the temper and difficulties of the situation in France.

19 Feb., 1919.

I have been hoping that you would be able to drop in on us here before our departure. We are slated to leave here at 4 A.M. on the 21st supposedly aboard the *Aquitania.* It was my desire to talk with you about the offer to officers and men in the A. E. F. to attend a school in France or England. I made application and was shown the endorsement by the Regt. Commander, that the offer did not apply to transient officers. The knowledge was obtained from a telegram received from Hdq. One of our officers went to the Commanding General of this Camp to obtain a copy of the telegram which could not be or was not produced. Capt. —— —— went in person to the General and requested permission to attend stating that he volunteered for service, left his practise and family at a sacrifice and that he thought the Govt. owed it to him to give him a chance and attend school here. The General took his name and the Organization to which he belongs promising to let him hear from him, but as yet nothing has been done. This Camp is practically a penal institution and prejudice against us is very strong. Some day there is likely to be some grave disturbance here. The conditions are simply awful: mud everywhere, leaky tents and barracks and lack of sufficient and proper toilets. The men are worked quite hard, some at night and others in the day, rain or shine. As a consequence there are quite a number of sick men in our organization. Since our arrival here, the roads have been improved quite a bit (due to the work of the 92nd div.) and you do not have to wade in ankle deep mud. Board walks here to nearly all the tents and barracks. There is so much talk about the rotten conditions that the Camp Officials are making feverish efforts to be ready for the proposed inquiry.

The work of each organization is graded by the Camp Officer in Charge of details and if not satisfactory, the organization may be placed at the bottom of the sailing list or removed temporarily. Commanding Officers of separate units or regiments are practically helpless and if they complain too much against the treatment accorded them are kept here until the Commanding General sees fit to let them go.

I am beginning to wonder whether it will ever be possible for me to see an American (white) without wishing that he were in his Satanic Majesty's private domain. I must pray long and earnestly that hatred of my fellow man be removed from my heart and that I can truthfully lay claim to being a Christian.

MARCUS GARVEY

In the following essay W. E. B. Du Bois raises questions about the bookkeeping of Marcus Garvey's organization, the Universal Negro Improvement Association (U.N.I.A.). Du Bois also questions the feasibility of Garvey's philosophy and goals. This essay was published in January 1921.

When it comes to Mr. Garvey's industrial and commercial enterprises there is more ground for doubt and misgiving than in the matter of his character. First of all, his enterprises are incorporated in Delaware, where the corporation laws are loose and where no financial statements are required.[2] So far as I can find, and I have searched with care, Mr. Garvey has never published a complete statement of the income and expenditures of the Negro Improvement Association or of the Black Star Line or of any of his enterprises, which really revealed his financial situation. A courteous letter of inquiry sent to him July 22, 1920, asking for such financial data as he was willing for the public to know, remains to this day unacknowledged and unanswered.

Now a refusal to publish a financial statement is no proof of dishonesty, but it *is* proof that either Garvey is ill-advised and unnecessarily courting suspicion, or that his industrial enterprises are not on a sound business basis; otherwise he is too good an advertiser not to use a promising balance-sheet for all it is worth.

There has been one balance sheet, published July 26, 1920, purporting to give the financial condition of the Black Star Line after one year of operation; neither profit or loss is shown, there is no way to tell the actual cash receipts or the true condition of the business. Nevertheless it does make some interesting revelations.

The total amount of stock subscribed for is $590,860. Of this

$118,153.28 is not yet paid for, leaving the actual amount of paid-in capital charged against the corporation, $472,706.72. Against this stands only $355,214.59 of assets (viz.: $21,985.21 in cash deposits and loans receivable; $12,975.01 in furniture and equipment, $288,515.37 which is the alleged value of his boats, $26,600 in real estate and $5,739 of insurance paid in advance). To offset the assets he has $152,264.14 of other liabilities (accrued salaries, $1,539.30; notes and accounts payable, $129,224.84; mortgages due, $21,500). In other words, his capital stock of $472,706.72 is after a year's business impaired to such extent that he has only $202,950.45 to show for it.

Even this does not reveal the precariousness of his actual business condition. Banks before the war in lending their credit refused to recognize any business as safe unless for every dollar of current liabilities there were *two* dollars of current assets. Today, since the war, they require *three* dollars of current assets to every *one* of current liabilities. The Black Star Line had July 26, $16,485.21 in current assets and $130,764.14 in current liabilities, when recognition by any reputable bank called for $390,000 in current assets.

Moreover, another sinister admission appears in this statement: the cost of floating the Black Star Line to date has been $289,066.27. In other words, it has cost nearly $300,000 to collect a capital of less than half a million. Garvey has, in other words, spent more for advertisement than he has for his boats!

This is a serious situation, and even this does not tell the whole story: the real estate, furniture, etc., listed above, are probably valued correctly. But how about the boats? The *Yarmouth* is a wooden steamer of 1,452 gross tons built in 1887. It is old and unseaworthy; it came near sinking a year ago and it has cost a great deal for repairs. It is said that it is now laid up for repairs with a large bill due. Without doubt the inexperienced purchasers of this vessel paid far more than it is worth, and it will soon be utterly worthless unless rebuilt at a very high cost.

The cases of the *Kanawha* (or *Antonio Maceo*) and the *Shadyside* are puzzling. Neither of these boats is registered as belonging to the Black Star Line at all. The former is recorded as belonging to C. L. Dimon, and the latter to the North and East River Steamboat Company. Does the Black Star Line really own these boats, or is it buying them by installments, or only leasing them? We do not know the facts and have been unable to find out. Under the circumstances they look like dubious "assets".

The majority of the Black Star stock is apparently owned by the Universal Negro Improvement Association. There is no reason why this association, if it will and can, should not continue to pour money into its corporation. Let us therefore consider then Mr. Garvey's other resources.

Mr. Garvey's income consists of (a) dues from members of the U. N. I. Association; (b) shares in the Black Star Line and other enterprises, and (c) gifts and "loans" for specific objects. If the U. N. I. Association has "3,000,000 members" then the income from that source alone would be certainly over a million dollars a year. If, as is more likely, it has under 300,000 paying members, he may collect $150,000 annually from this source. Stock in the Black Star Line is still being sold. Garvey himself tells of one woman who had saved about four hundred dollars in gold: "She brought out all the gold and bought shares in the Black Star Line." Another man writes this touching letter from the Canal Zone: "I have sent twice to buy shares amounting to $125 (numbers of certificates 3752 and 9617). Now I am sending $35 for seven more shares. You might think I have money, but the truth, as I stated before, is that I have no money now. But if I'm to die of hunger it will be all right because I'm determined to do all that's in my power to better the conditions of my race."

In addition to this he has asked for special contributions. In the spring of 1920 he demanded for his coming convention in August, "a fund of two million dollars ($2,000,000) to capitalize this, the greatest of all conventions." In October he acknowledged a total of something over $16,000 in small contributions. Immediately he announced "a constructive loan" of $2,000,000, which he is presumably still seeking to raise.

From these sources of income Mr. Garvey has financed his enterprises and carried on a wide and determined propaganda, maintained a large staff of salaried officials, clerks and agents, and published a weekly newspaper. Notwithstanding this considerable income, there is no doubt that Garvey's expenditures are pressing hard on his income, and that his financial methods are so essentially unsound that unless he speedily revises them the investors will certainly get no dividends and worse may happen. He is apparently using the familiar method of "Kiting"—*i. e.,* the money which comes in as investment in stock is being used in current expenses, especially in heavy overhead costs, for clerk hire, interest and display. Even his boats are being used for advertisement more than for business—lying in harbors as exhibits, taking excursion parties, etc. These methods have necessitated mortgages on property and continually new and more grandiose schemes to collect larger and larger amounts of ready cash. Meantime, lacking business men of experience, his actual business ventures have brought in few returns, involved heavy expense and threatened him continually with disaster or legal complication.

On the other hand, full credit must be given Garvey for a bold effort and some success. He has at least put vessels manned and owned by black men on the seas and they have carried passengers and cargoes. The difficulty is that he does not know the shipping business, he does not understand the investment of capital, and he has few trained and staunch assistants.

The present financial plight of an inexperienced and headstrong promoter may therefore decide the fate of the whole movement. This would be a calamity. Garvey is the beloved leader of tens of thousands of poor and bewildered people who have been cheated all their lives. His failure would mean a blow to their faith, and a loss of their little savings, which it would take generations to undo.

Moreover, shorn of its bombast and exaggeration, the main lines of the Garvey plan are perfectly feasible. What he is trying to say and do is this: American Negroes can, by accumulating and ministering their own capital, organize industry, join the black centers of the south Atlantic by commercial enterprise and in this way ultimately redeem Africa as a fit and free home for black men. This is true. It is *feasible*. It is, in a sense, practical; but it will take for its accomplishment long years of painstaking, self-sacrificing effort. It will call for every ounce of ability, knowledge, experience and devotion in the whole Negro race. It is not a task for one man or one organization, but for coordinate effort on the part of millions. The plan is not original with Garvey but he has popularized it, made it a living, vocal ideal and swept thousands with him with intense belief in the possible accomplishment of the idea.

This is a great, human service; but when Garvey forges ahead and almost singlehanded attempts to realize his dream in a few years, with large words and wild gestures, he grievously minimizes his task and endangers his cause.

To instance one illustrative fact: there is no doubt but what Garvey has sought to import to America and capitalize the antagonism between blacks and mulattoes in the West Indies. This has been the cause of the West Indian failures to gain headway against the whites. Yet Garvey imports it into a land where it has never had any substantial footing and where today, of all days, it is absolutely repudiated by every thinking Negro; Garvey capitalizes it, has sought to get the coöperation of men like R. R. Moton on this basis, and has aroused more bitter color enmity inside the race than has ever before existed. The whites are delighted at the prospect of a division of our solidifying phalanx, but their hopes are vain. American Negroes recognize no color line in or out of the race, and they will in the end punish the man who attempts to establish it.

Then too Garvey increases his difficulties in other directions. He is a British subject. He wants to trade in British territory. Why then does he needlessly antagonize and even insult Britain? He wants to unite all Negroes. Why then does he sneer at the work of the powerful group of his race in the United States where he finds asylum and sympathy? Particularly, why does he decry the excellent and rising business enterprises of Harlem—intimating that his schemes alone are honest and sound when the facts flatly contradict him? He proposes to settle his headquarters in Liberia—but has he asked permission of the Liberian government? Does he presume to usurp authority in a land which has successfully withstood England, France and the United States,—but is expected tamely to submit to Marcus Garvey? How long does Mr. Garvey think that President King would permit his anti-English propaganda on Liberian soil, when the government is straining every nerve to escape the Lion's Paw?

And, finally, without arms, money, effective organization or base of operations, Mr. Garvey openly and wildly talks of "Conquest" and of telling white Europeans in Africa to "get out!" and of becoming himself a black Napoleon!

Suppose Mr. Garvey should drop from the clouds and concentrate on his industrial schemes as a practical first step toward his dreams: the first duty of a great commercial enterprise is to carry on effective commerce. A man who sees in industry the key to a situation, must establish sufficient businesslike industries. Here Mr. Garvey has failed lamentably.

The *Yarmouth* for instance, has not been a commercial success. Stories have been published alleging its dirty condition and the inexcusable conduct of its captain and crew. To this Mr. Garvey may reply that it was no easy matter to get efficient persons to run his boats and to keep a schedule. This is certainly true, but if it is difficult to secure one black boat crew, how much more difficult is it going to be to "build and operate factories in the big industrial centers of the United States, Central America, the West Indies and Africa to manufacture every marketable commodity"? and also "to purchase and build ships of larger tonnage for the African and South American trade"? and also to raise "Five Million Dollars to free Liberia" where "new buildings are to be erected, administrative buildings are to be built, colleges and universities are to be constructed"? and finally to accomplish what Mr. Garvey calls the "Conquest of Africa"!

To sum up: Garvey is a sincere, hard-working idealist; he is also a stubborn, domineering leader of the mass; he has worthy industrial and commercial schemes but he is an inexperienced business man. His dreams of Negro industry, commerce and the ultimate freedom of Africa are feasible; but his methods are bombastic, wasteful, illogical and ineffective and almost illegal. If he learns by experience, attracts strong and capable friends and helpers instead of making needless enemies; if he gives up secrecy and suspicion and substitutes open and frank reports as to his income and expenses, and above all if he is willing to be a co-worker and not a czar, he may yet in time succeed in at least starting some of his schemes toward accomplishment. But unless he does things and does them quickly he cannot escape failure.

Let the followers of Mr. Garvey insist that he get down to bed-rock business and make income and expense balance; let them gag Garvey's wilder words, and still preserve his wide power and influence. American Negro leaders are not jealous of Garvey—they are not envious of his success; they are simply afraid of his failure, for his failure would be theirs. He can have all the power and money that he can efficiently and honestly use, and if in addition he wants to prance down Broadway in a green shirt, let him—but do not let him foolishly overwhelm with bankruptcy and disaster one of the most interesting spiritual movements of the modern Negro world.

THE FAITH OF THE AMERICAN NEGRO

In this essay, Mordecai Wyatt Johnson writes about the depth of the suffering endured by African Americans following emancipation. However, they held on to a mighty faith that sustained them in hope that their situation in America would change. This essay was published in August 1922.

Since their emancipation from slavery the masses of American Negroes have lived by the strength of a simple but deeply moving faith. They have believed in the love and providence of a just and holy God; they have believed in the principles of democracy and in the righteous purpose of the Federal Government; and they have believed in the disposition of the American people as a whole and in the long run to be fair in all their dealings.

In spite of disfranchisement and peonage, mob violence and public contempt, they have kept this faith and have allowed themselves to hope with the optimism of Booker T. Washington that in proportion as they grew in intelligence, wealth, and self-respect they would win the confidence and esteem of their fellow white Americans, and would gradually acquire the responsibilities and privileges of full American citizenship.

In recent years, and especially since the Great War, this simple faith has suffered a widespread disintegration.

When the United States government set forth its war aims, called upon Negro soldiers to stand by the colors and Negro civilians, men, women and children, to devote their labor and their earnings to the cause, and when the war shortage of labor permitted a quarter million Negroes to leave the former slave states for the better conditions of the North, the entire Negro people experienced a profound sense of spiritual release. For the first time since emancipation they found themselves comparatively free to sell their labor on the open market for a living wage, found themselves launched on a great world enterprise with a chance to vote in a real and decisive way, and, best of all, in the heat of the struggle, they found themselves bound with other Americans in the spiritual fellowship of a common cause.

When they stood on the height of this exalted experience and looked down on their pre-war poverty, impotence and spiritual isolation, they realized as never before the depth of the harm they had suffered, and there arose in them a mighty hope that in some way the war would work a change in their situation.

For a time indeed it seemed that their hope would be realized. For when the former slave states saw their labor leaving for the North, they began to reflect upon the treatment they had been accustomed to give the Negro and they decided that it was radically wrong. Newspapers and public orators everywhere expressed this change of sentiment, set forth the wrongs in detail, and urged immediate improvement. And immediate improvement came. Better educational facilities were provided here and there, words of appreciation for the worth and spirit of the Negro as a citizen began to be uttered, and public committees arose to inquire into his grievances and to lay out programs for setting these grievances right. Colored people in these states had never experienced such collective good will, and many of them were so grateful and happy that they actually prayed for the prolongation of the war.

At the close of the war, however, the Negro's hopes were suddenly dashed to the ground. Southern newspapers began at once to tell the Negro soldiers that the war was over, and the sooner they forgot it the better. "Pull off your uniform," they said, "find the place you had before the war and stay in it." "Act like a Negro should act," said one newspaper, "work like a Negro should work. Talk like a Negro should talk. Study like a Negro should study. Dismiss all ideas of independence or of being lifted up to the plane of the white man. Understand the necessity of keeping a Negro's place." In connection with such admonitions there came the great collective attacks on Negro life and property in Washington, Chicago, Omaha, Elaine, and Tulsa. There came the increasing boldness of lynchers who advertised their purposes in advance and had their photographs taken as they stood around the burning bodies of their victims. There came vain appeals by the colored people to the President of the United States and to the Houses of Congress. And finally there came the reorganization and rapid growth of the Ku Klux Klan.

The swift succession and frank brutality of all this was more than the Negro people could bear. Their simple faith and hope broke down. Multitudes took weapons in their hands and fought back violence with bloody resistance. "If we must die," they said, "it is well that we die fighting." And the Negro American world looking on their deed with no light of hope to see by, said, "It is self-defense; it is the law of nature, of man and of God, and it is well."

From those terrible days until this day the Negro's faith in the righteous purpose of the Federal Government has sagged. Some have laid the blame on the parties in power, and some have laid it elsewhere, but all the colored people in every section of the United States believe that there is something wrong, and not accidentally wrong, at the very heart of the government.

Some of our young men are giving up the Christian religion, thinking that their fathers were fools to have believed it so long. One group among us repudiates entirely the simple faith of former days. It would put no trust in God, no trust in democracy, and would entertain no hope of betterment under the present form of government. It believes that the United States government is through and through controlled by selfish capitalists who have no fundamental good will for Negroes or for any sort of laborers whatever. In their publications and on the platform the members of this group urge the colored man to seek his salvation by alliance with the revolutionary labor movement of America and the world.

Another and larger group among us believes in religion and believes in the principles of democracy, but not in the white man's religion and not in the white man's democracy. It believes that the creed of the former slave states is the tacit creed of the whole nation, and that the Negro may never expect to acquire economic, political and spiritual liberty in America. This group has held congresses with representatives from the entire Negro world, to lay out the foundations of a black empire, a black religion and a black culture; it has organized the provisional Republic of Africa, set going a multitude of economic enterprises, instituted branches of its organization wherever Negroes are to be found, and binds them together with a newspaper edited in two languages.

Whatever one may think about these radical movements and their destiny, one thing is certain. They are home grown fruits, with roots deep sprung in a world of black American suffering. Their power lies in the appeal which they make to the Negro to find a way out of his troubles by new and self-reliant paths.

The larger masses of the colored people do not belong to these more radical movements. They retain their belief in the Christian God, they love their country, and hope to work out their salvation within its bounds; but they are completely disillusioned. They see themselves surrounded on every hand by a sentiment of antagonism which does not intend to be fair. They see themselves partly reduced to peonage, shut out from labor unions, forced to an inferior status before the courts, made subjects of public contempt, lynched and mobbed with impunity, and deprived of the ballot their only means of social defense. They see this antagonistic sentiment consolidated in the places of power in the former slave states, and growing by leaps and bounds in the North and West. They know that it is gradually reducing them to an economic, political and social caste. And they are now no longer able to believe with Dr. Booker T. Washington or with any other man that their own efforts after intelligence, wealth and self-respect can in any wise avail to deliver them from these conditions, unless they have the protection of a just and beneficent public policy in keeping with American ideals. With one voice, therefore, from pulpit and from press, and from the humblest walks of life, they are sending up a cry of pain and petition such as is heard to-day from the citizens of no other civilized nation in the world. They are asking for protection of life, for the security of property, for the liberation of their peons, for the freedom to sell their labor on the open market, for a human being's chance in the courts, for a better system of education, and for the boon of the ballot. They ask, in short, for public equality under the protection of the Federal Government.

And that request is sustained by every sentiment of humanity and by every holy ideal for which this nation stands. The time has come when the elemental justice called for in this petition should be embodied in a public policy initiated by the Federal Government and continuously supervised by a commission of that government representing the faith and will of the entire American people.

The Negro people of America have been with us here for three hundred years. They have cut our forests, tilled our fields, built our railroads, fought our battles, and in all their trials until now they have manifested a simple faith, a grateful heart, a cheerful spirit and an undivided loyalty to our nation that has been a thing of beauty to behold. Now they have come to the place where their faith can no longer feed on the bread of repression and violence. They ask for the bread of liberty, of public equality, and public responsibility. It must not be denied them.

We are sufficiently far removed from the Civil War and its animosities to see that such elements of justice may be given to the Negro with entire good will and helpfulness toward the former slave states. We have already had one long attempt to erect a wealth and culture on the backs of slaves. We found that it was a costly experiment, paid for at last in the blood of our best sons. There are some among our citizens who would turn their backs on history and repeat that experiment, and to their terrible heresy they would convert our entire great community. By every sacred bond of love for them, we must not yield. And we must no longer leave them alone with their experiment. The faith of our whole nation must be brought to their support until such time as it is clear to them that their former slaves can be made both fully free and yet their faithful friends.

Across the seas the darker peoples of the earth are rising from their long sleep, and are searching this western world for light. Our Christian missionaries are among them. They are asking these missionaries: "Can the Christian religion bind this multi-colored world in bonds of brotherhood?" We of all nations are best prepared to answer that question and to be their moral inspiration and their friend. For we have the world's problem of race relationships here in crucible, and by strength of our American faith we have made some encouraging progress in its solution. If the fires of this faith are kept burning around that crucible, what comes out of it is able to place these United States in the spiritual leadership of all humanity. When the Negro cries with pain from his deep hurt and lays his petition for elemental justice before the nation, he is calling upon the American people to kindle anew about that crucible of race relationships the fires of American faith.

Coöperation and the Negro

E. Franklin Frazier discusses the need for intelligent organization among black farmers. Frazier examines the liabilities of African-American farmers, and he offers some suggestions on how to overcome the obstacles they face. This essay was published in March 1923.

The recent impulse given to Coöperation through organization on the part of the farmers and the removal of legal barriers is sure to affect the Negro. This is inevitable since any attempt on the part of white farmers to sell directly to the consumer would be futile without the coöperation of the Negro. The products coming from the latter if under the control of speculators are sufficient to nullify to a large extent the collective action of white coöperators. Successful coöperation requires the organization of production in relation to the size of the market.

The types of coöperation in which the Negro will probably engage are: Coöperative Marketing Societies; Coöperative Supply Associations; and Credit Unions.

There are at present in the South sporadic suggestions of and attempts at coöperative marketing. The meat exhibits among Negro farmers under the direction of farm demonstrators where the products are sold collectively, carry with them the germs of a developed system of coöperation. More promising, though temporary, essays in coöperation are the occasional combinations to furnish carloads of hogs and other products which are sold at a more favorable price than individual bargaining could command. Even these ephemeral organizations have failed in most cases. They have failed partly because of the ignorance of the Negro farmer and partly because he, under necessity, has been compelled to sell prematurely. The absence of any organization to bind him to his promises and the economic domination of the white landlord have had a share in these failures. A more determined and consistent attempt to organize coöperatively can be seen in the coming meeting of peanut growers in Texas in the fall, when a cöoperative market association is to be formed.

Successful coöperative marketing among Negro farmers can be achieved only when they are placed on a cash basis in renting and, under intelligent leaders, are organized according to their mode of production and the area of the market. Moreover, the areas which will be organized as logical units will naturally contain white and colored farmers. The question arises immediately: Is the Negro farmer to enter these societies on equality with the white members? It should be the duty of rural colored leaders to see that Negro farmers enter on equal terms or form independent societies. In an organization where the size of one's holdings do not count in voting power the accident of color would certainly have no place. Certain social consequences implied in these organizations merit more consideration than can be given them here.

Under the caption of Consumers' Coöperatives we shall consider those organizations which maintain stores to supply their members daily with groceries; and those organized for the purchasing of feeding stuffs and farm implements. At present the writer has not at hand any data concerning the fate of the first type among Negroes; he has heard rumors of some stranded undertakings. There are, however, widely dispensed attempts at coöperation where Negro farmers, recognizing the economic advantage of collective buying of feed and implements, have combined. But these associations have been temporary and spasmodic. The rural leader, after acquainting himself with the principles of coöperation, should seize upon these favorable moments to organize permanent societies. Even where the necessary knowledge is available, there is another obstacle to be met. In many small rural communities of the South, the Negro consumer is absolutely powerless to free himself from the white landlord's commissary. White landlords who resent the teaching of scientific methods of agriculture to their colored tenants and even neighbors would not tolerate the inauguration of a system to eliminate their stores. It is useless, of course, as a colored rural worker remarked to me recently, to think of such stores in many sections. Nevertheless, a great step towards economic emancipation could be achieved through the development of coöperative enterprises in many centers of Negro population.

While considering the present progress and future possibilities of coöperation among Negroes it is necessary to take into account the question of credit. The coöperative movement in Europe took its inception in the credit unions of Germany; and in Denmark where coöperation pervades the economic structure, the crowning achievement has been a coöperative bank. The writer has been informed that there are several rural credit unions in North Carolina among colored people. This is a hopeful sign. But on the whole the subjection of the Negro farmer has been due to his inability to get credit. The writer has been informed by a man intimately acquainted with the condition of Negro farmers that Farm Loan Banks have discriminated against colored applicants. Even if these banks function impartially, there will still be need of rural credit institutions among colored farmers. But the organization of this fundamental branch of production must wait upon intelligent leadership and expert information.

In conclusion, it appears that if the colored people, especially the farmers, are to avail themselves of the economic and social advantages of coöperation, in spite of the large percentage of illiteracy, the following program is necessary:

(1) To disseminate among them literature on the principles of coöperative enterprises.

(2) To get rural leaders, after the study of the mode of production and the market of different communities, to organize consumers and farmers; and

(3) To liberate the Negro from the present share crop system of farming.

It is to be regretted that such an occasion as the recent Farmers' conference at Tuskegee Institute was not utilized to disseminate among Negro Farmers the principles of economic coöperation. The incidental references to spontaneous attempts at coöperative marketing by the farmers attending the conference not only should have invited an investigation of the progress of the movement among Negro farmers, but should have been the basis of a discussion of the problems connected with this new era in agriculture. With the proper information and encouragement the farmers could have used their initial undertakings as the foundation for further efforts.

JOHN BROWN DAY

John Brown, the great historical abolitionist, was honored during a ceremony held in North Elba, New York. William Pickens, the author of this essay, relates the events of this tribute to John Brown. The essay was published in July 1924.

On May 9, 1924, I stood on the great rock at North Elba, New York, to address the assembled people in the presence of "Old John Brown of Ossawatomie and Harper's Ferry." John Brown lay there as dust and crumbled bones buried at the foot of that rock, sharing his burial ground with twelve of his Knights, white and black, who shared his exploit at Harper's Ferry. And if I were not doing my best now to further the work in which they so gallantly engaged, I would rather be the dust and bones of any one of them than to be alive on the rock.

"Old John Brown" is a saint among the people of North Elba and Lake Placid, and the white people of the neighborhood turned out and grouped themselves with the brown people who had journeyed in a string of automobiles and by train from Philadelphia and New York City. Every accommodation was given and every courtesy shown to the visitors. The National Hotel, hard by the station, was turned over to the guests, and the proprietor held his car at the disposal of those who did not bring automobiles of their own.

Most of the delegation arrived on the evening of the 8th, and the Memorial Exercises at the grave were conducted on the afternoon of the 9th, the 124th anniversary of John Brown's birthday. Further exercises were held at the Town Hall auditorium on the evening of the 9th, at which the Rev. Mr. Imes, of Philadelphia, was the principal speaker. And on Saturday evening, the 10th, Miss Julia Gilbert, of Philadelphia, and a male quartet of Lincoln University, gave a musical concert in this same Town Hall of Lake Placid. Mr. Ralph Parman, president of the Lake Placid Chamber of Commerce, and also the president of the Chamber of Commerce of North Elba, called early on Dr. Jesse Max Barber, founder of the John Brown Memorial Association and leader of this expedition. These gentlemen and the local officers of the Lake Placid Club offered to Dr. Barber every assistance and courtesy which the guests might require.

At noon on the 9th, the great Lake Placid Club, the wealthiest and most richly appointed country club in the world, was opened for a detailed visit by the guests of the city. This Club is an institution that covers acres with offices, commodious lobbies, numerous parlors, a great theatre that seats 1500 and a chapel for religious services. The theatre and chapel are so built that the ample stage of the theatre is a sort of rear extension room for the chapel, and the same pipe organ serves both. The theatre is larger than the chapel—everybody goes to the theatre. When the guests reached the theatre there was an impromptu concert in which Miss Gilbert played and sang, the quartet rendered a few selections, and the whole delegation sang "John Brown's Body".

In the Pilgrimage of the afternoon many of the Lake Placid people tramped the two and a half miles to North Elba where is the John Brown Farm with the grave. There was a procession of little blooming children and old gray-haired people.

It was gratifying to see that the great state of New York, which is civilized enough to have a head of Frederick Douglass in its state house at Albany, was also brave enough to buy and preserve John Brown's Farm as state property, to install a caretaker there, and to erect a simple granite monument on a rock that rises from the ground just outside the high iron fence which surrounds the great rock and the graves of the Heroes. New York is a civilized state. A few steps from his grave is the old home of John Brown, a comfortable and well preserved house, where the caretaker now lives. But such interest in Brown has been awakened by these pilgrimages of the John Brown Memorial Association that a New York historical society is now planning to build a special house for the caretaker, so that Brown's home may be preserved as a museum.

Strangely enough, the great rock around which Brown and his knights are buried is the only great rock in the immediate neighborhood. Some mountain has been worn away here, and this remaining rock is its heart and essence, which like the spirit of Brown has not yielded to the abrasions of time. This jutting head of some cliff that descends to an unknown depth into the bowels of the earth, seems to have been set there by Mother Nature as a fitting tombstone for the greatest Hero of Conscience.

The audience gathered mostly within the enclosure of the high iron fence, wherein stands also a lofty white flagpole, flying the Stars and Stripes, against which Brown never raised a hand except to make it clean.

By a pair of steps at the rear the speakers ascend to the top of this rock—a rostrum erected by time and the elements, a fitting platform from which to recount the deeds and sing the praises of the greatest heroes.

From this rock the secretary of the Lake Placid Club presided; the Lincoln University quartet sang; the Rev. Mr. Logan, of Philadelphia, prayed; and then Jesse Max Barber, founder of the Memorial Association, spoke eloquently, and introduced the speaker.

There was present a little brown baby from Philadelphia, 11 months old. And there was present from the neighborhood Lyman E. Epps, who, when John Brown's funeral was held in 1859, was 8 years old and sang in the children's chorus. These two extremes were photographed at the grave, the brown veteran holding the brown baby. Other photographs were made.

These pilgrimages are awakening a new interest in John Brown as a great historical character, and the annual visits to his grave have increased five-fold since Max Barber led the first pilgrimage there in 1922. Until then no Negro had ever placed a wreath of flowers on the grave of John Brown!

Here while the highest Adirondacks, usually hooded with snow, look down on him, he sleeps, one of the greatest heroes of all time, a Man who would not barter principle for personal convenience or even for life—a man of "Action, action, action!"—a nineteenth century Prophet of God.

Temperament

In this essay, author Horace Mann Bond discusses many
of the stereotypes associated with the temperament of
African Americans. He argues that there is no intelligent basis for separating temperamental African Americans from the temperamental types of other peoples.
The essay was published in June 1925.

We are all intimately interested in the nature and amount in detail by
which one individual differs from another. This one is quick and
strong—that one slow and weak—to adapt Wundt's familiar classification of temperamental traits. This man devotes his energies with un-
flagging zeal to a disagreeable task; that one shirks the slightest
exaction upon his time or effort.

These are the manifest and evident peculiarities which are laid before our eyes daily, in a hundred interesting fashions. For them we have
an easy explanation and one which serves to satisfy the demands of science. It is quite logical to locate these differences in the inherited pattern of behaviour, granted always that environment may obscure
individual facts and mask the significance of group exhibitions of these
same factors.

In the same manner, we are apt to make classifications of races based
upon our observance of certain facts. The Italian is quick and emotional, we decide; while opposed to his warm, impassioned southern
temperament is the stolid determination and steadfast vision of the
Teuton and the child of the North. The Negro is governed by his emotions, docile and childlike; the Nordic is a thinker, an individualist and
self-assertive where the other is instinctively submissive.

So the man in the street runs the gamut of impression and belief. It
is not only this much maligned person who subscribes heartily to such

a credo, but the littérateur, the commercial man, the military man and in many cases the man of science. An explanation for this fact is not far in abeyance; temperament is one subject which heretofore has not been given scientific and experimental investigation. Anatomical differences have been discarded as superficial and unimportant; differences in intelligence have been admittedly reduced to vague and inconclusive ranges; but temperament represents a field whose soil is still virgin. It thus is the vantage ground for many of the weird and impossible speculations which formerly took refuge under the wing of other factors, now discredited as significant of total race cleavage.

That our conception of the factor of temperament is ill-defined is shown by the anomalous variety of adjectives used by differing commentators to describe one racial type. In the course of a study recently made, it was found that Negro temperament was considered to be cowardly, ferocious, loyal, treacherous, deceptive, truthful, docile, recalcitrant, submissive, individualistic, by as many different writers. As a concrete example of this confusion as to exact classification, we know the variant viewpoint contrasted in reports on the discussion of the Negro of Civil War days and the same Negro of ten or fifteen years later. Surely, we have the same Negro; yet there is an astonishing amount of literature existent on the loyal and faithful Negro of the former period and an equally astonishing amount of literature treating of the Negro of the latter period as thief, rapist and treacherous scoundrel.

It is such facts as these which serve to indicate that temperamental differences are no more to be relied upon as separating races than anatomical or intellectual differences. As one of the fruitful sources of data as to temperamental traits, the Negro in America affords a tempting subject for investigation as to the genuineness and authenticity of his inherent characteristics which have been so laxly considered racial in extent.

What are the temperamental features which are generally relied on in classifying the Negro? Although, as we have pointed out, there exists a conflicting mass of opinion relative to these features, there is almost general agreement in regarding the Negro as possessing a high degree of emotional tonicity. We hear him referred to as an emotional animal, as the child of his emotions and in other ways descriptive of a rather general crystallization of comment on this factor. Another temperamental characteristic which receives almost general approbation is that of a docile and submissive nature. Since attention is more concentrated upon these features than others, it is well to choose them as the starting off points in our investigation of the unique form of temperament, which, it is alleged, is the ear-mark of race and people.

In the first place, we are struck by the fact that it is not the emotion as such which causes an association of this temperamental characteristic with the Negro, but rather the mode of expression of emotional states of feeling. In other words, we do not know whether the weeping mourner is more or less emotional than the stolid mourner; we only know that one expresses his feeling in a less inhibited fashion than the other. Thus, with examples of emotional expression which lead to classification as characteristic of a racial, inherited pattern of feeling, we know nothing of the comparative depth of the subjective experience, but only are aware of the manner of manifestation.

Turning from consideration of this fact, it is evident that manners of acting and the expressions of emotions are controlled more by social pressure than by instinctive promptings. Although a naïve observer might so conclude, we are not to suppose that the Spartan youth suffered less agony of flesh and spirit than would some modern urchin. It was merely the stern form of social urge which meant action of a subdued nature as interpretative of emotional feeling.

This fact is so obvious that one feels like proffering an apology for its presentation. The casual way in which writers imply a contrary conclusion, however, must serve as palliative for the inclusion of such matter here.

It thus follows that all of the ways in which Negroes, as well as other people, express their emotional states of feeling are controlled by social forms of practice. Custom is the force which dictates exaggeration, on the one hand, or inhibition, on the other, of tendencies to action.

One of the evidences most usually relied upon in demonstrating the inferior control which the Negro—inherently—possesses over his emotions is his religious activities. There is no gain-saying the fact that the typical Negro religious gathering is replete with all sorts of emotional scenes and instances. The atmosphere is surcharged with impulsion; and the ejaculations, physical contortions and other phenomena indicate a freedom from "cloying convention" which might forbid any such expressions. In fact, it is quite probable that there exists a convention of *exhibition* rather than one of *inhibition*. It is the fashion to "shout", to see a "little white man", just as much as it is the fashion in the church across the street to be staid and sober in the matter of religious experience.

That this explanation is valid is shown by comparison of groups within the major limits of races. There is little difference, if any, between the actions of the backwoods Methodist and Baptist revivalists of the Middle West and the exhibition of religious conviction to be witnessed in Negro churches of today. One need not go beyond the limits of the race itself to find a contrast as striking as any which might be imagined. Witness the contempt with which certain Negro church people regard the form of procedure in other churches!

It is evident, then, that we have here a matter of convention, of custom, of social pressure and not of fundamental and racial import. It is conceivable that with further development of social disapproval of hyperemotional expressions, Negro religion and religious observances will approximate the forms found in the ecclesiastical life of other groups. This is a fact often overlooked by Negroes as well as whites. Many are prone to offer vicarious apologies for Negro excesses in religious affairs by claiming a distinct religious fervor as part of the Negro temperament. One prominent thinker goes so far as to claim that therein lies the hope of Negro contribution to civilization. The white man, it is said, has developed a highly mechanized form of society which is a child of Mammon, but sadly neglectful of the glories of theistic devotion. The Negro was divinely introduced into America in order to offer salvation to this mercenary people in the form of a fervid devotion to religion. The Negro faith is to be the leaven of American unrighteousness.

Such a statement is a typical instance of the beliefs which assign to various races different temperamental characteristics. It is forgetful of all of the facts of Negro life, it is careless of all of the facts of social psychology as well. If the Negro is to make a unique contribution to American religion, or to any other field, it will come as the result of a unique experience involving group pressure; and not as a result of a peculiarly constructed racial complex or psychosis.

To say that the folk songs of the American Negro were the result of a distinct racial endowment seems less of a correct explanation than to say that those songs would never have been produced if their authors had not suffered the experiences related in them. This is a proposition to which many may find it difficult to subscribe; yet it will be found to be the most consistent with the facts in the case.

If it be logical, in the light of this examination, to conclude that the Negro does not differ temperamentally from other peoples, in so far as a hyper-emotionalism is concerned, what shall we decide as to the other trait most confidently assumed to mark distinctively Negro temperament? So prominent and authoritative an observer as McDougall has asserted that the Negro is submissive by instinctive tendency; that he is temperamentally the ideal hewer of wood and drawer of water.

It is easy to dismiss McDougall's opinions in view of his well known "Nordic complex" and to consider them as the biased estimates of a prejudiced observer. However, it is better that the issue be met squarely and without shirking, for the one vulnerable point in the synthetic armor of the "Instinct psychologists", represented by McDougall, lies in this very assumption of a separate instinctive endowment for differing races.

The status of the Negro in America has always been that of a subject people, save in certain isolated instances where revolt has swept away the over-lordship of white masters. The very antecedents of the American Negro indicate that he has been the victim of an overwhelming culture. The Hebrew remains isolated and maintains his cultural identity because preservation is the law of the tribe; and never have the members of that race been totally divorced from their cultural affinities.

The Negro, however, was transported piece-meal to America; with every boat load came the transfusion and mingling of diverse types of culture. Not any of the material evidences, upon which a culture must largely be built, were retained; they were left behind absolutely. No race-transportation in history parallels that of the Negro; and nowhere in history can be found such an abrupt disruption of home ties and native culture.

Add to this the fact, the social law, that a superior culture tends to supplant the less-developed one and we have an explanation of the manner in which the Negro found himself wholly at the mercy of white culture. As a result, there was no escape from imitation; the alien group had the bitter alternative of accommodation or elimination; and with the cultural bands which might have made for a death struggle lacking, the choice, inevitable in the light of circumstances, was adaptation to the desires and wishes of the master class.

For some three or four hundred years this accommodation has persisted. In America, the Negro has always had the choice of submission or extermination. As we have pointed out, a more vigorous cultural background might have prompted the latter; but the way in which the Negro was brought to this country totally deprived him of any such background. We then have as a necessary and perfectly natural corollary the fact of accommodation, of submission in the face of the master class.

But to reason from this fact to a belief in submission as a hereditary element of Negro temperament is manifestly absurd. As the above alternative becomes less imperative, so also becomes less evident the tendency to submission. The comment, not uncommonly heard, that northern Negroes are not as "polite" as southern Negroes is relevant.

Even without this modification in response which can be seen developing, even without the ferment of revolt which is becoming more and more apparent on the part of the Negro today, we have the evidence of members of the race in other parts of the world. It would be hard to classify the Sudanese Negro, the "big, black, bounding beggar" whom Kipling praised because he broke the British squadron at Khartoum, as possessing an instinctive tendency to submit to authority; nor does it seem quite in order to regard as particularly submissive the Zulus with whom Boer and Englishmen waged bitter warfare for a century or more. These peoples are certainly more representative of the Negro type than the mixed Negro races of America; and the only answer to their spirit of resistance, compared to the attitude of the American Negro, is to be found in the fact that they have not been the victims for centuries of a propaganda and instruction calculated to enervate the strongest.

Are we not justified, then, in rejecting any conclusion which would intrude submission as a hereditary trait of Negro temperament? Surely no other opinion ever demonstrated its fallacious nature more strikingly.

And if there is no basis for separating Negro temperament from the temperamental types of other peoples, in the facts of emotionalism and submission, there is even less of reason in considering it separable on the basis of other traits. For these are the major traits in which it is considered the Negro temperament is unique: and removal of these traits leaves only a vague and ill-defined belief in difference which cannot be maintained in the face of further investigation.

The importance of such a demonstration is obvious. Because of the false ideas now in vogue relative to the unique temperament of the Negro, most impossible things are expected of us and the most illogical conclusions drawn. If different races have different temperamental types, it is thought, there can be no objection to the proscription of well defined avenues of expression for these types. If the Negro is temperamentally different from the white, it follows that different treatment is necessary for the two. If the white is temperamentally individualistic, independent and aggressive, democracy may be said to constitute his ideal of government; while for a people who are highly emotional, dependent and submissive by nature, domination by another group is the most logical treatment, and that calculated to obtain the best results.

The distinguished literary critic of the Chicago Tribune, Miss Fanny Butcher, was only expressing the naïveté of the unthinking when she criticized Miss Fauset's novel "There Is Confusion" on the ground that it did not catch "that essential something which makes the Negro what he is". People actually believe that there is something strange and mysterious in the psychological make-up of those of other races. The Slav has earned such a reputation; and literature is replete with references to the "inscrutable Orient", as though the phenomena of human existence there apparent were woven in an occult fashion to make the woof of reality.

A more scientific approach will place the mystery, not in our differences, but in the factors of which we must confess ignorance. The mystery of the Orient is not of the germ-plasm but of the social mechanism. The presence of a Tartar beneath the veneer of Russianism is not genetic but conventional.

We have long since foregone attempts to call the anatomical differences of races insuperable; they have been exposed as superficial, transitory, unimportant. Even those who would make intelligence a scale for race differentiation admit that overlapping and social factors can obscure the pattern of intellectual traits which might otherwise indicate actual differences.

Temperament remains as the only refuge for those intent on setting up barriers to the full participation in society of all races. Temperament is called upon in justification of those who brand Jeffersonian democracy as a glittering generality and regard the words of Christ as the dream of an impossible visionary. Investigation must doom such reliance to the fate which has befallen its predecessors. The results of scientific research are slightly appreciated when first proposed in the face of universal ignorance and opposition, but powerful in their ultimate conquest.

The Negro is beginning to develop a race-consciousness which is of utility in destroying the submissive and dependent attitude he has hitherto assumed. But too strong a race-consciousness may be as disastrous as none at all. One wonders whether the preservation of Hebrew culture and family life has been worth the price paid—the travail of centuries and the hatred of the world. What we should value as more enduring and important than any race consciousness is a realization of ourselves as simply and wholly human; not separable by any anatomical, or intellectual, or temperamental barriers from our fellows. To realize that we are but human beings; prone to err, subjected to the vices of others, heirs of the virtues of the saints and fellow beneficiaries of the common weal. Than this there can be no diviner racial goal.

THREE ACHIEVEMENTS AND
THEIR SIGNIFICANCE

The following address was given by James Weldon
Johnson before the eighteenth annual N.A.A.C.P. conference and was published in 1927. This address examines the purposes and effects of three significant
achievements of the N.A.A.C.P. during the preceding
year.

We came together this year in this Eighteenth Annual Conference
after a year of what we might call a year of triumph, a year of victory.
At our opening session on last Wednesday morning I rehearsed briefly
to our delegates a general summary of the direction and of the
processes which this organization has followed since its foundation.
This organization began as an organization almost exclusively of agitation. When the National Association for the Advancement of Colored People was founded, when it was organized, the fundamental
citizenship rights of the Negro and the estimation in which the Negro
was held by the general American public had reached the lowest point
possible. In fact, America in general was not concerned about the
Negro in America as a man and a citizen. It was concerned about him,
perhaps, as a factor in labor or in politics, a negative factor, but was not
very much interested in him otherwise. So the first job of this organization was the awakening, a quickening, a pricking, of the American
conscience, of public opinion and we began with the only weapon
which we had at hand and that weapon was intelligent and persistent
agitation about the right and the wrong. We began to agitate about
what was at that time and still is in a very large measure the great
American crime, the great American disgrace and in some states the
great American pastime—lynching. And we brought the cruel, naked,
raw savage facts about lynching and began placing them before the

American public and before the civilized and the uncivilized world. The uncivilized world included a very large section of the American people themselves.

This organization has always sought to use the weapons which were most effective and which were possible for us. When we first started the most effective weapon that we had, the most available weapon, was intelligent agitation and we used it. Now we have gone on further; we do not depend entirely upon agitation. The greatest victories of the organization during the past twelve months have been victories in the courts of America, from the lowest to the highest. Yet we still agitate and for some of the conditions, for some of the situations which confront colored people in America, agitation is still the most effective weapon that can be used.

THE AIKEN LYNCHING

The latest effective piece of agitation which we have been able to launch was against lynching. We have been fighting lynching for a generation but we still have to fight it and we agitated against the Lowman lynching at Aiken, South Carolina. South Carolina, known as one of the proud states of the South, the home of Southern aristocracy. Aiken, the winter resort of Northern aristocracy. Yet it was in this old state and in this select community in this state that within these recent months occurred an incident which should cause every American to hang his head in shame. Three humble Negroes accused of a crime, accused of murder, hastily tried, farcically tried, convicted and condemned; a few days still awaiting them when their cases were taken up by a colored lawyer of South Carolina, Mr. N. J. Frederick. Mr. Frederick appealed these cases to the Supreme Court of South Carolina and to the credit of that court and to the state, the cases were remanded to the Circuit Court for trial. And so, in the re-trial Mr. Frederick, assisted by a Southern white lawyer, Mr. L. G. Southard, represented the Lowmans. These three Negroes, two of them men and one a woman, were being re-tried in the courts of South Carolina and in the course of the trial, upon motion of Mr. Frederick, the Judge directed a verdict of not guilty for one of the defendants and it is most probable that the other two would have been acquitted. But what happened? On that night a mob gathered and entered the jail through the connivance of the officers of the law and those two men and that woman were taken out and shot to death.

Now, the National Association for the Advancement of Colored People did play a great part in focusing the attention of the American people upon this lynching. It is most likely that the Aiken lynching would have passed as an ordinary piece of news, not even law-abiding Americans being in any way shocked or disturbed about it. But the National Office of the N. A. A. C. P. sent Walter White to Aiken. He went there and I need not tell you that it was no matter of play for him to do it. He went there and as a result of his visit he secured the names of a score or more of the men who had taken part in the mob and those names were placed in the hands of the Governor of South Carolina. Following Mr. White's investigation the *New York World* sent one of its star correspondents to the scene and the whole Aiken disgrace was upon the front pages of the *New York World* and other great Northern newspapers as well as the newspapers of the South, especially the newspapers of South Carolina.

We could not save the Lowmans and we have not been able to indict or punish their murderers, their foul and cowardly murderers, but at least we have made the decent citizens of South Carolina aware of the shame and the degradation of their state and we have no doubt made it easier for law-abiding citizens in South Carolina to stand up for common justice and common decency than it would have been without the assistance of this organization.

That was a piece of agitation; and may I stop here long enough to say that I want you to get a comprehension of the fight against lynching which this organization makes. Does anyone for a moment suppose that it is merely to save a few miserable Negro wretches from the sufferings which they undergo at the hands of these savage barbarians? That, of course. But that is not all. What are we fighting for? Eventually everybody must die and some must die terrible deaths, but there is more behind it. This fight against lynching is not merely a fight to save a few men who are put to a swift death and a few women, too. The Negro—and the National Association for the Advancement of Colored People—is fighting as much for the whole of America as for Negro America. In fact, this fight against lynching is merely an illustration of what this organization stands for in the whole idea of American democracy. Look at all the organizations at work in America today and make an estimate of their work and what they are doing and you cannot find a single one that has higher ideals or ideals that are more vital to the happiness and the security of this country than the National Association for the Advancement of Colored People. This organization has nothing to hide. It can declare its principles anywhere in America and they square up with everything that every decent American stands for. Compare it if you will with the Ku Klux Klan—the Ku Klux Klan subversive of everything that is in the Constitution and the Declaration of Independence, and the National Association for the Advancement of Colored People standing for everything that is fundamental to a democracy. The ideals that the National Association stands for, the ideals that the Negro stands for—they are the ideals that are at the bottom of our democratic government. If the National Association fails, if the Negro fails in what he is fighting for, then American Democracy fails with him. And so, in this fight against lynching, it goes much further than the poor Lowmans and hundreds and hundreds of others that could be cited.

———

Take the case of lynching a few days ago in dark and benighted Mississippi. While in New York City millions of people were acclaiming Lindbergh who had made an achievement which added to the glory of America, to its name throughout the whole world which added to scientific effort and achievement, at that very hour when millions of Americans, not only white but black, in the city of New York were acclaiming Lindbergh, a mob of a thousand or more barbarians in Mississippi had taken charge of two Negroes, brothers, accused of killing a slave-driving overseer in a sawmill. They took them from the hands of the constituted authorities and what did they do with them? They chained them to a telegraph pole, baptized them in gasoline and set them afire.

Now, what do you think the fight against lynching means? Does it mean so much the mere saving of two solitary black men from being made into a bon fire, or does it mean saving the civilization of a whole state? I shall try and put it more graphically. Try to balance if you can the momentary sufferings of those two black men, their physical suffering, against the moral degradation, the degeneracy of the white people of that community. I have sometimes tried to put it this way, that after all the Negro problem, so far as it is involved in lynching, may mean this: the saving of black America's body and of white America's soul. That is why we are agitating about lynching and all the other grievances and outrages perpetrated against the American Negro.

LOUISIANA SEGREGATION DECISION

All of the injustice against the Negro is not obvious, blatant, like lynching. After all, there are lots of Negroes in the United States who never have, up to this time, been lynched. But let me say to you that there is lynching of the spirit and of the soul as well as lynching of the body. For instance, take a great Southern city like Atlanta, Georgia. In 1920 this Association held its annual conference in Atlanta. Some people thought that we would not do it. It was after the terrible summer of 1919 when Negroes were mobbed and beaten to death in a dozen civilized American cities including the capital of the nation and our friends said: "Do not do it. Call your conference off. Cancel it." We did not. We went to Atlanta. Going down, Mr. Arthur B. Spingarn and I were in the same seat riding in a Pullman car, which of course is a crime down there. We got out together and a red cap seized his bag and mine. I do not know whether Mr. Spingarn noticed it or not, but it was a psychological study to me to see through the back of that red cap's head what was going on in his brain. Now, what was his great problem? What was the poor man trying to solve? It was whether to violate the law by taking Mr. Spingarn through the Jim Crow exit with me or by taking me through the white folks' exit with him. I say this to his credit: he finally resolved that if he had to go to jail he would go to jail for taking me through the white exit and so he did.

———

Now that sounds ridiculous. It sounds trifling and I have heard a number of our friends say: "Why worry about such trifling things?" But perhaps after all the absurdity of it is what makes it in some measure tragic. Here is a great city where Negroes and white folks live pretty close together, much closer than they do in lots of Northern cities; where they live on terms of intimacy; their food prepared, their babies nursed, their sick taken care of by black hands. Yet an entrance to a great railroad station almost as wide as this Tabernacle is too narrow for the two races to walk through together. An effort at sheer humiliation. An absurd effort at lynching the Negro's spirit. Why should a white person who is not too proud to eat biscuit mixed by black hands be afraid to walk through the same entrance of a railroad station? That is merely one of the absurd efforts—and sometimes quite successful in spite of the ridiculousness of it—to lynch the Negro's spirit.

A more serious effort of that same kind are the segregation laws. Here we have white households which for many hours of the day are tenanted by both white and black people and they want laws on the statute books saying that whites and blacks cannot live in the same block or in the same street or in the same section of the city. What is it? What is behind it? An effort at lynching the Negro's spirit.

———

And so this Association has not only fought these outside manifestations of this damnable thing but we fight that which is more insidious, the thing which is concealed and under all the rest. And we have fought these segregation ordinances wherever they have poked their heads up. Sometimes that fight has had to be doubled. There have been cases in which we have had to fight the idea through the heads of Negroes themselves. I do not know what it is—I suppose it is some sort of a Freudian complex—I cannot explain it—I am not a psychologist—but Negroes sometimes get thrown back on themselves and it robs them of what they need in making a fight of this sort and they make use of this sort of defense and say: "We do not care; we want to be to ourselves. It makes no difference. We do not want any law which will allow us to live where the white folks live." Of course we want to be with ourselves. That is very natural. It is very natural that colored people and various other groups, for reasons which need no explanation, love to be together. People who speak the same language—I mean who have the same ideas—find it easier to be together. They do not have to think. You cannot be lazy and lazy-minded and be a citizen of the world. The more lazy-minded we are the more we want to get right into the center of what we call our group. It takes no effort to live. You do not have to know very much. And so we have had to fight this thing first of all through the heads of many Negroes. We should love to be together but this is a very different thing from having a law upon the statute books of the city or the state or the nation saying you have got to live together. I heard my friend Pickens put it the other day in his own inimitable way. He said: "I would not think of wearing a red hat now, but if they passed a law that colored men could not wear red hats, I would insist on having nothing but a red hat."

Now, we have fought segregation by enactment in this country. We have fought it and beaten it down so that it cannot even appear again. We won the Louisville Segregation Case in 1917. We reaffirmed it and strengthened it in the New Orleans Segregation Case and we drove a nail in its coffin and clinched it on the other side in the Indianapolis case. Segregation by law in the United States is dead and it is dead because the National Association for the Advancement of Colored People killed it. And, my friends, if we had not done it you may rest assured that there would have been segregation laws in every state and every city in the United States where there is any considerable colored population.

THE WHITE PRIMARY CASE

Now I can come to the last achievement which I shall mention. These three achievements during the past year will give you some idea of the purpose and also of the effects and the results of the work this organization is doing. We now come to what has been the most far-reaching victory ever achieved by this organization and that is the decision of the United States Supreme Court in the Texas White Primary Case. The State of Texas had a law—and this law is very much like the laws of other Southern states—and that law said that no Negro should vote in a Democratic primary. Now what does "Democratic primary" mean in Texas? "Democratic primary" means "white primary". It therefore means that no Negro shall vote in a white primary, because there is no Republican primary. I could go into that and tell you why there are no Republican primaries, but that is another speech. What does a primary election amount to in Texas? It amounts to all the election there is or is to be. A primary election is an election intended for the selection of candidates. They have one primary, a second primary and sometimes even three primaries. Then they have the general election as understood by the people at large. By the time they get to the general election in Texas everybody with any sense at all is tired of voting because they know the whole thing has been settled. So for colored citizens in Texas not to be able to vote in the primaries and content themselves with voting in the general election would be like rising to third or fourth a motion, having no effect whatever.

Our Branch in El Paso, Texas, took up a case which is now history. As soon as they took it up and took the first steps, they got in touch with the National Office and we carried that case through the Federal courts of Texas on up to the Supreme Court of the United States and gained a unanimous decision which declares laws of that kind to be unconstitutional. Let me just interpolate this: that in gaining that unanimous decision of the Supreme Court we did more than merely kill that kind of legislation. The United States Supreme Court went on record as re-writing and re-affirming the Fourteenth Amendment in more emphatic language than was used by the Congress which originally passed it. I do not know whether you realize the importance of that. But if you are familiar at all with the history of the Fourteenth Amendment you will know that from the time of its passage on down the Supreme Court has been busy whittling it away, splitting it into shreds so thin and fine that the Fourteenth Amendment up to a few months ago meant actually nothing.

There have been more than six hundred decisions rendered by the United States Supreme Court based on the Fourteenth Amendment, an amendment which was passed specifically for the protection of the newly enfranchised Negro citizens and out of those more than six hundred decisions only about thirty have anything to do with the Negro at all and the majority of these are against him. And so the Supreme Court's recent decision was more than to declare such primary laws unconstitutional.

—

Now I must get away from that because I want to say a practical word about this victory. I want to ask what are we going to do about it. All of these victories that the National Association wins, if the Negroes of America do not themselves take advantage of them, will be ineffective. For example, going back a moment to the segregation decision, the National Association by these victories has given the Negro a weapon by which he can kill any segregation law anywhere in the United States, but you have got to use that weapon. If in some city a city council, ignorant of the fact that there is a Supreme Court, should pass a segregation ordinance and colored citizens do not use the weapon which this Association has given them, we cannot help it. We have put the weapon into their hands.

We have done something of the same kind in this White Primary Decision and we want to know if the Negroes of the United States and especially of the South are going to take advantage of it. You might justly ask: "Well, give us your opinion as to how we might take advantage of it." I will tell you quite plainly. In every state where there are such primary laws on the statute books now Negroes should register locally as Democrats and vote. (Applause). Now, that is very encouraging—to get that many hands on that statement. When I made that statement four years ago I got a few groans. Some of the brethren really moaned in spirit. I will tell you why you ought to do that. Because it is a Democratic primary. You cannot go in and vote in a Democratic primary by declaring yourself to be a Republican or a Socialist. I am giving you just practical advice, what I consider to be common sense. But there is something back of it bigger and broader. I feel that the time has come for the Negro in the South to make himself a political factor locally and it is worth more than being a political factor nationally. I am going to tell you a little more to back up that statement. It is worth a great deal more for a Negro in Mississippi to help elect the sheriff, the prosecuting attorney, the police judge, the board of education and the various other local officers than it is to help elect the President of the United States. Why? If you are a Negro in Mississippi the President of the United States cannot help you one bit. Of course if you are a Negro citizen and move to China he can order out the army and the navy to protect you. Now, that is just the common sense of it and my advice to colored citizens in all these Southern states would be to qualify and take advantage of this decision recently rendered by the United States Supreme Court, making themselves political factors locally, which has in it some intrinsic worth beyond glorying in the fact: "I helped to elect Coolidge."

———

Now, my friends, we have got a big job; but we are going at it. When I sat with Miss Ovington and watched this great crowd filing in I wondered what must have been her thoughts when she remembered the two or three people who gathered together in a little room in New York City eighteen years ago and conceived the idea of this organization. At that time we could get only a few people together and here we have these ten thousand people this afternoon. But we have got to go on further. We have a big job but it is a mighty interesting job. We get discouraged sometimes, but after all it is such a big fight, such an interesting fight, such a glorious fight, that I could not do anything else but want to be in it. I want to do my part, at least, because I know that what this Association stands for and is working for will some day come to pass. The Negro fighting for his citizenship rights knows, as far as the human mind is capable of knowing a thing, that he is right. He has right on his side and he has his enemy at a great disadvantage in that respect. And so we are going to win. We cannot help but win. As I said a moment ago, if we do not win, Democracy fails with us.

The Present South

Robert W. Bagnall was director of branches for the
N.A.A.C.P. at the time he wrote this essay. In his role as
an N.A.A.C.P. official, he traveled extensively across the
nation. In the following essay, he recounts some of the
conditions he found as well as some that were reported
to him in the South regarding race discrimination. This
essay was published in September 1929.

It is Mississippi. "*The* River" is on its annual rampage. Wastes of water
spread over the landscape. Houses are submerged up to the second
story. Boats have replaced automobiles and buggies. Boys and women
and a few white men fish for "cat" where the plow stood a few weeks
ago. At any time, any and every Negro may be impressed to save the
levees. Now convicts from all over the state are assembled under
prison guards to strengthen levees and railroad embankments. Bags of
concrete are piled high while the sullen yellow river gnaws at the banks
like a hungry rat. Everywhere there is unrest and an atmosphere of fear
and suspense. Along with it is irritation and a sullen ugliness of temper occasioned by the frustration of hopes.

The railroad embankment runs like a ribbon flanked by the flowing
waters—but as we get away from Vicksburg we find fields above
ground. Looking out of my car window as my train scuttled across the
state as if it feared the rising waters might engulf it, I was riveted by a
scene in the field opposite me. A Negro was desperately fleeing. Behind him ran two white men. I saw the flashes of their pistols as they
fired at him. All at once, he stumbled, threw up both arms and fell. In
a moment he was on his feet once more. Again, the two whites running
towards him blazed away, as he haltingly fled before them. My train
whisked me out of sight and I shall never know whether the Negro was
killed. He probably was. Who were the whites—officers or civilians? I

shall never know. I scanned the papers for days afterwards but saw no word of what had happened. When I told my friend in Louisiana, he merely shrugged his shoulders and said—"Why, that was merely an incident"—a common one. "The world never hears of many things like that." In Baton Rouge they told me how Negroes dared not report whippings and lynchings. Right across the river, a few days before I reached that city, a Negro working in front of the home of a white butcher indulged his proclivity to oaths and obscene language, so the butcher's wife proclaimed. At any rate, her husband, when she told him, got together a gang of his friends and took the Negro out and lynched him. Nobody was arrested. No inquest was held. No newspaper carried any account. It was just another dead Negro. Negroes say the woman has lost her mind since and has been committed to an insane asylum—but that may be only a myth. They whispered dark things and hint that the lynched Negro's profanity was not what really angered the woman.

In the upper part of Louisiana—as in most places of the South—the whites believe that Chief Justice Taney's decision that "a Negro has no rights which a white man is bound to respect" yet holds. A Negro sued the parish for damages he had suffered. His was a good case. Therefore, persons close to the affairs of the parish determined to settle the matter out of court. They took him for a ride, flogged him until his clothing had been cut to ribbons and his back was in shreds, broke his arm, threw him out in the road and ordered him never to return to the parish. The encouraging thing is that he has courage enough to continue his fight in court. I understand, too, action is to be started against his assailants whom he recognized, it is stated, as officers of the parish.

But it is "the magic city" of Birmingham which holds the prize for terrorism. There police and courts are run by that order of thugs—the Ku Klux Klan. Without provocation police shoot Negroes so frequently there, that it is no longer news. Negroes are beaten up daily for standing on the streets. Recently the police killed a school teacher because he was standing on a corner and didn't move with sufficient alacrity at their orders. Somewhile before, they found an undertaker asleep in his own car at night, in front of the house in which he was boarding. Thieves somewhile before had stripped his car of tires. He decided to sleep in it so as to guard against further theft. Two police officers came along late in the night and saw him asleep with his pistol on the seat between his legs. They put a gun to his breast and fired, killing him instantly, and then woke the people in the house and told what they had done. What was done about it? Nothing! When the N. A. A. C. P. offered to send an investigator concerning this and other atrocities, prominent Negro citizens of Birmingham insisted that he should not be sent.

In fact, Negroes are so afraid in Birmingham that out of twenty-four outstanding persons written to about reorganizing the work of the Association there, not one answered. They frankly tell you—"We are afraid." An aura of fear that presses upon one like a black cloud surrounds Negroes in this city. They have wealth and live in nice houses but they cringe before whites and curry favor with the whites in power by sacrificing all their rights. There are a few exceptions among the younger men.

Not only are the police brutal and sadistic, but the civilians are of the same type. A short while ago in one of Birmingham's suburbs a young Negro woman, a college graduate from a well-to-do family, went into a drug store a block or so from her home. The clerk ignored her presence and waited on several white persons who had come into the store after her entrance. She started to leave. Upon this, the clerk burst into abuse and slapped her. The girl ran to her home and told her brother, an undertaker and a graduate of Howard University. When he ran to the drug store an officer in the doorway seized him as he attempted to enter. Back in the store stood another officer and the clerk, both with drawn pistols. The young Negro and his sister were arrested and charged with disorderly conduct. The man was given a suspended sentence and the woman was fined $10 for being slapped. The young undertaker procured a warrant against the white drug clerk for assaulting his sister but the charge was dismissed.

Down in South Georgia at Americus some one reported that liquor was being sold in a restaurant. In Americus there are no comfort stations for Negroes—only whites. A hard working respectable Negro, from the country, had gone into this restaurant at the demands of nature. He was just coming out when the police entered and an officer drew his gun and pushed it in the Negro's stomach as he tried to pass him. The colored man, believing the officer about to shoot, grabbed the gun and prevented him using it. He was about to twist it from the officer's hand, when the brave representative of the law yelled for help. Two officers rushed to his aid and putting their guns against the body of the Negro emptied them, killing him. Nothing has been done about it although our branch there is trying to push the case.

They tell me that Tennessee is much better. But they also told me how two fine colored women, one a school teacher, were held up on the road between Murfreesboro and Nashville and raped. A white man acted as witness for them and our branch in Nashville prosecuted. But Tennessee has no intermediate punishment for rape—it's death or acquittal. And it would not do for a jury to send a white man to the electric chair for raping Negro women. So the jury acquitted them. They were then rearrested and charged with having liquor in their car and sentenced to the chain gang. Thus the conscience of white justice in Tennessee was salved.

Up in Rome, Ga., a little colored boy of eight and a little white girl of seven were playing together. It began to rain and the children ran into an open church for shelter. A timid and suspicious Negro janitor saw them and called a policeman. This guardian of the law knew things criminal must be going on when a black boy dared to play with a white girl. He arrested the boy and charged him with rape. There was no evidence of anything wrong—but nevertheless the colored boy was sentenced to the reformatory until he shall be twenty-one years of age.

This is a black picture but there is another side. Here and there white citizens are protesting and acting against these injustices. In the country side countless atrocities occur of which the world never hears. Negroes dare not speak. But now and then as in the case of Eros, La., white men both speak and act. Their numbers steadily increase. Added to these are the new whites of the South we find occupying some of the chairs in the universities and colleges and the great number of Southern white college students who have come to the light as the result of the interracial conferences in colleges. Many of these have thrown on the scrap heap the traditional views of the white South as to race relations. Down in a college center in Tennessee white and colored college students met regularly, ate, drank, discussed and played together—even to the extent of dancing until a nasty newspaper article frightened the authorities in their schools. I know Southern whites who are as much at home teaching in Negro schools as any of their colored colleagues and just as free in their relations. I know Southern whites who have given up father, mother, home and hopes of inheritance, in order to cling to their beliefs, that men and women are to be made comrades on the basis of congeniality regardless of color. "My father died in my arms without forgiving me," said one of these to me, "because of my position on race matters but I am happy, for I have found something worthwhile in life."

And the number of these is increasing in geometrical ratio. The University of Georgia admits colored students to its summer school now and gives them full credit towards a degree for the work done. In certain places one finds anomalies that astonish. I stopped with a

Negro physician in a town in central Georgia whose practice was sixty per cent white. He was called into white homes to deliver children without any fear of public opinion for any hesitancy. Yet his brown face clearly evidenced his race to the most casual observer. In this same town, I was told of a remarkably queer situation. On its outskirts a Negro trusty ran a store for both races. The only objection his white neighbors had to him was that this convict trusty dressed in the height of fashion *and wore spats*!

The most hopeful thing in the South, however, is the growing realization of colored people that without organization destined to mould public opinion, to modify laws and to gain justice in courts and safety of life, limb and property, Negroes can have no freedom nor ending of danger. If they get wealth they will be only rich serfs.

Along with this is the rapidly spreading conviction that a voteless people must be a powerless people. Birmingham has nearly eighty thousand Negroes. Not 300 vote Registrars crossly refuse them. Few persist in their attempts to register or insist.

Mobile has thirty thousand Negroes and only one hundred fifty-five vote. And this is indicative of the entire South with the exception of a few places. Nowhere in the South can be found a place where Negroes vote in representative numbers. Hence the judge whose office is not at all affected by the Negro vote often gives a colored boy ten years for an offense for which a white boy receives a sentence of one year. School boards whose tenure of office is not affected by Negro votes; police commissioners, sheriffs, town councils forget the rights and needs of Negroes because Negroes can do nothing towards putting them in or casting them out. Segregation ordinances would seldom have to be fought in courts at large costs if Negroes voted and could defeat councilmen who favored such ordinances. Where Negroes vote in any numbers, paving, lighting and sewerage in their districts improve, schools become better, justice more frequent. The South would be transformed if Negroes would organize to secure the ballot and use it to vote for friends of the race and against its enemies. They would have to fight for a while in courts. In some instances they would at times have to run certain physical risks. But if freedom is worthwhile, what are risks? And here is one way to freedom for the Negro in the South.

In the past, the dyed-in-the-wool Republican Negro leaders, often professional politicians, have guided them into a morass. The Republican party has been the party of blacks and the Democratic, that of whites. Hence whites have had corruption, robbery, and demagoguery and the blacks have been holding to a shadow. When Negroes in the South vote for friends without regard to party, the South will become normal in its political status—a two party region. When a sufficient number of Negroes are Democrats, it will become respectable for whites to be Republicans, for both parties will contain both races. The obvious reason why, in municipal and state politics, Negroes in the South should vote in the Democratic primary and election was well expressed by my friend who said to me: "No one can be elected here except a Democrat. A Republican has just as much chance to be elected here as a celluloid cat would have in an attempt to catch an asbestos mouse in hell. We mean to support the most friendly Democrat, and if he fails us, we will do our best to put him out." When Negroes everywhere in the South realize this and act upon it a new day will come for whites and blacks in that region.

AFRICA–OUR CHALLENGE

Susie Wiseman Yergan, wife of Y.M.C.A. official and activist Max Yergan, was the first African-American woman to work in Africa. In the following essay she relates a firsthand account of the social, cultural, and political conditions facing the continent. She also addresses what was being done to implement change. This essay was published in June 1930.

Africa which centuries ago lost step in the march of civilization is now forced once again into the line of procession. Whether she desires it or not, the impact of Western Civilization is upon her, compelling her to proceed in its direction or be trampled under foot. Although she can not yet advance with the same strides as the West, yet it cannot be denied that she is progressing. Her pace is necessarily tedious and irksome because the road over which she must travel is perhaps the stoniest in the world today, and the obstructions she must overcome are some of the greatest man has to encounter.

She moves forward so slowly that she appears to be merely marking time. Therefore it seems that those of us whose steps are a little quicker and firmer should reach out a hand to help her on this arduous march. This is a real challenge which we as American Negroes cannot well afford to ignore. It is true that as yet, we are just finding our own stride, for we face many of the same difficulties, but because of our long contact with Western civilization and the bitter experience through which we passed, we are better prepared to face them. Too, I believe that one great stimulus to advancement is self-sacrifice. When we are willing to help carry the burdens of the weaker along with our own, we will gain more strength as we go on our way. Africa realizes the superior advantage of her American brothers and sisters and is looking to them to help her, if all others fail.

Europe and America are just within recent years realizing the magnitude of Africa and the vastness of her potential wealth. This continent is said to be no less than one fifth of the land area of the world. It is three times as large as Europe and half again as large as the continent of North America. This huge continent which is the home of the black races is so chopped up and divided among the European powers that the native races, with the possible exception of those within the few Mandates, are foreigners in their own country. The country is in reality an immense extension of the continent of Europe. It is said that in the nineteenth century the population of Europe increased threefold. This meant an enlarged demand for food, for more abundant supplies of raw material, and for new markets for the products of the factories. Then there was a great scramble by the powers of Europe for the possession of Africa whose mineral, agricultural, as well as animal wealth make it one of the most valuable quarters of the globe.

South Africa, where the climate is delightful for the greater part of the year and where the scenery is beautiful and inspiring, is a lovely garden spot for the Europeans who come to settle permanently in the country. After the over crowded conditions in Europe where the struggle for existence is keen, it is a paradise. This is true of the poorer classes who go out there to better their conditions. Although certain parts of Africa are unhealthy to the white man, South Africa is a resort for some of the health seekers of Europe. For various reasons Europeans have gone to South Africa to the extent of a million and a half.

The problems of South Africa are some of the most perplexing in the world today. These problems are created by this sudden impact of what is considered a highly developed civilization upon the lives of peoples for the most part in the primitive stages of human development. The Western capital which is being poured into the country to develop her rich resources creates a perplexing economic problem. The government of one people by another presents a complicated political problem. The presence of a European population attempting to make a permanent settlement in the country alongside of a race whose background is essentially different develops an acute racial problem.

Lord Balfour once said that the economic, political and racial problems are all inter-connected so that they constitute a problem novel in history to which there is no precedent or parallel in the memory or experience of man. The difficulties of the African brought about by the European in South Africa are very real indeed. The Negro appreciates the benefits arising from occupation such as the suppression of human sacrifice, or incessant warfare and of slavery. The introduction of roads and railways have been a boon to the progress of the people. Trade, Education and Medical service have all contributed to the prosperity of the country. It is also true that Mission work can be carried on more effectively than before. The African realizes these benefits from the European; but at the same time he knows that he has lost so much that he will have to change his whole outlook on life in order to fit into the new state of things. He finds that his ancient customs, beliefs and social organizations have all been destroyed. He is left bewildered and devoid of anything to guide him over the confusing road Europe has mapped out for him.

The West which has such a superiority complex that it is difficult for her to understand the value of that which is unlike her own, does not realize the value of Africa's past heritage. Africa had a culture all her own. It was not necessarily inferior to Western culture but rather it was different. Since culture is said to be adapted to its environment and is in a certain degree created by it, the African had real culture—the full expression of racial life. His social organization was simple but adjusted to the needs of his simple life. His code of ethics embodied some of the highest ideals. For instance, the "Lobola Custom", which means the exchange of cattle for the bride, viewed superficially, is considered a mercenary act, yet it has a deeper ethical significance in that it insures protection to the bride. I know certain well educated girls who still hold that they want to be Lobolaed.

The African had his art. His sculpture is now attracting the interest of the West. His music, though not well known, deserves high appreciation. His imagination had found adequate expression, in an almost inexhaustible store of folk-lore which is often real poetry. In the caves of the Zimbabwe ruins I found not only paintings on the walls but also gold ornaments which showed that Africa had its culture.

Now in South Africa this heritage has been lost and the very foundation of the African's life has been swept from under him. He is left impoverished, bewildered and confused. He cannot follow the old lines which are broken, but he must follow new lines of Western civilization.

It is true that there are great regions in South Africa where primitive conditions still prevail; where the African still lives and works much as his forefathers did under a modified tribal rule. There are also large agricultural regions which are the natural home of conservative traditions, but the general system of government forced upon him is that of a highly civilized country.

The old system of tribal rule, with all of its defects, was suited to the needs of a primitive people. The presence of the European in the country has caused a gradual decay of this system. This tribal disintegration has brought about dangers and difficulties with which the Africans have been unable to cope. Numbers of them who have broken away from tribal life have sunk into a condition of misery and social degradation.

Under the ancient tribal system, the African had enough land for his needs because the struggle for existence was not keen. When that land proved worthless he moved on to another place and built his hut; but now the reserves where he can live are over crowded and the land often inferior. Very little is done to train him as an agriculturist. Therefore he can scarcely make a livelihood for his family from the soil.

When droughts, which prevail in many parts of South Africa, come as they have done in the last four years, he almost starves. When I and my husband returned to South Africa, the country had passed through a serious drought. As we rode along on the trains it was a sad sight to see the little nude children whose protruding ribs and thin legs showed signs of extreme hunger. Every time the train stopped, they ran along its side begging us to throw out the remnants of our lunch to them. When we did so they scrambled in the dust hungrily searching for the least morsel. At such time as this, the hospitals are filled to overflowing.

The result of this land system is that men must go away for periods of several months at a time while the women struggle on with the family at home. The young men who go to the mines form the largest single groups. It is said that annually they average 180,000 of the best specimens of manhood between the ages of 18 and 30, south of the Zambesi. In these great mining centers we find them herded together in the close, unsanitary quarters, imbibing the immoralities of the lowest classes of Europeans and catching their diseases. Very often they return broken in health or perhaps injured by some accident. One of our most frequent visitors was a blind man, 40 years old, who lost his sight by an explosion in the mines and was paid $100 for the injury. These figures indicate the dangerous character of the mine: during the years 1916–21 inclusive 15,954 casualties occurred, the deaths being 2,936. The commonest source of accident is overhanging rock. During the same period 18,331 died of disease. This is a great sacrifice to the race when one considers that the workers are chosen from the best physical types of manhood. There is some improvement in conditions since that time but still the death total is heavy.

The females also flock to these areas by the thousands and sink along with the males into the lowest depths of shame and degradation.

Drink and illicit liquor traffic are some of the overwhelming evils. Not only the men and women drink, but young children. Women because of the cut of their garments conduct illicit liquor traffic more successfully than men and more are engaged in it. Fatal brawls are frequent. It is said that in one school of a hundred children, only fifteen or twenty pupils came from homes having paternal protection.

Besides finding employment in the mines, big strapping men accept employment as household servants in certain parts of South Africa. Although they may be bearded men, these "boys" as they are called, perform the tasks of cook, housemaid, and even nurse maid. It is estimated that about 50,000 of them are admitted to European homes during the course of eighteen months. Since sweeping, dusting, making beds and the like, are duties which take them through all parts of the house during any part of the day, they are often exposed to immodesty and indiscretion on the part of the women of these homes. This tends to lower their respect not only for these women but for all womanhood. These male household servants morally and spiritually are a neglected group.

The change from a primitive, pastoral life in the free open country where there is plenty of sunshine and fresh air to the squalid crowded slums in the cities creates a situation calamitous to the race, for these people are in every way unprepared for the sudden transition. Contrasted with the simple life in the kraal huts, we find them huddled together in iron shanties, sometimes eight or ten living in one room. One writer has said that in Johannesburg the slums are so disgraceful and immoral that the thought of them murders sleep. The conditions under which people live in locations outside of South African towns are awful beyond description. We do not say that the old life was always pure and clean but it was wholesome compared with this slum life.

Before the advent of the European into the country, the amount of work that the African did was regulated by his immediate needs which were not great. In South Africa cattle breeding was his chief occupation. This easy pastoral life together with the climate had such an effect upon his character that it is exceedingly difficult for him to make adaptation to regular work under modern conditions. Accustomed to a world without clocks, where time is of little consequence, and where they can do what they like and when they like, the regular and persistent methods of European industry soon become irksome to them, so that they must go home and rest a while. They are therefore accused of Indolence and are paid a very low wage for their work.

Under changed conditions when the African's life is no longer simple and primitive, he finds it very difficult to make a livelihood for his family on the low wage he receives. When his maximum wage may be $15 per month it is very hard for him to feed a family which may consist of a wife and from 5 to 7 children especially when civilization demands that he adopt European dress, etc. When he has to pay from four to five dollars for a bag of corn, which is his staple diet, it is barely possible for the family to exist.

Again the Color Bar Bill, which was passed in 1926, discourages his efforts to become a skilled laborer, for he would hardly be given a certificate by the government which would entitle him to seek employment. This Color Bar Bill was introduced as a measure of protection to the 130,000 "poor whites" whose degeneracy is assumed to be due to the black man's competition and upward rise. It is a cruel blow to the African for it condemns him always to bottom unskilled work while the skilled work to which he naturally aspires is reserved for the white man.

The health of the people is greatly affected by this new life for they not only suffer from their own diseases, with which many of the witch doctors could very well cope, but they suffer from the diseases of the white man; these the African does not understand. Therefore tuberculosis, sleeping sickness and the like play havoc with the people, whose poverty and ignorance do not allow them proper medical attention. The death rate is high especially among children.

Under the changed conditions the people do not know how to care for children properly for they know nothing of disease, germs, flies, mosquitoes, etc. One day I read these startling figures: In one year, of the 575 born at Port Elizabeth 154 died; at East London, of 597 born, 131 died; at Johannesburg, of 470 born, 173 died. All these deaths occurred before the age of twelve months. One report I read showed an infant death-rate at Johannesburg of 455 deaths per thousand against 60 per thousand in a European town a mile away. In the same year in an enlightened country like England only 12 out of a thousand died. These are some of the appalling situations in South Africa.

Although I said South Africa has lost heavily, and because of her impoverished condition there is moral and physical degeneracy, yet we believe the trend is upward. The missionaries who have borne the burden these long years are seeing results. Out of the scanty funds which are provided largely by the poor in their homelands, they have carried on the work in spite of indifference, oft times opposition. They even persevered when the African himself saw no need of mission work. As a result the young Africans are clamoring for education. It is through this group of students that we hope to help Africa find her way over her precipitous roads.

Another important aspect of our work has been along interracial lines, for the hope of Africa rests not only with the African students but with the European students who will perhaps have the largest responsibility in shaping her destiny. At first it was barely possible to get a hearing but now Mr. Yergan has responded to pressing invitations to address large European gatherings in the colleges of South Africa. It is encouraging to find numbers of these Christian students not only willing to study these situations concerning the welfare of the Africans, but actually ready to pay the price.

In a small conference at Lovedale both European and African students met and it was a joy to see how frankly and fearlessly both groups discussed the most delicate interracial questions. At a European student conference in a small Dutch village, Mr. Yergan spoke in a public meeting at the city hall. When he had finished some of the most conservative of the older Dutchmen mounted the rostrum and shook his hand, tears almost streaming down their cheeks, and exclaimed that they now saw this whole racial problem in a new light and intended to live their last years according to that light. Truly great spiritual forces are at work in Africa even as they are in other parts of the world today. It is the dawn of a new day for Africa.

Our task now is to try to raise up among the students we reach through our associations a number of strong leaders who will give their lives unreservedly to the people in the years to come. This we believe to be a new era upon which we are now entering and this era will demand well educated, deeply consecrated, inspired men and women who will lead the people. We hope our movement will soon be in position to provide this leadership.

The building which we hope to erect at Fort Hare will serve not only as headquarters for the work (I might say just here that our headquarters are now on our back veranda), but also a training center for this new leadership. We hope that this building will serve as a kind of experimental laboratory for trying out different types of social work.

In the second place it is now time to begin a type of work for the nonstudent groups who live in the town. If we do not then the purpose of this leadership will be lost. The Associations will be the channels through which inspired, trained men may guide the lives of other young Africans. Something of this kind is so much needed for this nonstudent class of young people. It is a deplorable sight to see them gathered on the street corners at night and on Sunday afternoons with nothing to do, for life for them is meaningless and purposeless.

Next, an effort must soon be made to begin work in the rural districts. For, after all, the masses of the people are still in these sections and it is a dreary life too. As we ride through these sections we always feel the loneliness of it. Sometimes one sees no sign of human life—bare huts—not a shrub or bush, a few straggly chickens, and nothing else. The people are inside the huts with nothing to do. This kind of life for bright, vigorous youth is sad and monotonous.

With my mind's eye I can see all these types of work going on during the next twenty-five years. In this transitional period of Africa from the old to the new life the Young Men's Christian Associations have a wonderful opportunity to help a great race in the making. As Dr. Mott said to the Student Federation: "Now is the time to get into Africa on the ground floor". If we lose this opportunity, it may not come again.

I have a mental picture of the needs which are tremendous. A great race with a heritage lost; its foundations of life swept away; left empty of soul, impoverished, bewildered, confused. On the other hand, a Christian student group inspired, ready to consecrate their lives to their people, just waiting to be trained and used. Again a nonstudent city group steeped in ignorance and poverty living an aimless life. Then the country youth full of life and vigor, yet living an idle, dreary life. And yet these are people, human beings, living in a great age, moved and controlled by great forces.

Again there is another picture—I speak in a detached way—A man with a vision; unable to sleep because of that vision; a man on the field well prepared because of his long experience, and by reason of his great love for Africa and yet bound fast by inhibitions which can be easily removed. I hear him crying out, a long voice in the wilderness, not only for financial aid, but for a man, yea, men to help him. During the great war, that same voice cried out for help in East Africa and three men answered the call. Then peril lurked on land and sea and yet these men volunteered for Y. M. C. A. work. Two gave their lives for Africa and only one returned to tell the story.

Biographical Notes of Contributors

Bagnall, Robert W. (1864–1943), clergyman and civil-rights worker, was born in Norfolk, Virginia. He was educated at Bishop Payne Divinity School (Virginia) and was ordained an Episcopal priest in 1903. He served pastorates in Pennsylvania, Maryland, and Ohio. In 1921, Bagnall became director of branches for the N.A.A.C.P. In 1931, he accepted the pastorate of Saint Thomas's Episcopal Church in Philadelphia. Bagnall was a man of broad knowledge and possessed great writing and oratory skills. His writings appeared mainly in *The Crisis.*

Bennett, Gwendolyn (1902–1981), painter, writer, and educator, was the daughter of a Texas lawyer. She refined her artistic talents through fine-arts study at Columbia University, the Pratt Institute, and in France. Upon her return to the United States, she became assistant editor of the Urban League's *Opportunity.* Bennett contributed short stories and poems to *American Mercury, The Crisis, The Messenger, Opportunity,* and *Fire.* She taught art at Howard University and was director of the Harlem Community Art Center from 1937 to 1940.

Bond, Horace Mann (1904–1972), educator, author, and college president, was born in Nashville, Tennessee. Bond received his B.A., M.A., and Ph.D. from the University of Chicago. He taught at a number of colleges before serving as president of Lincoln University (Pennsylvania) from 1945 to 1957. His books include *The Education of the Negro in the American Social Order* (1934). He was the father of the present N.A.A.C.P. board chairman, Julian Bond.

Bonner, Marita O. (1899–1971), essayist, poet, and educator, was born and educated in Brookline, Massachusetts. She graduated from Radcliffe College with a degree in English and comparative literature. She contributed a number of prize-winning essays to *The Crisis* and *Opportunity.* Following teaching positions at Bluefield Colored Institution in Virginia and Armstrong High School in Washington, D.C., she married accountant William Occomy and moved to Chicago, where she taught at Philips High School and the Doolittle School for the Educationally Retarded.

Bontemps, Arna (1907–1972), poet, librarian, and novelist, was born in Alexandria, Louisiana. He moved with his family at the age of three to Los Angeles. Educated at San Fernando Academy and Pacific Union College, in 1924 he moved to Harlem, where he was soon welcomed into the "Talented Tenth" club, was published, and received awards for poetry from both *Opportunity* and *The Crisis* as well as a Rosenwald fellowship for Caribbean travel. Following some career-enhancing collaborations with Countee Cullen, Harold Arlen, and Langston Hughes, he spent his final years as curator of the James Weldon Johnson Memorial Collection of Negro Arts and Letters at Yale University.

Braithwaite, William Stanley (1878–1962), poet, educator, and literary critic, was born in Boston, Massachusetts. Educated at home, Braithwaite became interested in literature while working in a bookstore. From 1908 to 1929, he was literary editor of the *Boston Transcripts.* His publications include *Selected Poems* (1946) and an autobiography, *The House under Arcturus* (1941). He was a recipient of the N.A.A.C.P.'s coveted Spingarn Medal.

Brawley, Benjamin Griffith (1882–1934), educator and author, was born in Columbia, South Carolina. He received B.A.s from Morehouse College (1901) and from the University of Chicago (1906) and an M.A. from Howard University in 1908. He taught at a number of colleges and universities, including Howard University, Morehouse College, and Shaw University (Raleigh, North Carolina). His books include: *A Short History of the American Negro* (1913); *A Social History of the American Negro* (1921); *The Negro in Literature and Art* (1918); and *A Short History of the English Drama* (1921).

Brown, Sterling (1901–1989), poet, critic, folklorist, and educator, was born in the District of Columbia, where he graduated from the famed Dunbar High School. He was elected Phi Beta Kappa while earning a B.A. from Williams College and an M.A. from Harvard University. Following positions at Virginia Seminary, Lincoln University in Missouri, Fisk University, and Howard University, he published his first book of poetry. Through the greater part of the 1930s, he was literary editor of *Opportunity* and served as Negro-affairs editor for the Federal Writers Project.

Chesnutt, Charles W. (1854–1932), essayist, educator, and novelist, was born in Cleveland, Ohio. He was educated in Cleveland and in North Carolina. He served as principal of the State Normal School in Fayetteville, North Carolina, beginning in 1880. While serving as principal, he studied shorthand dictation and ultimately landed a job as a legal stenographer for Dow Jones. During this period, he published his first short story, "The Gophered Grapevines." This work was followed by a volume of short stories. Praised by the great literary critic William Dean Howells, Chesnutt is considered by some to have been the first serious craftsman among African-American writers.

Coleman, Anita Scott (1890–1960), poet, short-story writer, and essayist, was born in the city of Guaymas, Mexico. Her father, a Cuban, purchased her mother as a slave. Coleman was educated in the school system of Silver City, New Mexico. She published in *The Crisis, Opportunity,* the *Messenger, Flash,* and other magazines. Under the pseudonym Elizabeth Stapleton Stokes, she published a book of poems: *Small Wisdom* (1937).

Corrothers, James D. (1869–1917), was born in Cass County, Michigan. He worked in the mills and lumber camps of his native state. He was also a sailor, a coachman, and a janitor. He entered the ministry and remained in this profession throughout his life. He authored two volumes of poetry: *Selected Poems* (1907) and *The Dream and the Song* (1914).

Cotter, Joseph Seamon, Jr. (1895–1919), poet and playwright, was born in Louisville, Kentucky. He attended Fisk University for one year. He left during his second year because of tuberculosis. Most of his poems were written during his illness. His work showed great promise, but unfortunately his life was cut short. He died at the age of twenty-four.

Cotter, Joseph S., Sr. (1861–1949), poet and essayist, was the illegitimate son of a prominent white citizen in Louisville, Kentucky. Cotter spent his early adolescence as poor ragpicker, brick maker, and cotton and tobacco picker. After completing his education during an intense period of night study, he eventually became principal of the local high school. Inspired by poet-scholar Paul Laurence Dunbar, Cotter began to write and publish his own dramatic, autobiographical, and poetic writings in magazines such as *The Crisis* and *Opportunity.*

Cullen, Countee (1903–1946), poet, essayist, and educator, was the adopted son of the prominent Harlem minister Reverend Frederick Cullen. Though born in Lexington, Kentucky, he attended De Witt Clinton High School in New York City, where he was editor of the school newspaper. His first poetry was published at age fifteen. Cullen earned his B.A. and election to Phi Beta Kappa at New York University and his M.A. in English at Harvard. He received the Witter Bynner Poetry Prize at New York University, the Harmon Foundation Gold Medal Award, *Opportunity* poetry prizes, and in 1928, the first Guggenheim fellowship awarded to an African American. He taught in the public-school system of New York City.

Davis, Allison (1902–1983), psychologist, educator, and author, was born in Washington, D.C. He received a B.A. from Williams College in 1924, a B.A. from Howard University in 1925, and his Ph.D. from the University of Chicago in 1942. He taught at the University of Chicago, Columbia University, the University of Michigan, the University of California at Berkeley, and the University of Illinois. Davis's writings include *Children of Bondage*, coauthored with John Dollard (1940), and *Psychology of the Child in the Middle Class* (1960). He also contributed many essays to professional journals.

Dett, R. [Robert] Nathaniel (1882–1943), composer and college choir director, was born in Drummondsville, Ontario, Canada. The Dett family moved to Niagara Falls in 1893. He received a Bachelor of Music degree in composition and piano. Dett taught at Lane College, Lincoln Institute, and Hampton Institute. His published compositions include five piano suites and eight Bible vignettes; forty or more choral works; two orations; twenty-four vocal solos; one violin solo; and two collections of Negro spirituals.

Diton, Carl (1886–1969), musician and educator, was born in Philadelphia, Pennsylvania. He graduated from the University of Pennsylvania in 1909 and did further study in Germany. Between 1911 and 1918, he was director of music at Paine College in Georgia. After 1918, he returned to Philadelphia, where he held concerts and continued to teach. His works include "Four Spirituals" (1914) and the oratorio "The Hymn of Nebraska" (1921).

Du Bois, William Edward Burghardt (1868–1963), historian, sociologist, novelist, essayist, editor, civil-rights leader, and educator, was born in Great Barrington, Massachusetts. As an undergraduate, he matriculated at Fisk and Harvard Universities, earned an M.A. in history from Harvard, studied at the University of Berlin for two years on a grant from the Slater Fund, and was the first African American to receive a Ph.D. from Harvard, in 1896. Following two years of research at the University of Pennsylvania, he produced one of the first studies of urban sociology in the United States. His many moving and insightful books and essays cemented his roles as principal opponent of Booker T. Washington and fiery exponent of civil rights for African Americans. Du Bois was the first editor of *The Crisis* for the N.A.A.C.P. and, as such, was a major influence on black writers and cultural activists during the Harlem Renaissance.

Fauset, Arthur Huff (1899–1983), author, was born in Flemington, New Jersey. He received his B.A., M.A., and Ph.D. from the University of

Pennsylvania. He was a teacher and principal in the public schools of Philadelphia between 1918 and 1946. His books include *Sojourner Truth: God's Faithful Pilgrim* (1938) and *Black Gods of the Metropolis: Negro Religious Cults of the Urban North* (1944).

Fauset, Jessie (1882–1961), essayist, poet, teacher, and novelist, was born into a prominent old Philadelphia family. She graduated with honors and was elected to Phi Beta Kappa at Cornell University, earned an M.A. in romance languages from the University of Pennsylvania, and studied at the Sorbonne. She taught Latin and French at Washington, D.C.'s academically rigorous Dunbar High School but is most noted for her extensive affiliation with *The Crisis*, where she became literary editor. She excelled as a prolific novelist and was convinced of the power of "arts and letters" to help extirpate racial prejudice and change the chemistry of race relations in the United States.

Fisher, Rudolph (1897–1934), physician, roentgenologist, musician, and novelist, was born in Washington, D.C., but was reared in Providence, Rhode Island. He graduated Phi Beta Kappa from Brown University. He received his M.D. at Howard University but completed two years of specialized training in biology at Columbia University's College of Physicians and Surgeons. He then moved to Harlem, where he began writings novels, short stories, and essays, which were published in magazines such as *The Atlantic Monthly, The American Mercury, McClure's, The Crisis*, and *Opportunity*. Fisher also served as an arranger for many years of the Negro spirituals sung by Paul Robeson. He eventually died from the chronic effects of exposure to his own X-ray machines.

Frazier, E. [Edward] Franklin (1894–1962), educator, sociologist, and author, was born in Baltimore, Maryland. He graduated with honors from Howard University, earned an M.A. in sociology from Clark University in Atlanta, and received his Ph.D. from the University of Chicago. Frazier taught at Atlanta and Fisk Universities and was chairman of the Sociology Department at Howard University. Though primarily an educator and sociologist, he wrote insightful essays that appeared in *The Journal of Social Forces, The Nation, The Crisis*, and *Opportunity*. His books include: *The Negro Family in Chicago* (1932); *Traditions and Patterns of Negro Family Life* (1934); and *The Negro in the United States* (1949). His most popular and controversial book was *Black Bourgeoise* (1957).

Hare, Maud Cuney (1874–1936), pianist and author, was born in Galveston, Texas. She received her musical training at the New England Conservatory in Boston, Massachusetts. She served as director of music at the Deaf, Dumb, and Blind Institute of Texas. Her books include: *Creole Folk-Songs* (1921), *Negro Musicians and Their Music* (1936), and *The Message of the Trees* (1918).

Hill, Leslie Pinckney (1880–1960), educator and poet, was born in Lynchburg, Virginia. He received a B.A. (1903) and M.A. (1904) from Harvard University. He taught at the Tuskegee Institute and Manassass Industrial Training School and was president of Cheyney State College (Pennsylvania) for twenty years. He authored *Wings of Oppression* (1921) and *Toussaint L'Ouverture: A Dramatic History* (1928).

Horne, Frank (1899–1974), physician, public official, and poet, was born in New York City. He graduated from the City College of the City University of New York in 1921. Horne received a degree in ophthalmology from Northern Illinois College of Ophthalmology and Otology in 1923. He joined the staff of Fort Valley State College (Georgia) as dean and for a time was acting president. Among his publications is a book of poems, *Haverstraw* (1963).

Hughes, [James] Langston (1902–1967), poet, playwright, novelist, anthologist, and historian, was born in Joplin, Missouri. His parents separated when he was a child. His maternal grandfather was the abolitionist Charles Langston, who fought with John Brown at Harper's Ferry. He was a half-brother of John Mercer Langston, U.S. congressman from Virginia. While his childhood was rather peripatetic, his literary talents brought him notice in elementary and secondary schools. As a merchant seaman, Hughes saw much of the world. He was "discovered" by poet Vachel Lindsay as a "busboy poet" in Washington, D.C. Having dropped out of college at Columbia University, he returned to Lincoln University with the financial assistance of Amy Spingarn, wife of the N.A.A.C.P. board chairman, J. E. Spingarn. His touching and lyrical poetry won him notice from both jazz and literary patrons; but he began to lose favor after he chose voluntary exile for a time in Cuba, Russia, and Spain. He later collaborated with Arna Bontemps on anthologies and children's works and funded theater groups in Harlem, Chicago, and Los Angeles.

Jamison, Roscoe C. (1888–1918), poet and essayist, was born in Winchester, Tennessee. James Weldon Johnson wrote that Jamison falls into the class of poets of one poem because his poem "The Negro Soldiers" stands so far above all else that he wrote.

Johnson, Charles Bertram (1880–?), educator, minister, and poet, was born in Callao, Missouri. He was educated in the public schools of his native town and at Western College, Lincoln Institute, and the

University of Chicago. He authored two pamphlets of poetry—
Wind Whisperings (1900) and *The Mantle of Dunbar* (1918)—and one
volume, *Songs of My People* (1918).

Johnson, Fenton (1888–1958), playwright, poet, and editor, was referred
to by James Weldon Johnson as "one of the first Negro revolutionary poets." While yet in his teens, several of his plays were per-
formed by the repertory company at Chicago's Old Pekin Theatre.
He was later publisher of his own magazines, *Correct English* and the
crusading monthly *The Champion Magazine.* Johnson attended college in his hometown at the University of Chicago, as well as at
Northwestern University. He also spent some time at Columbia
University's School of Journalism.

Johnson, Georgia Douglas (1886–1966), poet, essayist, and educator, was
educated at the Oberlin Conservatory of Music and Atlanta Uni-
versity, where she met and married her husband, Henry Lincoln
Johnson. They settled in Washington, D.C., where she was employed
by the federal government and he became a prominent figure in the
Republican party. Georgia Douglas Johnson was a founder of "The
First Nighters," a literary club whose membership included Mary
Miller, Angelina Weld Grimké, Alain Locke, Jean Toomer, Richard
Bruce Nugent, James Weldon Johnson, W. E. B. Du Bois, Jessie
Fauset, and Langston Hughes. She was the first African-American
woman to be widely recognized as a poet in the early twentieth cen-
tury, received considerable acclaim as a poet and teacher, and won a
first prize in an *Opportunity* contest for one of her plays.

Johnson, James Weldon (1871–1938), poet, educator, novelist, lawyer,
diplomat, newspaper editor, and civil-rights leader, was born in
Jacksonville, Florida. He attended Atlanta University Preparatory and
received a B.A. from Atlanta University in 1894. Upon returning to
Jacksonville, he accepted a position as principal of Stanton
School—the school that he ultimately made the first high school for
blacks in the state of Florida. During this time, he founded a weekly
newspaper, the *Daily American,* and passed the Florida bar exam. He
moved to New York City in 1902, where he and his brother, J. Rosamond Johnson, collaborated with musician Bob Cole to produce
highly successful light operas, musical comedies, and more than two
hundred songs. Johnson authored a number of books, including *The
Autobiography of an Ex-Colored Man* (1912), *God's Trombones: Seven
Negro Sermons in Verse* (1927), *Black Manhattan* (1930), and *Along This
Way* (1933), an autobiography.

Johnson, Mordecai Wyatt (1890–1976), clergyman, essayist, and college
president, was born in Paris, Tennessee. He received his B.A. from

Morehouse College in 1911, a second B.A. from the University of Chicago in 1913, a B.D. from the Rochester Theological Seminary in 1916, and a M.th. from Harvard University in 1922. He taught at Morehouse College and served as pastor of a church in Charleston, West Virginia. In 1926, he became the first black president of Howard University. Johnson received the N.A.A.C.P.'s Spingarn Medal in 1929. A gifted orator, Johnson retired from Howard University in the early 1960s.

Locke, Alain (1885–1954), philosopher, educator, literary critic, and anthologist, was born in Philadelphia. Locke was elected to Phi Beta Kappa and became the first African-American Rhodes scholar. After two years at Oxford, he studied at the University of Berlin and the Collège de France, and later earned his Ph.D. in philosophy from Harvard University. From 1912 until his retirement, he taught at Howard University. His best-known work is the anthology *The New Negro* (1925).

McKay, Claude (1889–1948), author and poet, was born in Jamaica. His initial training was in agriculture at the Tuskegee Institute, from which he later transferred to Kansas State College. Upon his arrival in New York City, he entered the bohemian and revolutionary lifestyle in Greenwich Village. His first American poetry was published under the pseudonym Eli Edwards. In 1919, McKay moved to London, where he read the works of Marx and Lenin and joined the staff of the Communist newspaper, *The Worker's Dreadnought*. Disenchanted with America's race relations, with Marcus Garvey's Universal Negro Improvement Association (U.N.I.A.), and with editorial politics at the *Liberator*, where he had become editor, he traveled to France and North Africa, where he wrote many of his prize-winning works. With the exception of James Weldon Johnson, McKay sharply criticized many senior notables of the Harlem Renaissance.

Miller, Loren R. (1903–1967), lawyer, judge, and author, was born in Pender, Nebraska. He received his B.A. from Howard University and his LL.B. from Washington College of Law (Topeka, Kansas) in 1929. He practiced law for thirty years in Los Angeles and was subsequently appointed municipal judge. His critically acclaimed book, *The Petitioners: The Story of the Supreme Court of the United States and the Negro*, was published in 1966.

Nelson, Alice Dunbar (1875–1935), author, social worker, and poet, studied at Straight College (now Dillard University), New Orleans; the University of Pennsylvania; Cornell University; and the School of Industrial Arts (Philadelphia) before she married the poet Paul Laurence Dunbar in 1898. Dunbar died in 1904. In 1916, she married Robert J. Nelson. Alice Dunbar Nelson was a probation and parole officer and served as associate editor of the *AME Review* of the African Methodist Episcopal Church, and she was editor of the Wilmington, Delaware, *Advocate.* She was also a weekly contributor to the Associated Negro Press. Her books include *Goodness of St. Rocque, and Other Stories,* a book of short stories (1899), and two edited volumes: *Masterpieces of Negro Eloquence* (1914) and *The Dunbar Speaker and Entertainer* (1920).

Newsome, [Mary] Effie Lee (1885–1979), poet and columnist, was born in Philadelphia. She attended Wilberforce University, Oberlin College, the Philadelphia Academy of Fine Arts, and the University of Pennsylvania. While she contributed much of her work to children's magazines, she maintained a regular column for them in the Urban League's *Opportunity.* She was also a regular contributor to *The Crisis.*

Pickens, William (1881–1954), educator, dean, civil-rights worker, and government worker, was born in Anderson County, South Carolina. He received his B.A. from Talladega College (Talladega, Alabama) in 1902. He received a second B.A. from Yale University in 1904, where he was elected to Phi Beta Kappa. He earned his M.A. from Fisk University in 1908. He taught at Talladega College and Wiley College (Marshall, Texas), and he served as dean of Morgan College from 1915 to 1920. He then served as field secretary for the N.A.A.C.P. for twenty-two years. He left the N.A.A.C.P. in 1942 to work for the U.S. Treasury Department, where he remained until 1950. He published his autobiography, *Bursting Bonds,* in 1923.

Richardson, Willis (1889–1977), playwright, was born in Wilmington, North Carolina, and reared in Washington, D.C. He studied at Dunbar High School. Among those who encouraged and inspired him were his teacher and aspiring playwright Mary Burill, author Angelina Grimké, and W. E. B. Du Bois. From 1910 to 1955, he supported himself as a clerk at the U.S. Bureau of Engraving. His play *The Chip Woman's Fortune* opened on Broadway in May 1923. The Howard Players staged his *Mortgaged* in 1924. Other relevant works include *Plays and Pageants of Negro Life* (1930) and *Negro History in Thirteen Plays* (1935).

Savage, Augusta (1900–1962), sculptor and educator, was born in Green Cove, Florida. She studied at Cooper Union (New York City), the Grand Chaumière (Paris), and the Academy of Fine Arts (Rome). In 1939, she was commissioned to create a sculpture that was to make her famous—the harp-shaped *Lift Every Voice and Sing,* which was displayed at the 1939 World's Fair in New York City. Her work was exhibited at the Harmon Foundation in New York City and Société des Artistes Français in Paris. Her sculptures are part of the permanent collections of Morgan State University in Baltimore, Maryland, the Schomburg Center for Research in Black Culture of the New York Public Library, and the National Archives in Washington, D.C.

Sheen, Edwin Drummond (1901–?), short-story writer and editor, was born in Decatur, Illinois. He received his B.A. from James Miliken University in 1925 with honors, and a B.A. from the University of Illinois in 1927. He wrote for several Chicago newspapers during his career.

Spencer, Anne (1882–1976), poet and librarian, was considered one of the more talented of the "new Negro" poets. It has been said that her home and garden in Lynchburg, Virginia, served as a literary "haven" during segregation, much as Georgia Douglas Johnson's Washington, D.C., home did. She was born in Bramwell, West Virginia, but was educated at Virginia Seminary and College in Lynchburg, where she was librarian at the town's Dunbar High School until her retirement in 1943. Her first poetry, which was adjudged to be "temperate, noble and mildly feminist," was published in James Weldon Johnson's *Book of American Negro Poetry* and Alain Locke's *The New Negro*.

Toomer, Jean [Nathan Eugene] (1894–1967), poet and novelist, was born in Washington, D.C. He was the grandson of the lieutenant governor of Louisiana during Reconstruction who had challenged U.S. Senator Pinckney Benton Stewart Pinchback for political office. He was raised by his grandparents and introduced to literature by his uncle Bismarck. For brief periods, he attended the University of Wisconsin, Massachusetts College of Agriculture, a physical training institute in Chicago, and some lectures at New York University. After short stints as a shipfitter, car salesman, and teacher, he found himself amid the stimulating atmosphere of Greenwich Village, where his poetry and short stories were published in the pages of *Double-Dealer, The Dial, Broom,* and *The Liberator.* While his early writings received enthusiastic and critical acclaim, his later writings (following his return from the Continent—a period during which he claimed that he was no longer a black man) seemed to show less promise.

White, Walter (1893–1955), author and civil-rights leader, was born in Atlanta, Georgia. Blue-eyed and blond-haired, White was considered a "volunteer Negro." However, his experience in the Atlanta riots of 1906 rendered him unalterably committed to the struggle of

African Americans for civil rights. After graduating from Atlanta University, he accepted the position of assistant executive secretary of the N.A.A.C.P.—a position offered him by James Weldon Johnson. In his early days with the N.A.A.C.P., he "passed" to infiltrate vigilante and Klan groups of the Deep South for evidence of mob violence against blacks and published articles and stories that stunned America and the world. White was an indefatigable lobbyist for furthering the goals of civil rights through arts and letters and was said to be a riveting speaker and tireless organizer. He published well-received novels propagandizing against white supremacy, which were widely sold. He soon took on the role of agent and senior literary adviser to many painters, poets, entertainers, and novelists of Harlem.

Wright, C. Ruth held a strong literary and cultural interest in black letters. She was the wife of Dr. R. R. Wright, Jr., editor of the *Christian Recorder* and pastor of Jones Tabernacle A.M.E. Church of Philadelphia.

Yergan, Susie Wiseman, a native of Salisbury, North Carolina, and an honor graduate of Shaw University (Raleigh, North Carolina), became the only African-American female worker in South Africa during the 1920s.

BIBLIOGRAPHY

Aptheker, Herbert, ed. *A Documentary History of the Negro People in the United States, 1910–1932,* vol. 3. Secaucus, N.J.: Citadel Press, 1977.

Bontemps, Arna, ed. *The Harlem Renaissance Remembered.* New York: Dodd, Mead, 1972.

Brown, Sterling, Arthur P. Davis, and Ulysses Lee. *The Negro Caravan.* New York: Dryden Press, 1941.

Du Bois, W. E. B. *The Autobiography of W. E. B. Du Bois.* New York: International Publishers, 1968.

Gates, Henry Louis, Jr., and Nellie Y. McKay, eds. *The Norton Anthology of African American Literature.* New York: W. W. Norton, 1996.

Huggins, Nathan Irvin. *Black Odyssey: The Afro-American Ordeal in Slavery.* New York: Vintage Books, 1979.

———. *Harlem Renaissance.* New York: Oxford University Press, 1971.

Johnson, James Weldon. *Along This Way: The Autobiography of James Weldon Johnson.* New York: Viking Press, 1933.

———. *Black Manhattan.* New York: Alfred A. Knopf, 1930.

———. "Race Prejudice and the Negro Artist." *Harper's* 157 (1928): 769–76.

Johnson, James Weldon, ed. *The Book of American Negro Poetry.* New York: Harcourt Brace Jovanovich, 1959.

Johnson, James Weldon, with J. Rosamond Johnson, eds. *The Books of American Negro Spirituals.* New York: Viking Press, 1958.

Lewis, David Levering. *When Harlem Was in Vogue.* New York: Oxford University Press, 1981.

Lewis, David Levering, ed. *The Portable Harlem Renaissance Reader.* New York: Viking, 1994.

National Association for the Advancement of Colored People. "Minutes of the National Board of Directors, 1909–1914." *Crisis* (1910–1931).

Singh, Amritjit, William S. Shiver, and Stanley Brodwin, eds. *The Harlem Renaissance: Revaluations.* New York: Garland Publishing, 1989.

Watkins, Sylvestre C., ed. *Anthology of American Negro Literature.* New York: Modern Library, 1944.

Wilson, Sondra Kathryn, ed. *The Selected Writings of James Weldon Johnson,* vol. 2. New York: Oxford University Press, 1995.

ABOUT THE EDITOR

DR. SONDRA KATHRYN WILSON is an associate of Harvard University's W. E. B. Du Bois Institute and executor of James Weldon Johnson's literary properties. She has published two volumes of Johnson's writings. Her upcoming books include *The Opportunity Reader* and *In Search of Democracy: The N.A.A.C.P. Writings of James Weldon Johnson, Walter White, and Roy Wilkins (1920–1977)*.

A NOTE ON THE TYPE

The principal text of this Modern Library edition
was set in a digitized version of Janson,
a typeface that dates from about 1690 and was cut by Nicholas Kis,
a Hungarian working in Amsterdam. The original matrices have
survived and are held by the Stempel foundry in Germany.
Hermann Zapf redesigned some of the weights and sizes for Stempel,
basing his revisions on the original design.